A MICKEY MOUSE READER

A
MICKEY
MOUSE
READER

Edited by

GARRY APGAR

© Disney

UNIVERSITY PRESS OF MISSISSIPPI   JACKSON

www.upress.state.ms.us

The University Press of Mississippi is a member of the Association of American University Presses.

First printing 2014
∞
Library of Congress Cataloging-in-Publication Data

A Mickey Mouse reader / edited by Garry Apgar.
    pages cm
  Includes bibliographical references and index.
  ISBN 978-1-62846-103-9 (hardback) — ISBN 978-1-62846-104-6 (ebook) 1. Mickey Mouse (Fictitious character) 2. Mickey Mouse (Fictitious character) in mass media. 3. Popular culture—United States. 4. Walt Disney Company. I. Apgar, Garry, editor.
  N8224.M47M53 2014
  791.43'75—dc23
                                2014017814

British Library Cataloging-in-Publication Data available

published with support from

Figure Foundation

now next may man grow up.

CONTENTS

Born in Chicago in 1901, raised in rural Missouri and Kansas City, Walter Elias Disney was a child of the new century, a son of the Heartland. Never a stranger to hard work, as a boy, Walt delivered papers—morning and evening—, sold refreshments on passenger trains, and dreamed of drawing political cartoons for a big city daily.

He served in France as a Red Cross driver at the end of World War I. When he returned to the States, Walt applied to the *Kansas City Star* for a job as editorial cartoonist, but was rejected and went instead into the field of commercial art where he got hooked on filmmaking. In 1923, he moved to Hollywood and in partnership with his brother, Roy O. Disney, formed the Disney Brothers Studio. Their first venture was the "Alice Comedies," a string of short subjects that combined live action and animation. "Alice" was followed in 1927 by an all-cartoon series, *Oswald the Lucky Rabbit*.

Starting in 1928—with Mickey Mouse—and throughout the 1930s, Walt was an innovator in sound and color motion-picture technology as well as animation. In the early 1930s, he and Roy pioneered the year-round marketing of children's toys. By linking the distribution of their cartoons to sales of consumer goods bearing the image of Disney characters (school supplies, food, etc., in addition to toys), they helped develop the notion of corporate synergy. In 1955, with the *Mickey Mouse Club*, Walt transformed the field of children's television programming, and, with Disneyland (also 1955), reinvented the amusement park as a travel destination. Walt Disney World, his last great inspiration, spawned the global theme park industry.

At his death in 1966, Disney had been active in the film industry for almost half a century, from the heyday of silent pictures and the advent of talkies into the Golden Age of the studio system, and its decline. By the start of the new millennium, the two-man shop established by Walt and Roy had become the biggest operation in Hollywood, and the most far-flung and profitable entertainment empire in history. Both an entrepreneurial and an artistic genius, Disney was part Aesop and P. T. Barnum, part Henry Ford, Cecil B. DeMille, and Ray Kroc.

Blessed with a fertile imagination and a rare gift for visualizing and communicating a story, no individual has dominated the cultural land-scape in as many ways as Disney did, while he lived . . . and still does to-day. Indeed, if popular culture *is* culture—be it Shakespeare in the Park, Elvis, or Bart Simpson—then Walt Disney was arguably the foremost figure in American and world culture over the past hundred years. That is particularly true if one accepts the view, articulated by Neal Gabler in his book, *Life the Movie*, that motion pictures, television, and other mass-cult amusements are "the most pervasive, powerful, and ineluc-table force of our time." Henry Luce, in a *Life* magazine editorial in 1941, famously called the twentieth century the "American Century." It could as easily be dubbed the "Age of Disney."

Each of Walt's future exploits—Donald Duck, *Snow White*, Disney-land, *Mary Poppins*, Epcot, and so much more—sprang from the un-precedented success of Mickey, whose eager, can-do attitude mirrored Disney's own persona. The story of how Mickey came about (and what he "means" in sociocultural or mythic terms) is, at bottom, the story of Walt himself. That is one of several themes in my book, *Mickey Mouse: Emblem of the American Spirit*, scheduled to be published in 2015, by the Walt Disney Family Foundation Press. The idea for the *Mickey Mouse Reader* grew out of an urgent need to organize the mass of mate-rial gathered in the course of my research on that project.

Nearly half of this anthology tracks Mickey's rise to glory from 1928, when his first sound film, *Steamboat Willie*, was made, into his seventh anniversary year, and his first Technicolor release, *The Band Concert*. Thereafter, the readings chronicle or critique Mickey's continued as-cent to the status of a true icon and the position he still enjoys today as an enduring, frequently charged emblem of America and the American way of life.

From virtually the instant Mickey Mouse appeared in *Steamboat Willie*, he was embraced as a graphic analogue to Charlie Chaplin's Little Tramp, trying to get by (and have a little fun) in a not-always-friendly world. In the beginning, he was rather risqué, too. In *The Gal-lopin' Gaucho*, his third cartoon release, he smoked and drank beer—and in that film, and a few others, was seen visibly lusting after Minnie.

Within a few years he would lose much of that raw, primitive vigor, though he did have one last grand turn on the big screen, in 1940, as the Sorcerer's Apprentice in *Fantasia*.

The early Mouse and his progenitor were embraced by film stars and directors like Chaplin, Mary Pickford, Frank Capra, Sergei Eisenstein, and composer-songwriters Cole Porter and Jerome Kern. Two essays in this volume—"Mickey Mouse and American Art" (1932), by the Mexican muralist Diego Rivera, and "Mickey and Minnie" (1934), by the English novelist E. M. Forster—reflect the esteem of eminent artists and writers for Walt Disney and Mickey Mouse. Mickey also was acclaimed by the German theorist Walter Benjamin, who, in the 1930s, advanced the notion of "machine-age art," a concept that fueled a perception in the prewar era that Walt's modest one-reelers, produced with the collaborative aid of a loyal band of gag men, animators, musicians, in-betweeners, inkers, and painters, constituted a fundamentally modern, democratic mode of artistic expression.

Disney's Mouse and even more tuneful Silly Symphonies series likewise were hailed in the '30s as examples of a home-grown art form unfettered by Old-World esthetics, much like jazz, itself a key component in many of the first Mickeys. Among those who saw "genuine artistry" in Disney's work, and perceived in Mickey Mouse specifically "the embodiment of a new art," were a Philadelphia art critic, Dorothy Grafly ("An Artist of Our Time: Walter E. Disney, 1901–"), and the Manhattan publicist and future doyenne of haute couture, Eleanor Lambert ("Notes on The Art of Mickey Mouse and His Creator Walt Disney").

After World War II, the studio quit making cartoons featuring Mickey. His future looked grim until Disneyland and the *Mickey Mouse Club* gave him a new lease on life. Ironically, the squeaky-clean, un-hip qualities of the Mouse as seen on TV and at Anaheim, Mickey's most palpable presence in postwar America, factored decisively in fixing the words "Mickey Mouse" (originally a pejorative expression in jazz jargon) as a slur on anything thought to be petty or pointless. By the 1980s and '90s, as terms like "Disneyfication" and "Disney discourse" entered the lexicon, Walt and Mickey—in a complete reversal of how they'd been received in the 1930s—were derided by critics on the left as symbolic of everything that was wrong with the country (i.e., Disney = McDonalds = Coca-Cola = Amerika).

Starting in the 1940s, Walt and his runic rodent fell from favor among the intelligentsia. But they still had their defenders. For Mickey's exact contemporary, Maurice Sendak, who wrote "Growing Up With Mickey" (1978), and Sendak's junior by four years, John Updike, author of "The Mystery of Mickey Mouse" (1991), Walt's formerly antic progeny was a Proustian reminder of their childhood. By the 1980s, Mickey benefited as well from a whimsical or irony-laced, retro revival among the leading Pop artists, Roy Lichtenstein, Claes Oldenburg, Andy Warhol, all members of Sendak and Mickey's generation. Their imagery of Mickey—Warhol's especially—helped lift the Mouse back to the top of the mass-cult heap, and the dual distinction he maintains even now, reviled by some, beloved by many more.

This book is intended to serve as a compendium of the liveliest, most instructive, and influential texts on Mickey Mouse from 1928 to the present day. It contains not just the musings of scholars or the literati, but also less solemn fare, geared toward what the French call *le grand public*.

Journalism in America has long had a reciprocal relationship with popular culture. In the 1930s, publications like the *New York Times*, *Time*, and *Reader's Digest* were not averse to publicizing the Mouse or promoting the critical and financial fortunes of Walt Disney. Many, often front-page newspaper stories about Mickey were squibs. They are no less important for that, and their inclusion here, along with other relatively short or minor (or fanciful) items, provides an occasional, perhaps welcome, respite from weightier reads written by the likes of Forster and Updike.

The sixty-nine principal texts in the *Reader* are organized chronologically into seven sections, followed by:

- appendices containing the original versions of six texts in the anthology proper, written or first published in French, German, or Spanish;
- a list of key books on Walt Disney and Mickey, plus complete bibliographical references for each article, essay, or news item reproduced herein, and for every article or (in a few cases) book cited in my commentary;

- concise profiles of all fifty-one named writers represented in the anthology.

Three of the sixty-nine texts are excerpts of articles not devoted entirely to Mickey. As a rule, only minor changes have been made to any of the material, typically for typos, misspelling, or lapses in punctuation, although some stylistic peculiarities have been spared (e.g., "Micky" instead of "Mickey," "animaters" and "cells," instead of "animators" or "cels"). All substantive editorial intrusions are clearly indicated. References to texts elsewhere in the *Reader* are indicated with an asterisk.*

Some basic, recurrent inaccuracies—even my own—were left as is: for instance, the factual error that Walt had been a student at the Art Institute of Chicago (it was the Chicago Academy of Fine Arts), the notion that *Steamboat Willie* moved two blocks east to the Roxy after its debut at New York's Colony Theatre (as reported in *Film Daily*, "'Mickey Mouse' at Roxy," it was not until May 1931 that Disney's diminutive star "crashed the world's largest picture palace," in the Mickey Mouse cartoon *Traffic Troubles*), and the oft-told tale that "Mickey Mouse" was a password or codeword on D-Day (it was, as we shall see, the password for a pre-D-Day briefing).

Finally, to all who dip into these pages, I offer this advice by P. G. Wodehouse from the introduction to the first omnibus edition of his Jeeves and Wooster stories: "I would not recommend anyone to attempt to finish this volume at a sitting." Nor should anyone feel obliged to turn this page and dutifully proceed from there. A good place to begin, actually, may be near the back of the book, with two excellent surveys of Mickey's "career" and how he has been received over the years by John Canemaker (1995) and M. Thomas Inge (2006). Having digested one or both of those essays, one might do well to heed the further counsel of Wodehouse: "Take it easy. Spread it out. Assimilate it little by little." In other words, take in the short with the long—the flip or droll with the more studious or academic—, either randomly or methodically, as the spirit moves you.

Either way, enjoy.

A MICKEY MOUSE READER

1. The Early Years

1928–1931

In March 1927, Universal Pictures hired Walt Disney to produce *Oswald the Lucky Rabbit*. Five months later, in a squib labeled "Short Subjects," the trade paper *Film Daily* termed the feature "a riot." Despite *Oswald's* success, however, when Walt's contract came up for review, he was offered a reduction in pay, not the raise he felt he deserved. He rejected the proposed terms and, in short order, in concert with his ace animator, Ub Iwerks, and brother Roy, created Mickey.

No one then imagined Mickey Mouse becoming "one of the most famous actors on the screen," as journalist Harry Carr, in "The Only Unpaid Movie Star" (March 1931),* put it. For Walt, making a go of Mickey was all about the survival of his studio, not the making of an idol for the ages.

Disney's shabby treatment by Universal was too painful, or embarrassing, to be discussed at length (if at all) in early accounts of how Mickey was conceived. According to Harry Carr, Walt could only say that "we were rather indebted to Charlie Chaplin for the idea." There was more to the story than that, of course. Not only was Mickey Mouse born of necessity, he arose from a wide array of sources, including—but not limited to—Chaplin, Douglas Fairbanks, Felix the Cat, Oswald the Rabbit, and frisky cartoon mice like those that abounded in mid-'20s animations such as the Farmer Al Falfa and Krazy Kat series and Disney's own Alice and Oswald one-reelers.

Plane Crazy, the very first Mickey cartoon chronologically, though not the first to be released, was inspired by the exploits of a real-life hero, aviator Charles Lindbergh. It was animated at almost warp speed by Iwerks, whose role in crafting the original Mouse films was so crucial that the opening credits read: "A Walt Disney Comic by Ub Iwerks." In 1930, after Ub and Walt had gone their separate ways, several critics intimated or, as Maurice Bessy did, affirmed outright that Mickey was the "offspring of the cartoonist Ub Iwerks."* Bessy was wrong. As will be evident in the pages that follow, Walt, who, for over two decades, provided Mickey's voice, was always the driving force behind the invention and animated adventures of Mickey Mouse.

Work on *Plane Crazy* commenced in March or April 1928, and was previewed in mid May at a theater on Sunset Boulevard. A second cartoon, *The Gallopin' Gaucho*, went into production almost immediately, but both films were silent, and Disney could find no takers for the series. Although Al Jolson's *The Jazz Singer* had, in October 1927, presaged the coming of talking pictures, distributors and theater owners in the spring and summer of 1928 were still unsure of what lay ahead for the movie business. Sound versions of *Gallopin' Gaucho* and *Plane Crazy* would not be released until December 30, 1928, and March 17, 1929, respectively, after *Steamboat Willie* had proven a hit.

Animation on *Steamboat Willie*—Walt's first cartoon planned from scratch as a talkie—was completed by late August 1928. The soundtrack was recorded on September 30th. Which is why, throughout the 1930s, the studio fêted Mickey's birthday on or about October 1st. In the 1970s, The Walt Disney Company began celebrating the event on November 18th, since it was on that date in 1928 that *Willie* premiered at the Colony Theatre on Broadway, as part of a lavish bill featuring a live orchestra and the now-forgotten mob movie, *Gang War*. *Steamboat Willie* was applauded by audiences and critics alike. Walt must have been especially gratified when he and Mickey were singled out in a review of the day's doings by Mordaunt Hall in the *New York Times*:

> On the same program is the first sound cartoon, produced by Walter Disney, creator of "Oswald the Rabbit." This current film is called "Steamboat Willie," and it introduces a new cartoon character, henceforth to be known as "Micky Mouse." It is an ingenious piece of work with a good deal of fun. It growls, whines, squeaks and makes various other sounds that add to its mirthful quality.

The *New York Times* has committed countless column inches ever since to Mickey, by way of hundreds if not thousands of news briefs, wire service reports, full-length articles, and opinion pieces. On November 21st, two days after Hall's critique appeared, the trade paper *Variety* printed the first item focused exclusively on the Mouse.* The *Times* and *Variety*, like several other publications at the time, raved about how novel and amusing *Steamboat Willie* was. They also commended Disney and the Powers Cinephone System—whose product was used to make the film's soundtrack—for demonstrating that, as *Variety* put it, "interchangeablity" among competing sound technologies was feasible for "all wired houses."

Mickey, circa 1930, didn't just growl, whine, and squeak. He was, as previously noted, more impish than the little guy we now know, and periodically made headlines for running afoul of the censor, both abroad (Canada and Germany) and at home. In February 1931, in "Regulated Rodent,"* *Time* magazine gleefully reported that Clarabelle Cow, a prominent member of Mickey's supporting cast, was reproached for too readily revealing her "famed udder," and for being seen on screen reading a mildly erotic novel, *Three Weeks*, by Elinor Glin.

These spicy contretemps merely added to Mickey's charm at a time when intellectuals, notably in Europe, like the motion picture critics Caroline (C. A.) Lejeune,* Maurice Bessy, and Pierre Scize,* were starting to sing his praises. In November 1929, a private group of elite enthusiasts, the London Film Society, organized a program that featured Sergei Eisenstein's *Battleship Potemkin* and a Mickey Mouse cartoon, *The Barn Dance*. Ten months later, Eisenstein visited Walt's studio, proudly posing for photos with a cut-out image of Mickey, and in November 1930 the Soviet director was quoted in the *Manchester Guardian* ("Art & Hollywood: Sergei Eisenstein Gives it Up") saying "that the only artistic success yet achieved by the talkies" was in the Mickey Mouse cartoons. In Germany in 1931, a cardboard effigy of Mickey was glimpsed in a pastry shop in Fritz Lang's proto-noir masterpiece, *M*, and Walter Benjamin, also in 1931, commented favorably on the character in his private journal.*

Meanwhile, in the world of commerce, the Mouse was taking on a life of his own. In an article in the *Windsor Magazine* in October 1931,* Disney would boast that "manufacturers of every kind of commodity" were "using Mickey to promote the sale of their goods." By late December 1931, it could be said that Walt and Mickey had truly "arrived" after Gilbert Seldes, the nation's most distinguished media maven, published an extensive profile of the young producer in the *New Yorker*, entitled "Mickey-Mouse Maker."*

Steamboat Willie

Land (Robert J. Landry)

Variety, November 21, 1928. Copyright ©2012 Reed Business Information,
a division of Reed Elsevier, Inc.

Not the first animated cartoon to be synchronized with sound effects but the first to attract favorable attention. This one represents a high order of cartoon ingenuity cleverly combined with sound effects. The union brought forth gags galore. Giggles came so fast at the Colony they were stumbling over each other.

It's a peach of a synchronization job all the way, bright, snappy and fitting the situation perfectly. Cartoonist, Walter Disney.

With most of the animated cartoons qualifying as a pain in the neck it's a signal tribute to this particular one. If the same combination of talent can turn out a series as good as "Steamboat Willie" they should find a wide market if interchangeability angle does not interfere.

Recommended unreservedly for all wired houses.

• This item was published four days after Mordaunt Hall lauded *Steamboat Willie* (and Mickey Mouse by name) in the *New York Times*. *Willie* and its star had, however, been mentioned one week earlier, both perhaps for the first time in print, by *Film Daily*, in its November 13, 1928, issue ("First Four Cinephone Cartoons Under Way"):

> Four of a series of 26 new all sound animated cartoons to be made by Walter Disney, creator of the Oswald cartoons, are now in work at the new Powers Cinephone studio in New York. The new series is tentatively titled "Micky Mouse." The first subject has been fully completed and three others will be ready for screening within the next week or ten days.
>
> Each of the 26 subjects will have a distinguishing title. The first will be known as "Steamboat Willie" to be followed by "The Barn Dance," "The Galloping Gaucho" and "Plain [*sic*] Crazy."

"Steamboat Billie" /
Walt Disney Cartoon /
Real Entertainment

Film Daily, November 25, 1928

This is what "Steamboat Willie" has: First, a clever and amusing treatment; secondly, music and sound effects added via the Cinephone method. The result is a real tidbit of diversion. A maximum has been gotten from the sound effects. Worthy of bookings in any house wired to reproduce sound-on-film. Incidentally, this is the first Cinephone-recorded subject to get public exhibition and at the Colony, New York, is being shown over Western Electric equipment. Distribution has not been set.

• Distribution in the United States for *Steamboat Billie* [*sic*] and the other early Mickey cartoons would be managed on a state-rights basis by Patrick A. Powers (1869–1948), a colorful and rather ruthless figure in movie history, whose career is touched upon in "Mickey Mouse's Financial Career" by Arthur Mann* and Jim Korkis's "Secrets of Steamboat Willie."* Powers had a propensity for legal entanglements, among them a lawsuit with Buffalo Bill Cody, in which the fiercely competitive Irishman prevailed.

The Barn Dance/Draughtsman . . . Walt Disney

London Film Society

The Film Society Programme, November 10, 1929

The Mickey Mouse series of films presents a model of synchronisation. It consists of animated cartoons, of that kind of which *Mutt and Jeff*, *The Katzenjammer Kiddies* (renamed during the war *The Prohibition Children*) and *Æsop's Fables* were among the earliest examples and of which Felix the Cat is perhaps the most celebrated. The personality of Felix is no doubt more individual than are those of the protagonists of Mickey Mouse, but the drawings of the latter series are superior in fertility of invention. In his limited field, Mickey Mouse has achieved that perfect blend between visual and aural impulses towards which other sound-film technicians are yet striving, and of which Mr. Meisel's scores for 'Potemkin' and 'Berlin' were the first hints. The film is shown courtesy of British International Film Distributors Ltd.

• *The Barn Dance*, the fourth Mickey Mouse cartoon released by Walt Disney, was screened for The Film Society of London at the Tivoli Palace, on the Strand, Sunday afternoon, November 10, 1929. It was part of a bill comprised of three full-length motion pictures, *The Fall of the House of Usher* (1928), directed by Jean Epstein, John Grierson's *Drifters* (1928), and Sergei Eisenstein's *Battleship Potemkin* (1925). Eisenstein and Aldous Huxley were in attendance. The Disney animated short and three feature films formed the thirty-third in a series of programs presented by the Society, established in 1925 by Ivor Montagu and Sidney Bernstein. Iris Barry, film critic for the *Observer*, and later first director of the Film Library at the Museum of Modern Art in New York, established in 1935, was a founding member of the Society. In 1930 Ivor Montagu would accompany Eisenstein to New York and Hollywood, where, as already noted, the Soviet director visited the Disney studio.

Mickey Mouse

C. A. (Caroline Alice) Lejeune

Observer, December 8, 1929. Copyright Guardian News & Media Ltd 1929.

To my mind, Walt Disney's cartoons of Mickey Mouse are the most imaginative, witty, and satisfying productions that can be found in the modern cinema. It is surely beside the point to argue that cartoon is not, and never can be, the highest form of expression in any medium. The cinema has not yet discovered its highest form of expression, but it has discovered, and perfected, the cartoon. I can imagine finer films than Mickey Mouse, but I cannot walk into a theatre and see them. Walt. Disney's work is here, and it is good; that somebody else's work must eventually be better does not affect my pleasure in Mickey to-day.

* * *

The tradition of cartoon in the cinema goes back to a very early stage of film development, and springs directly from the comic strip of the American newspapers. The minute draughtsmanship and endless labour required in arranging these drawn figures in a sequence close enough and long enough to provide material for the film has always limited the output: but the few artists who have seriously employed themselves in cartoon-photography have proved, by series after series of successes, the remarkable aptness of this kind of production for the screen. Walt. Disney's cartoons have a fine genealogy, in which Felix the Cat is perhaps the most famous name. But Mickey Mouse, while drawing so much from the past, is a real creature of the present; his line is freer and richer in comedy than that of any of his predecessors, and combined with it is a line of burlesque music, a kind of animal obbligato, with a scale and rhythm altogether its own.

* * *

Every Mickey Mouse cartoon is complete in itself, a single manifestation of its hero's activities, but the whole series is linked together by cast, environment, and idea. Mickey, like Krazy Kat of the comic strip, is always a lover; his mouse "sweetie" inspires and shares in all the best of his music; they are a country couple, finding their adventures among the other creatures of the farmyard and countryside. As a rule they move in front of a static drawn background, and such accessories as the story needs are developed one out of another, transformed, with the barest economy of line. There is something reminiscent of Chaplin's method in the integral use of accessory in the Mickey Mouse cartoons; Mickey dances on the platform boards, and creates a xylophone, pulls the spaghetti out of the tin and plays on it with a 'cello bow. Every line in the film is pregnant with the next; every movement is resolved, every gesture has its structural use. And matched with the burlesque tripping measure that runs through all the cartoons is a burlesque patter of music—a kind of musicbox jingle with thin, tinkling silences. The whole cunning of Mickey lies in its deliberate sub-tones—it is a whispered and wicked commentary on Western civilization through the medium of civilisation's newest and most cherished machine.

* * *

Perhaps the surest proof of the value of the Mickey Mouse cartoons is their acceptance by men and women of every type of understanding. I often hear complaints that the really good things of the cinema fail through lack of recognition. My own belief is that anything good enough in entertainment compels recognition in time. The first Mickey Mouse pictures came into the cinema quietly enough. So did the first Chaplins. Now Mickey, like Chaplin, is snapped up by every live exhibitor. Twice last week I heard a West End audience cheer the appearance of Mickey on the screen, and I am ready to believe that wherever he goes he gets the same ovation. I know that at my local cinema the Mickey Mouse cartoons are advertised in letters as large as those of the "feature" film, and on several occasions have been the only "attraction" to get an advance line. Mickey, in a few months' time, has become a star and won a star's billing—an achievement quite unprecedented in the history of the one-reel film.

* * *

The Mickey Mouse cartoons go into every sort of programme and appeal to every sort of audience; our enjoyment only differs according to the measure of our understanding of its cause. Some of us know that the joke is dependent on the unbroken flowing line that makes flat designs of all the pictures—others feel the beauty of the line and stick to the joke that the line suggests. It is possible to know too much, as well as too little, about an entertainment. We can spoil Mickey, just as we can spoil Chaplin, by losing the fun in the technique, or the technique in the fun. The balance of the two is the nice point of appreciation, and the man who gets the most out of the Mickey Mouse cartoons is neither the "highbrow" nor the "hick," but the ordinary intelligent picturegoer, who allows his appreciation of talent to multiply his pleasure, and a knowledge of the means to increase his enjoyment of the end.

• This essay by C. A. Lejeune, under her recurring rubric, "The Pictures," may represent the first serious effort in print to analyze what made Mickey tick cinematically. Lejeune's *consœur*, Nicole Boré-Verrier, critic for *Le Figaro*, who covered Disney's visit to Paris in 1935 ("Mickey Mouse at the Gaumont-Palace"*), used the masculine pseudonym "Jean Laury" to mask her gender. But Lejeune, one of the earliest full-time movie critics in journalism, male or female, simply hid her sexual identity behind her initialed byline.

The Cinema (*excerpt*)

Pierre Scize (Michel-Joseph Piot)

Jazz: l'actualité intellectuelle, December 15, 1929

Today, 15 December 1929, *Jazz* can, without fear of inciting laughter among those who will leaf through its pages in 1960, proclaim the following: "Technically perfect sound films are now being shown in the cinema."

Remember that it is barely a year since the first mediocre attempts at talking films were presented to the public. What the future has in store we can only guess.

—What pictures are we talking about: *Broadway-Melody*, *Les Trois Masques*, imperfect or impossible films that are, by turns, both astonishing and ridiculous?

—Not at all. We are referring, rather, to the phenomenal series of "Mickeys."

Animated cartoons. Synchronized with sound on film, these new creations offer a hundred pure delights. Of course, they would be remarkable even if silent. Their technique, their lyrical fantasy combined with the freedom, nay, the incredible imagination that informs their production would touch the soul of a mute. Never have pictures achieved greater, more varied effects, never has freer rein been given to lively antics and subtle humor. The inventiveness of their creator is astounding. Nothing impedes his verve, nothing limits it. At each instant, the wit summoned forth by the most whimsical and amiable extravagance seems to push back the bounds of the medium—when suddenly, the next instant, a new and unexpected twist sends it off, towards even more drollery, and an ever greater and more astounding level of laughter.

What compounds the quality of these little masterpieces is the synchronization of action and sound. Here we touch upon the miracle. Amazed technicians look at each other and ask: "How do they do it?"

When you know the painstaking care and trouble required to make a soundtrack, you quake, and say, like the sound engineer with whom I discussed the matter a short while ago: "It is pure mathematics!"

But the public, blissfully unaware of such intricacies, sits back and takes in this new wonder—a wonder, whose enjoyment is based at least in part on sheer astonishment. Like the devotees of a new religion, we ask with a knowing wink: "Did you see *The Opry House*? Ah! And *The Jazz Fool*? Oh! And the joy as your memory recalls this or that savory touch, sequence of musical notes, or gag.

The horse in *The Opry House*, and his orchestra wherein we see the violinist saw his violin in half, then carry on with the tune using the four whiskers of his beard, the tonal range of muted trumpet sounds executed by the cats whose tails are being pulled, the soap bubbles used to produce pizzicatti and, for a final crowning touch, the spectacular piano scene!

Ah! That piano! We see its sketchy, unreal graphic contours on the screen, and out of this arbitrary silhouette, from this abstract suggestion, suddenly issues forth, with the magnificent strains of a great Steinway concert piano, the prelude by Rachmaninoff, played by a splendid virtuoso.

The superposition of a real noise and a virtual image produces a staggering effect. One laughs, and, yet, one is troubled. A magical spell enthralls and gladdens us. We are seized with a kind of nervous admiration, like children admiring their first mechanical toy.

Then, suddenly, the piano frees itself from the grasp of its pianist. The keys execute their own interminable trills. They must be stretched like taffy, braided and tied together to keep them still. Is that all? No! The stool dashes out from beneath its occupant, and the piano, now in full rebellion, delivers a mighty kick and sends him off to dreamland; after which, the whimsical instrument, its keyboard giving a broad laugh, starts to dance and, with the aid of its front legs, plays a pulsing Charleston unassisted.

Where are we, if not somewhere in the uninhibited world of dreams, in the lawless realm of inanimate objects? And, in the end, what are Mickey and his friends? Animals, people? No one knows. It goes beyond simple artistic design, for it impossibly combines various species, such as the ox, dog and turkey which, colliding, fuse miraculously into a twelve-footed creature, with three heads, feathers and fur, before it flees, barking, over hill and dale . . .

All this madness, supported by brilliant sound-effects and appropriate musical accompaniment plays out to the tune of a burlesque symphony full of unexpected sounds. We never tire of the music because everything is perfectly *allied to the action* on the screen, striking just the *right tone*, and supporting the truly humorous, profoundly expressive visual spectacle. Certain inventions, through their rhythm and their apposite tonality, enchant musicians. There are in the various *Mickeys* we have been able to see, scenes now and forever famous, and deservedly so. I was talking to you a moment ago about *The Jazz Fool*. But just talk to those who are familiar with the scene of the horse and the wasp . . . There is only one word, to describe these triumphs. That word is "masterpiece."

• Pierre Scize (real name: Michel-Joseph Piot) was another pseudonymous critic. In the final two-thirds of this rundown of current Paris cinema listings in the Parisian monthly *Jazz: l'actualité intellectuelle* ("intellectual news"), Scize commented on the German film *Melodie der Welt* ("Melody of the World"), among other feature films. *The Broadway Melody* had been released in the U.S. on June 6, 1929, *Les Trois Masques* ("The Three Masks") was released in France on November 1st. Scize's original text in French (see Appendix A) was reprinted, with a few minor errors of transcription (mistakenly dated "1930" and also mistitled as "Éloge de 'Mickey'"), in Maurice Bessy's biographical treatment of Walt Disney (Paris, 1970).

An International Language:
The Animated Cartoon (*excerpt*)

Maurice Bessy

Pour Vous, March 27, 1930

It seems that everything has been said already about the marvelous "talkartoons" which have, no doubt, converted more people to talking pictures than either *Trois Masques* or *Broadway Melody*.

Who today can possibly be unaware of that great star of sound animated cartoons, the mischievous mouse Mickey, offspring of the cartoonist Ub Iwerks? Mickey, emperor of the inkwell and king of the microphone!

Mickey's fame justifies our providing a few details about his father, one of the most accomplished American "cartoonists," too often overlooked in favor of the well-deserved praise bestowed upon his creations.

Ub Iwerks was not an overnight sensation. In fact this marvelous artist has been working for fourteen years in "cartoons"; his success has been the result of a long and concerted effort.

Iwerks started out as an assistant for two years to an artist specialized in the field, then worked as a "commercial artist" in an advertising agency. It was at the Commercial Film Company of Kansas City, where he was head of the art department, that he made his first animated shorts.

There he became acquainted with the cartoonist Disney who soon became his partner and the two men began to turn out animated cartoon shorts on a regular basis.

The two friends remained partners until February 1930.

It was Ub Iwerks, in fact, creator of *Mickey*, of *The Skeleton Dance*, who sought to distance himself from Walt Disney, father of *Oswald*, the "Lucky Rabbit," which was amusing but in no way comparable to

Mickey, in order to set up as an independent producer and, ultimately, to launch his new creation: *Flip the Frog*, a new animated character that New York has only recently begun to appreciate.

Iwerks is convinced that that the frog closely resembles human beings and that it is a symbol of both human idleness and exuberance.

Iwerks's work is of exceptional and remarkable interest.

Let us make clear in passing that this new series of cartoons will be made available in color versions and that Iwerks is prepared to produce one film per month.

Since, with the exception of the familiar image of Mickey and the soon to be equally well-known Flip the Frog, the French public is unacquainted with Ub Iwerks's other characters, let us present his ant and his heron, his chameleon and his crow, his rabbit, his tortoise, his cat and his spider.

• "Talkartoons" were produced by the Fleischer Studios. On January 21, 1930 Roy Disney (1893–1970) was informed by Ub Iwerks (1901–1971) that Ub wished to end his partnership with the Disneys (Walt was in New York at the time). Just one Flip the Frog color cartoon has been confirmed, *Fiddlesticks* (released August 16, 1930). None of the creatures listed at the end of this *hommage* to Iwerks ever figured prominently in Iwerks's new series, and none are known to have had names. The final third of Bessy's article was devoted to a discussion of Russian animators including Nikolay Khodatayev. For the original text in French, see Appendix B.

Miraculous Mickey

Creighton Peet

Outlook and Independent, July 23, 1930

Should I ever visit Hollywood—that golden land where other people's ideas are used until they are threadbare and then patched a hundred times—there is but a single studio I should insist on visiting. This is the modest establishment which turns out the Walt Disney "Mickey Mouse" and "Silly Symphony" animated cartoons. These charming drawings, ingenious and often refreshingly original, are something of a high climax in the cinematic art—yes, art. They are "free" in the fullest and most intelligent sense of the term. They know neither space, time, substance nor the dignity of the laws of physics. They are the quintessence of action. They thumb their beautiful, elastic noses at the very movies between which they are sandwiched. While even Charlie Chaplin must contend with a more or less material world, Mickey Mouse and his companions of the "Silly Symphonies" live in a special cosmos of their own in which the nature of matter changes from moment to moment. Mickey can play the great lover, the great hunter or the great toreador, after which he can reach inside the bull's mouth, pull out his teeth and use them for castanets . . . he can lead a band or play violin solos . . . his ingenuity is limitless . . . he never fails . . . he is the perfect hero of all romance. He overcomes skyscrapers, mountains, oceans or even the expanse of planets without so much as getting out of breath or singeing his whiskers.

But it is in the "Silly Symphonies" that the animated cartoon, now the musical cartoon, has achieved real triumphs. Here Walt Disney deals with ideas rather than characters. There is no story in *Springtime*—we see spring coming to the plants, the insects, and the animals. Potato-bugs tap dance on the petals of a daisy—the daisies themselves go through an Albertina Rasch routine, while the whole landscape sways, taps, and vibrates with happiness. In *Autumn* the squirrels, the beavers, the skunks, the porcupines, the owls, etc., are shown stowing themselves away for the winter, while the ducks fly south and the crows crawl into the scarecrow for shelter. All this goes on, of course, in perfect synchronism with the provocative music.

The humor of the Disney cartoons is sharp, fast, and universal. They should be (and are) equally entertaining to Americans, Germans, Frenchmen, Russians, Chinese, and our great grandchildren. In a way, Mr. Disney and his associates (it takes a dozen men about two weeks to produce one eight-minute cartoon) are performing an act of charity when they release their joyful and intelligent little India-ink characters. They may not realize it, but there is a faithful and steadily increasing audience which finds their gay, witty and civilized foolery is the only tolerable moment in an entire evening of inevitably dreary servant-girl romances.

I don't know who is the real genius back of these drawings. Until recently they appear to have been planned by a certain Ub Iwerks—and who he may be I cannot say. Their really superior musical scores are arranged by Carl Stallings [*sic*].

It is true that there are other cartoons—many of them excellent, many of them imitations of the Disney films. "Looney Tunes," for instance, substitutes petty vulgarities and smirks for ingenuity and invention. It can't be done. There is but one Mickey Mouse. Amen.

• "Miraculous Mickey" constituted the bulk of Peet's highly regarded weekly column, "The Movies," published July 23, 1930. Albertina Rasch was a dancer and choreographer for Broadway and Hollywood. Carl Stalling (1891–1972), Disney's first music director, was with him at the Colony Theatre for the premiere of *Steamboat Willie*, but quit the studio in early 1930 at about the time Ub Iwerks did. The *Looney Tunes* series was animated for Warner Bros. at this time by ex-Disney cartoonists Rudolph Ising and Hugh Harman.

Peet's salute to Walt (and Ub's) "genius" did not sit well with everyone, however. "Reading Mr. Peet's eulogy of 'Miraculous Mickey,'" the *Literary Digest* declared ("Europe's Highbrows Hail 'Mickey Mouse'"), "we realize that the funny little fellow at whom we have laughed so often, has met the same fate as many others who have set out to be merely amusing," and like Krazy Kat, Charlie Chaplin, among others, "is being 'discovered' by the intelligentsia." Walt's brother Roy mentioned "the write-up in the *Literary Digest*" in a letter to their parents dated August 25, 1930. "We are getting to be publicity hounds, and never miss that kind of stuff. We have a great number of very good write-ups like that," Roy reported (Thomas, *Building a Company*, 88).

On Mickey Mouse

Walter Benjamin

Notebook entry written in 1931, unpublished during the author's lifetime.
"Mickey Mouse" reprinted by permission of the publisher from *Walter Benjamin,
Selected Writings, Volume 2, 1927–1934*, translated by Rodney Livingstone and
Others, edited by Michael W. Jennings, Howard Eiland, and Gary Smith, p. 545,
Cambridge, Mass.: The Belknap Press of Harvard University Press, Copyright
© 1999 by the President and Fellows of Harvard College.

From a conversation with Glück and Weill.—Property relations in
Mickey Mouse cartoons: here we see for the first time that it is possible
to have one's own arm, even one's own body, stolen.

The route taken by Mickey Mouse is more like that of a file in an office than it is like that of a marathon runner.

In these films, mankind makes preparations to survive civilization.

Mickey Mouse proves that a creature can still survive even when it
has thrown off all resemblance to a human being. He disrupts the entire
hierarchy of creatures that is supposed to culminate in mankind.

These films disavow experience more radically than ever before. In
such a world, it is not worthwhile to have experiences.

Similarity to fairy tales. Not since fairy tales have the most important and most vital events been evoked more unsymbolically and more
unatmospherically. There is an immeasurable gulf between them and
Maeterlinck or Mary Wigman. All Mickey Mouse films are founded on
the motif of leaving home in order to learn what fear is.

So the explanation for the huge popularity of these films is not
mechanization, their form; nor is it a misunderstanding. It is simply the
fact that the public recognizes its own life in them.

• There may be a faint echo here of C. A. Lejeune's comment in December
1929 that Mickey's cartoons were "a whispered and wicked commentary on
Western civilization." The banker Gustav Glück was one of Benjamin's best

friends; the composer Kurt Weill was another acquaintance. Maurice Maeterlinck was a Symbolist poet and playwright, Wigman a German dancer and choreographer. For the original text in German, see Appendix C.

Regulated Rodent

From the pages of TIME. February 16, 1931.
TIME is registered trademark of Time Inc. Used under License.

Motion Picture Producers & Distributors of America last week announced that, because of the complaints of many censor boards, the famed udder of the cow in Mickey Mouse cartoons was now banned. Cows in Mickey Mouse or other cartoon pictures in the future will have small or invisible udders quite unlike the gargantuan organ whose antics of late have shocked some and convulsed other of Mickey Mouse's patrons. In a recent picture the udder, besides flying violently to left and right or stretching far out behind when the cow was in motion, heaved with its panting when the cow stood still; it also stretched, when seized, in an exaggerated way.

Already censors have dealt sternly with Mickey Mouse. He and his associates do not drink, smoke or caper suggestively. Once a Mickey Mouse cartoon was barred in Ohio because the cow read Elinor Glyn's *Three Weeks*. German censors ruled out another picture because "The wearing of German military helmets by an army of mice is offensive to national dignity." (TIME, July 21). Canadian censors ruled against another brand of sound cartoon because a leering fish in it writhed up to a mermaid and slapped her on the thigh. But censorship is only a form of public testimony that Mickey Mouse and other animated cartoons are an important and permanent element of international amusement. Sergei Eisenstein, famed Russian director, has said, "They are America's most original contribution to culture. . . ."

. . .

Mickey Mouse Features are produced by the same modern processes as other feature pictures except that artists and an art process take the place of actors. First, in the Walt Disney Studios in Hollywood a "gag" meeting is held, ideas talked over, roughly outlined. Scenario writers compose a regulation script: adapters break it down into sequences, scenes, shots. The scenic department designs the background. Then three kinds of artists begin to work: 1) "animators" who sit at two long rows of specially made desks and work by light that streams through a central glass. They develop the gags, draw only the beginning and the end of an action. Their sketches are passed to 2) the "in-betweeners" who draw the small intricately graded changes that make a motion kinetic. Then 3) the "inkers" place a transparent square of celluloid on the drawing and outline boldly in ink on the celluloid. Action is photographed by superimposing these transparent drawings over the painted backgrounds which have been placed under a camera.

Cartoonist Walter Disney, 30, thin and dark, gives his collaborators no publicity. He is the originator and so far as the world knows the sole creator of Mickey Mouse's doings. Eleven years ago he was working on the Kansas City *Star*, drifted to Hollywood where he produced pictures combining people and cartoons. When the sound device was invented he originated his famed rodent, devising a method to make the Mickey Mouse musical scores synchronize perfectly with the action. It takes from 6,000 to 7,000 drawings to make one reel (650–750 ft.) of Mickey Mouse films. Walter Disney produces 26 films a year, 13 Mickey Mouse cartoons, 13 Silly Symphonies.

Like Charlie Chaplin, Mickey Mouse is understood all over the world because he does not talk. The Germans call him Michael Maus, the French Michel Souris, the Spaniards Miguel Ratonocito and Miguel Pericote, the Japanese Miki Kuchi. Although his Christian name might be understood as an affront to Irish dignity, he has been respectfully reviewed in the *Irish Statesman* by Poet-Painter George ("AE") Russell. Great lover, soldier, sailor, singer, toreador, tycoon, jockey, prizefighter, automobile racer, aviator, farmer, scholar, Mickey Mouse lives in a world in which space, time and the laws of physics are null. He can reach inside a bull's mouth, pull out his teeth and use them for castanets. He can lead a band or play the violin solos; his ingenuity is limitless; he never fails. Best of Mickey Mouse competitors is Koko the Clown, of Fleischer Bros.' *Out-of-the-Inkwell Series*. Others: Paul Terry's *Aesop's Fables*, Charles Mintz's *Krazy Kat*, Warner Bros.' *Looney Tunes*.

• Soon after this story appeared, the *New York Times* reported ("Danes Ban 'Mickey Mouse'") that the first Silly Symphony, *The Skeleton Dance*, was deemed "too macabre to be put on the screen" by the state censor in Denmark. An account of Mickey's travails in Germany the previous summer, in the *Times* of London ("'Mickey Mouse' in Trouble: German Censorship"), cited a statement by the German Board of Film Censors that "the victorious mouse," in an unnamed Disney cartoon, was "distinguished by the French *képi*, his enemies the cats are clearly recognizable as the German Army by their German steel helmets." Thus, the Board banned the film (*The Barnyard Battle*) for being "calculated to 'reawaken the latent anti-German feeling existing abroad since the War' and 'to wound the patriotic feelings of German cinema-goers.'" Elinor Glyn's novel, *Three Weeks*, had been made into a movie in 1914. Walt Disney never worked for any newspaper, though he did apply unsuccessfully for a job as editorial cartoonist on the *Kansas City Star* in 1919. Finally, it is interesting that A. E. Russell's protégé, P. L. Travers, whose Mary Poppins stories would be turned into a multiple-Oscar-winning film by Disney in 1964, also wrote (though less "respectfully" than Russell) a piece about Mickey. In a decidedly sour critique of Disney animated shorts in the *New English Weekly* ("Mickey Mouse," Feb. 3, 1938), she said of "Mickey's country" that it was "a grown-up world dwindled to a pinpoint, not only in size but in quality." Travers also declared that Mickey was "lopping off the boughs of the tree upon whose roots he lives—the fairy tale."

Advertisement in *Film Daily*, April 19, 1931.
© The Walt Disney Company.

The Only Unpaid Movie Star

Harry Carr

American Magazine, March 1931

Even though you may be a citizen of the world, you really must have a place to hang your hat. Just so with the illustrious, world-famous, pen-and-ink talkie star—El Señor . . . Herr . . . Monsieur . . . Mister . . . "Mickey Mouse."

He is known in Paris and Paraguay; in Norway and Northampton; in every capital of Europe and America; and in the far islands of the sea. But he has his abode on the edge of Hollywood. One would reasonably expect him to be living in a palatial Edam cheese. But—alas—the mansion of "Mickey" is a small, concrete factory-studio on a side street next door to a gasoline service station.

"Mickey Mouse" is only an animated pen-and-ink drawing, but he has become one of the most famous actors on the screen. He is known and adored for his side-splitting antics in every country in the world where there are motion picture screens. He has his own fan mail, his own storybooks. Almost everything from razor blades to German toys has been dedicated to his fame. He is asked to inscribe his autograph in books adorned with the signatures of kings and queens.

What is more to the point, he has become one of the greatest "box office" actors in the world—though he is the only one who doesn't receive a salary.

For the rest, "Mickey Mouse" is an impossible little creature with a funny tiny nose and big ears, who has mad adventures with cats and cows and elephants that dance hornpipes, or with mountain lions that join paws and dance the *Spring Song* in a modern picture landscape.

Incidentally, he is a mirror of the times. He represents the modern fairy tale—"Puss-in-Boots" adapted to a flapper jazz age. Old Hans Christian Andersen would turn in his grave if he knew that the one fairy tale capable of seizing the imagination of the entire modern world is being dreamed in a concrete factory where the front gate clicks with an electric lock.

Like many another beloved fairy, "Mickey Mouse" had a tough time breaking his way into the hearts of children—children from eight to eighty.

About twenty years ago, the animals in the Chicago zoo had an admiring friend who came to see them often. He was a little boy of nine. His name was Walt Disney. His life's ambition was to own a circus filled with animals. (And now, in a way, he does.)

With his parents he moved to Kansas City, where his life's ambition veered a little. He decided to become a newspaper artist. He found the way as difficult as owning a circus. Wistfully he hung around the office of the *Kansas City Star*, wishing he could be an office boy or something. The nearest he got to fame as a newspaper cartoonist was delivering papers at three dollars a week.

He stayed with this job—his ears always tuned in on an office job—from the time he was nine until he was sixteen—going on seventeen.

When the war broke out, he forgot all about animals and cartoons. In spite of his youth he somehow managed to get himself attached to the Red Cross and went to France.

After the war, he found himself in the same predicament as other returned soldiers—broke and out of a job. Back home, the *Kansas City Star* was advertising for an office boy. Walt felt that his life's ambition was about to materialize, and he hustled over to the office. But they looked him over and decided he was too tall. If he hadn't sprouted up so, "Mickey Mouse" might still be living in that far-off dreamworld with the fairies who can't find their way into anybody's heart.

At last Disney got a job in a commercial art department, drawing pictures to be used as advertisements in a farm magazine. He drew cows that beamed with innocent joy at the prospect of licking somebody's patent salt boxes, chickens almost transported with enthusiasm at the sight of Whozit's Lay-More-Eggs Food. He learned a lot about drawing barnyard animals, but—in spite of the emotional frenzy of the cows and the chickens—his artistic yearnings were not satisfied.

Being a movie fan, he drew some animated—that is to say, moving—cartoons of local Kansas City celebrities and cartoon comments on local events. He managed to sell the idea to Frank Newman, a Kansas City movie magnate.

But Disney still yearned. He saved some money from his two jobs and organized a little company to make motion pictures—with pen-and-ink drawings for actors. They were all famous fairy tales, such as *Jack and the Beanstalk* and *Jack the Giant-Killer*. They interested everybody except the public. The modern young lady and gentleman in rompers had become too sophisticated. They said, "Aw, that's hooey," when they saw Disney's fairy tales in animated drawings. The corporation promptly went bankrupt.

Out on the cold, wet pavement again, Disney decided to storm the citadel of the movies. He set out for Hollywood. He had forty dollars in cash and three hundred dollars' worth of debts.

His idea was to start a motion picture series which should be partly pen-and-ink drawings and partly a motion picture of a real little girl playing with the fairies. This was "Alice" of the films. He convinced one of the motion picture releasing companies that the idea was good; but he would have to make the pictures at his own expense. He was to receive fifteen hundred dollars when the negative was delivered. But the problem of producing motion pictures on a capital of forty dollars was not easy. His brother threw in two hundred and fifty dollars, and together they managed to borrow a few hundred more. Not having money to hire artists, Disney had to make thousands of drawings himself. Under pressure, he could make one hundred to two hundred a day. There was plenty of pressure.

While their first picture was in the making, they lived chiefly on California climate. Their one real meal of the day was in a cafeteria on the corner. Disney bought whatever meat order they could get the most of for the money. His brother bought "filling" vegetable orders. Then they had a clearing house at a corner table.

Their first "Alice" picture was made for about half of the fifteen hundred dollars they received. This enabled them to let out a notch in their belts and have a meat order apiece.

"Alice" didn't last long. Disney says that "she was terrible." The public agreed with him. "Alice" was chased back to fairyland, and "Oswald the Cat [*sic*]" was born. He was more successful—even acquired some celebrity. "Oswald" enabled the firm to save about fifteen thousand dollars and hire some help. But "Oswald," too, gave up the ghost as the result of a dispute between Disney and a motion picture releasing company.

It was then that "Mickey Mouse" was born.

"I can't say just how the idea came," said Disney. "We wanted another animal. We had had a cat; a mouse naturally came to mind. We felt that the public—especially children—like animals that are 'cute' and little.

"I think that we were rather indebted to Charlie Chaplin for the idea. We wanted something appealing, and we thought of a tiny bit of a mouse that would have something of the wistfulness of Chaplin . . . a little fellow trying to do the best he could.

"Did I realize that I had hit upon an idea that would go around the world? Well, we always thought every new idea was a world-beater. And usually found out that it wasn't. We were enthusiastic over the idea of 'Mickey Mouse' but we had been just as enthusiastic over 'Alice.'"

One of the appealing things about Disney is his modesty. He is now twenty-nine years old—a slim, shy, pleasant-looking young fellow who gives you the impression he has stepped in from a golf course. He lives in a modest rented house in Hollywood and is married—not to a "professional." He has no children for "Mickey" to play with. He has very little time for amusements, but is a movie fan.

Having produced "Mickey Mouse" in a glowing first attempt, Disney dashed away to announce the news to an eager industry. He was turned down cold. He went from door to door—the round of the studios—to every picture company in Hollywood. The best he got was a sniff of contempt. Not a producer in Hollywood could get even a wan smile out of "Mickey."

In the end, Disney joined the army of the forsaken in "Poverty Row"—the Hollywood name given to those who release pictures in the open market—for those to buy who will. He made two pictures which were fairly successful. Both were silent pictures. Then Disney found the idea that made "Mickey" famous. The talkies came in. He decided to set him to music, to make him dance and talk. That was the beginning of these fantastically comic effects in the "Mickey" drawings where the elephants sway and pirouette and prance like chorus girls.

Within a year, every producer who had turned thumbs down on "Mickey" was wildly bidding for him. And here's irony. The first big laugh that came to "Mickey" was from England . . . where we think they have no sense of humor!

When "Mickey Mouse" rang the bell, Disney started another cartoon feature called *Silly Symphonies.* These were much on the same order, but a little wilder—trees and animals and birds and flowers that danced. The most successful one had skeletons that arose from their graves and danced. It had just as hard going as "Mickey Mouse." The first "symphony" lay for six months on the shelves—rejected and scorned.

After two years and a half, "Mickey" is established, in the language of Hollywood, as a box office riot, perhaps the greatest box office actor on the screen. He is known in every country which has a motion picture theater. He is even more popular in Europe than in America—especially Paris.

The most successful of the *Silly Symphonies* earned about sixty thousand dollars. "Mickey" makes about the same per picture. About one third of the receipts is profit. "Mickey's" earnings do not, however, stop with the pictures. Royalties pour in from many sources. Disney turns out a newspaper comic strip, showing the adventures of the mouse. It is sold to sixty newspapers in the United States and to newspapers in twenty foreign countries. "Mickey's" picture is on toys, dolls, storybooks, and his name is on safety razors, candy boxes, and what not.

The process of translating "Mickey Mouse" into films starts with a scenario conference—just like any motion picture. Disney employs thirty artists—mostly enthusiastic young fellows, many of whom have been newspaper cartoonists. Every other Friday night they have a story conference in Disney's office.

A "Mickey Mouse" story doesn't just happen; neither is it "sort of made as you go along." The amazing adventures of the mouse must have a clear dramatic story—usually with a definite villain, a climax, and a "chase."

The stories are "talked" first; then written down. One conferee bursting with mighty inspiration says, "I'll tell you what will be a wallop; have him meet a lion and . . . "Then the others groan and say, "Aw, get out with that old stuff."

Disney says that they usually eat candy—lollipops preferred—as the drama is evolved. Some of the artists are good at gags, others at plot.

After the story has been written comes the big job of drawing it. First, one of the star artists makes a series of key drawings—something like a long comic strip in a newspaper—portraying the important situations and showing "Mickey" and the cows, horses, bears and pigs in certain key positions. For instance, one drawing shows "Mickey" entering a scene; another shows him in the center of the stage; and so on. It is for the other artists to supply the gaps.

Very early in the game, the musical director takes a hand. One of the reasons why "Mickey" has been a success where so many others have failed is that no attempt is made to fit the music to "Mickey's" antics. The director decides first on the musical theme; then the artists make "Mickey" and the other animals dance to the music. The most difficult problem is to make "Mickey's" dance motions exactly correspond to the music. This is done by a secret process. All that can be said is that experts have figured out exactly how many motions the mouse can make to each musical "beat."

An average "Mickey" picture usually requires about nine thousand drawings for a run of seven and a half minutes on the screen. Let us say that "Mickey" is about to stroke his whiskers reflectively. One drawing as he starts to raise his paw; another picture showing the paw farther up; then another and another, until his paw finally caresses the whisker. If the "shot" proceeds at the normal speed of twenty-four pictures a second, this little gesture will require about eighty drawings.

In the older and cruder days of "animated cartoons," stencils were used to make multiple reproductions of all but the moving parts of a drawing. That is, "Mickey's" body would have been stenciled in for each successive picture, and original drawings would have been required only to show the moving arms and legs. But now, for greater realism, a complete drawing is made each time. The pictures even show the contraction and expansion of the mouse's body as he breathes.

Each of these thousands of drawings is made at first on cardboard to the required size. The chief problem is to give the impression of action—to make the motions natural; especially in the dance scenes. Often the neighbors of the "Mickey Mouse" studio think they have moved next door to an insane asylum as they see young artists in shirt-sleeves cavorting in the back yard. The young men are trying to discover what their legs do in the *Spring Song*. If the neighbors could peek inside the studio they would be certain they were in a lunatic neighborhood . . . young men leering and grinning into hand mirrors to see what on earth an eyebrow does during a laugh. The average competent artist makes from sixty to seventy-five action drawings a day.

The scenic backgrounds for the pictures are made by another gang of artists who are especially skilled in drawing the quaint fairy landscapes. Since one landscape will serve for several hundred motions of the action figures, an ingenious labor-saving method is employed in photographing the drawings. After the action drawings are completed, each is traced in India ink on a small celluloid sheet. The photographer then places these transparent sheets, one after another, over the desired landscape drawing. Since the landscape shows through, a complete picture is photographed in each case. The cutter joins these separate shots into a continuous film—ready to go to the ends of the earth.

An anxious moment comes when the film is run off to see if "Mickey's" motions fit the music. At first the producers tried giving "Mickey" theme music—like a motion picture drama. This didn't work. It made the picture seem long and dragged out. They found that a continuous flowing "piece" gives the desired effect. The gent who composed *Poet and Peasant* wrote great "gag" music. It goes with action.

"Mickey's" papa—Mr. Disney—has learned a lot about the American public from these pictures.

"In the beginning we thought we had to make the mouse very small in order to win the sympathy of the audiences. We have learned that we can make him as big as a horse. Sometimes we do.

"Another mistake we made was in thinking that American audiences always want brand-new gags—surprises and cute turns. We have found out that they want most to laugh. They easily forget the original turns but if a picture has given them a good laugh, whether by old gags or new, they always remember it and tell other people.

"We learned after hard lessons, too, that the public wants its heroes. In some of the pictures we tried to let other animals steal the honors from Mickey. There was an immediate reaction against this. Mickey has to be the whole thing, especially in the matter of brains. No one must outdo him. Most of all we learned that the American public loves dance music. It also demands villains with human characteristics."

Disney told me that the boys in the art department get great glee out of making the villains of the screen. They make rough cat villains to resemble Wallace Beery and smooth, polished cat villains to look like Erich von Stroheim. Much of the glee comes from the knowledge that all of these gentlemen, in private life, are charming and amiable fathers of families.

"Mickey Mouse" receives great stacks of fan mail. Some of the letters are addressed to "Mickey Mouse—Hollywood." Others are addressed to Disney. More grown people than children send fan letters. Sometimes they offer suggestions; more often they ask for Disney's autograph.

"Mickey Mouse" has even had the distinction of being censored. In Germany, the government barred a mouse film which showed an army of cats wearing German infantry helmets—thus heading off any suspicion that Germany might be mobilizing an army.

In Canada, the authorities were horrified to observe that the cow in one of the pictures was entirely in the nude. Whereupon Disney drew skirts for the lady.

The censors in one state in this country turned thumbs down on the same picture because the cow wore skirts. You just can't please everybody.

Of late, "Mickey" has been experiencing the grief that came to many movie actors with the advent of the talkies. He had to learn to talk. As a matter of policy, Disney limits the dialogue to as few words as possible. Of course, the audiences in Germany have resented their beloved mouse speaking in any other language. Just so the French. . . . So it looks as if "Mickey" were due to become the world's great linguist, as his pictures are shown to audiences who speak something like thirty-seven different languages.

Disney's job has become a big one. He escorts "Mickey" through every act of his life. He keeps in constant touch with the daily work of every artist. "Mickey" has an extremely critical and exacting papa. Perhaps that is why the little fellow seldom falls down on the job.

• As in *Time* magazine's "Regulated Rodent," * Harry Carr—a renowned writer and editor at the *Los Angeles Times*, with intimate ties to the movie industry—placed great emphasis on how Mickey's cartoons were made. Walt Disney's article in the *Windsor Magazine* (Oct. 1931)* and Gilbert Seldes's piece in the *New Yorker* (Dec. 1931)* were two among a number of others in the early to mid-1930s that aimed to satisfy reader curiosity on the same subject. All such reportage, Carr's included, must have been based—entirely, perhaps—on promotional material supplied by the studio, Mickey's distributor, Columbia Pictures, or both. In a two-page ad in the *Motion Picture Herald*, Columbia touted "what the big magazines" were saying about the feature it represented, specifically citing "Regulated Rodent" and Carr's piece in the *American Magazine* (Heide, *Mickey Mouse*, 38–39).

Carr's vivid description of Mickey's "abode on the edge of Hollywood," in "a small, concrete factory-studio on a side street next door to a gasoline service station," may reflect the fact that Carr himself lived under a mile from Walt's base of operations on Hyperion Avenue, in the Los Feliz section of Los Angeles. But Carr might not have actually interviewed Disney personally for this story. In his daily column for the *Los Angeles Times* (Jan. 28, 1935), he noted that he had just "met a young man whom I dimly remembered to have seen somewhere. We fell to talking about Mickey Mouse." However, Carr declared, he "did not seem to share my enthusiasm" for Mickey, and "I walked away," convinced "there was no use talking to a dumbbell like that." "Was my face red when I discovered that I had been talking to Walt Disney!"

Mickey and Walt may have been first mentioned in print by Carr in his column for December 29, 1930: "'Mickey Mouse' now stands at the head of box-office movie stars; but Walt Disney was thrown out of every studio in Hollywood when he tried to sell the series." Presumably, Carr wrote this squib at about the time he was composing his story for the *American Magazine*. In a subsequent column (Jan. 2, 1934), Carr had this to say with respect to Walt, Mickey and "the idiocy of the comic strip":

> Walt Disney, papa of Mickey Mouse and Three Little Pigs, is a bigger figure in literature than any of us have perhaps realized. He is comparable with the art of Hans Christian Andersen in the realm of pure fantasy.

Mickey Mouse is growing in quality all the time. I predict that these films will last forever as classics. They are more than comedy. They belong in the realm of literature that at times approaches greatness.

Mickey has chased every comedian off screen. He has something behind his laughs. He is a reproach to the idiocy of the "comic strip." With a salute to the myriad readers of The Times who can't live without them, I say that enjoyment of a comic strip is a sure symptom of arrested mental development.

You Can See Mickey Mouse Dancing . . .

Film-Kurier, July 28, 1931

"Die Diktatur," the Pomeranian regional organ of the N.S.A.P., published the following appeal:

"The Mickey Mouse Scandal!!!"

"Blonde, freethinking, urban German youth tied to the apron strings of Jewish finance. Young people, where is your sense of self? Mickey Mouse is the shabbiest, most miserable ideal ever invented. Mickey Mouse is a recipe for mental enfeeblement sent over with capital from the Young Plan. Healthy instinct should tell every decent girl and honest boy that those filthy, dirt-caked vermin, the greatest carriers of bacteria in the animal kingdom, cannot be made into an ideal animal type. Have we nothing better to do than decorate our garments with filthy animals because Jewish business in America wants profits? Down with Jewish brainwashing of the people! Kick out the vermin! Down with Mickey Mouse, and up with the swastika!"

*

Mickey Mouse, come on! We will brandish you as a cheerful emblem for all sensible people who oppose impiety, denial, and murder.

Pin little Mickey Mouse to yourself as a distinguishing mark against the swastika and provocation.

• As indicated here by the Berlin daily *Film-Kurier*, "The Mickey Mouse Scandal!!!" was an article or editorial (it's not clear which) published by a Nazi affiliate of the N. S. A. P. (*Nationalsozialistische Arbeiterpartei*, or National Socialist Workers Party) in Pomerania, a northern region of Germany near Poland. The Young Plan (1929–1930) was devised to relieve the oppressive terms of German reparations imposed by the Allies after World War I. It was named after the head of the committee that drafted the plan, Owen D. Young, founder of RCA (1919) and co-founder of the NBC radio network (1926). For the

35

original in German, see Appendix D. This translation is a reworking by Esther Leslie of an earlier rendition in her book, *Hollywood Flatlands* (Verso, 2002). "The Mickey Mouse Scandal!!!" inspired the epigraph in vol. 2 of Art Spiegelman's Pulitzer Prize-winning graphic novel *Maus: A Survivor's Tale*, which began, "Mickey Mouse is the most miserable ideal ever revealed," and ended, "Away with Jewish brutalization of the people! Down with Mickey Mouse! Wear the Swastika Cross!"

"Mickey Mouse": How He Was Born

Walt Disney

Windsor Magazine, October 1931

Filmgoers in this enlightened age are more or less familiar with the inner mysteries of a motion picture studio. Almost anyone can explain how the studio scene-shifters can produce at a moment's notice, so to speak, a storm at sea, an earthquake, snowclad mountain-tops, sun-parched plains, a mediaeval castle or a modern skyscraper, all within a space of a hundred square feet or so, and within a stone's-throw of the busy thoroughfares of Hollywood.

What puzzles them, however, is how the ingenious Mickey Mouse can gambol and gyrate across the screenland landscape without the aid of studio "props," stage carpenters, scene-shifters or electrical devices of any kind.

Mickey can do things which even the acrobatic Douglas Fairbanks would hesitate to attempt. This little inky "star," whose pictures ranked among the "10 Best of 1930," can hop and skip and kick his heels. He can play any kind of musical instrument; can run faster than the fastest kangaroo; can climb the highest mountain with no effort whatever; and can swim the Atlantic Ocean more quickly and more easily than the swiftest ocean greyhound. Such stunts are simply child's play to Mickey. He can straddle a continent or two before breakfast without so much as blinking an eyelash.

Who is the power behind this little mouse—the motive force that makes him do all these things apparently of his own volition? He is so real to some people that they have tried to mortalise Mickey—to put him in a class with real human actors. But that can't rightly be done, as Mickey after all is only a mouse—and not even a live mouse at that!

Mickey has no reality whatever outside the artist's brain. He owes his precarious screen existence solely to a whim of mine—translated by my corps of cartoonists (who act as "make-up men" and "wardrobe mistresses" to Mickey and his friends) using nothing but pen, ink, pencil and lots and lots of paper!—as well as an orchestra and one or two "effects men," who synchronise the completed cartoon with a musical score and occasional scraps of dialogue and song.

To go back a little further, however, the idea of Mickey originated long before the days of sound-films and I will try to relate some of the incidents that led up to his first appearance on the screen.

When I returned to the United States, after serving as an ambulance driver in the Red Cross during the war, I went to work as a cartoonist on the *Chicago Tribune.* Later I took a similar position on the *Kansas City Star.* I bought a second-hand camera and in my spare time worked as a free-lance in taking news-reel pictures. A few animated cartoons had been shown on the screen at that time, and, believing that there was an opening in that field, my brother Roy and I went to Los Angeles in 1923 with the firm determination to enter the animated cartoon business. Our combined capital was less than $500, but we had plenty of energy and enterprise, and originated the "Alice Cartoons."

Although this series proved popular from the first, I thought it might be improved through the introduction of a live character. So I elaborated upon the original cartoon idea by "double-exposing" a young girl along with the animated drawings of animals. It was really "Alice in Cartoonland" rather than "Wonderland." This series was produced for about two years, after which I went to the Universal Studio and originated Oswald the Rabbit. It was during the production of this series that I first conceived Mickey Mouse, and in order to increase his value as a cartoon subject I desired to give more attention and thought to the plot, gags and stories, more detail to the animation of the figures. In a word, I wanted to put more money into my product. As the studio executives demurred to my proposals, we agreed to part company, and I set up in business for myself.

Why did I choose a mouse for my principal character? Principally because I needed a small animal. I couldn't use a rabbit, because there already was a rabbit on the screen. So I decided upon a mouse, as I have always thought they were very interesting little creatures. At first I

decided to call him Mortimer Mouse, but changed his name to Mickey
as the name has a more friendly sound, and Mickey really is a friendly
sort of character. We have become great pals, Mickey and I. And I'm
not fooling when I say that he is just as much a person to me as anyone
I know. He is full of vitality and youth, and has the most endearing
childlike ways. He is unassuming and modest—not at all like all those
temperamental film stars we hear so much about!

While returning from a visit to New York, I plotted out the first story,
which was later to be released to the public as "Plane Crazy." I made
two of these subjects and tried to sell them. It was at this time that
sound was first becoming known. Al Jolson's first picture, "The Jazz
Singer," had been released and was creating a sensation in every cinema
in the country. All the large producers and distributors were hurrying
and scurrying to equip their studios and theatres with sound apparatus.
The consequence was that I could not get the ear of any producer, because of the changing conditions in the industry. Realising what I was
up against, I immediately set about producing a cartoon which could
be synchronised with sound. I then evolved my present system of syn-
chronising sound with animated drawings, which was later to take the
amusement world by storm.

After making this cartoon—which was especially drawn to be synchronised with music—I returned with it to New York to have it synchronised, as there was no available independent sound apparatus on
the Pacific Coast at that time.

Even in New York I had to go to an independent manufacturer of
sound apparatus to get my work done. I then tried to dispose of my
product to all the producers. In fact, I peddled it everywhere, but no
one would listen to me, until, finally, as a last resource, I entered into
a contract with the person who had furnished me with my first sound
equipment. It was not until "Steamboat Willie" was released to the
public, however, that Mickey Mouse was recognized at his true worth,
and from then on his path—and incidentally mine!—was one of roses.

The success of these musical cartoons is indeed universal, as they appeal not only to the American public, but to the world, and particularly
continental Europe. To-day manufacturers of every kind of commodity are using Mickey to promote the sale of their goods. He is repre-

sented in jewellery, earthenware, dolls, soap and candy. His features are embroidered on linen, on children's frocks and toys of all descriptions. Mickey is a symbol of laughter to countless thousands.

Strange that so much fame and popularity should be achieved by just a little splotch of ink!

How is the cartoon built up? Something like this.

Having prepared my scenario, I make sketches of the principal characters in front, profile, three-quarter, and back view, and, as far as possible, the size fixed for these figures is maintained throughout the film, in order to save as much re-drawing as possible. This is important when one considers that for every 500 feet of film something like 2,000 drawings are required.

In the old days of silent cartoons the procedure was simple. "Animators" decided upon a theme. Scenes were allotted to each of his assistants and the drawings begun. With the synchronised cartoon, however, not only has it been necessary to treble the staff of artists, but it takes at least three times as long to complete a subject.

Supposing, too, that a Censor in some foreign country objects—as one did in Canada—to the cow in one of my pictures reading a copy of Elinor Glyn's *Three Weeks*, or—as they did in Germany—to my army of cats wearing military uniforms—I must be prepared to cut out the offending scene and send another in its place. That means that I have to draw an entirely new scene to fit the synchronised record on the sound disc, and send it away without delay, by air mail if necessary, to the film local exchange.

You see, everything must be in time with the music. The characters that dance must be given dance steps that are not merely a jumble of hops and jumps and twirls. Funny gags must be enhanced by appropriate music. First of all, a conference is held and a theme decided upon, and the musical director brings to the attention of the animators various musical *motifs* that he considers befitting the proposed picture.

So soon as Mickey's supporting cast of animal characters has been selected the scenario is developed in detail. Scenes, actions and titles are put into proper continuity in the same manner as a scenario for an eight-reel extravaganza.

Backgrounds are the first pictures to be drawn. These are sometimes exterior scenes, showing woodland country or mountains, or, if it is a picture of the Frozen North, the background is an Arctic one. Interiors of rooms are drawn, or "close-ups " of windows or doors, as the case may.

After the backgrounds have been made, the artists immediately set to work animating the various scenes, each working with a sheet of music before him. This means that thousands of drawings must be made for each release so that a lifelike effect is the optical illusion when the various drawings are shown on the screen consecutively and in rapid succession. Each "animator" is given a series of scenes, and his drawings are made on translucent tissue paper. Thus the "animator" may see the lines of the preceding drawings as he places a new paper over each completed sketch. On the new paper he traces the previous drawing, but moves the arm or leg or head, as the case may be, to give the started or completed action of the character. This means that each drawing of the character is made in an entirely different position and the mere action of Mickey blowing his saxophone or striking the notes of the piano may mean a series of forty to fifty separate drawings.

When the picture has been completed by the total number of drawings being made on tissue paper, these pictures are handed to the "tracers," who transfer the drawings from the tissue to celluloids, or "cells," as they are commonly called. Tissue paper and "cells" have been perforated at the top with two holes an exact distance apart, and they fit snugly on two pegs that are at the top of the animators', as well as the tracers', drawing-boards. The completed drawings are numbered by the supervising artist, and the number of photographic exposures necessary to register the desired action is made. The entire cartoon release at this stage consists of about twenty thousand sheets of celluloid!

So soon as the "master print" has been made from the film negative, Mickey and his friends are ready to be synchronised with music, and the scene shifts to a sound studio, where in front of a motion picture screen is seated an orchestra of twelve pieces or so under the leadership of Carl Stallings, who writes the amusing "Scores" to each of my pictures. The players sit with their backs to the screen, facing the conductor, and a few feet from the orchestra is a long table upon which are scores of peculiar instruments to be used for the "effects" by the men who stand behind the table for that purpose.

At a given signal the lights in the studio go out and the animated cartoon is flashed on the screen. Stallings leads his orchestra through each stage of the picture, keeping time with the actions of Mickey Mouse and the other animals exactly as he planned to do during the making of the original design. The "effects men" watch for certain spots in the film where "effects," such as the barking of a dog, the slamming of a door, the ripple of water, the hoot of an owl, are needed.

Five rehearsals are held, and the film projected five times, before the services of the microphone are called in to give Mickey Mouse that last semblance of reality—the screen voice that has carried him straight into the hearts of a friendly world.

• Disney's byline for this story bore the editorial notation, "In an interview." But it was surely stitched together from other sources by a *Windsor Magazine* staff member, someone working for Walt or Columbia Pictures, or a combination thereof. Portions of the text were cribbed from a pair of articles published in 1931, one by Dan Thomas ("How They Make Animated Cartoons"), the other a promotional piece in *Motion Picture Daily* ("The Evolution of Mickey Mouse").

Three glaring inaccuracies suffice to confirm that Disney did not write this text: the comment that he was a cartoonist for the *Chicago Tribune* and the *Kansas City Star*, the claim that he "first conceived Mickey Mouse" while he was making Oswald, and the fact that Carl Stalling ("Stallings" here) had quit the Disney studio on January 24, 1930, nearly two years before the *Windsor* article was published. If this essay was composed in the U.S., in whole or in part, it may have been authored by Harry Hammond Beall, who, by June 1931, was Director of Publicity at the Disney studio, and was described by Kaspar Monahan in a July 1932 column in the *Pittsburgh Post* as "Mickey's chief press agent."

It was Dan Thomas, incidentally, in 1931, who may have been the first person to disclose in print what Walt stated here, that originally he wanted to call his cartoon mouse "Mortimer."

Mickey-Mouse Maker

Gilbert Seldes

New Yorker, December 19, 1931

In the current American mythology, Mickey Mouse is the imp, the benevolent dwarf of older fables, and like them he is far more popular than the important gods, heroes, and ogres. Over a hundred prints of each of his adventures are made, and of the fifteen thousand movie houses wired for sound in America, twelve thousand show his pictures. So far he has been deathless, as the demand for the early Mickey Mouses continues although they are nearly four years old; they are used at children's matinees, for request programs, and as acceptable fillers in programs of short subjects. It is estimated that over a million separate audiences see him every year.

Thirteen Mickey Mouses are made each year. The same workmen produce also thirteen pictures in another series, the Silly Symphonies, so that exactly fourteen days is the working time for each of these masterpieces which Serge Eisenstein, the great Russian director, called, with professional extravagance, America's greatest contribution to culture. The creative power behind them is a single individual, Walt Disney, who happens to be such a mediocre draughtsman, in comparison with the artists he employs, that he never actually draws Mickey Mouse. He has, however, a deep personal relation to the creature: the speaking voice of Mickey is the voice of Walt Disney.

He is a slender, sharp-faced, quietly happy, frequently smiling young man, thirty this month. He is married to Lillian Marie Bounds, whom he met in Hollywood, where she was probably unique, as she had nothing to do with pictures. She has enough to do with them now, because she is the first receiver of her husband's ideas. Mickey Mouse pictures are talked into being before they are drawn, talked and cackled and groaned and boomed and squeaked and roared and barked and meowed, with every variation of animal sound, with appropriate gesture, and with music. If strange outcries and queer noises awaken Mrs. Disney at night, it is only Walt working on a new story. He never stops; he swims and rides and he plays baseball with his staff, but all the time he is inventing. He is one of the lucky ones who can make a fortune out of the work they love and he does not love Mickey for his wealth alone. He was just as keen when exhibitors refused to look at the Mouse, and just as keen over earlier efforts which were, as he now says, "pretty awful."

He is fortunate also in having as his chief co-worker his elder brother, who is the businessman of the firm. Roy Disney and five assistants attend to finance; Walt and about a hundred others—a quarter of them are artists, the rest are gagmen, story-men, and technical experts—make the pictures. The distribution and sales are in other hands.

When a Mouse or a Silly Symphony is finished, the business side and most of the artists watch it carefully for commercial value, for those mysterious qualities which they think, or guess, will make it popular. They find their congratulations to Walt Disney accepted without enthusiasm. He is not putting on artistic airs; he is not indifferent to profits. What he is frequently doing is referring each finished picture back to the clear idea with which it started, the thing he saw and heard in his mind before it ever came to India ink and sound tracks. In the process of making the picture, something often escapes, and Disney wanders moodily away from the projection-room grumbling: "Where did it go to?" and often will begin outlining the original idea again, with gestures and sound effects, to prove that he is right.

The mechanics of creating Mickey Mouse are complicated and, to the workers, tedious. Six or seven drawings are required for every movement, and the first and last, the position of the Mouse at the beginning and at the end of any motion, are drawn by the principal artists, or "animators." After them, the "in-betweeners" fill the intervening space, with minute changes in the figure. The final step in preparing for the camera is the photographic transfer of these drawings to celluloid. As the background changes less frequently, dozens of celluloid drawings may be placed over a single background scene.

The drawings are now ready for the camera, which photographs each separately. The tracing of the moving figure is placed on its background, the photograph is taken, and the next drawing is moved into position. About eight hundred photographs can be taken in one day—some fifty feet of film.

The sound track is made after the picture has been completed. A short section of the film is projected; the music, which has been selected in advance, is rehearsed by musicians, who watch the screen as they play; and when the timing has been perfected, the music is recorded.

The two advantages of the animated cartoon over the feature picture are only implied in the above description: there are no stars and only as much film is taken as will be used. A few feet are allowed for adjustments, but the filming of a hundred and fifty thousand feet for a six-thousand-foot picture does not occur.

Walt Disney is, as I have said, thirty, and that means that he is too young to have had a history, too young to have developed oddities and idiosyncrasies. He is a simple person in the sense that everything about him harmonizes with everything else; his work reflects the way he lives, and vice versa. Mickey Mouse appears on the screen with features and super-specials, but Mickey Mouse is far removed from the usual Hollywood product, with its sex appeal, current interests, personalities, studio intrigue, and the like. And Disney, living in Hollywood, shares hardly at all in Hollywood's life. He has not only made a lot of money (between forty and fifty per cent of the return on each film is net profit); better than that, his potential income is enormous: he has the surest bet in filmdom; experts think that he is only at the beginning of his great success. In these circumstances, Hollywood builds itself a palace and a pool; Disney lives in the house he built five years ago when he and his brother were too poor to buy a lot for each, and combined on a corner so that both the houses they built would have sufficient light and air. His house is a six-room bungalow, the commoner type of middle-class construction in Hollywood; the car he drives is a medium-priced domestic one; his clothes are ordinary. He goes to pictures, but rarely to the flash openings; he neither gives nor attends great parties. Outside of the people who work with him, he has few friends in the industry. The only large sum of money he ever spent was one hundred and twenty-five thousand dollars; it was the cost of his new studio. Everything he earns and everything his brother earns, on the fifty-fifty basis they established years ago, is reinvested in the business.

Walt Disney's life before he went into movie-making divides into two almost equal and almost entirely undistinguished sections. He was born in Chicago in 1901, his father was an Irish-Canadian builder and contractor, his mother a German-American. He went to the Chicago public schools and studied drawing for a few months at the Art Institute. Arguing, perhaps, from his present enthusiasms, friends of the Chicago days now say that he was exceptionally fond of going to the Zoo. The second period a little shorter in time, is more varied. The family moved to Kansas City; from there Disney, too young for service in the trenches went to the war with a Red Cross unit; to Kansas City he returned and tried to become a newspaper cartoonist. He found no job. He went to work as a commercial artist and saved up enough money to make his first animated cartoons.

These were animations of well known fairy tales and children's classics. In competition with the highly developed product of the experts, they were crude and uninteresting, and they failed. Disney felt that if he wanted to make pictures, he would have to go where pictures were made and, in 1923, departed for Hollywood. His brother, who had come out of the war in shattered health, expected to live only a short time, and thought that California would be an agreeable place for his few remaining months of life. Walt had forty dollars when he arrived in Los Angeles, Roy contributed about two hundred and fifty; they borrowed enough to make a total of five hundred dollars and made their first picture. It was done in a bastard medium, using human beings and drawn figures simultaneously, ordinary movie photography and pen and ink; the inspiration comes from "Alice in Wonderland" and the series was called after the heroine which is interesting because since the success of Mickey Mouse, Disney is continually receiving requests to make the original Alice in his own medium.

The first picture brought in fifteen hundred dollars; half of this was profit, if you figure that the brothers were not entitled to salary. During the making of the picture they had lived skimpily, on one full (cafeteria) meal a day, Roy ordering the most filling vegetable, Walt the most filling meat, and then sharing, as they shared everything in those days, including their bank account. The lean time was soon over; the pictures were moderately successful, and after about four years, Disney went, in 1927, to Universal, where he created Oswald the Rabbit, the true forerunner of Mickey Mouse. Oswald was left behind when, in the middle of 1928, the Disneys, with fifteen thousand dollars saved, started out again on their own.

Sound was just coming in and Disney's still-silent cartoons were unacceptable. Instantly he adapted his idea to the new medium. Unlike the producers of feature pictures he had nothing to scrap, no equipment to save, and hardly any public to worry about. He made a drawn comic and took it to New York for synchronization. When he was finished he took it to the great producers and distributors—the men who had a few months earlier turned down the whole talking mechanism and were now furiously witnessing the success of the Vitaphone. Unanimously they informed Disney that no one would care for animated cartoons with sound. After several weeks, he found an independent backer, and on the nineteenth of September, 1928, the audience at the Colony Theatre in New York was "panicked" by "Steamboat Willie," the first adventure of Mickey Mouse. A few days later Mickey was the hit at Roxy's. Almost at once England all-hailed him. The rest has been roses, roses all the way.

Roses and children. Leaving the distribution of the films to others, the Walt Disney Corporation concentrates commercially on the creation of movie audiences. Disney's own connection with the vast enterprise which now enrolls three-quarters of a million children in Mickey Mouse clubs is not close. The clubs are the invention of an enterprising member of the business staff, and Disney's only interest in them is as a source of knowledge; he learns from them what children like. The club members attend morning or early-afternoon performances at movie houses, led by a Chief Mickey Mouse and Chief Minnie Mouse; they have a club yell, and official greeting, a theme song, and a creed. As I find myself a little unsympathetic to this activity, I shall limit myself to an exact quotation of the creed:

"I will be a square-shooter in my home, in school, on the playground, wherever I may be. I will be truthful and honorable and strive always to make myself a better and more useful little citizen. I will respect my elders and help the aged, the helpless, and children smaller than myself. In short, I will be a good American."

For the good Americans there are commercial tie-ups with local businessmen, such as druggists who may feature a Mickey Mouse sundae, florists with Mickey Mouse bouquets, and so on; Parent-Teacher Associations are enlisted; the films at the matinees are swift-moving Westerns and other clean films, with a rather elaborate ritual of patriotism and good-fellowship before and after.

It was reported that at the great Leipzig Trade Fair this year, forty percent of all the novelties offered were inspired by Mickey Mouse. One American company lists a velvet doll, a wood-jointed figure, a mechanical drummer, a metal sparkler, and half-a-dozen other toys; there is a "Mickey Mouse Coloring Book" and another book of the adventures of Mickey Mouse; you can have Mickey Mouse on your writing paper; you can have him as a radiator cap. He appears in a comic strip in twenty-seven languages. From all of these exploitations, the originators receive royalties, since they own both the name and the design of the figure. (Infringements have been successfully prosecuted.) On the screen, Mickey Mouse appears in every country to which equipment for projecting sound films has penetrated. His name in Japan is Miki Kuchi.

Neither at home nor abroad has Mickey's career been without accidents. In Germany the appearance of an army of animals in Uhlan helmets was considered an affront, and the film was censored. In more dainty Ohio a cartoon was barred because a cow was discovered reading "Three Weeks." Cows seem to have given more offence than any other beast in the Disney jungle, for many State Boards of Censorship protested against the grotesque and emotionally expressive udders which Nature and Disney gave them, and hereafter udders are to be at least partially concealed under a small provocative skirt. Disney himself is amused by the fuss; quite justifiably he takes it as a tribute to the remarkable reality of his totally unreal figure.

The process of creating this unreality begins in Disney's mind. By this time it is only necessary for him to think of Mickey running to a fire, or Mickey skating; the rest is worked out in discussions with the artists and the gagmen. The automatic thing, the formula of the present, is the creative work of years ago, when Disney saw a series of pictures, saw moving forms across landscapes, rhythmic dances, compositions in black and white. These are still the essence of his pictures; his imagination is still largely visual. Only now that his assistants know the kind of picture he wants, his work has to be selecting the general idea, thinking out the tiny plot (even if it be only a modern version of "Little Red Riding Hood" or a burlesque of some popular feature film), leaving the rest to experts.

I have kept Mickey Mouse in the foreground because in general it is with Mickey that Disney is identified; but I belong to the heretical sect which considers the Silly Symphonies by far the greater of Disney's products. Although there is a theme in each one, Disney's imagination is freer to roam than it is in the more formal Mouse series. The Symphonies, moreover, are true sound pictures, without dialogue; the Mouse series has a tendency, lately, to run to verbal fun which is a little out of place.

Unlike the Mouse pictures, the Symphonies have no central character and no clearly defined plot. In them the animals and vegetation, purely incidental to Mickey Mouse, are brought into the foreground, and go through a wide range of activity—dances, skating contests, and so on—to the accompaniment of a reiterated musical theme.

The Symphonies reinforce what the Mouse tells us about Disney's character: his delight in quick surprises, his uncomplicated sense of fun, his keen observation (Mickey Mouse has, correctly, four fingers, not five). In addition they suggest his passion for all animals—he dropped his work and ran all over the vacant lot near his studio when he heard that a gopher snake had been seen there; he watched some sparrows for hours while they beat off a hawk and set up their nest. And he likes enormously the kind of laughter he himself creates; laughter at absurdities and impossibilities. Out of these natural, simple interests, backed by enormous files of pictures, cross-sections, and data on every animal extant, he creates the Silly Symphonies.

Like the first Mouse, the first Silly Symphony was long rejected by exhibitors; once shown, it ran six weeks at one house, an exceptional occurrence for a short subject. It was the Skeleton Dance, a theme naturally macabre, but treated with such humor and fantasy that no child has ever been frightened by it. Soon after followed a masterly series on the four seasons.

In one of these occurs a moment typical of Disney's method. A frog dances on a log, its shadow following in the pool below. Presently the frog moves to the opposite end of the picture, the shadow stays where it is, but continues to reflect the dance; then it joins its owner. Perhaps fifteen seconds cover the incident; it is a grace-note of wit over the broad humorous symphony of the whole picture.

With a picture to make every two weeks, both Disney and his associates have to use certain formulas, like the dancing of animals and chairs, chases and the sudden elongations of necks and legs. But the freshness of picture after picture proves that the creative force behind the formula is still powerful, and the combination of ingenuity and innocence (which was typical of prewar America) can still give pleasure. At the end of three and a half years, Disney's ingenuity seems more fertile than ever. And his innocence is attested by the fact that he can think of nothing better to do with his time, his talent, and the five thousand a week (or thereabouts) which he earns, than to put all of them back into the work he enjoys.

• In the fifth paragraph of the text, the phrase given here as "not putting on artistic airs" originally appeared as "not putting on artistic side," presumably a typo—something rare in the *New Yorker*.

2. Into the Realm of High Art

1932–1933

Walt Disney and Mickey Mouse reached the airy strata of high art half a century before their now far more familiar association with Pop Art maestros like Roy Lichtenstein, Claes Oldenburg, and Andy Warhol.

In November–December 1931, as Diego Rivera readied a one-man show at the Museum of Modern Art, he authored an essay, "Mickey Mouse and American Art," published in February 1932 in a short-lived literary magazine called *Contact*. In Rivera's article, he predicted that Mickey would be seen as "one of the genuine heroes of American Art in the first half of the 20th Century." *

Also in 1932, the American Regionalist painter Thomas Hart Benton painted a set of murals, "The Arts of Life in America," for the library of the Whitney Museum of American Art, then located in lower Manhattan, one panel of which included Rivera's heroic mouse. In 1934, Benton's friend and fellow Regionalist, John Steuart Curry, executed two fresco designs, *Tragedy* and *Comedy*, on the walls of a school auditorium in Westport, Connecticut, in which, as Alexander Eliot, writing in *Time*, commented, Curry "gaily jumbled" Chaplin with Mickey, Hamlet, and other figures from high and low culture.

From September 1932 till the start of World War II, scores of exhibits (no two the same) comprised mainly of production art from the Mickey Mouse and Silly Symphonies series went on display in museums, galleries, and libraries across the nation and in Canada, England, and Ireland. Dorothy Grafly and Eleanor Lambert summed up the basis for this unparalleled attention. Grafly characterized the Symphonies as "genuine artistry," * while Lambert declared Walt's "engaging, lovable little adventurer" (Mickey) to be "the embodiment of a new art, an art in motion and an art in rhythm, the keynote of a new epoch in the history of æsthetics." *

Mickey Mouse transcended boundaries of nationality, age, and class. Plebs and eggheads alike regarded him, in the words of Terry Ramsaye, editor of the *Motion Picture Herald*, as "the Great Common Denominator of the great common art of the commonality," and as a latter-day "Everyman."* Disney's diminutive Everyman did occasional battle with villains both foreign and domestic. But he was prized primarily as just a regular kind of guy, one who, as Edwin C. Hill put it, "will never 'go Hollywood.'"*

In 1933, a torrent of publicity was generated by Disney and its current distributor, United Artists, to mark Mickey's fifth-anniversary year. As part of the promotional process, a backstory to the saga of the Mouse took hold, circulated by writers like Lambert, who described a youthful Disney observing "the antics of a pair of little mice," and Hill, who spun a tale of "mice that played about in Walt's room," which he "tamed and taught to pose for him." This emergent, PR-driven theme conveyed a comforting impression of Walt as a genial, twentieth-century counterpart to St. Francis of Assisi, devoted friend of all creatures great and small.

Disney did not, of course, talk to the animals. Instead, he made the animals talk . . . and sing and frolic about, to the delight of movie-goers the world over. This gentle, reassuring image, established circa 1932–1933 by Mickey's poppa, helped lay the groundwork for the nickname "Uncle Walt," by which Disney would be widely known after World War II.

Mickey Mouse and American Art

Diego Rivera

Contact: An American Quarterly Review, February 1932. D.R. © 2013 Banco de México, "Fiduciario" en el Fideicomiso relative a los Museos Diego Rivera y Frida Kahlo. Av. 5 de Mayo No. 2, Col. Centro, Del. Cuauhtémoc 06059, México, D.F.

The other night after a lecture on The Functions of Art and of the Artists in Present Day Society we prolonged the same theme and arrived at length at the discussion of things which are not taken seriously, not even by those that make them.

I remember innumerable things made in Mexico which are destined to be destroyed—sculptures in sugar, made to be eaten; sculptures in cardboard and paper made especially to be torn to pieces or burnt (The Judases*). And those things are the ones which really possess the greatest plastic value in the art of Mexico.

If some day a famous artist were not to look for but to stumble onto the way to attain, to create one of those objects, the "world of art" would be gaping and the museums of the entire world would be offering anything to acquire the marvelous object.

But all those playthings for children and grown-ups live and die without disquieting the realm of the esthetes.

It may be that some day an esthete will "find" or "discover" the beauty of those things. The people of good taste will be astounded by them.

Probably at that moment, such things will cease being produced; or will become as boring as the art of the artists.

Don't be alarmed! I do not believe that I am discovering the theory of unconscious creation; others have sought and found it long ago. I am only referring to the subject of our discussion of the other night.

If we look at the characteristics of the animated cartoons which are shown in the movies, we find them to be of the purest and most definitive graphic style, of the greatest efficacy as social products, drawings joyous and simple that make the masses of tired men and women rest, make the children laugh till they are weary and ready for sleep and will let the grown-ups rest undisturbed.

Note the style, the standardization of the drawing of details, the infinite variety of the groupings, as in the painted friezes of the Egyptians and the earthenware vases of the Greeks! And with all that, the added quality of motion!

And their representation in the movies, which according to Mr. Eisenstein is the only art of today!

If that be so, lucky for the oculist! And also for the insomniac, if he is fortunate enough to find a quiet sound film and a comfortable loge.

Let us admit that those animated cartoons express the most logical yet most unexpected rhythms by the necessity of their technique—the most direct expressions, uniting the greatest efficiency with the greatest economy.

Finally we may conclude that perhaps if the films can be preserved, the people who at last will possess a theater, will refuse to accept the cine-dramas most admired today. The masses which will have realized by then the genuine revolution, will not interest themselves greatly in the "revolutionary films" of today. And all that, together with the pictures and statues and poetry and prose which may have survived the general cleansing of the world, will be looked at with compassionate curiosity. But probably the animated cartoons will divert the adults then as now and make the children die laughing.

And the esthetes of that day will find that MICKEY MOUSE was one of the genuine heroes of American Art in the first half of the 20th Century, in the calendar anterior to the world revolution.

* (*Effigies with fire-work attached representing Judas and made to burn on the Saturday of Easter-Week.*)

• This brief essay appeared in *Contact: An American Quarterly Review*, co-founded and co-edited by the poet William Carlos Williams. It faithfully follows a manuscript in Rivera's hand penned in brown ink on Barbizon-Plaza stationery, now in the collection of the Walt Disney Family Foundation, San Francisco. Only minor revisions of spelling, capitalization, and wording were made, though two mistakes crept into the piece as published, both rectified here: where Diego had written, "Note the style, the standardization of the drawing," the printed text read "Not the style," and where, in his original Spanish-language text, he had written, "en el cine," those words appeared in *Contact* as "in the movie," rather than "in the movies."

Diego's essay was written in Spanish and translated by his friend and fellow Marxist, Bertram D. Wolfe, a founding member of the Communist Party of America. By the 1950s, however, Wolfe had become a fervent anti-Communist, and was a Senior Fellow at the Hoover Institution Library and Archives, Stanford University. Diego's manuscript in Spanish, also on Barbizon stationery, is among Bert Wolfe's papers at the Archives, along with a draft by Wolfe of the English translation, entitled "Mickey Mouse." For the text in Spanish, see Appendix E.

Like the original version in Spanish, Wolfe's translation must date from between mid-November 1931 and January 1932, while Rivera was in New York preparing a solo exhibition of his work at the Museum of Modern Art, which ran from December 22, 1931, to January 27, 1932. Diego and his wife, Frida Kahlo, stayed at the Barbizon-Plaza at MoMA's expense during the ten-week period leading up to and during the run of his show. Diego and Walt, incidentally, met at least once. In December 1942, they were photographed chatting with film star Dolores Del Rio at the opening of Ciro's, a posh nightclub in Mexico City.

Mickey Mouse:
He Stays on the Job

Terry Ramsaye

Motion Picture Herald, October 1, 1932

Mickey Mouse is the crystalline, concentrated quintessence of that which is peculiarly the motion picture. He is at one with the Great Common Denominator of the great common art of the commonality in terms of expression, while in production he is a logarithmic derivation of the whole of screen technology. He is as simple as a dandelion and we do not know what makes it grow.

❡ Mickey is most humbly superhuman. He is an evolutionary product with everything that ever was made for the screen in his ancestry and with Charlie Chaplin as his closest human relative.

❡ The irrepressible Mickey in charmingly typical expression of his own psychology, which is based on the principle of the triumph of the boob, the cosmic victory of the underdog, the might of the meek, has in a very certain sense paid tribute to Mr. Chaplin by becoming his successor in certain considerable sectors of the world of the motion picture.

❡ Due to assorted forces, as variant as commercial demands and personal ambitions, to say nothing of human limitations, Mr. Chaplin who began and became famous by endless, continuous industry in single reels, on the screen every day in thousands of theatres the world around, has become consciously symbolic, esoteric, multiple reeled, rich and infrequent. Mickey Mouse, like Mr. Chaplin used to, makes one reelers frequently, always sings something simple and scatters prints over the world across all linguistic and geographical boundaries, as lightly as he defies the law of gravity and all other laws thereunto pertaining.

❡ In the four years of his rise Mickey Mouse has become in a world sense the most famous personality of the screen of the day, and is likely in fact to become as well known as his collateral ancestor Mr. Chaplin was in the period 1916–1918, when he was, beyond doubt, known to more persons than any prior or subsequent figure of human history.

❡ In his consistent and continuous screen performances at a high standard of quality, Mickey Mouse is today the screen's own best contributor to the creation and maintenance of the habit of attending the screen theatre. His success is a service to the industry. He stays on the job.

❡ Mickey confers distinction and honor upon the motion picture by his peculiar and lone capacity to utilize and demonstrate all of those capacities of the camera and screen as an instrument which especially distinguish it from other media of expression.

❡ In turn this amazing little creature of the cinema promises to share in the glory of the great immortals, in a hall of fame with Santa Claus, Don Quixote, Leather Stocking, Paul Bunyan, Rip Van Winkle, Long John Silver and Odin, Wodin, Thor & Co.

❡ Even as Chaplin was, Mickey Mouse is all things to all men. He is a gust of thoughtless fun to the casual, the lowbrow, the thoughtless. He is the voice and personification of the weltschmerz to the sophisticate and a blood brother to the philosopher.

❡ Mickey is more of a man than a mouse and in all humility, not irony, we must admit that it takes a mouse to be Everyman.

An Artist of Our Time: Walter E. Disney, 1901–

Dorothy Grafly (unsigned)

Philadelphia Public Ledger, October 23, 1932. Used with permission of Philadelphia Inquirer. Copyright © 2013. All rights reserved.

Walter E. Disney, American artist, creator of Mickey Mouse and Silly Symphonies, was born in Chicago, December 5, 1901, of Irish-Canadian and German-American ancestry.

Disney's early impressions of life were various, as the family was continuously on the move, remaining six years, however, on a farm in Missouri, where the boy became acquainted with barnyard characters. City life followed, and at 17 Walt, although under age for the army, enrolled with an ambulance unit for a year in France. At the close of the World War he returned to Kansas City to eke out a living as free lance news reel cameraman.

Due to the family's nomadic tendencies, Walt's schooling was anything but orthodox, the greater part of his information and inspiration deriving from nature and life contacts. He did spend some time in Chicago public schools, with a period of training in the rudiments of drawing at the Chicago Art Institute. His ambition then was to become a newspaper cartoonist, but the opening never presented itself.

The camera job evaporating Disney entered a commercial art concern, where he turned farm experience to good account in devising advertisements for a farm journal. With his first savings, plus funds from a local financier, he decided to try his luck at the animated cartoon. The venture yielded much experience and more debts. Nothing daunted, Disney decided to go to California, where he could be near Hollywood and where his brother, Roy, once a banker, might regain his lost health.

In 1923 the Disney team set out for new soil.

For five years Walt Disney developed his idea with no particular success. His early ventures combined photography with the cartoon. Gradually, however, he purged his story of such photographic aids. It was not until 1928 that he hit upon Mickey Mouse as star. Mickey was not born in a flash. His beginnings go back to the midnight hours that Disney spent in that Kansas City advertising concern, when he watched the antics of the office mice, and even trained one to sit on his drawing-board.

Fortunately for Disney, Mickey was born just when the talkies were playing havoc with American film distribution abroad. The animated cartoon, providing entertainment independent of speech, had an enthusiastic tryout in New York and became an instant favorite in Europe.

The Silly Symphonies followed Mickey Mouse, and give Walt Disney claim to genuine artistry. Mickey Mouse, however, is more popular, and it is said that Disney receives approximately $100,000 a year from royalties derived mainly from the sales of such by-products as Mickey Mouse dolls, toys and other articles.

Mickey Mouse, the star, is a producer, ranking today with Charlie Chaplain, Douglas Fairbanks, Mary Pickford and Ronald Colman. He also employs a staff of some 300 workers, has blossomed forth in a comic strip and is patron saint of some 1,000,000 children who are members of Mickey Mouse clubs.

Roy Disney finds outlet for his banking talents in the managing and advertising of the Disney projects, which in the field of American art are unique and fabulous.

• This unsigned piece by Grafly accompanied her review, also unsigned ("Disney Has Debut in Art Circles"), of the first-ever exhibition of Disney production art, presented at the Art Alliance of Philadelphia from October 22 to November 6, 1932. In a signed article on the same page, "Animated Cartoon Gives the World an American Art," Grafly declared that, with motion picture cartoons like Disney's, "we have witnessed the birth of an American art, something that has yet to be given us in the realm of paint." In that same article she also said that the "symphonic treatment of the animated cartoon" in Walt's Silly Symphonies series "joins the potentialities of drama, music and art.

It lacks precedent, and is consequently reviled by established art. In its Mickey Mouse phase," Grafly went on, the animated cartoon "gives us a contemporary folk art."

He Gave Us Mickey Mouse

Jack Jamison

Liberty, January 14, 1933. Copyright Liberty Library Corporation.

There is a young man, in Hollywood of all places, who could be a millionaire if he liked, but who smiles and shrugs and says, "No; I'm having too much fun this way, thanks."

He is Walter Disney, creator of Mickey Mouse and the Silly Symphonies.

In 1919 a young Red Cross ambulance driver came home from France to Kansas City, Missouri. He became a ten-dollar-a-week apprentice in a commercial art firm. Let out when business was slow, he carried mail for Uncle Sam, and shortly teamed up with another youngster who liked pencils and paper. They drew pictures of oil wells.

"The firm that was selling the oil wells told us to draw them the way they would look when the oil came in," Walter recollects. "You should have seen the amount of oil we got into those drawings!"

Always interested in cartoons, he next experimented with a motion-picture cartoon reel for a Kansas City chain of theaters, depicting local happenings and personalities. Finding that he had a knack for it, he laid out a series of fairy-tale cartoon reels to be shown in schools and churches. His backers failed, and he found himself reduced in assets to a pair of trousers, a sweater, a motion-picture camera, and a pair of shoes bought with five dollars borrowed from a friend; those, and a great faith in the possibilities of motion pictures.

Hollywood was motion-picture headquarters. Always impetuous, he sold the camera and arrived there with $40 to spare. His brother Roy was in Hollywood selling vacuum cleaners. He had $250 in a savings account. Walter talked fast, and a few hours later Roy discovered himself to be in the motion-picture business. Walter's initial idea was to hire a child actress and let her act in the cartoons along with the drawn figures. For the first reel he did all the drawings himself—fifteen hundred of them. Its entertainment value was instantly recognized, and a studio gave him a contract to do a series.

"Success!" thought Walter, and promptly expanded his staff, hiring a young lady to help him ink in his drawings. She was an exceedingly pretty girl—and, as day after day they bent their heads together over a drawing board, Walter became increasingly aware of the fact. The upshot was inevitable, because she had as much faith in his cartoons as he had. In short, he married her.

Soon other people had to be hired, for Universal Studios invited the budding young concern to manufacture a cartoon having to do with a rabbit named Oswald. Walter thought rabbits were too meek and not up to enough devilment, but he made twenty-six Oswalds. The trouble, the studio found, was that he was always trying out new ideas and gadgets, wanting to spend money instead of just settle down into a rut and make it. They allowed his contract to lapse. He was in New York when he got the news, and his first thought was for the twenty young fellows out in Hollywood now working for him. He couldn't bear to let them know that they were out of jobs. With Mrs. Disney, he caught the first train for Hollywood, and on the train he wrote the scenario for the first feature production of Walt Disney Studios, Ltd.

The hero, he decided, would be a mouse. Mice were little and cute, and always up to mischief.

Of course he had no backing. But that was nothing.

The first Mickey Mouse reel was produced in a cramped room over the Disney garage. It had approximately one chance in a thousand of succeeding. Talkies had come in. Walter offered that tin can of celluloid to every studio in town. Not one of them showed interest in it. A year later every one of them was to bid frantically for it, but at the moment all they were interested in was bringing vaudeville acts to the screen. Anybody else would have been discouraged. Walt wasn't. He was having fun. Finally he located an independent producer who, in a flight of wild daring, agreed to risk a few dollars on the mouse. And that is how Mickey, born in an attic, first saw the light of the projection-machine arc lamps.

A few days before I last saw Walter Disney he happened by chance to run into the studio executive who let his contract run out because he "wasted the studio's money to have fun." They shook hands, and a deep silence fell. Finally, with a groan, the executive shook his head. "And I let you get away from me!" he commented.

For Mickey, today, is the most popular film star in the world. This is not exaggeration but the literal truth. Whether as Miki Kuchi in Japan or Mikkel Mus in Denmark, he lays honest claim to more enthusiastic fans than Greta Garbo, Clark Gable, and Marie Dressler put together. More than a million American youngsters belong to Mickey Mouse clubs. A hundred manufacturers all over the globe—thirty in England alone—are kept busy turning out Mickey Mouse novelties; to name a few, souvenir spoons, all-day suckers, wall paper for nurseries, toys, drawing books, cards, pillows, pennants, jewelry, and, unbelievably enough, razor blades.

Children in Manchester, England were afraid to ride in the black ambulance of the Royal Manchester Children's Hospital. It was decorated with paintings of Mickey and the other cartoon characters, and now the kids can't get tummyaches often enough.

In Europe alone sixty newspapers beguile their readers with Mickey comic strips. Fan mail at the studio has reached a peak of eight thousand letters a week, the letters coming from every country and every town where there is a theater. Naturally, quite a few nickels are jingling into Mr. Disney's jeans today. The garret over the garage has been succeeded by a modern $150,000 studio housing a hundred employees who turn out one Mickey reel and one Silly Symphony a month. And yet—

A friend who used to know him in the old Kansas City days, when he was drawing pictures of hens and cows for farm journals, dropped in at the studio and asked him: "Well, Walt, how does it feel to be rich?"

"I don't know," Walter said, "and I don't care."

He doesn't. It's the simple truth. He lets someone else take care of all the figures. He doesn't want to know. He might begin to let his mind dwell upon figures rather than ideas, and that would spoil the fun.

The figures are interesting, just the same. Per foot of film, it costs as much to make a Mickey picture as it does to make a full-length feature film. Although he has invented any number of efficient labor-saving devices, Walt absolutely refuses to economize. For the comfort of his animators, the men who lay out the drawings, he has installed a variety of devices ranging from an air-washing system to ping-pong tables. He refuses to let them work at night, or overtime lest they get tired. He keeps a much larger staff on hand than is really necessary, paying men well to do nothing but sit in a comfortable chair and play with new ideas and methods—"feeling around," he calls it. And, depression or no depression he refuses to reduce his men's salaries. With a smile, Mrs. Disney accuses him of having more affection for his animators than he has for her, and of turning all his profits back into the studio. The latter he does. Today, as ten years ago, the Disneys live in a six-room English-style bungalow in which the greatest luxury is an electric refrigerator. The neighborhood is a quiet residential district close by the studio, so that Walt, if he gets a good idea at 3 A. M., can scramble out of bed and walk to his drawing board in three minutes.

Up and down Hollywood Boulevard roll the imported cars of stars, directors, executives, glittering with chromium and enameled in bright orange, or yellow, or orchid. Mr. and Mrs. Disney share a moderate priced car of American manufacture, now in its third year. None of those executives would be likely to be much impressed by the young man slouched behind his own steering wheel. Walt is not what could be called a fancy dresser. His only extravagance along that line is sweaters, of which he owns dozens. If he has a coat, he doesn't know it—and as for neckties! It requires threats of fire and flood, assault and battery, desertion and divorce, for Mrs. Disney to get one around his neck.

And yet, nine out of ten of those personages in the huge automobiles Walt could buy or sell outright and not lose a cipher of his bank statement. I doubt if he's ever thought of that, either. He's having too much fun.

Walter Disney was born December 5, 1901, on Chicago's North Side, where his father was a building contractor in a small way. His mother was the daughter of a Warren, Ohio, school-teacher. The children were four boys and one girl. When Walter was five the family moved to a farm near Marceline, Missouri and it was there that he acquired his love for animals. In the five years he spent on the farm he came to know horses, cows, ducks, chickens, all the regular roster of farm beasts, and all of them he made his pets.

His particular favorites were the colts and the pigs. The family left the farm to try city life again in Kansas City when he was ten years old, and he got up every morning at three thirty, carried newspapers until six, went to school all day, and carried papers again in the evening, for six years. But it is really the farm that molded his character. All he recalls of his paper route is that he got to know every dog in the city. Always, in his mind, he was yearning back to the friendly animals of the farm.

There, at the age of five, he drew his first cartoon. His ink was rich, sticky black tar, and his paper was the white side of the farmhouse— "and I got my pants warmed with a razor strop," he remembers. There, when he was not much older, he drew his first animated cartoon. He discovered, as many a small boy has that if he drew figures in graduated poses on the margins of a book, and then thumbed the pages rapidly, the figures would move. Shortly there was not a book in the house in which he had not scrawled sketches. They weren't bad sketches, either. At least, they were good enough so that his parents did not oppose his decision, when he made it a few years later, to study art.

Today, a strange combination of ingenuousness and ingeniousness, he lives, breathes, eats, and sleeps Mickey—and his notion of a holiday is to go off to a zoo with his personal eight-millimeter movie camera and photograph still more animals!

"I," laments Mrs. Disney, "am a mouse widow."

Not a golf widow. Walter joined a golf club once, paid ten dollars for the membership, lost his card the next day, and has never seen the course since.

• This piece, with the amusing line by Lillian Disney (1899–1997) about being "a mouse widow," marks one of the first times Walt's wife entered into the narrative of how Mickey was born.

Notes on the Art of Mickey Mouse and His Creator Walt Disney

Eleanor Lambert

College Art Association, spring 1933 (unnumbered 6-page booklet).
Printed with permission of William Craig Berkson, executor of the
Eleanor Lambert Berkson Estate.

Walt Disney and Mickey Mouse

In a five dollar-a-month room over a garage which he proudly termed his "studio", a boy named Walt Disney used to sit at night and watch the antics of a pair of little mice. After weeks of patient persuasion, he had tamed them beyond the precincts of their hole in the base-board, across the floor and at last onto his drawing-board. There they sat up and nibbled bits of cheese in their paws or even ate from his hand. As he watched them, he sometimes wrote letters to his niece, aged six, daughter of his older brother who carried mail in Los Angeles. The letters described the activities of the mice and were sometimes illustrated with drawings of them, doing funny, fantastic human things.

Walt Disney (his name is Walter, but no one but his mother ever thinks to call him by it) first saw the light of day in Chicago on December 5, 1901. His mother is German, his father Irish-Canadian. The family was large; four sons already when Walt was born and a sister later. Mr. Disney's business, contracting, caused the family to move frequently, chiefly between Chicago and Kansas City. When Walt was four years old, his parents decided to make a try at country life, and the next six years, until Walt was ten, were spent on a farm in Marceline, Missouri. Here he grew to know and love the animals, cows, horses, ducks, chickens, pigs—the regular roster of farm beasts who now move through Mickey's adventures and the Silly Symphonies to the marvel of all beholders. It was those five years, he believes, that did the most to shape his character. At any rate his unconscious absorption in the way animals looked and moved stamped his mind with impressions that have never failed him since.

When the family returned to Kansas City, Walt earned his first money with that resource of many enterprising middlewestern small boys, a paper route. Every morning he got up at three-thirty, delivered papers until six, returned home for breakfast, went to school at eight and carried papers again at five in the evening. At school he was bright-looking, quiet, apparently studious, but to the surprise of his teacher, seldom able to recite. Investigation revealed that it was the white margins, rather than the contents of the book which held Walt's attention. He had hit upon the trick of drawing people in graduated poses on succeeding pages, and flipping the leaves rapidly, so their figures would move. This fascinating pastime filled all his school books, and the whole of the modest library at home.

So unusual was his talent for drawing that, about this time, he was forced to defend it in the face of the school art teacher's open suspicion that he had traced a figure drawing from a book. Standing before the whole class, he drew another, and was vindicated.

A short interlude in Chicago for the Disney family gave their son his only opportunity for specialized training and he studied for a few months at the Chicago Art Institute.

In Kansas City again when he was seventeen, Walt drew a funny picture each week, usually of animals in human situations, for the neighborhood barber in return for a haircut. The picture in the window attracted crowds. When he didn't need a haircut, he drew the picture anyway and collected twenty-five cents.

One of the barber shop's patrons, the owner of a movie theatre, offered Walt a job drawing animated cartoon slides as screen advertisements. It was then that he rented his "studio" and made the acquaintance of the two mice.

With a capital of about forty dollars, savings from his first job, he made a serious attempt at a motion picture of his own. Animated cartoons were not new, but in Kansas City, he had no way of learning their technique, and was forced to work out every step of the process for himself. It took him months to develop a feasible method, and he executed literally thousands of drawings for his first picture, each one complete, even to the background. His enthusiastic letters to his brother in Los Angeles at length brought some real cooperation in the loan of a few hundred dollars, with part of which Disney promptly purchased a ticket to California. The rest went to pay for the photography of the picture, which proved, because of its obvious lack of mechanical perfection, an unqualified flop. But the drawings themselves showed enough talent to interest a Hollywood producer, and Disney was eventually ensconced in a studio job, feeling that he had repaid his brother's faith, if not his investment. The character of "Oswald the Rabbit" was his next creation. The success of this series was not by any means great, but this disappointment would probably not have driven the producer to summary action if it had not been simultaneous with the sudden introduction of sound and dialogue into picture, which completely demoralized the industry. Out of a job, he again found his brother (now, if anything, more confident in Walt than he was in himself) ready to back him on a new venture, one wholly new and completely his own, of synchronizing the actions of animated cartoon characters to music and dialogue. It was then, in the Spring of 1928, that the idea of the mouse as a character recurred in Disney's mind. At first he was to be known as Mortimer Mouse but the name Mickey was soon introduced, and it stuck. The memory of the second little mouse who had nibbled the cheese so friendly back in Kansas City was realized in Minnie, Mickey's companion and leading lady. Soon Mickey and Minnie were dancing in time to music, tripping off together on extravagant adventures, meeting the animals of the Missouri farm, who also danced and talked in perfect rhythm.

For several discouraging weeks, the brothers peddled the finished film of Mickey Mouse to Hollywood producers and at last found a backer in New York. In September 1928, the film was shown in a small uptown New York theater. Within a week it was playing to enchanted audiences at the Roxy. Soon exhibitors everywhere were wiring for it and United Artists, as distributors of the films, were besieged with requests from every country in the world.

At five years of age, Mickey and Minnie Mouse are the undisputed monarchs of a hundred and fifty thousand dollar studio. Every rule is for them, every effort has been expended for their ease and comfort. So definitely do they dominate the atmosphere that suggestions of their actual existence, such as a miniature two-car garage with two very small limousines on which name-plates are engraved "Mickey" and "Minnie", do not seem at all peculiar.

Their "father," at thirty-one, is a happy example of the young man who has made good, not because he has made a fortune out of an idea, but because he has made a success at work that he loves. All but the most modest portion of his income is turned back into production, perfecting processes and buying experimental equipment. So absorbed is he in the studio that his wife terms herself a mouse widow. Although he has surrounded himself with a staff of more than a hundred talented artists, musicians and writers, he is himself responsible for the major portion of the ideas and drawings.

The Silly Symphonies, the new series which the Disney studio introduced last year, and which is now making use of color photography, have never achieved the fabulous popularity of Mickey Mouse, but their creator feels that in some ways they are superior, and has great hopes for them.

Mickey's meteoric rise to stardom will always remain a legend in the film industry. He has more millions of fans than Garbo, Dietrich, Chevalier and Marie Dressler put together. The use of Mickey's portrait on novelties; souvenir spoons, toys, sofa cushions, jewelry, sweaters, underwear and candy has become a sort of sales insurance, so that over a hundred manufacturers in England and America are turning them out. Sixty newspapers chronicle Mickey's adventures daily in a comic strip.

The eighteen films which cover the famous mouse's life for each year are shown in ten thousand theatres in America, and more than half that many in Europe.

In Germany, his name is Michael Maus, in France, Michel Souris, in Denmark, Mikkel Mus, in Japan, Miki Kuchi and in Spain, Miguel Ratonocito. If, in any of these countries, Mickey has a detractor, that misanthrope has never been heard from.

In spite of all this no one was more surprised than Mr. Disney when the College Art Association invited him to lend a collection of his original Mickey Mouse and Silly Symphonies drawings to form a circuit exhibition of leading museums and colleges throughout the United States. He has been too busy to realize that his engaging, lovable little adventurer has become the embodiment of a new art, an art in motion and an art in rhythm, the keynote of a new epoch in the history of æsthetics.

Creating Mickey Mouse

The cost of creating a Mickey Mouse reel of one thousand feet is perhaps greater, per foot of film, that that of making a full-length feature picture. This is taking into account the salaries of living stars, stage settings, and studio production costs. Between eight and ten thousand drawings, produced entirely by hand, are required for each film, and about eight weeks are spent between the time the idea is first accepted and the finished film reaches the United Artists distributing office. The production system is "staggered" however, so that a new film, either Mickey Mouse or a Silly Symphony is ready every two weeks.

The first step is, naturally, the selection of the subject. Usually, but not always, the title is Disney's. Around a conference table the studio staff sits and plays with the idea, adding to it, changing, until a rough plot is worked out. It is then the task of the humorists to supply the "gags"—to introduce funny situations that will bring laughs from the audience.

Next, the story is turned over to the artists, and a series of key drawings, covering the main situations in the plot are made. Usually these are made by Disney himself—an artist at the Mickey Mouse studio must serve a long term of apprenticeship doing just ears or tails or feet before he is entrusted with more finished drawings.

Simultaneously, the music department of the studio has been busy working out the musical score. This is enormously important, since the number of beats in a phrase of the music determines how many movements Mickey can make in as many feet of film. This calculation, timed to a fraction of a second, is the duty of a chief lay-out man, who corresponds to the director of an ordinary motion picture. When his work is finished, he compiles a detailed list of drawings, usually about nine thousand, which are to be made by the artists, termed animators. Each drawing must be made separately, but for a series where backgrounds are the same, they are transferred to celluloid sheets and photographed after being laid over one drawing of the background.

The recording of the music and sound effects begins as soon as the lay-out man has marked out the score for the artists. In a sound-proof room, similar to a radio broadcasting studio, an orchestra plays the music, and five men interpose the dialogue and give perfect imitations of every imaginable sound, from pigs to rain, thunder and tap dancing.

The finished drawings are photographed one at a time on the film and that film is then merged with the sound track containing the music. The negative is delivered to the United Artists distributing office, and the necessary number of prints are made.

• The booklet containing Eleanor Lambert's essay was sold (at ten cents apiece) at stops on the tour of Disney art organized by the College Art Association that kicked off at the Kennedy Galleries in New York in May 1933. The C.A.A., founded in 1911, is still today the national professional organization for American art historians and college-level art instructors.

The statement by Lambert that the "key drawings, covering the main situations in the plot" of each Disney cartoon were usually made by Walt was a widespread misperception. Also: in 1928, Mickey's distributor was Pat Powers. Walt and Roy Disney did not sign a distribution deal with United Artists until December 1930, and even then the "first cartoons under the new agreement with UA did not appear until mid-1932" (Barrier, *Animated Man*, 89). As reported in May 1931 in the *Washington Post* ("That Rodent Now Rates a Top Ranking"), the Disney brothers' arrangement with United Artists was "the first time a cartoon screen subject has gained sufficient importance to rate recognition alongside the screen's biggest stars." Foreign exhibitors everywhere, the *Post* added, "are clamoring for 'Mickey,'" and in light of Mickey's universal appeal, Walt Disney "recently decided to make his comedies with music and sound, using only those verbal expressions common to all languages."

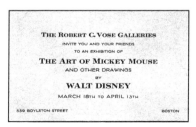

Invitation to "The Art of Mickey Mouse" at the Robert C. Vose Galleries, Boston, Mass., from March 18 to April 13, 1935, courtesy Vose Galleries, LLC.

Mickey Mouse Invades Gallery

Art Digest, May 1, 1933

May, the month of merriment and gay festivals, marks the appearance in a New York art gallery, of that cheerful little creature, indigenous to America, but welcomed heartily in other countries, Mickey Mouse.

Heretofore, Mickey has only executed his capers on the motion picture screen, but due to the efforts of the College Art Association in co-operation with the United Artists Corporation, 50 black-and-white drawings of him by Walt Disney, his creator, will be on view at the Kennedy Galleries, all month. There will also be 50 water color drawings of the Silly Symphonies.

The College Art Association feels that Mr. Disney's works constitute art and that to see the original drawings which are weekly metamorphosed into Mickey Mouse and Silly Symphony comedies will be a treat for the art loving public.

• In its May 15, 1933, edition, *Time* ("Profound Mouse") reported that "art critics piously eyed a collection of original Mickey Mouse cartoons" at the Kennedy Galleries. "From Manhattan," *Time* noted, "the cartoons will go to leading U.S. colleges and museums for exhibition." In 1934 Disney's art traveled to, among other venues, the Evansville Temple of Fine Arts, Milwaukee Art Museum, Smith College Art Gallery, Art Gallery of Toronto, and in 1935, Leicester Galleries, London, two other cities in England, Belfast, Northern Ireland, and the Vose Galleries in Boston (see illustration, p. 71). It was at the Kennedy Galleries that Eleanor Lambert's essay first went on sale.

Mickey Mouse Goes to Hollywood—How Young Artist Tamed His Models

Edwin C. Hill

Boston Evening American, August 8, 1933.
Printed with the permission of the *Boston Herald*.

Behind the news that Artist Walt Disney will hereafter do all his work and transact all his affairs in Hollywood, lies one of those human stories which make news live. For the announcement means that Mickey Mouse has gone to California—Mickey and his beloved Minnie and all the little mice.

Well, Mickey should have quite a few years to enjoy the golden sunshine of beautiful Southern California. He is only five years old which, while fairly well along in years for the ordinary mouse, is nothing for the irrepressible, ageless Mickey. For Mickey Mouse, like Alice in Wonderland, will never grow up, and the chances are that children of years to come—yes, and the grown-ups of years to come will still be squealing with laughter or chuckling apologetically over the antics of that invincibly gay, gallant and resourceful little creature who makes kings and presidents laugh as well as humbler folk.

One thing is certain. Mickey will never "go Hollywood." He is too real for that—too genuine. His rise to popularity is one of the most amazing stories of the times. This writer is certain that more people follow his doings and the doings of his little group than pay heed to the heavy sessions of economic conferences or the doings of legislatures.

Perhaps Mickey's celebrity is not so amazing, after all, when one remembers that he came to us at the time the country needed him most—at the beginning of the depression. He has helped us to laugh away our troubles, forget our creditors and keep our chin up. And now that good times are returning, I think Mickey Mouse, as well as Franklin D. Roosevelt, his good friend and ardent admirer, is entitled to take a bow.

Mickey was born in Kansas City. He was really a live mouse, playing unafraid over the drawing board of an ambitious art-crazy kid of 17, who was working in a five-dollar-a-month room over a garage in the Missouri city. That was how and where Walt Disney, Mickey's creator, got his inspiration, his model and his start. Perhaps one should say, really that there was actually a live Mickey and a live Minnie scampering over Walt Disney's drawing board as the young artist dreamed his dreams, for there were two mice that played about in Walt's room, and which he tamed and taught to pose for him. It's really a fascinating story.

Walt Disney, who looks like a simple and unsophisticated Adolphe Menjou, is 31 now, and one of the most celebrated persons in the world, with an income that millionaires might well envy, and a fame that reaches all around the curves of the world. You can see Mickey at his pranks if you wander up to the Arctic Circle and sit in a little movie house illuminated by whale oil lamps. And you can see him in some sizzling hot little cinema theater down under the Equator, in Borneo or Central America, or China or Japan. For Mickey, good American though he is, is an international character, who speaks all languages because he speaks the language of the heart.

When Walt Disney was a small boy his teachers had a great deal of trouble with him because he was dull with his lessons. Arithmetic and grammar simply could not be got into his head. All he could think about was drawing. He covered his school books, his writing pads and his examination papers with drawings of people and of animals. Before he was out of his teens he knew what he wanted to do and was sure he could do. And when he was 17 years old he paid for his haircuts because a barber discovered that Walt's drawings of animals doing humanlike things pleased people, when he put the pictures in his window, and drew customers to the shop.

And presently Walt was making a little money, just enough to live on, just enough to take a room over a garage in Kansas City, a room which he proudly called his "studio." And that was where fate stepped in. Fate in the persons of Mickey and Minnie.

Working away in the hot little room above the smelly garage, Walt caught sight of two mice, one night—two timid creatures that had come out of the wall for coolness, perhaps, or to get the crumbs that even a hungry artist leaves around. Walt was amused by the tiny little creatures and began to make friends with them, finally luring them, by a trail of crumbs and cheese, to his drawing board. And it wasn't long until they would sit on the drawing board while he worked, combing their whiskers and licking their chops and telling each other, probably, what funny people these artists are.

Walt began to draw them, actually using them as live models, working them into human situations, making them tell human stories. And suddenly in the spring of 1928 the country awakened to the fact that there was a new character in films, a comedy character different from anything that had ever been seen before. Within a few weeks the whole country was rocking with laughter and still is.

Today, Mickey Mouse's studio is in a large building just off Hollywood Boulevard, in the outskirts of Los Angeles. In that studio Walt Disney and a large staff of carefully trained assistants turn out eighteen Mickey Mouse cartoons every year.

Mickey Mouse, Big Bad Wolf Reach Walls of Art Museum

United Press

Cleveland Press, December 14, 1933

CHICAGO, Dec. 14—The antics of Mickey Mouse and fantasies from Silly Symphonies ascended to the stately walls of the Chicago Art Museum today for the winter exhibits of the Art Institute.

Beside the grim Russian morbidities of Boris Grigoriev, Walt Disney's big, bad wolf squared off for a good huff and puff at the house of straw and the little piggies wiggled their way under the bed.

Grigoriev's "Theodore Karamazov" squinted with a leer trying to watch Minnie Mouse chase Pluto, the dog, just across the gallery.

Sandwiched between Rockwell Kent's austere paintings of Greenland ice fields and the classically conceived cows from the brush of the young Frenchman, Eugene Berman, were four rats from Disney's Pied Piper of Hamlin.

The rats, perched on a high molding, craned forward and down, their little tongues protruding in a whole-souled gesture of "giving the bird" to the goodly burghers of Hamlin town. That was before the piper came along.

Thus Mr. Disney returned to the Chicago Art Institute, where a few years ago instructors told him there was no future for him as an artist. Sadly, Mr. Disney laid down his palette and brush, at that time, and turned to newspaper cartooning.

• In early December 1933, it was announced that "The Art of Mickey Mouse" would be seen in early January 1934 at the Temple of Fine Arts in Evansville, Indiana. This must have been the first stop on its national tour after Chicago ("Mickey Mouse Exhibit Will be Shown Here"). One year later, in December 1934, an Associated Press piece published in the *Washington Post* ("Cartoons

Invade Chicago Institute Of Art For Exhibit") and in other papers around the country described a repeat visit by Disney's creations to the Art Institute of Chicago:

> Mickey Mouse, the Three Little Pigs, the Katzenjammer Kids, Jiggs and Maggie, Mutt and Jeff, and others of their ilk took their places alongside austere and venerable canvasses that grace its walls. The exhibit is part of a salon of American humorists which will open to the general public tomorrow.

In this 1934 visit to the Art Institute of Chicago, reported on by the Associated Press, Walt's characters were part of a display of cartoon art "from the Revolutionary period to the present day," described as marking "the first occasion the cartoon has been exhibited as an art form, except for one or two individual shows in the past."

3. "You're the Top"

1934–1935

The *New York Times* was truly the "Newspaper of Record" where Mickey Mouse was concerned. One-sixth of the texts in this book appeared in the *Times*, which, in 1928, thanks to Mordaunt Hall's glowing review, had given Mickey his first critical mention by the fourth estate. Hundreds, if not thousands, of items, short and long, were to follow during the course of the next eight decades, including a half-dozen feature articles in the *Times* Sunday magazine. But it was not until 1934 that the paper's devotion to the character began to manifest itself in force.

"Now Mickey Mouse Enters Art's Temple," an uninspired essay (despite its enticing title) by Douglas W. Churchill, appeared in the June 3, 1934, issue of the magazine section. However, more substantial pieces were to come: L. H. Robbins's "Mickey Mouse Emerges as Economist," in 1935,* Herbert Russell's "L'Affaire Mickey Mouse," in 1937,* and, during the postwar period, Frank S. Nugent's "That Million-Dollar Mouse" (1947)* and Barbara Berch Jamison's "Of Mouse and Man" (1953).*

The twenty-four months covered in this section, 1934–1935, mark, in many ways, the apogee of Mickey's career. In January 1934, the earliest appreciation of the character by a distinguished man of letters, the novelist E. M. Forster, was published in England in the *Spectator*.* In April 1934, the future Poet Laureate of Britain, John Betjeman, declared—in a sidebar to his regular column, "London After Dark," in the *Evening Standard*—that the "Silly Symphonies and Mickey Mouse are still, in spite of everything, the best entertainment the cinema provides."

In May and July 1934, respectively, Arthur Mann in *Harper's*,* and Pulitzer Prize–winning journalist Alva Johnston, a former Timesman, in *Woman's Home Companion*,* each generated over 4,400 words about Mickey and his maker. It would be another thirty years or so before another magazine or newspaper would expend as much ink on either subject.

Cole Porter's musical, *Anything Goes*, opened on Broadway in late November 1934. Among its show-stopping tunes was "You're the Top," which included the lines,

> You're a Bendel bonnet,
> A Shakespeare sonnet,
> You're Mickey Mouse.

A week later, Mickey took part for the first time in Macy's Thanksgiving Day parade. Prior to the event, the *New York Times* ("Santa Is Coming Early for Parade") announced that St. Nick would be preceded "by blaring bands, bulging likenesses of Mickey Mouse, Pluto the Pup and other childish idols." Hundreds of balloons were "to be released from airplanes of the Mickey Mouse squadron of the Naval Reserve" stationed at Floyd Bennett Field in Brooklyn. Also scheduled to march were the Big Bad Wolf, a "helium-filled figure of one of the Three Little Pigs," "Pegleg Pete, villain of the Mickey Mouse world," Minnie Mouse, and a forty-foot-high balloon of Mickey secured "by twenty-five husky attendants."

As glorious as 1934 had been, 1935 may be considered Mickey's *annus mirabilis*. In February of that year, his first color animation, *The Band Concert*, was released. (Gilbert Seldes, writing in *Esquire* magazine, would call it "Disney's greatest single work.") In June and July 1935, Walt, Roy, and their wives embarked on a triumphal tour of Europe that included stays in London, Paris, and Rome. In the City of Light, according to journalist Jean Laury in *Le Figaro*,* "over five thousand children cheered 'Mickey Mouse' and his father, Walt Disney" at the Gaumont-Palace, Paris's grandest movie theater. That summer as well, according to the *Times* ("Gain in Television"), an experimental TV broadcast showcased "a group of chorus girls, an orchestra and Mickey Mouse."

By 1935 Disney's cartoon star was so firmly fixed in the firmament of popular culture that, when journalist and future novelist Graham Greene wished to praise Fred Astaire in the pages of the *Spectator*, he could think of no higher compliment than to compare the debonair hoofer to Mickey:

> *Top Hat* is a vehicle, a little better than *Roberta*, for Mr Fred Astaire's genius.
> It doesn't really matter much that the music and lyrics are bad. Mr Astaire is
> the nearest approach we are ever likely to have to a human Mickey Mouse;
> he might have been drawn by Mr Walt Disney, with his quick physical wit, his

incredible agility. He belongs to a fantasy world almost as free of Mickey's from the law of gravity, but unfortunately he has to act with human beings and not even Miss Ginger Rogers can match his freedom, lightness and happiness.

Finally, it was in this period, 1934–1935, that the circumstances of Mickey's birth were revisited in a second article published in the *Windsor Magazine* under Disney's name. In 1933 a narrative had emerged that publicized his kindly affection for mice. In Walt's 1934 *Windsor* piece, "The Life Story of Mickey Mouse,"* the emphasis shifted from compassion for the "little guy" to the resolve of Mickey's creator in the face of adversity—after he'd lost Oswald. This new, more muscular wrinkle to the story, no doubt anchored in truth, must also have been at least partly calculated to project an image even more appealing to a nation still in the throes of the Depression: that of a man staring defeat in the face and, "out of the trouble and confusion," coming up roses by conjuring up a "romping, rollicking" "dream mouse" named Mickey.

The Life Story of Mickey Mouse

Walt Disney

Windsor Magazine, January 1934, Weidenfeld & Nicolson, a division of The Orion Publishing Group.

The creator of "Mickey Mouse" tells how the most famous star in the world (unpaid, too) came to be born, and describes the methods pursued in presenting him. Incidentally, we learn that "Mickey" keeps 200 people constantly employed and receives 800,000 letters a year.

Perhaps it is one of the many paradoxes of the picture business that a star who has taken the screen by storm should receive no salary for his services, and should have been made, not born.

His exploits have brought in many thousands of pounds, though the star himself is just something out of an ink-pot—if you view him in a literal light, which I don't. Mickey Mouse is a very real personality to me.

It has been said that Mickey is the only star who satisfies high-brows, broad-brows and low-brows alike the world over. Well, I am proud of him, and of the great success he has brought me personally. It was a pleasure to create him.

Everything has to have a beginning—even a mouse. My care-free, cartooned little rodent did not find his way to the world's screens in five minutes. His "life story" really goes back to a day before his time.

Thirteen years ago a young, obscure commercial artist used to work late at night in a studio where a company of mice scratched around for any stray crumbs. The young man made friends with those mice, adopted a family of them in a cage, and even tamed one sufficiently to sit on his drawing-board.

Time passed, as time will, and one day the young man stepped off the train in Los Angeles with very little money and no more idea of where to get any than a rabbit. That young man was myself.

I had a straw suitcase in my hand, a cartoon in my head, and heaps of hope. Put me down as Mickey Mouse's potential papa from that moment, although Mickey had yet to be born.

My brother, Roy, and I at once set serenely about making movie cartoons in a tiny, empty store-room. The chief character in the cartoons was a little girl, a real little girl, who played with cartoon animals, swam in cartoon water, and ate cartoon food.

I wrote the scenarios, drew the cartoons and built the sets. I hammered in nails, laid floors, and went home night after night dog-tired and generally caked solidly in misplaced cement. I directed the pictures, and acted any part that lay around loose.

I used back alleys and vacant lots for their sets, and had never seen a Klieg light, let alone used one. Brother Roy was camera man, the like of whom has never before nor since been seen in Hollywood. He got everything jumbled up.

But real camera men were expensive, twenty-five dollars a day. So I learned to keep one eye on the camera, and so as not to embarrass brother camera man before the usual crowd of onlookers, I would mutter in a loud stage whisper, "Shove her over," or, "Switch the lens." Whereupon Roy, with a look of well-I-was-going-to-do-it-anyhow, would "shove her over."

It was work. Hard, heart-breaking work. But fun, too.

And all the time, in the back of my mind, lurked the germ of an idea: an idea that was one day to dance wildly across the wall paper, in hot red velvet pants and two huge pearl buttons, of little Princess Elizabeth's bedroom in a English castle.

The Alice cartoons, as my first ones were called, eventually caught on. Then I conceived the idea of an animal for the chief character of the cartoons. Someone chose a cat [sic]. We called it Oswald.

For three years I slaved with Oswald. I moved to a larger room. My staff grew. I still drew and wrote and laboured. But my heart wasn't in it. Sometimes Oswald could be pretty much of a dumb animal.

Trouble had started, too. I wanted more money to work with, and my releasing agent wanted to cut down my expenditures. Some of my men became discontented. There was a regular hullabaloo over it all.

So I hurried to New York for advice.

"Get together," I was told. "Times aren't so good. So sign again." (They were saying it even again, several years ago.)

When I made my advances I received a shoulder so cold that the chill was felt for miles around. So with no contract signed and just six months left to go on the old one, I boarded a train for home. But was I downhearted? Not a bit! I was happy at heart. For out of the trouble and confusion stood a mocking, merry little figure. Vague and indefinite at first. But it grew and grew and grew. And finally arrived—a mouse. A romping, rollicking, little mouse.

The idea completely engulfed me. The wheels turned to the tune of it. '*Chug, chug, mouse, chug, chug, mouse*' the train seemed to say. The whistle screeched it. '*A m-m-m owa-ouse*,' it wailed.

By the time my train had reached the Middle West I had dressed my dream mouse in a pair of red velvet pants with two huge pearl buttons, had composed the first scenario, and all was set.

Up in the loft of my private garage, my brother and I and a group of faithful workers drew and copied and toiled, and finally brought the first Mickey Mouse cartoon to life.

And he wasn't even named Mickey. He was called Mortimer. But the name "Mortimer" threw the first producer into such spasms of Hollywood sarcasm that I soon decided to rename my mouse "Mickey."

And now Mickey was ready for a waiting world. But a waiting world was past being ready for Mickey. For just at that time Al Jolson yodelled "Sonny Boy" from the talking screen. Sound had come in and little Mickey couldn't even speak.

Here was a setback. Now came the problem of how to get sound into Mickey. I actually went around Hollywood begging for sound—offering to pay for its use. But no one would even look at Mickey.

Once again I took myself off to New York. Finally, after weeks and weeks of discouragement, I arranged through an independent company to add sound to Mickey. But, even so, nobody seemed to want him.

Then one day I succeeded in placing Mickey Mouse in the Colony Theatre in New York. He was a riot. *Variety*, the trade paper, raved about him. Daily newspapers praised him. For the first time a cartoon, the lowest form of cinema life, was hailed.

To-day there is a lot of hand-wringing by the people who turned down Mickey Mouse. For no star ever had such a cosmopolitan appeal.

What was once a store-room has blossomed into a white stucco mansion. Not a house that Jack built—but a castle a mouse built.

Mickey has enabled me to sit in one of those business sanctums which is only reached after you have traversed miles of padded stairs and suites of offices. You know the sort.

There I sit behind a massively carved desk—but I always remember the Walt Disney who tramped the streets looking for help a few years ago, and keep my feet on the ground. I may have made Mickey—but Mickey made me. Brother Roy is now my business manager—and makes a darned sight better manager than he did a camera man.

I am the subordinate of Mickey. The little mouse is a personage of the place. He is treated seriously and almost reverently by everyone in the studio. An unseen star, he rules supremely—as a Chaplin or Fairbanks.

Artists by the dozens labour diligently for Mickey. Musicians compose and rehearse for him. Truck drivers, electricians, carpenters, writers, and typists labour day by day for him. His own little car stands quietly in a miniature garage. Above the door is painted MICKEY. In a similar garage adjoining, the name MINNIE is inscribed over the portal—Mickey's leading lady and partner in pranks. A professor of heraldry has designed a coat-of-arms for Mickey, and the shield hangs prominently in the studio. I still prepare Mickey's scenarios. Then a "gag" conference is called, and sometimes it may last two or three days before the artists can get out their drawing-boards and proceed with the actual drawings.

Every "gag" must be an idea that has appeal to all. Views are exchanged. Often someone will say, "No; Mickey wouldn't do that. He's not that kind of a fellow."

All the "gags" finally arranged, the artists then go to work, while I supervise. Fifty men in the studio go to the making of a Mickey Mouse cartoon that takes only a few minutes to show on the screen—fifty men, who devote their time exclusively to drawing, are divided into three groups of artists, or animators, tracers and inkers.

Fifteen artists sketch their drawings on tissue paper. The average cartoon, 700 feet of film only, requires from 10,000 to 15,000 drawings, with twenty to thirty backgrounds. This is not so impossible as it may seem, as some of the drawings merely consist of a hand or a foot which is later superimposed over another sketch to make a complete picture.

The artists work over a glass board with a light underneath it. This method enables every artist to follow the action of his drawing through several layers of paper.

Supposing the particular scene in making shows Mickey walking. The sketch would show him starting a step; in the next he would finish the action. By placing two drawings above the light, the animator is able to see the start and finish of the action, and must fill in the intervening drawings to give the process smoothness.

The drawings are numbered according to scenes and groups, and the action is synchronised with the music—which is set up by the beats of a metronome.

Some artists draw nothing but backgrounds—never draw Mickey at all. Others are concerned wholly with the action. Every artist is handed a sheet of paper bearing a certain number of movements and a certain number of music beats. They are synchronised to the twenty-fourth of a second. The faster the action, the fewer the drawings.

Every new artist is a heartbreak. It takes months of training before he becomes "Mickey conscious."

And it takes about two years for an artist, skilled in cartooning, to master the technique of animation. Many well-known cartoonists have tried the job, and thrown it up in disgust and exasperation.

Dozens of girls in another department transfer the drawings to celluloid, tracing the outlines of the figures in ink so that they stand out in brilliant black. Next they pass to the opaquing department, to be filled out with black, white, or grey paint. Then into the camera room they go. The photographer sits at a desk with the lens of the camera pointed downward and the drawings laid flat underneath. So really, you see, Mickey is always photographed from above.

When the photography is completed, the scenes are arranged in order and a master print is made. Mickey is silent in this form, but all the time the musical director has been working away rehearsing and arranging the music, and having it recorded for synchronisation.

It is only necessary now for the picture negative and the sound-track negative to be delivered to the laboratory, matched up correctly, and hundreds of prints made, for the world to have another eight minutes of Mickey Mouse.

All told, there are something like 200 people on the payroll to produce those eight minutes regularly every month!

We make one Mickey Mouse cartoon in a fortnight, and one Silly Symphony in the other two weeks of the four. Working alone, it would take one man about two years to turn out a Mickey Mouse reel. And if all the Mickey Mouse cartoons produced in one year were laid end to end . . . But who wants statistics anyway? Let me just say that if these same cartoons—one year's work of a big organisation—were shown at one sitting, the performance would only take three hours and twenty minutes.

That Mickey is a real person to millions is proved by the fact that his "fan mail" runs into 800,000 letters a year. But I shall see to it that adulation never goes to his head. Not that it would. He's much too shrewd.

Mickey and I are firm friends. We have weathered the storms together. I have tried to give him a soul and a "keep kissable" disposition. And Mickey has given me a little bar behind a panel, a carved desk, two-hundred-and-forty-one golf sweaters. All blue.

• This text, which cannot have been written by Walt himself, reveals more about the making of Mickey than any previously published piece, although no mention is made of Lillian Disney and her role in the naming of the Mouse. Nor, of course, does Ub Iwerks's name arise. Not only had Ub quit the studio four years before, but from a practical business standpoint, Mickey needed to be marketed as a strictly Disney product.

As was the case with "Mickey Mouse: How He Was Born,"* the first *Windsor Magazine* article published under Walt's name (Oct. 1931), some of "The Life Story of Mickey Mouse" was cribbed from at least one earlier source: "The True Story of Mickey Mouse," by Sara Hamilton (*Movie Mirror*, Dec. 1931). In October 1934, on the occasion of Mickey's sixth anniversary, yet another ghost-written piece "signed" by Walt, "Mickey Mouse's Birthday: How the Famous Cartoons Are Made," would appear in an Australian newspaper, the *Age*. However, rather than lift material from the second *Windsor* article, whoever cobbled together the text published by the *Age* harkened back to the Harry Carr story from March 1931,* with words like these:

It is difficult to say precisely how Mickey came about. He just put in an appearance. I wanted something appealing, something wistful; a grand little fellow trying to do the best he could.

Mickey and Minnie

E. M. Forster

I am a film-fanned rather than a film-fan, and, oh, the things I have had
to see and hear because other people wanted to! About once a fortnight a puff of wind raises me from the seat where I am meditating
upon life or art, and wafts me in amiability's name towards a very different receptacle. Call it a fauteuil. Here art is not, life not. Not happy,
not unhappy, I sit in an up-to-date stupor, while the international effort unrolls. American women shoot the hippopotamus with eyebrows
made of platinum. British ladies and gentlemen turn the movies into
the stickies for old Elstree's sake. Overrated children salute me from
Germany and France, steam-tractors drone across the lengths and
breadths of unholy Russia, with the monotony of wedding chimes. All
around me, I have reason to believe, sit many fellow film-fanneds, chaff
from the winnowing like myself, but we do not communicate with one
another, and are indistinguishable from ecstasy in the gloom. Stunned
by the howls of the Wurlitzer organ, choked by the fumes of the cigars—and here I break off again, in a style not unsuited to the subject.
Why do cigars and cigarettes in a cinema function like syringes? Why
do they squirt smoke with unerring aim down my distant throat and
into my averted eyes? Where are they coming from? Where are they
going to? Before I can decide, the greatest super-novelty of all time has
commenced, Ping Pong, and the toy counter at Gamage's is exhibited as
a prehistoric island. Or mayn't I have a good laugh? Why certainly, why
sure, that's what we take your money for, a good laugh, so here's a guy
who can't swim and finds he can racing a guy who can swim and pre-
tends he can't, and the guy who can't get a laugh out of that had better—

But now the attendant beckons, a wraith in beach pyjamas, waving her electric wand. She wants someone, and can it be me? No—she wants no one, it is just a habit she has gotten into, poor girlie, she cannot stop herself, but fanned by she knows not what sits skirted and bloused in the audience she lately patrolled. I do not think though—for it is time for optimism to enter—I do not think she will choose a performance which bills a Mickey Mouse. And I do hope that Mickey, on his side, will observe her fidelity and will introduce her into his next Silly Symphony, half glow-worm and half newt, waving, waving. . . .

What fun it would be, a performance in which Mickey produced the audience as well as the film! Perhaps Mr. Walt Disney will suggest it to him, and I will provide the title gratis: "Plastic Pools." We should see some gay sights in his semi-darkness, and more would get squirted about than smoke. Siphons that pour zig-zag, chocolates exploding into fleas—there are rich possibilities in the refreshments alone, and when it comes to Miss Cow's hatpins and fauteuils for the dachshund sisters, why should there be any limits? Yet I don't know. Perhaps not. "Plastic Pools" is withdrawn. For much as I admire Mickey as a producer, I like him as a lover most, and rather regret these later and more elaborate efforts, for the reason that they keep him too much from Minnie. Minnie is his all, his meinie, his moon. Perhaps even the introduction of Pluto was a mistake. Have you forgotten that day when he and she strolled with their kodaks through an oriental bazaar, snapping this and that, while their camel drank beer and galloped off on both its humps across the desert? Have you forgotten *Wild Waves*? Mickey's great moments are moments of heroism, and when he carries Minnie out of the harem as a pot-plant or rescues her as she falls in foam, herself its fairest flower, he reaches heights impossible for the *entrepreneur*. I would not even have the couple sing. The duets in which they increasingly indulge are distracting. Let them confine themselves to raptures appropriate for mice, and let them play their piano less.

But is Mickey a mouse? Well, I am hard put to put it at moments certainly, and have had to do some thinking back. Certainly one would not recognize him in a trap. It is his character rather than his pieces that signifies, which one could surely recognize anywhere. He is energetic without being elevating, and although he is assuredly one of the world's great lovers he must be placed at some distance from Charlie Chaplin or Sir Philip Sidney. No one has ever been softened after seeing Mickey or has wanted to give away an extra glass of water to the poor. He is never sentimental, indeed there is a scandalous element in him which I find most restful. Why does he not pick up one of the coins thrown to him in that Texas bar? Why does one of the pillows in *Mickey's Nightmare* knock him down? Why does Pluto—Or there is that moment in *Wild Waves* when Minnie through some miscalculation on her part is drowning, and he rushes for a boat. As he heaves it out of the sand two little blobs are revealed beneath it, creatures too tiny to be anything but love-items, and they scuttle away into a world which will scarcely be as severe on them as ours. There are said to be "privately shown" Mickeys, and though I do not want to see one, imagination being its own kingdom, I can well believe that anyone who goes so far goes further.

About Minnie too little has been said, and her name at the top of this article is an act of homage which ought to have been paid long ago. Nor do we know anything about her family. When discovered alone, she appears to be of independent means, and to own a small house in the midst of unattractive scenery, where, with no servant and little furniture, she busies herself about trifles until Mickey comes. For he is her Rajah, her Sun. Without him, her character shines not. As he enters she expands, she becomes simple, tender, brave and strong, and her coquetry is of the delightful type which never conceals its object. Ah, that squeak of greeting! As you will have guessed from it, her only fault

Minnie and Mickey Mouse, figures from two original production animation drawings for the 1936 Walt Disney Studios animated cartoon *Mickey's Rival*, private collection. © The Walt Disney Company.

is hysteria. Minnie does not always judge justly, and she was ill advised, in *Puppy Love*, to make all that fuss over a bone. She ought to have known it belonged to the dogs. It is possible that, like most of us, she is deteriorating. To be approached so often by Mickey, and always for the first time, must make any mouse mechanical. Perhaps sometimes she worries whether she has ever been married or not, and her doubts are not easy to allay, and the wedding chimes in *Mickey's Nightmare* are no guide or a sinister one. Still, it seems likely that they have married one another, since it is unlikely that they have married anyone else, since there is nobody else for them to marry.

What of their future? At present Mickey is everybody's god, so that even members of the Film Society cease despising their fellow members when he appears. But gods are not immortal. There was an Egyptian called Bes, who was once quite as gay, and Brer Rabbit and Felix the Cat have been forgotten too, and Ganesh is being forgotten. Perhaps he and Minnie will follow them into oblivion. I do not care two hoots. I am all for the human race. But how fortunate that it should have been accompanied, down the ages, by so many cheerful animals, and how lucky that the cinema has managed to catch the last of them in its questionable reels!

• This was a rare instance—perhaps the first—in which Minnie and Mickey got equal attention in print. Elstree's was a major British movie studio (founded 1927), Gamages, a London department store known for its toy section. The ancient Egyptians venerated Bes as a champion of good against evil; Ganesh was an elephant-headed Hindu deity.

Several years after "Mickey and Minnie" was first published, the American humorist James Thurber came across the essay in Forster's collection of writings, *Abinger Harvest* (Harcourt Brace, 1936). In a letter to his *New Yorker* colleague and friend, E. B. White, sandwiched between two quotes from the essay (one of them beginning, "But is Mickey a mouse?"), Thurber remarked: "This guy [Forster] is full of swell lines."

Mickey Mouse's Financial Career

Arthur Mann

Newfound wealth, regardless of its source, is viewed with the same fact-distorting enthusiasm as that which greets a gold strike. News and rumors fly thick and fast, gathering exaggeration as one wild-eyed narrative whispers to another.

The latest gold-strike gossip concerns Walt Disney, pied piper of the nation's children—of the world's children—and his supposed record-breaking financial harvest from the popularity of his animated cartoon sound pictures. The contagious national enthusiasm over the Mickey Mouse films has given impetus to an erroneous belief that the creator of these quaint characters is gaining fabulous riches from the movie-going public.

This widespread misapprehension may be due to subtle film publicity. From time to time official publicity items have placed peculiar emphasis on the fact that Disney takes a modest salary, $150 or $200 a week, and "puts the rest back into the business." No publicity items have attempted to explain what is meant by "the rest."

On several occasions the artist has personally denied the rumors of his vast income from the films. As an obvious attempt to correct the misconstruction, he declared that his net profits on the amazing "Three Little Pigs" would total about $25,000 from world-wide sales. And this picture is the most popular short feature ever produced.

A study of Mickey Mouse's film finances seems to uphold Disney. His revenue from other sources may attain unprecedented heights, but a few actual film figures and contract clauses indicate that Disney's wealth from the motion pictures has been exaggerated. The story of his financial adventures constitutes a significant chapter in the unhappy chronicle of the artist among the business men.

Disney has been successful for only five years. That is, his product has been marketed successfully for the past five years. Prior to that he was woefully unsuccessful for five bitter years.

He was born in Chicago thirty-two years ago, and he absorbed a smattering of knowledge of art before his family left Kansas City. There he tried a variety of art jobs. He failed at newspaper cartooning. He limped through trade-paper drawing and commercial art, where he developed his "steel-die" taste in drawing.

When Disney sank to the level of making barber-shop signs for his Kansas City haircuts he felt that a change of medium was necessary. He tried the animated movie cartoon business. He began by raiding the fairy-tale classics for his productions. They were free from copyright entanglements. Evidently his mind has always been drawn to the fantastic material in fairy stories, for his determination to produce them in the face of repeated financial losses amounted to stubbornness. But the Kansas City film venture failed.

Disney's brother, Roy, had $250 and poor health. Walt had $40 and good health. They pooled their resources. Roy agreed to a fifty-fifty split, if and when.

They headed for Hollywood. Walt was the artist. Roy was the business manager. They borrowed enough money to make $500 capital and began to make animated film cartoons. That was in 1923.

Disney's first production on the Coast was a curious mélange called "Alice." He used a few real actors, photographic wonderland settings, and pen-and-ink animals. It failed. The Disneys joined the independent shoe-string producers of "Poverty Row." They went hungry. Nothing seemed to succeed; and Roy's health didn't improve on a diet of financial worry and little else.

The pioneer animated cartons, "Little Nemo," "Colonel Heezaliar," "Krazy Kat," "Felix the Cat," etc., had resembled one another pretty closely, and none of them had caused any dancing in the streets. The picture people very naturally refused to buy something that had already been done. Disney had nothing worth while for them, not even a copy of something good.

His funds were exhausted. His plans for independent production were thwarted, temporarily at least. For some time he made "Alice comedies," on the basis of an outright sale contract (at prices ranging from $1,500 to $12,250 each), for Charles Mintz. The Universal Film Company wanted some animal cartoons. "Krazy Kat" was the most successful and popular in the field. They asked Mintz to submit samples. This was done and, of those submitted, they liked a rabbit cartoon best. P. D. Cochrane, a Universal official, named the animal "Oswald the Lucky Rabbit." Mintz put Disney to work on the rabbit film and it sold pretty well. It is still selling. It did not, however, attain the popularity of Krazy Kat and her companion, Ignatz Mouse.

George Herriman's Krazy Kat, you may or may not recall, is somewhat masochistic. She loves to be socked with a brick, especially if it is thrown by her sadistic companion, Ignatz Mouse. It usually lands on Krazy Kat's head in the last picture, and its force is indicated by a boldface "Pow!" Ignatz Mouse was an important part of the supporting cast of Krazy Kat cartoons.

Singularly enough, it was while Disney was working for Mintz that he conceived the idea of making a mouse picture. He worked out ideas and stories. To this end, he saved every nickel he could spare, and so did his brother Roy.

II

Enter at this point—in 1928—the first of Disney's mouse pictures. Two reels were made up by Disney and Ub Iwerks, who was then and still is the best animator in the film cartoon business. Ub Iwerks was the artistic genius behind the early Disney animated cartoons, and his name appeared on the title flashes.

Straightaway a new partnership was drawn up for production, Iwerks received about a fifth, and the Disneys divided the remainder equally.

Walt Disney arrived in New York City in the spring of 1928, armed with fifteen hundred dollars in cash and two silent films, his first mouse pictures. The pictures were essentially of the same sort that had been created for fifteen years. They were, however, admittedly better. The motions of the figures were fluid. The ideas were crisp and ingenious. Disney and Iwerks were an excellent combination.

Up and down Broadway marched Disney, peddling his two films from door to door among the distributors.

Realizing that his difficulty in selling these silent pictures was partly due to the rising popularity of sound effects, he returned to the coast and started work on "Steamboat Willie," which was to be a sound picture. On his reappearance in New York with the partly finished "Steamboat Willie," he met Patrick Powers, an independent film producer, who had once been Treasurer for Carl Laemmle's Universal Company. Powers was a pioneer in the film business from the old General Film Company "trust" days. Powers had seen the old silent films develop into a national institution for the multitude. A shrewd Irishman, he had foreseen the approach and significance of talking pictures. At the time he met Disney, in the fall of 1928, he was trying to find a marketable outlet for his Cinephone, a process of placing sound on film, which he controlled through the Powers Cinephone Equipment Corporation.

They entered into a ten-year recording agreement. Powers agreed to distribute the films, to promote the idea generally, and to lend money to Disney to finance the making of the pictures.

Powers went to work at once and peddled the animated cartoons. The addition of sound made them easy to sell. "Steamboat Willie," the first Mickey Mouse picture, was shown in the old Colony Theatre in September, 1928.

After surmounting several difficult obstacles, Powers succeeded in getting a second Disney film into the Roxy Theatre. When Roxy saw it and observed the significant reaction of the audiences he ordered it held over for two additional weeks.

Those were the first steps in Mickey Mouse's march to fame.

Disney, back on the Pacific Coast, turned out pictures on a fairly heavy schedule. Six months later, or about midway through 1929, the demand for Disney pictures was so heavy that another series, the Silly Symphonies, was offered to the market. These cartoons were then without color, but they were cleverly synchronized with music and rhymes.

Here, however, the artist ran over his budget. He encountered unexpected expenses, such as the high rates which had to be paid to union musicians, the retakes for perfect synchronization, and so forth. But Powers advanced the extra capital.

Powers' success with releases and distribution continued, but he ran into the usual difficulties which beset the independent distributor. He found that theaters in certain desirable territories were bound by pledges to other distributors. In order to get the pictures widely shown, he had to "sub-let" them to rival distributors and holders of state-rights privileges. There was no other way to get the Disney pictures into the desired theaters.

One of these concerns through which Powers had to deal was the Columbia Pictures Corporation. Columbia handled Mickey Mouse in certain portions of the United States. The Silly Symphonies were distributed or sub-let exclusively through Columbia to the United States or Canada. Business boomed for more than a year.

By January of 1930 Disney had turned over to Powers a unit of twelve Mickey Mouse pictures, a unit of six Silly Symphonies, and three pictures of a second Mickey Mouse unit, a total of twenty-one productions.

Disney had produced these films at a total cost of $116,500, or an average of over $5000 per picture. This was much greater than the amount which he had originally figured on. And yet this sum was less than a third of the gross income obtained by Powers from the leasing of the films to April 1930. By that time the pictures earned $354,000, or an average of $16,848 each.

Ordinarily this might permit of a substantial profit for the creator of the series. But the motion picture industry is not an ordinary business, as a few of the following figures, taken from the actual record of the earnings, will show.

Powers, as distributor, took the customary 35 per cent of the $354,000 gross. From the remainder he deducted the $116,500 which had been advanced to Disney for production. By agreement the distributor was also permitted to be reimbursed for additional expenses incurred outside of actual distribution, Cinephone fees, and so forth. Specifically, these expenditures were for extra prints, print processing, negative and laboratory expense, advertising (more than $3000), censorship and licensing, insuring negatives, music copyrights, recording fees and print royalties, and territorial recording (in foreign languages).

This left a net profit of less than $100,000, which was further reduced, for Powers as backer was entitled to one-fourth of the net as a return on his investment. After a few other charges and costs to meet,

Disney came out of it all with about ten per cent of the entire gross for himself. He had only Roy to share with, because some enterprising employee in the Powers organization had persuaded Ub Iwerks to sign an independent producing contract, similar to the one under which Disney was working. Since then Iwerks has produced a clever piece called "Flip the Frog," which was released through Metro-Goldwyn-Mayer.

And Disney didn't even get his profit, because at this point he and Powers had a disagreement. Disney wanted to look at the business end of the Mickey Mouse films, but Powers refused to show his books, not because there was something to hide, but because he wanted Disney to sign a regular distributor's contract. They had been working under a mutual agreement, executed through a series of letters. The Mickey Mouse idea had grown into more than just a program filler. The demand for Disney films pointed to unprecedented business. Powers realized that he must have something stronger and more legal than an exchange of letters to protect himself and his investment. They parted company and Powers received no more Mickey Mouse or Silly Symphonies pictures. He was left in something of a predicament, for he had orders and contracts for the Disney pictures from all parts of the world; it looked as if the business for 1930 would double that of 1929.

Presently Disney came to New York with a motion picture attorney, who insisted upon seeing the gross income figures. Powers, buttressed by the batch of orders and contracts for the pictures, felt certain that Disney would weaken first. But he did not, and the break between them became final.

III

The Columbia Pictures Corporation now persuaded Disney to negotiate with them. They gave the artist a contract that was indeed a contract. It assured him of an advance of $7,000 per picture—three times the sum agreed upon with Powers. More important, however, was that Columbia contracted to advance to Disney money to the extent of $25,000 to defray the legal costs of settling the disagreement with Powers and actually did advance $10,000 for this purpose.

Powers realized at once that he was up against a stone wall. He suggested a cash settlement for complete release of Disney and his twenty-one films. The figure was more than $100,000. Disney, like a true artist, agreed. He wanted to get things straightened out, so he could work in peace.

But, since he had considerably less coming from Powers than the distributor wanted, Disney had to borrow $50,000 from Columbia to close the deal!

Having shaken off, as he supposed, his business troubles, the Mouse man went back to the Coast to resume production of his brain children.

Disney worked with Columbia for two years under a contract that could hardly be expected to make him independently wealthy. To begin with, after turning over to Powers every cent of his profits on his first twenty-one creations, he went to work owing his distributors $60,000. The Columbia contract stated that Columbia, as distributor, was privileged to exact the usual 35 per cent of all collections taken from film exchanges and exhibitors direct. It further stated that Columbia, as distributor, was to retain all balances until reimbursed for the advances made to Disney for the production of pictures. Columbia was also given the privilege of regaining all moneys spent which were not attributable to actual distribution, such as ". . . to defray costs of prints, recordings, transportation charges, insurance on negatives, advertising and furthermore, with respect to Canada and foreign countries, duties, censorship fees, censorship reconstruction charges . . ." etc.

Whatever chanced to be left over after all this had taken place was divided into two equal parts, one of which went to Columbia Pictures, and the other to Disney.

Late in 1930 Disney wisely reorganized his partnership with brother Roy and formed the Walt Disney Productions, Ltd. Membership in the corporation is confined to Mr. and Mrs. Walt Disney and Mr. and Mrs. Roy Disney.

The two-year association with Columbia may or may not have been as profitable as Disney expected; but it is significant to note that in the two years he produced about fifty pictures, and that each of these pictures was saddled with a deficit before he drew a line because of the $60,000 which Columbia advanced to finance the break with Powers.

That the artist was dissatisfied is probable for, when his contract was about to run out, Columbia refused a request to double the amount advanced to him for production, that is, to make the advance per picture $15,000 instead of the prevailing $7,000. The gossip went through Hollywood that the Mouse Man was getting "tough."

A meeting on a Hollywood thoroughfare with an executive of United Artists—once the haven of dispirited creative geniuses of the film industry—was all Disney needed to select a new distributor. What apparently won him over to United Artists was that they handled no other short pictures and therefore would be able to sell the Disney pictures by themselves, instead of selling them along with others in "block booking" arrangements. But they also agreed to pay him the much-desired $15,000 advance for each picture.

So Disney signed a contract to release through United Artists. Hadn't this fifteen-year-old "declaration of artistic independence" made Charlie Chaplin, Mary Pickford, and Douglas Fairbanks the three richest artists in the film business?

But Disney's financial tangle soon became deeper. He was thrust into a whirlpool, an endless chain of debit and credits. The money advanced for production was not an out-and-out gift to have and to hold. Would things were as simple as that.

IV

Briefly, the new arrangement was as follows: The artist, or his company, received the cash advance from a finance unit, which took his note of indebtedness for the amount. The note was underwritten by United Artists as distributors, but the indebtedness remained on the books against Disney. If, when, and as the distributor took in the dollars for Mickey Mouse rentals, it paid them over to the finance unit until Disney's obligation was liquidated. But by the time one of these obligations was settled, Disney or his bookkeeping department obtained another substantial advance on a second production, and possibly money for a third or a fourth. He was likely to be charged with from $45,000 to $75,000 for advances against subsequent productions before sizeable returns began to come in from the first release.

Profits? Theoretically there are no profits until a unit of pictures—usually thirteen—is completed. At the completion of a unit an accounting is rendered and the profits, if any, are relinquished to the artist or his company.

Yet still the profits, if any, may not be relinquished. For by the time the accounting on the first unit is completed, Disney has obtained an advance or advances to finance one or two or more productions of the succeeding unit of Mickey Mouse or Silly Symphonies!

Why doesn't he use his own money for productions? He does—but it does not reach very far, for he is engaged in a very expensive business. And the advance, even though not actually used, is there "in case." Disney's pictures of to-day are vastly superior to the productions he made for $5,000 each when he was distributing through Powers. They are works of art. The Silly Symphonies are works of both science and art. The famous "Three Little Pigs" required 12,992 drawings. Disney not only animates figures to-day; he animates color. And he matches every move with sound effects or measured music. All this work is done in an up-to-date studio, built two and a half years ago at a cost of $250,000. The studio is devoted solely to the Disney Productions, which include newspaper cartoons, the designing of figures, and supervision of the various royalty-bearing items which have a wide market.

For the making of his films Disney has a staff of at least a dozen story men, gag men, and scenarists. There are forty animators who draw the movements of the figures, and forty-five assistant animators. There are thirty girls who trace and color non-moving parts and paint backgrounds. There is an orchestra of twenty-four skilled musicians. Then there are sound-effects workmen, special voices, electricians, photographers, and Technicolor experts, film developers, laboratory chemists, a fully equipped and staffed projection room, a "dubbing" outfit for scoring and synchronizing sound tracks after the silent film is made, and, of course, menial workers about the plant and offices. In all, there are 187 people in the organization.

Over in a secluded corner of this cozy-looking white building which is far out from Hollywood Boulevard, Roy Disney and his staff of bookkeepers endeavor to keep pace with the finance unit. The studio is identified at night by a large figure of Mickey Mouse and a sign which blaze forth to the world. Probably the most unique feature of the Studio is that it is owned solely by Disney and is free of mortgage.

Film production at the plant is done on schedule, and it is not a light schedule. Thirteen Mickey Mouse pictures are made each year, one every four weeks. Thirteen Silly Symphonies are fashioned annually, one every four weeks. And that is only one phase of it. The sound track is dubbed in two foreign languages. (In France he is Michel Souris; Germany, Michael Maus; Japan, Miki Kuchi; Spain, Miguel Ratono-cito, also Miguel Pericote; Greece, Mikel Mus; Italy, Michele Jopolino. Other Latin-speaking people call him Michael Mus.)

It is a far cry from "Steamboat Willie." Maintaining the heavy sched-ule and running a fully equipped studio requires a steady stream of cash. The income from film rentals does not come forth in a steady stream of cash. The flow is spasmodic and, alas, sometimes not at all. The earning life of a short talking picture is anywhere from six months to five years. That life can be prolonged only by salesmanship, like the life of any product on the market.

Meanwhile, however, the money guaranteed by the distributor for the making of each picture is ready in advance of every new produc-tion, regardless of how well or poorly the preceding film may have fared in the open market. Disney therefore used to be constantly "in hock" for the advances, which mounted up when passed out in regular sums of $15,000 each.

He is now out of debt, it is said, and able to finance his picture-mak-ing without using the advance; but even now he has only enough cash to run the business, and no more.

Furthermore, the prospective earnings on the pictures he is making will be slow in coming in, and the successful ones will have to help pay the cost of making the less profitable ones.

Take the "Three Little Pigs" as an example. The cost of this picture was $20,500 and it took four weeks to make, although Walt Disney had been trying for a year to persuade his story staff that the idea was a good one. This picture has turned out to be a freak in the matter of sales. Nothing has ever been seen to equal the demands. A total of over 400 prints were made so that all parts of the country could have it when they wished. Of course, all 400 prints are not earning money simultaneously, but all have produced income. The gross returns on this eight-minute picture have been unofficially estimated at anywhere from $150,000 to $200,000, and of course rumor has set them at much higher figures even than those. But the profits, whatever they may be, will never be announced, for "Three Little Pigs" is only part of a unit. Its income will be pooled with that of the preceding and subsequent films in the unit. In short, much of the profit of the "Three Little Pigs" may have to cover the weaknesses in the earning record of other pictures which have failed to return a profit, if such films exist.

V

Meanwhile a barrier in Disney's path to wealth is still Columbia Pictures. That organization's contract with the artist, dating from January, 1930, was not merely for two years of production. It reserved the right to rent out each picture for five years after the date of initial release!

This privilege has brought about an unusual state of affairs. Columbia Pictures have on their books more than sixty Disney pictures. These include the twenty-one productions obtained from Powers, and two years of shorts made under contract. The Powers pictures are running past the five-year date line now, and each film must be withdrawn from the market when it passes this five-year line. But many old Mickey Mouse and Silly Symphonies films are still obtainable. This is a sharp competitive weapon against all of Disney's new productions.

For instance, suppose the children of your neighborhood want to see Mickey Mouse pictures, and refuse to tolerate other animated cartoons. They threaten to leave the neighborhood theater. The manager is in a quandary.

He first calls up United Artists or its territorial agent. The new Mickey Mouse, he is told, can be rented for, let us say, $20 for three days. He winces at the price, but he must have a real Mickey Mouse. Happily, however, his distributors' bulletin shows him that he can save money. Columbia has shelves full of Mickey Mouse prints. He can have his choice of the lot for, let us say, $5 for three days.

Does he take the "New Mickey Mouse" at $20 or one of the old series at five dollars? In these times there is no alternative for the neighborhood theater manager.

The first-run houses in the large cities welcome the new productions as the best of their kind, and Mickey frequently gets top billing on the canopy. Silly Symphonies go into the RKO Music Hall in New York City for a rental of $500 a week. But there is only one Music Hall.

It is in the smaller cities and neighborhood theaters that the costly new productions face serious opposition from ghostly Mickey Mouse productions of the past. And Disney's productions are costly. The Mouse films average $18,000 and the Silly Symphonies $20,000. Color-print costs add another $18,000 to $20,000. This necessitates high rental prices, which are pro-rated so as to wipe out all existing costs within eighteen months. Only unusual demand for a picture produces a profit before the eighteen months have expired.

Three more years will elapse before Columbia's supply of Mickey Mouse and Silly Symphonies prints becomes nullified by contract. And there is no telling through whom Disney will be releasing three years hence. At present he is releasing through the specific outlet of a big producing company, for the controlling stock in United Artists was purchased recently by 20th Century Pictures.

It is quite true that Walt Disney is not exactly in need of sympathy, for he has other channels of revenue over which he has better control. His newspaper cartoon strip returns a handsome profit, largely because there is no distributor soaking up 35 per cent and "extras" for mailing out the mats. There are several varieties of Mickey Mouse books. A half-million were printed recently exclusively for one group of the five-and-ten-cent-stores. There are Mickey Mouse toys, writing paper, printed card insertions for gum and candy, cloth prints, novelties, effigies, gramophone records—in fact, anything that will produce a royalty for the use of the name or figure. Of late the "Three Little Pigs" have invaded the Mickey Mouse territory, vying with the mouse for popularity and royalties. Fortunately Disney has copyrighted and registered his various brain children in every possible way to protect himself from infringement and gross imitators.

So long as he can keep Mickey Mouse films popular, these various royalties will continue to pour in, and he will shed no tears over profitless films. But it remains a curious fact that his chief returns thus come from by-products, not from the pictures themselves which have given delight to so many million people.

• The bulk of this article is not concerned with Mickey Mouse, the cartoon character, but rather the financial side of the house of Mouse. From that unique perspective, Mann reveals more than any other writer for years to come about how Walt and Roy built and managed their operation. Mann was also, apparently, the first writer to reveal that Ub Iwerks once owned shares in the studio.

Mickey Mouse

Alva Johnston

Woman's Home Companion, July 1934

Charlie Chaplin and Mickey Mouse are the only universal characters that have ever existed. The greatest kings and conquerors, gods and devils, have by comparison been local celebrities. Mickey's domain is today even more extensive than Chaplin's. Charlie's mustache, hat, pants, shoes and cane belong to western civilization and make him a foreigner in some regions. Mickey Mouse is not a foreigner in any part of the world.

Mickey's appeal extends to and beyond the frontiers of civilization. He has for example an Eskimo following in Alaska. Douglas Fairbanks on his world tour endeared himself to cannibals and headhunters by showing them movies of Mickey Mouse. Tribes of Kaffirs in South Africa recently declined to accept any cakes of soap which did not bear the image of Mickey, just as formerly they declined to accept coins which did not bear the image of Queen Victoria. Tribes of connoisseurs in the big cities have taken up Mickey Mouse and lorgnettes are focused on original drawings of him on the walls of fashionable galleries.

Mickey has received greater honors abroad than at home. He was recently created a citizen of France at a carnival in Granville. His fifth birthday, on September twenty-eighth last was almost unnoticed in America, but was the occasion of impressive column-long editorials in newspapers in England. Mickey's greatest triumph in Germany was Hitler's denunciation of young Nordics who were wearing Mickey Mouse emblems instead of the swastika. Since Stalin ordered the people to laugh and be gay, Mickey Mouse films have been smuggled into Russia in considerable numbers, although there is no authorized distributing agency there. There are theaters in Sweden and in India which run seven or eight Mickey Mouse epics one after the other as their main programs. The animated cartoon is the life of the movie business in Japan where the feature picture is often cut to pieces because of the prejudice of the Orientals against scenes where lovers are shown frying in the deep fat of passion.

The little hero is billed as Miki Kuchi in Japan, Michel Souris in France, Miguel Ratoncito in Spain and Micky Maus in Germany. The number of admissions to theaters where Mickey Mouse played last year is calculated at four hundred and sixty-eight million. King George, Queen Mary, Mussolini and President Roosevelt are among his fans. More than six hundred manufactured articles ranging from doormats to jewels bear his portrait. The Ingersoll factory turned out more than a million Mickey Mouse watches in eight months but was unable to keep up with the demand. Mickey, like Chaplin, was discovered by the mob before he was discovered by the art world. It was another case in which the masses gave a lesson in art appreciation to the intelligentsia. Mickey is America's greatest esthetic achievement, according to Eisenstein, Russian director, who is a little bitter toward Hollywood. "Mickey is Art," declared Robert Harsche, director of the Art Institute of Chicago, in installing a permanent Mickey Mouse exhibit among the great moderns. The little star of the animated cartoons promises to eclipse Picasso and Matisse in the chatter of the salons. In short, poor Mickey is in the hands of the dilettantes. After escaping hundreds of other dreadful perils, he is now in the most desperate plight of his career.

The creator of Mickey Mouse is Walt Disney, a small, wiry bright-eyed and eager-faced chap of thirty-two years, a little bewildered but wholly unspoiled by his sudden rise to fame. Disney's own personal fame in fact is not so great. He basks to a certain extent in reflected glory, but only a small percentage of the Mickey Mouse fans have any interest in Disney. Mickey was discovered on his first appearance more than five years ago; Disney is just beginning to be discovered. He has tremendous prestige within the film colony, although he is not widely known there personally. He seldom attends Hollywood parties and premieres, but in the last two years he has gone Hollywood to the extent of taking up polo, a game in which he has an official rating of zero.

Will Rogers and other stars praised him to the skies and Chaplin did a Chaplin walk in his honor at a dinner tendered to Disney last fall by the Hollywood Writers' Club. Disney, who is as shy as Chaplin himself, was quite overwhelmed.

An example of Walt's high standing in Hollywood occurred when he visited the studio where Rasputin was being made. The Barrymores are not ordinarily given to effusiveness toward strangers, but when Ethel was asked whether Disney could come on the set she said, "I'll go home if he doesn't." She introduced him to John who threw both arms around him and then demanded that a group photograph be taken of the three Barrymores and the creator of Mickey Mouse. On being told no camera was available for taking still pictures, John exclaimed, "There are thousands of them around every time an Iowa politician comes here. Do you mean to tell me there is no camera when Disney visits us?" Barrymore clamored about this until a still camera was found and the Barrymore-Disney group picture was taken.

The only part of Disney's sudden renown which disturbs him is the art appreciation. He is apprehensive that his studio will become art-conscious. Even now a few of Disney's able cartoonists worry over their work and ask themselves, "Is this art?" When the publicity department receives a magazine or newspaper article discussing the dynamics, the rhythm, the fluidity of line, the symbolism and the expressionism of Mickey Mouse, Disney orders the publication taken away so that no one in the studio can read it.

Disney is a product of the system of child rearing which, although it has developed more than its share of American notables, is seldom recommended in modern treatises on education. This is the system which regards a boy as an economic asset who should at least pay for his keep and, if possible, pay dividends. Elias Disney, the father of Walt, had been reared on this plan and he believed in it for the sake of both the child and of the family. The philosophy of it is summed up in one of Frank Sullivan's simplified adages, "All work and no play makes jack." First as a chore boy on a farm in Marceline, Missouri, and later as a newsboy in Kansas City, Walt carried on the old Disney tradition. His father had been a building contractor for twenty years in Chicago, but moved to the farm when Walt was an infant.

The chore boy still manifests himself both in Mickey Mouse and in the Silly Symphonies. One of his earliest farm assignments was that of feeding pigs. He had hardly outgrown infancy when he became an expert milkman, and the cow has always been a leading Disney character. Both Walt and his brothers fed their kittens by shooting streams of milk directly from cow to kitten. Twenty years later this became one of the Mickey Mouse gags. Flying streams of milk figured in the early Disney work as custard pies figured in the glorious Mack Sennett days. The censors of Ohio and some other states held that Disney's milking scenes were improper and that the sight of a cow's udder was indelicate. Disney met the issue by putting a brassière on the cow.

The family moved from the farm to Kansas City when Walt was almost eight years old. From the age of nine to fifteen he delivered newspapers, getting up every morning at three-thirty, finishing about six and then selling papers on a corner. He repeated this routine after school in the afternoon. At times he floundered through three feet of snow with his papers and in bitter cold weather he warmed himself now and then in hallways of apartment houses. His earnings went into the family funds. When he wanted pocket money he had to take on extra tasks. Responsibility and hard work at an early age gave him his drive and industry; his talents for fun and pictures were inborn and insuppressible.

Disney began to draw almost as soon as he began to walk. He was an old hand with crayons before he was of school age. His first art patron was a veterinarian who lived near the Disney farm in Missouri. When Walt was seven the old horse doctor held a stallion by the halter and compelled him to pose for his portrait. All of the important early Disneys were acquired by this connoisseur. When Walt was nine years old his ambition shifted; he now wanted to become an actor instead of an artist. His first two roles were those of Abraham Lincoln and Charlie Chaplin. In the fourth grade he recited the Gettysburg address at school exercises, his make-up consisting of penciled lines of care, a wart made of putty, a tall hat of cardboard blackened with shoe polish and a solemn coat belonging to his father, who was an official of the Congregational church. Disney played Lincoln at school for five years. This was tempting fate, for the hardened Lincoln actor usually spends his whole life playing Lincoln both on and off the stage. The plight of the professional Lincoln was summed up by Gene Buck who said, "That guy will never be happy until he is assassinated."

Luckily for Disney, he soon became a better Chaplin than a Lincoln. He perfected himself in the art of springing a cane into the air with his feet and catching it nonchalantly. Sneaking out of the bedroom he would attend amateur nights where he won several small cash prizes and became known as the second best Chaplin in Kansas City. He still believes that he was jobbed, as the winner of the first prizes broke the rules by departing from pantomime and singing songs. Amateur nights in Kansas City had a great influence on the career of Disney.

Chaplin was a kind of godfather to Mickey Mouse. It is now and always has been the aim of Disney to graft Charlie's psychology upon Mickey. The two universal characters have something in common in their approach to their problems. They have the same blend of hero and coward, nit-wit and genius, mug and gentleman. The emotional subtleties of Chaplin, his repose, wistfulness and pathos are not for the animated cartoon; the action is too rapid for effects which must be gradually developed. Laughs can be produced in the fraction of a second; tears require time. Disney has, however, succeeded in introducing occasional heartthrobs. Once for example when Mickey Mouse was elk-hunting, he shot his dog which happened by a curious set of circumstances to be wearing antlers, but the artist did not dare to tamper with the feelings of his public. The tragic note was quickly silenced. The dog opened an eye to reassure the audience as Mickey rushed into a close-up and cried, "Is there a doctor in the house?"

When Charlie Chaplins became too common in Kansas City Disney took a partner and appeared on amateur nights in a singing and patter act. At fifteen years, he got a job as peanut butcher on trains running out of Kansas City. Later that year, 1917, the family moved to Chicago where Walt attended high school.

In Chicago an acute conflict developed between his ambition to be an actor and his ambition to be an artist. He did illustrations for the high school magazine and studied cartooning at night at the Chicago Academy of Fine Arts; at the same time he and a friend worked up an imitation of Weber and Fields and sought unsuccessfully to go on the amateur stage. He also tried to break into two other fields of public entertainment. He sent for all kinds of books on magic and sleight-of-hand but could not find the time for practice in these arts. He paid the first installment on a small cinema outfit and planned to produce pictures written and acted by juveniles for juveniles, but he could not raise the money to buy films or to pay the second installment on the camera, which was repossessed by the company.

In the summer of 1918, Walt, then sixteen years old, needed a job and applied for a position as a letter carrier. He said that he was seventeen years old. His conscience would not let him lie by more than one year, and he was rejected as being too young. He went home, put on his father's clothes, deepened his voice, hardened his conscience and reapplied for the position, saying he was eighteen years old. This time he was hired. He was rejected on account of his youth at army and navy recruiting stations and at a Canadian enlistment office, but in September, 1918, he joined the Red Cross as a chauffeur. He arrived in France after the armistice but served for a year as chauffeur for Red Cross officials.

Returning from France he worked as a commercial artist in Kansas City, drawing illustrations for advertisements in farm journals . . . pictures of happy cows eating patent salt blocks, of triumphant hens hatching out dollars after eating patent hen foods, and oil wells spouting seas of money.

It was pure accident that started Disney at work on animated drawings. By answering an advertisement in a newspaper he got a position with the Kansas City Slide Company, which formerly made stereopticon slides and had recently been making advertising cartoons for motion picture projections. Disney's first animated cartoon pictured a steamboat propelled by a series of nervous twitches. Human figures were activated at that time like stop-go signals. Paper arms and legs were pinned to a paper torso. The figure was photographed in one attitude, the arms and legs were then moved, the second photograph taken and so on, the animation being very jittery. Walt induced his company to get away from the Mexican jumping bean effect by drawing a fresh cartoon for each photograph.

Disney was only nineteen years old when he made his first independent production, but the haphazard experiences and enthusiasms of his early years had furnished him with an ideal equipment for his life work. He owed very little to schooling. His impressions were all first hand;

he had never peered at life through the spectacles of books. Recently, when Disney was discussing his rules for keeping Mickey Mouse true to his own character and for avoiding any violations of the laws of nature as they exist in Cartoonland, an interviewer said, "That's a paraphrase of Hamlet's advice to the players." Disney said that he had never seen or read Hamlet, but that he had had a vague idea that it was a part ham actors liked to play. He had never heard of holding the mirror up to nature. Disney is as free as Al Smith from the taint of book-learning; no man could be clearer of the curse of sophistication.

Disney's first independent effort was an animated weekly saga of the news events of Kansas City. This ran for six months. Its success inspired him to attempt Little Red Riding-hood. He worked on it for six months, using his father's garage as a studio. Goldilocks, The Town Musicians of Bremen and then children's tales followed. Walt, who had just come of age, then formed a corporation, hired a staff of artists and started to work on a large scale; but his distributing agency went into bankruptcy and failed to pay him for his films. This gave him his first introduction to business trouble, which has since become an old friend. The crash in Kansas City made him decide to go to Hollywood. To get the money for the trip he wrote a song film for a theater organist and made motion pictures of the offspring of his friends.

He arrived in Hollywood in August 1923, with one suit of clothes, very ancient and greatly patched. Walt and his brother Roy, who furnished capital of two hundred and fifty dollars, set up a studio in Hollywood. They lived for months on a starvation diet with the sheriff at their heels. Finally an eastern film distributor became interested in him and Walt started his series called Alice in Cartoonland which was a combination of a flesh-and-blood heroine with a supporting company of pen-and-ink characters, the photographs of the girl being superimposed on the photographs of the cartoons. After making sixty Alice films Disney started to produce Oswald the rabbit. Oswald was a great success and Disney ventured to ask a higher price for his work. The distributor's reply was to raid Disney's staff and start making his own Oswalds.

This was the first of three such raids which have been made on Disney's studio. Many film producers had the theory that Walt Disney was not particularly important to his cartoons. Their idea was that to duplicate Disney's success it was only necessary to capture some of his able workers. This theory has not justified itself. Disney has survived three almost complete changes in the personnel of his organization and his pictures have steadily increased in popular favor.

Disney was in New York when he had the trouble over Oswald. He then decided to make a new series and distribute it through some other company. The idea of Mickey Mouse was forced on him by process of elimination because the cat, dog, rabbit and other feasible animals were already cartoon heroes. Disney also had a sentimental attachment to mice because of the friendship which had sprung up between him and a mouse which used to drop around and play on his desk in the advertising office in Kansas City. It occurred to Disney that if he used a mouse hero he had a made-to-order villain in the cat, with unlimited possibilities of dramatic conflict. Of course Mickey is a mouse in name only; he is a biped that wears shoes and has a human soul. Walt, with the help of his wife, the former Lillian Bounds, wrote the first Mickey scenario on the train from New York to Hollywood. For a long time Mickey was closely guarded against the kidnappers in which Hollywood abounded; any new brain child was then likely to be abducted from its rightful parents. It was considered dangerous to let the mouse idea become known even at the studio, and the first Mickey picture was made in a garage used by Walt and his brother.

As the new cartoon character was coming into existence, Al Jolson was revolutionizing motion pictures by the success of his singing in The Jazz Singer. Walt decided to gamble with the new new medium and took his picture, which was entitled Steamboat Willie, to New York to be fitted up with music and sound effects.

The synchronization of Steamboat Willie was one of the major ordeals of Disney's life. The art of matching noise to action was then in great confusion. Effects came before causes, thunder preceded lightning, dull thuds resounded before objects fell. A musical director was engaged who had had experience in recording music for feature films, but this experience was a hindrance rather than a help. He knew how to set the pace for his musicians in an ordinary screen play, but the action in Steamboat Willie was so rapid that the orchestra had played only half of the musical accompaniment before the film was finished.

Disney got a metronome for the guidance of the musicians, but the director scorned to use it. "What am I here for?" he demanded. "Am I a machine?" Again the orchestra tried to keep its music abreast the high speed action of Steamboat Willie. It was like a group of nervous amateurs shooting at quail; the musicians blazed away too early and too late. This wild performance was repeated again and again. The weather was hot, the musical director was fat and he melted away in his effort to get the sound and action on speaking terms. Finally Disney induced him to let the orchestra keep time by watching a film on which a bounding ball acted as a metronome. Even then the musicians were distracted by watching Steamboat Willie and finally they were turned with their backs to the picture. The results at last were pretty satisfactory. Disney found it necessary, however, to spend a whole night clipping out bits of film here and there in order to bring the music and noises into their true relation to the action.

Mickey Mouse made his debut in Steamboat Willie at the Colony Theatre on September 28, 1928, and was an enormous success. The audience went wild when he played a xylophone solo on a cow's teeth and gave a concert with a set of dishpans. There was a great variety of sound effects all pretty well timed. Disney's next picture was The Skeleton's Dance, his first Silly Symphony. This was rejected by many motion picture exhibitors as being gruesome, but audiences loved the jolly skeletons as they loved the jaunty mouse. After breaking all precedent by playing an encore at Roxy's, The Skeleton's Dance became a cartoon classic. After five years it is still playing and has earned more money than any other "short," unless the lead has recently been taken by the Three Little Pigs.

When making the first Mickey Mouse picture Disney threw in all the wild gags he could think of. Later, however, Mickey began to assume a definite personality, and Disney would reject good comedy ideas, saying, "Mickey isn't like that." Today the mouse has matured, as Mr. Pickwick did, from a madly farcical comic to a being with a consistent though dizzy personality. Disney will not for example permit what he calls "camera puns" in connection with his celebrated creation. A rival used this gag: a lady character in an animated cartoon presses a handkerchief to her mouth and her lips are printed on the handkerchief in lipstick; the impression of the lips then delivers a monologue.

This was a "camera pun" which was highly rewarded with laughter, but such devices are held to be unworthy of the dignity of Mickey Mouse. He is not permitted to be cruel or arrogant except with villains. If he is vainglorious one moment he is deflated the next. Extreme vigilance is exercised to keep him from becoming a smart Alec. Too much whimsey and fantasy are objectionable. In Disney's own words there should be "just enough exaggeration to take the characters out of the real and into the imaginary; it must be natural to be effective."

One of Mickey's comparative failures was as a violinist. He fiddled divinely, but he fiddled too much to suit the audience. Since then it has been a rule that Mickey must never be allowed to be arty. The hands of Mickey Mouse and the rest of his physique are the work of other artists, but the voice is the voice of Disney. Walt started squeaking out the Mickey Mouse dialogues in the early days and has stuck to it for a good reason: if an actor or announcer were hired to speak Mickey's lines, the man might be hired away and it would disturb fans to have Mickey's voice change from time to time.

There are seventy-five artists employed at the Disney studios. A few others turn out the comic strips and designs for Mickey Mouse novelties. Nearly fifteen thousand separate drawings are made for each film. The backgrounds are drawn separately and remain on paper. Mickey and the other animated characters are drawn on sheets seven by nine inches and then traced on celluloid. The celluloid is superimposed on the paper backgrounds and then photographed. After one picture is taken, the celluloid drawing is removed, a new celluloid action picture is superimposed on the background and the camera clicks again. When Technicolor is used, the color is painted on thousands of drawings and transferred to film by the color cameras.

Even after the success of Steamboat Willie and The Skeleton's Dance the Disneys had a difficult time. It was a slow process to equip theaters with talking pictures apparatus. Many exhibitors doubted whether a mouse had the stuff of which heroes are made, but audiences never objected to Mickey on that account. For some reason or other the mouse, though unfavorably regarded in real life, has been kindly treated in art and letters from the time of Æsop to that of Robert Burns and later.

Even after Mickey had been established as a world character, the Disneys were still working their way through perilous financial shoals. Only four years ago Walt and Roy sold their jointly owned automobile to meet their payments and for six months thereafter they walked to work. Their claim is that the value of the animated cartoon has never been adequately recognized. When it was reported a few months ago that the profits of the Three Little Pigs had passed the million-dollar mark, the Disneys examined their books and reported that the profits from that record-breaking film were less than four thousand dollars. It will have a long run here and abroad and they estimate that its net earnings will eventually be about forty-five thousand dollars. Technicolor has recently proved an important factor in winning recognition for the Silly Symphonies. Walt and his brother have been afraid of what they call "commercializing the business." Both of them have turned deaf ears to promoters who have approached them with dazzling schemes for selling stock, refinancing and expanding, but the idea of having Mickey Mouse bossed by Wall Street is horrifying to the Disneys.

Because of the prejudice of the theater chains against paying handsome sums for short films, Walt is eager to make a long feature in animated color cartoons. Fan mail runs strongly in favor of a full-length Alice in Wonderland in this medium. Others think The Wizard of Oz is made to order for the animated cartoon. James Thurber has demanded in stern accents that Disney, putting aside business and excuses, proceed to make the Odyssey.

The difficulties in handling the animated cartoons increase geometrically with the length of the film, and the experiments suggested would all be heavy gambles. Walt Disney is convinced that tragedy and triangles and other heavy stuff cannot be conveyed by his medium. The ability of the animator to express varieties of emotion has, however, increased enormously in the last three or four years. Disney is eager to attempt an ambitious opus in the comic adventure field. He believes that the animated cartoon is only at the beginning of its career.

• Lengthy articles like this one by Alva Johnston (and Arthur Mann's from May 1934) were increasingly common in the mid-1930s, reflecting not only the growing body of Walt's work, but an intensified, unrelenting interest among the public in Mickey and Disney.

Mickey Mouse
Makes the Britannica

The most significant item of the week's film news was the announcement that Mickey Mouse had crashed the Encyclopaedia Britannica.
The editors of that voluminous publication—according to United Artists—intend to present the history and mechanics of the animated cartoon in their next edition. Rather than keep all their subscribers on
tenterhooks until it appears, they will issue in their September bulletin
an article entitled "The Story of the Animated Cartoon; from the Phen-
akistoscope to Mickey Mouse."

The article was, or is being, prepared by Earl Theisen, honorary cu-
rator of motion pictures at the Los Angeles Museum, and will be illustrated with sketches and photographs of Mickey, Minnie and other
creatures of the Walt Disney Studios. About the only honor yet unat-
tained by Mickey or Mr. Disney is the unveiling of a portrait in the Hall
of Fame. The list of distinctions is so great that one cannot help asking
the time-honored question: "What is he: Mouse or man?" Look at the
chronological record for the last year:

Mickey's Honors.

July 4, 1933—Walt Disney receives tailless Manx cat, the gift of the
Lieutenant Governor of the Isle of Man.

September, 1933—The King of England refused to go to a motion-
picture performance until he was assured there was a Mickey Mouse
on the program.

Sept. 30, 1933—Will Rogers, Joseph Schenck, Charles Chaplin and Dr. R. B. Kleinsmid, president of the University of Southern California, among speakers at Mickey's fifth birthday party.

Oct. 11. 1933—Walt Disney awarded diploma by the Academy of Fine Arts in Buenos Aires for his cartoons.

Nov. 17, 1933—Mr. Disney wins "extra special" award of the Academy of Motion Picture Arts and Sciences for his creation of Mickey.

Dec. 14, 1933—Sketches of Mickey and the Silly Symphony creatures were hung at the Winter exhibition of the Art Institute in the Chicago Art Museum.

Dec. 21, 1933—Mrs. Marion Sabin of New York presented a medal to Walt Disney for his "distinguished service to children."

Dec. 29, 1933—Mr. Disney rates mention in British "Who's Who" as creator of Mickey.

Jan. 18, 1934—The Poor Richard Achievement Medal, awarded yearly to an outstanding American, went to Mr. Disney as "a creator of laughter."

March 17, 1934—A gold statuette awarded Mr. Disney by the Academy of Motion Picture Arts and Sciences.

March 20, 1934—National Academy of Arts and Letters in Havana presents special honor diploma to Mr. Disney.

April 19, 1934—The League of Nations Committee on Child Welfare endorses Mickey Mouse. Mr. Disney elected honorary member of British Art Workers Guild.

May 9, 1934—Mr. Disney is one of four recipients of American Art Dealers Association gold medals for "service to American art."

• In 1936 Earl Theisen began a distinguished thirty-five-year career as a photographer for *Look* magazine. A version of Theisen's article cited here (upon which his Britannica entry was based), entitled "The History of the Animated Cartoon," also appeared in the *Journal of the Society of Motion Picture Engineers*, in September 1933, and was distributed in mimeograph form to staff at the Disney studio at some point after late April 1933.

In a front-page story three months earlier, the *New York Times* also had reported ("British Art Guild Honors Mickey Mouse Creator") that the guild, whose members included the architect Sir Edwin Luytens, George Bernard

Shaw, and "a host of Royal Academicians, artists, architects, sculptors and craftsmen," had "paid public tribute to Walt Disney, creator of Mickey Mouse and the Silly Symphony films."

Mickey Mouse
Emerges as Economist

L. H. Robbins

New applause is heard for Mickey Mouse, riding high above the general acclaim for him that already rings throughout the earth. The fresh cheering is for Mickey the Big Business Man, the world's super-salesman. He finds work for jobless folk. He lifts corporations out of bankruptcy. Wherever he scampers, here or overseas, the sun of prosperity breaks through the clouds.

Cutting up on the screen in every clime, entertaining a million audiences a year in eighty-eight countries, Mickey Mouse is the best-known and most-popular international figure of his day. One touch of Mickey makes the whole world grin in a very dark hour. But he does not stop with entertaining.

He rolls up his sleeves and grapples with the world's economic problem. He puts his shoulder to the stalled wheel of trade, and the wheel that won't budge for the statesman and the international bankers turns for the small and mighty Mickey.

Assisted by faithful Minnie, he pumps a key-winding handcar around a track of tin and pulls a two-million-dollar toy-making concern out of receivership. Then by himself he restores a famous but limping watchmaking company to health—after eight weeks of his treatment the company throws away its crutches, adds 2,700 workers to its payroll and proceeds to sell 2,000,000 watches.

Again, through three lean years he keeps a knitting mill busy making sweatshirts with his portrait in color on them—a million shirts a year, and one-third of the population of the mill town assured of three meals a day from the overtime work alone.

* * *

Mickey Mouse has his commercial headquarters in Seventh Avenue, just off Times Square. He lives in Hollywood, of course, pursuing there the fine art of the funny films with his creator, Walt Disney. Their art yields by-products worth millions to businessmen, hence Mickey's New York offices, with his name on the directory board downstairs and also in the telephone book.

A neat sign on the door says: "Kay Kamen: The Walt Disney Enterprises." Mickey himself, portrayed in bright hues and heroic size, greets you from the wall of the pleasantly appointed reception room. Beyond are showrooms where Disney commodities fill glass cases with color and humor; also workrooms where Disney artists, trained in the technique of the Hollywood studio, draw the countless pictures used in Mickey's commercial undertakings.

The office controls the by-products of the Disney art. If you wish to manufacture a Mickey Mouse roller-skate or a Mickey Mouse electric refrigerator, you come here for Mickey's permission, and Mr. Kamen, his merchandising representative, grants you a license, provided no one else is making the article you desire to make, and provided you convince him that your wares will measure up to the quality standard of the Disney animated cartoons.

It is a busy place. While you wait, an official of a national metal institute is 'phoning about Mickey Mouse book-ends, and a maker of optical instruments comes in to discuss Mickey Mouse thermometers. The first concession went to a doll maker in 1930. Now there are eighty licensees in the United States, fifteen in Canada, forty in England, eighty on the Continent and fifteen in Australia. There are branch offices in Chicago, Toronto, London, Paris, Copenhagen, Milan, Barcelona, Lisbon and Sydney.

The licensees make thousands of merchandise items—the latest in England is Mickey Mouse marmalade. Their royalties help to nurture the Hollywood art, which is laborious and expensive. An ideal arrangement it is, and highly suggestive of perpetual motion; for the better the art of the Disney studio, the better the by-products sell, and the better they sell, the better the art again. It is something novel in business cycles; it never gets worse. With commodity sales boomed periodically by the fame of the new films, the Mickey Mouse fad goes on as if forever—and Mr. Disney is still young.

Conservative business houses join in the rush to employ Mickey Mouse and his friends, the Three Little Pigs, the Wolf, the Grasshopper, Horace Horsecollar and Pluto, the dog. Among them are leading makers of pencils and of paper. The world's largest food-products company hires Mickey to sell a breakfast food and spends a million and a half to proclaim the tie-up. The manufacturer of half of the table silver in the United States dispenses Mickey Mouse cutlery in all grades, including sterling, and Fifth Avenue offers Mickey Mouse charms and bracelets in gold and platinum set with diamonds, retailing up to $1,200.

Mickey is such a literary lion, he has to have four publishers; one of his books last year sold 2,400,000 copies. His school notebooks and tablets go by the million. So do his neckties and handkerchiefs—the kerchief trade is keen for the cotton print that shows Pluto writing on the sidewalk, "Mickey loves Minnie." Department stores by hundreds, here and abroad, go Mickey Mouse, even to the length of spending $25,000 on a single window display, and a great rubber company pauses in making Zeppelins to turn out fifty-foot Mickeys for their street parades.

Undeniably and appallingly, it is Mickey Mouse's day. Shoppers carry Mickey Mouse satchels and briefcases bursting with Mickey Mouse soap, candy, playing-cards, bridge favors, hairbrushes, chinaware, alarm clocks and hot-water bottles, wrapped in Mickey Mouse paper, tied with Mickey Mouse ribbon and paid for out of Mickey Mouse purses with savings hoarded in Mickey Mouse banks.

At the lunch counter—Mickey Mouse table covers and napkins—they consume Mickey Mouse biscuits and dairy products while listening to Mickey Mouse music from Mickey Mouse phonographs and radios. Then, glancing at their Mickey Mouse wrist-watches, they dash away to buy Mickey Mouse toothbrushes that will make oral sanitation attractive to little Michael and Minerva.

And the children live in a Mickey Mouse world. They wear Mickey Mouse caps, waists, socks, shoes, slippers, garters, mittens, aprons,

bibs and underthings, and beneath Mickey Mouse rain-capes and um-
brellas they go to school, where Mickey Mouse desk outfits turn lessons into pleasure.

They play with Mickey Mouse velocipedes, footballs, baseballs,
bounce-balls, bats, catching gloves, boxing gloves, doll houses, doll
dishes, tops, blocks, drums, puzzles, games—

Paint sets, sewing sets, drawing sets, stamping sets, jack sets, bubble
sets, pull toys, push toys, animated toys, tents, camp stools, sand pails,
masks, blackboards and balloons—

Until day is done, when they sup from Mickey Mouse cups, porringers and baby plates and lie down to sleep in Mickey Mouse pajamas
between Mickey Mouse crib sheets, to waken in the morn smiling at
Mickey Mouse pictures on the nursery walls. In time, no doubt there
will be Mickey Mouse wallpaper for them.

After all, these material and tangible creations of the factories are
only shadows of the real thing; manifestations, as it were, of a spirit;
physical effigies of a vital reality who is but a shadow himself and has no
material existence, no tangibility at all. They merely reflect, they don't
explain the excitement over Mickey Mouse.

What is the secret of his appeal? How has an imaginary creature only
6 years old, going on 7, captured the interest of almost every tribe on
this terrestrial ball? Why is it that university presidents praise Mickey
Mouse, the League of Nations recommends him, *Who's Who 1934* and
the Encyclopaedia Britannica give him paragraphs, learned academics
hang medals on him, art galleries turn from Picasso and Epstein to hold
exhibitions of his monkey-shines, and the King of England won't go to
the movies unless Mickey is on the bill?

* * *

Crowds of ambitious folk looking for ideas and fortune would like to
know, to say nothing of people trying to interpret day-to-day phenom-
ena for the press, psychologists who must somehow account for human
behavior, and historians who will have to record this age for posterity's
eye. Mickey Mouse is Public Question No. 1 to a lot of people.

Sages in great argument try to explain Mickey Mouse, and, in the
fashion of the blind men of Hindustan who went to see the elephant,
they reason variously, each according to his feeling. To the timid among
us, Mickey represents mankind beset by grim circumstances and es-

caping whole and right-side up through luck. To them he is that dearest figure in fiction, the ill-used, defenseless, well-deserving Cinderella in disguise. To the aggressive and the predatory among us, on the other hand, he symbolizes cleverness and resource. He is "little, but oh my!" He outsmarts even Behemoth.

Again, world-weary philosophers find in Mickey's antics "a release from the tyranny of things." He declares a nine-minute moratorium on the debt we owe to the iron facts of life. He suspends the rules of common sense and correct deportment and all the other carping, conventional laws, including the law of gravity, that hold us down and circumscribe and cramp our style.

* * *

These observers tell us there is in human nature a streak of rebellion, a yearning to cut loose, to be free to overleap the moon if we like, even at the cost of a headache and an unpleasant taste in the cold gray dawn of the morning after. This craving of ours for Mickey, with his absurdities, his defiance of reason and his accomplishments of the impossible, gratifies for us vicariously.

We see Mickey, the bandmaster drawing dulcet strains out of the bell of the big brass tuba with his hands. We see him render the storm movement of the overture so convincingly that he brings on a tornado; and an umbrella is blown through the duck's flute, and the orchestra runs for cover, and the benches run, too; and at the last the musicians, high in the tree tops, go on playing, loyal to their dauntless leader, while the branches to which they hang beat time to the music.

After that excursion into the fantastic, the philosophers tell us, we are cured of our revolt. We leave the theatre calmed and stabilized to take up the humdrum of life in the right spirit again. Maybe so.

It sounds a bit highbrow to those who have most to do with Mickey's career. So does the explanation of educators who recall that folk tales have always been popular and fables of talking animals beloved; who cite the instances of Reynard the Fox and Brer Rabbit, and conclude that Mickey's creator has merely applied the old, tested method of Aesop.

There would seem to be more to Mickey Mouse than that, and besides, he is not an animal; he is a personality, along with Uncle Sam, John Bull, Mr. Dooley and the Tammany Tiger. He is not a mouse at all; he is Mickey Mouse. In one way or another, since there is a bit of Mickey's helplessness, shrewdness, madness and mischief in the best of us, he is an approach, the nearest one in our day, to that mythical and ubiquitous fellow, Everyman.

All these piecemeal explanations help in explaining Mickey Mouse, but they ignore the two obvious ones—that Mickey is superlatively funny, and that he is simple. The world, in all its continents and islands, wants to laugh, and never more than now. Mickey makes it laugh till the roof shakes. Moreover, the occasion of the laughter is always harmless, and the world likes decency. It is proudly boasted that no Disney film has given offense since the indiscreet day, long ago, when complaining censorship seemed to make lingerie desirable for Clarabelle, the cow.

The world wants also to understand, and Mickey is so simple that anybody of any age in any stage of the rather spotty civilization extant on this planet can understand him. His simplicity makes him so nearly universal that any land can take him for its own. Wherefore he is at once hot stuff in Chile, "it" in Italy, cheered in Algiers, pined for in the Philippines and a wow all over the map. Wherefore, also, he has many an alias—Michel Souris, Michael Maus, Miguel Ratonocito, Michele Jopolino, Miki Kuchi, according to locality.

Add to all this that his nine minutes on the screen contain as many plot situations and surprises and as much pathos and comedy as three hours of spoken drama; and that because all these are present the public is satisfied, yet because the thing is over so soon the public is left hungry for more.

Last, and most important of all, consider that Disney, as a dramatist and a producer, is a genius whose work the scholarly of the world hail as an immortal contribution to literature. Disney, who is modest, would probably offer the further explanation of Mickey Mouse's success that his distributors have excellent connections abroad.

After these three reasons have been recited, Mickey's professional friends confide that the real, final secret of Mickey's appeal is still a secret to them and to Disney himself. Why does one Disney film go big while one every bit as good fails to score? They wish they knew.

If the reason for the public response were surely known, Disney would make pictures to fit the response. He could have a formula and follow it. But he has still to discover the magic formula. He still adventures in the dark and mysterious terra incognita of popular taste, as he did in 1928, when he and Mickey Mouse, unhonored and unsung, came to town to seek their fortune.

• Disney merchandising genius Kay Kamen died in a plane crash in the Azores in 1949 along with his wife and Edith Piaf's husband, boxer Marcel Cerdan. The statement that Mickey "lifts corporations out of bankruptcy" at the start of Robbins's article alluded to a news story of fairly recent vintage. As the New York Times reported ("Mickey Mouse Saves Jersey Toy Concern") in January 1935: toy figures of Mickey and Minnie "pumping a red-painted hand car around a circular track" during the previous Christmas season, had saved the heavily indebted Lionel Corporation from ruin. "Mickey and Minnie's excursion into stem-winding railroads," the Times said, "chiefly raised the $296,197 by which all claims were paid in full."

Mickey Mouse at the Gaumont-Palace

Jean Laury (Nicole Boré-Verrier)

© Jean Laury/*Le Figaro*, June 28, 1935 avec l'aimable autorisation du Figaro.

At the Gaumont-Palace yesterday morning over five thousand children cheered "Mickey Mouse" and his father, Walt Disney. A full report on this gala affair, organized by *Le Figaro*, which was a complete success, appears in our movie column.

The exploits of the famous mouse and the clever little pigs, the adventures of a boy and girl penguin and of the Goddess of Spring caused the beating of little hands and young hearts among a fresh new public, unrestrained in expressing its enthusiasm: Walt Disney, personally quite moved, was able to gauge the impact of his work and the popularity of the characters he created.

After the Silly Symphonies had flashed across the screen, the artists of the Petit-Monde performed the *ballet de Mickey*. On stage, his arms laden with garlands of flowers in the American national colors, Walt Disney listened to the charming poem composed for him by Mme Pierre Humble. Finally, Mlle Hélène Vacaresco, bestowing upon M. Walt Disney the gold medal of the C.I.D.A.L.C., presented him to the children of Paris. "You would have been delighted," she told them, "to know La Fontaine or Perrault . . ." And Mlle Hélène Vacaresco, in her uniquely vibrant and thoughtful manner, drew a parallel between the fabulist, the storyteller, and the author of animated cartoons, both joyful and poetic, whose glory is a "happy glory" . . .

However, in the midst of the stars of the children's ballet, Walt Disney knelt over, as if to put himself, once again, within reach of the youngsters who were, once more last night, indebted to him for so many charming dreams . . .

• The Gaumont-Palace was Paris's grandest movie theater. Pierre Humble was the founding director of the children's troupe, le Théâtre du Petit-Monde; Elena Văcărescu, an aristocratic Romanian exile, was president of the C.I.D.A.L.C. or Comité international pour la diffusion artistique et littéraire par le cinématographe. On June 18, 1935, one week before Walt arrived in Paris, the London Times announced that "the creator of 'Mickey Mouse' and the 'Silly Symphonies,' has been awarded a special medal by the International Film Committee of the League of Nations" ("League of Nations Medal for Mr. Disney"). However, Mme Văcărescu's group, the C.I.D.A.L.C., was not officially affiliated with the League. The Times also reported that, in "a letter to Mr. Disney's representative in Paris, M. Pillat, the permanent secretary of the committee, says that the award is to be considered an exceptional honour in recognition of the original and distinctive work done by Mr. Disney." The medal, now on display at the Walt Disney Family Museum in San Francisco, was formally presented to Walt on June 26th, during a reception at the Hôtel de Crillon in Paris. For the original text of this article in French, see Appendix F.

Mickey Mouse
Is 7 Years Old Today

Cholly Wood

Bridgeport Sunday Herald, September 29, 1935

There is no better-known actor on the screen. His name, his face and his personality are better known than those of Clark Gable and Greta Garbo. His personal and public life are so closely merged that his innermost habits and thoughts are public property. His fame extends beyond the screen right into the homes and the private lives of the millions who see him perform.

He is the most popular screen star ever to face a camera. Yet he has never asked for an increase in salary.

He is, in short, that truly amazing phenomenon of modern life—an actor whose single purpose is to bring happiness to others, with no thought of self. His name—if its alliterative syllables have not already suggested themselves—is Mickey Mouse.

Today Mickey Mouse has attained his seventh birthday, and his years have comprised no ordinary childhood.

The earth-spanning sprite was born—a few bold, humorous strokes on a sheet of clean paper—out of the imagination of Walt Disney, on Sept. 28, 1929. He ventured into the world of fun-loving humans on that date, in a vehicle called "Steamboat Willie," which flashed across the screen of the Colony theater in New York.

Immediately newspaper critics, magazine writers, radio commentators and the public at large contributed to the discovery that a new star had been born.

In the next five years this pen-and-ink actor lived a thousand lives in celluloid. He has invested each character drawn for him with a touch of madness which distinguishes the artist. Mickey, even at the age of three could do no wrong.

Detail of "Mickey Mouse is 7 Years Old Today."
© The Walt Disney Company.

On February 21, 1935, Mickey shed his sombre black and white raiment and revealed himself in all the glory of the spectrum. "The Band
Concert," in which he shared honors with Donald Duck, Pluto the Pup
and Clarabelle Cow, widened Mickey's horizon to include lovers of music as well as color.

At the age of seven, Mickey Mouse puts to shame all the child prodi-
gies that have ever warmed proud parents' hearts. Mickey Mouse has
had more honors showered upon him than many an international or
historical hero.

How many youngsters of seven, for example, can claim the distinction of space in the Encyclopedia Britannica? How many children can
claim recognition by the League of Nations?

Ever since that day in 1928 when Mickey Mouse first came into the
world, the distinctions have been piling up on both Mickey and his
master. Diplomas, certificates, medals, cups, statuettes, testimonials—
every conceivable type of recognition—have come to them in a steady
stream.

The first symbol of this recognition came, strangely enough, in the
form of a tailless cat, sent to Disney by the lieutenant-governor of the
Isle of Man. The most recent manifestation, appropriately enough,
was the gold medal presented to Disney by the League of Nations last
month.

Mickey Mouse is responsible for the award of a gold medal to Disney by the American Art Dealers' association, and Disney's election to the British Art Workers' Guild.

The National Academy of Arts and Letters in Havana presented a special diploma in Mickey's honor. The American Academy of Motion Picture Arts and Sciences awarded a gold statuette to Disney on Mickey's account. The Poor Richard Achievement Medal, granted annually to an outstanding American for important deeds done, went to the creator of Mickey Mouse.

Mickey Mouse has been a subject for sculptors and painters throughout the world. He is represented in the literature of every civilized nation.

There was that time when King George of England refused to attend a motion picture performance until he was assured that Mickey Mouse was on the program.

There was that occasion when Mickey Mouse, blown up to gigantic size, was utilized to welcome the Normandie after her maiden voyage across the Atlantic.

And then there is the miracle performed by Mickey Mouse. He was performing at the Manoir Richelieu Casino in Murray Bay, Quebec. In the audience were numerous patients from the Murray Bay Convalescent Home nearby.

One patient, according to eye-witnesses, entered the Casino on crutches, navigating with considerable difficulty. During the showing he laid his crutches beneath the seat. For the next half hour he forgot all about his affliction as he laughed at the antics of the famous star.

When the show was over, he got up and walked from the theater, without even a limp, leaving the crutches behind him. It's now Mickey, the Miracle Mouse.

• A Mickey balloon ("blown up to gigantic size") greeted the Normandie as it arrived in New York. Walt, Roy, Lillian, and Edna Disney (1890–1984) went on board June 7, 1935, for the ship's return voyage, as they embarked on their grand European vacation. Mme. Albert Lebrun, wife of the president of France, who came across on the Normandie, made the return trip as well, and dined with the Disneys. She also attended the grand reception for Walt in Paris at the Hôtel de Crillon.

Fox, Disney Add
to Museum Film Group

Motion Picture Daily, November 30, 1935

Further additions to the collection of historic films being made by the Museum of Modern Art include a group of 13 subjects from Twentieth Century-Fox and a number of cartoons from Walt Disney.

The Twentieth Century-Fox subjects presented by S. R. Kent, are: "A Fool There Was" (Theda Bara), 1914; "Carmen" (Theda Bara), 1915; "A Daughter of the Gods" (Annette Kellerman), 1916; "Cleopatra" (Theda Bara), 1917; "Riders of the Purple Sage," 1918; "Sky High" (Tom Mix), 1921; "The Iron Horse," 1924; "Three Bad Men," 1926; ""Sunrise," 1927; Movietone Newsreel (Mussolini, Shaw, Tilden), 1927; "Sex Life of the Polyp" (Benchley), 1926; "Cavalcade," 1933; Special "Cavalcade" film, not issued commercially, taken of the London stage production.

The Disney subjects are: First animated cartoon by Disney produced in 1920 for the Newman, Kansas City; "Plane Crazy" (First Mickey Mouse); "Steamboat Willie," 1928 (First Mickey Mouse in sound); "Skeleton Dance," 1929 (First Silly Symphony); "Flowers and Trees," 1932 (First cartoon in Technicolor); "The Band Concert," 1935 (First Mickey Mouse in Technicolor).

• This article was based on publicity material provided by MoMA. A second PR release, printed in full by the *Springfield* (Mass.) *Evening Union* ("Add Vamp and Mouse"), quoted Walt as saying: "The aim and purpose of the Museum of Modern Art Film Library are highly commendable and it gives me great pleasure to cooperate by supplying certain of our cartoon films selected by you. Good luck and success." Disney's gift included "material selected to show step by step the various processes in the production" of his films in addition to the 1920 Laugh-O-gram ad for the Newman Theatre and the Mickey and Silly Symphony cartoons cited by *Motion Picture Daily*. MoMA's

Film Library, organized and managed by Iris Barry, was incorporated in May 1935. In November 1943, Disney would be named to the Board of Trustees of the museum.

4. Glory Days in Color

1936–1939

Praise and honors, public and private, some more glorious than others, continued to be heaped on Mickey and Walt in the second half of the thirties. In January 1936, the Associated Press informed the world that "the red ribbon of the French Legion of Honor arrived today for Walt Disney, producer of 'Mickey Mouse.'" In a diary entry for December 20, 1937, cited by Esther Leslie in her book *Hollywood Flatlands*, the Nazi minister of propaganda, Joseph Goebbels, wrote: "I have given twelve Mickey-Mouse-movies as a present for the Führer at Christmas! He is pleased about it. He is absolutely happy about this treasure." And, as noted in *Art Digest*,* on consecutive days in June 1938, Disney received honorary degrees from Yale and Harvard. In New Haven, he was cited for having "brought forth a mouse" with which "he conquers the whole world."

Nearly half of all Mickey Mouse color cartoons ever made were released between 1936 and 1939. The best of the bunch may have been *Lonesome Ghosts* (1937), which provided the conceptual premise for the 1984 Columbia comedy *Ghostbusters*, with Bill Murray, Dan Aykroyd, and Harold Ramis in roles analogous to those originally played by Mickey, Donald, and Goofy. Among other gems in this period were *Brave Little Tailor* (1938), co-starring Minnie, and *The Pointer* (1939), with Pluto in the lead and Mickey in a supporting role. However, as production began on *Snow White and the Seven Dwarfs* in the mid '30s, journalistic and critical attention turned toward Walt's feature-length films. In the five or six years leading up to America's entry into World War II little serious notice was given in print to Mickey.

He was a source of interest in that period chiefly as a pop-culture phenomenon and emblem of Walt's endeavors and accomplishments as a whole. Hence, in a rather slapdash, error-filled tour d'horizon in 1936, entitled "'Mickey Mouse' is Eight Years Old," *Literary Digest* stressed the ongoing commercial appeal of the Mouse, with no mention of his current cartoon roles. By 1939, a professor of art history at Harvard, Robert D. Feild, had taken an academic interest in what the student newspaper, the *Harvard Crimson*, called "the merits of Mickey Mouse and associates." * Feild's research culminated in the first book-length study devoted to Disney (Macmillan, 1942), which, in fact, focused to a very limited extent on Mickey. It dwelt instead on the studio's feature-length animations and how they were made. Even so, as the *Crimson* related, Feild's work on Walt—his "Mickey Mouse scholarship," as it were—cost him his coveted Ivy League position.

Mickey's last great movie role was delivered to the public on November 13, 1940, when *Fantasia*, with its innovative stereophonic system, Fantasound, premiered at the same theater, since renamed, where *Steamboat Willie* had debuted in 1928. *Fantasia* was well received by almost all who saw it, including the *New York Times* film critic, Bosley Crowther, who declared:

> At the risk of being utterly obvious and just a bit stodgy, perhaps, let us begin by noting that motion picture history was made at the Broadway Theatre last night with the spectacular world premiere of Walt Disney's long-awaited "Fantasia." Let us agree, as did almost everyone present on the occasion, that the sly and whimsical papa of Mickey Mouse, Snow White, Pinocchio, and a host of other cartoon darlings has this time come forth with something which really dumps conventional formulas overboard and boldly reveals the scope of films for imaginative excursion. Let us temperately admit that "Fantasia" is simply terrific—as terrific as anything that has ever happened on a screen. And then let's get on from there.

Fantasia tended, however, to be scorned in highbrow circles. Typical of the naysayers was the architect-painter-author Christopher La Farge. Writing in *Theatre Arts* magazine, La Farge called *Fantasia* "another example of the failure of taste and of analyzed conception," although he admitted that the "abstractions of motion shown in the Frost Fairies, the Dancing Leaves, the Sorcerer's Apprentice are almost beyond cavil."

Mickey's appearance in *Fantasia* represented his swan song as an active Hollywood "leading man." While it was never the object of sustained contemporary critical analysis, the "Sorcerer's Apprentice" sequence was universally admired and Mickey quit the cinematic stage on a high note. As the *Time* art critic, Robert Hughes, later observed, with respect to one of the most memorable moments in *Fantasia*, when the Mouse mounted the podium to shake hands with the famed conductor of the Philadelphia Orchestra, Leopold Stokowski, "it was inevitably Mickey who made Stokowski more of a star by the handshake, not the other way round."

"Mickey Mouse" Is Eight Years Old: Disney's Squeaky Star Played to 468,000,000 in 1935

Literary Digest, October 3, 1936

Eight years ago this week, an unsuspecting audience sat in New York City's Colony Theater viewing a movie romance entitled "Lonesome," starring Barbara Kent and Glenn Tryon. As a filler, the management ran a short animated cartoon bearing the title "Steamboat Willie." It introduced a shrill, capering India ink character billed as *Mickey Mouse*. The audience expressed restrained approval, unaware that it was witnessing the beginning of a success story unparalleled in Hollywood history.

That date was September 28, 1928. This week, *Mickey Mouse* celebrates his eighth birthday, friskily aware that he played to 468,000,000 paid admissions last year, that the League of Nations has pinned a medal on his chest, that his ubiquitous likeness penetrates the great American home on cereal boxes, chinaware, toys, candy, jewelry, baby pants, belts and a thousand other items. Through it all, *Mickey Mouse* has kept his head, remained a fantastic, unpretentious, squeaking personality with a heart of gold. His creator, Walt Disney has seen to that.

Grown Up—At the mature age of eight, *Mickey Mouse* is not completely the child of whimsy he started out to be. Fantasy could not be laid on too thickly in early Disney scenarios; gag followed gag in whimsical procession. There's not so much of that to-day. *Mickey Mouse* has grown up as a character. For quite practical reasons, as will presently appear, *Mickey* abhors tobacco, uses no expletives, shuns liquor, comports himself with Algeresque probity. His smart-Alec tendencies are ruthlessly suppressed. He is never permitted to be cruel or arrogant. If

Mickey hurts the feelings of another character, he gets his come-up-pance at the end of the reel. A by-product of Disney's watchfulness is almost complete freedom from censorship troubles. (Exception: *Clarabelle Cow* wore a brassière in a milking scene, following protests by Ohio censors.)

Less well-known to the general public than his famous brain child, Walt Disney at thirty-five, is something of a Hollywood legend. Shy, slight, dark, Disney rarely attends movie parties and is not well known in the colony, tho his name is magic. He dresses informally but detests "artiness." Magazines which attempt to explain *Mickey Mouse's* phenomenal success in such abstractions as symbolism, rhythm, dynamics, fluidity of line, are barred from the Disney studio to protect his staff from introspection.

Garage Mice—Obsessed with the idea that animated cartoons could be made to pay, Walt Disney set up shop in Kansas City on his return from ambulance driving service in the World War. A local theater owner with a chain of three houses contracted for a series of cartoons, current events turned into animated form. Disney turned them out in an empty garage, alone with his drawing-board. But not quite alone. The barn-like structure was enlivened with the scamperings of mice. Friendly, inquisitive, companionable, they helped relieve the tedium of Disney's long hours. One gentlemanly frolicker, more daring than his fellows, became the artist's particular pal. With characteristic Disney whimsy, the rodent was dubbed *Mortimer Mouse*. Soon *Mortimer* was dropped for the more friendly *Mickey*. This early flair for alliteration endures to-day in "Silly Symphonies," *Donald Duck, Pluto the Pup, Clarabelle Cow.*

In 1923, Disney and his brother, Roy, $500 capital in their pockets, went to Hollywood. Soon Walt was producing "Oswald the Rabbit" for Universal. It was a success, but *Mickey Mouse* still frisked tantalizingly in the back of Disney's memory. In time, he produced two animated cartoons starring *Mickey*. Both flopped dismally. Exhibitors wouldn't touch them. For they were silent productions, and by 1928 sound had come to stay. Scrapping the two productions, Disney produced "Steamboat Willie," with sound effects. He himself was the squeaking voice of *Mickey Mouse*, as he is to-day. Other impersonators may be hired for various roles in Disney productions, but nobody can hire *Mickey Mouse's* voice away from him.

To-day, four hundred employees are required to turn out a *Mickey Mouse* and a "Silly Symphony" each month. Of these, some 300 are artists, thirty-five in the story department, most of the others musicians, sound crew or cameramen. The animated cartoon industry stubbornly resists mechanization. A short feature running six minutes on the screen is a composite of 10,000 drawings. The industry still cries for the genius who can provide a substitute for the draftsmen.

Demand for animaters so exceeds the supply that Disney sent representatives to interview 1,000 applicants in New York last March. With about 100 of these applicants, Disney founded a temporary school; twenty artists received diplomas in the form of a contract to work at the Walt Disney Hollywood studio.

Animaters are aristocrats of the profession; then come "in-betweener" men, inkers-in, opaquers. Cartoons are animated by photographing drawings, each succeeding sketch showing the characters' limbs in positions slightly further advanced. Sixteen drawings are needed to show *Mickey Mouse* taking a single step. The animater makes drawings 1, 8 and 15, showing *Mickey* at midpoint and extremes of motion. The in-between man fills in the supplementary drawings which smooth out the motion.

Original drawings, done in pencil on white paper, then go to the inking-in department. Here they are traced on transparent celluloid sheets, the backs filled in with opaque whites, blacks and grays to give substance to the line drawings. If it is to be a color production, tints are used instead of grays. Each drawing is carefully numbered and photographed in sequence.

"Cells," trade slang for the transparent sheets, are laid one on top of another over a background drawing. Half a dozen cells may be used in one scene, one showing *Mickey Mouse's* body, another his hands, legs, feet. Thus the limbs can be animated without repeating the body drawing each time.

Three Fingers—Master layout sheets insure uniformity in drawings, save time in figuring animations. If *Mickey Mouse* is called upon to clench his hand into a fist, the animater finds that bit of action already sketched on the layout sheets. Hundreds of repeated motifs are thus represented. Pluto the Pup, wrinkling his nose, worries the organ through four stages designated as the "sniff cycle." Close study of a *Mickey Mouse* film will reveal that he wears gloves with but three fingers and a thumb. The missing digit saves Disney several thousand dollars a year in artists' time.

Not all bits of animation can be thus standardized. When a fresh problem occurs, the animaters retire to a conference room, gravely dance together, shadow box, play the trombone, while artists soberly take note of their gyrations. Penguins may be brought in to capture their authentic waddle, a turtle imported to observe how it snaps.

Walt Disney does little of the actual drawing, but his influence is supreme in the story department. Three musicians sit in at story conferences known as "gag sessions." It is their duty to select sound effects which will synchronize with the action. If *Mickey Mouse* tap-dances, his toes must strike the floor in perfect rhythm. Musical beats are carefully plotted, calculated to fall within designated frames of the picture which animaters must rigidly respect in making their drawings. Sound tracks are recorded after the drawings have been filmed and dubbed in on the master negative.

Side-Lines Pay—Costly tho they are to produce, animated cartoons do not bring the big money returns chalked up by Hollywood's super-productions. But they have found in their back yards a private gold-mine all their own, toward which the biggest Hollywood studios cast a jealous eye. In Disney's case, this gold-mine functions under the name Kay Kamen, Ltd., and both organizations are unique in the history of corporate structures.

It all began casually enough a few months after *Mickey Mouse* made his début. A few manufacturers began writing in requesting permission to use *Mickey's* trade-marked countenance on dolls, toys, clothing. By 1933, Disney had licensed some fifteen manufacturers to use his character. In that year, he began distributing through United Artists.

Sensing golden opportunities, a shrewd merchandizing man was called in to take charge of Walt Disney Enterprises. He was Kay Kamen, who to-day, as head of Kay Kamen, Ltd., apportions *Mickey* licenses to a hundred manufacturers turning out a thousand different products. In four years, he has increased this phase of Disney's business 10,000 per cent, and it is no exaggeration to state that Walt Disney Enterprises has become the tail that wags the mouse.

Merchandise—In the dime stores you can purchase a piece of *Mickey Mouse* jewelry for ten cents, in an exclusive shop you can buy the same item, set in platinum, for $200. Between these price extremes, *Mickey Mouse* merchandise includes toy dishes, candy, moccasins, musical instruments, song sheets, chinaware, rubber boots, mirrors, play suits, tumblers, drawing sets, corn-poppers, radios, cookies, rubber stamps, lunch kits, blocks, greeting cards, a soap, electric trains, games, books, balloons, shirts, dresses, an endless array of other items. They are all listed in an elaborate catalog which Kay Kamen sends out to 25,000 purchasing agents for chain, department stores, small businesses.

In eight months, the Ingersoll Watch Company sold 1,000,000 *Mickey Mouse* watches at $2.95. This year, its fourth year with Kamen, it expects to dispose of 1,125,000 units. General Foods last year distributed 6,000,000 *Mickey Mouse* cereal bowls as box-top premiums. One of the shrewdest recent merchandising ideas was the use of *Mickey Mouse* cut-outs on Post Toastie boxes. Latest Kamen enterprises: purchase of *Mickey Mouse Magazine* from its founder, Hal Horne; closing of a contract with Libbey-Owens Glass Company for the distribution of *Mickey Mouse* tumblers by the millions.

World-Wide—Kay Kamen, Ltd., is a clearing-house for ideas. He has offices in Canada, Australia, London, Italy, Spain, Paris, Denmark, Portugal which license foreign rights to *Mickey Mouse*. A successful Australian merchandising idea immediately becomes available to American and European subscribers. Kamen maintains a staff of thirty-five in his Rockefeller Center office, including artists who design packages, advertising, promotional matter. Disney royalties are a trifle per unit, but turnover runs into several millions yearly.

Walt Disney himself has headquarters in Hollywood, keeps in close touch with the business. Roy handles executive details. Rivalry there is, both within and without the Disney organization. Within the last year, *Donald Duck*, a ferociously funny animated quackling in *Mickey Mouse* comedies, has emerged as a serious contender for *Mickey's* popularity crown. Disney, of course, by no means has the animated cartoon field to himself. Most formidable rival: Max Fleischer, who releases *Popeye the Sailor* and *Betty Boop* through Paramount.

New Project—Always a restless experimenter, Walt Disney's most ambitious project is now taking shape in his Hollywood studio. It is neither a *Mickey Mouse* nor a "Silly Symphony" release but full-length animated feature in colors designed for the carriage trade. Its working title is "Snow White and the Seven Dwarfs." It will flicker on no screen for two full years. Disney has allowed that period for completion of the necessary drawings!

L'Affaire Mickey Mouse

Herbert Russell

New York Times Magazine, December 26, 1937

Now that that unreconstructed international rebel, Mickey Mouse, has been thrown out of Yugoslavia for conspiring against the throne—he together with the newspaper correspondent who rashly reported the plot—the expulsions from foreign countries of this arch-enemy of nations have risen to two. Hitler once barred him from Germany because Mickey was accompanied by a brigade of animals wearing Uhlan helmets, which was a reflection on the honor of the German Army and too serious to be passed over. Of course, Mickey was eventually pardoned, because not even dictators are completely immune to his spell; Mussolini loves him.

The incident in Yugoslavia serves again to emphasize the international character of Mickey's activities, the boring within by means of which he is winning the populations of a good part of the world to his cause. He is apparently without principles and can be all things to all men. While Yugoslavia suspects him of communistic and revolutionary designs, the Soviet thinks he represents the meekness and mildness of the masses under capitalism, and has countered by creating a Russian Mickey, known as Yozh, or the Porcupine, an animal favorite of Russian children. But Yozh will probably turn out to be the old Mickey in disguise.

Mickey does not care what he does so long as he gains his ends—he is completely unscrupulous—and while his victims laugh he conspires. Or so one might think. Walt Disney, his father and Prime Minister, slyly deprecates the subtleties of Mickey's character. He says that all Mickey wants is laughter, that he has no ulterior thoughts, no philosophy of life, no hidden political, social or psychological motivations, none of the Eastern mysticism of which he is sometimes suspected, with reason, as will be seen. Those who read anything else into his life are all wrong, says Mr. Disney—but look at the record, as Al Smith used to remark.

In the first place there is no doubt that Mickey is an internationalist, and to be an internationalist these days is unorthodox to every one except Leon Trotsky. Mickey has been in thirty-eight countries in the world, and he is looking for the others. In all of these countries he has been popular and has captivated the masses; and that, to say the least, is suspicious. He promises them release for the time from worry and unhappiness, and speaks of a promised land where anything can, and does, happen.

That the great and near-great laugh at him merely proves his universality. He draws no distinctions of class, race, color or previous condition; he is kind even to jailbirds. President Roosevelt is his friend, and Queen Mother Mary sends for him regularly. He is the idol to savages, as Douglas Fairbanks found in Africa, and the Zulus refuse cakes of soap unless they bear his picture, just as natives used to refuse coins which did not have Queen Victoria's picture on them.

Reports from abroad continually show his increasing influence, an influence as mysterious as it is real. England, in self-defense is creating a rival to him. In France his black-shirted pictures are everywhere. The shortness of his trousers has caused him to be looked upon as almost a Sans Culotte, or revolutionary, and his creatures, similarly dressed, may be found serving as ushers in theatres. A traveler in the East found Mickey peeking from a store window in Manchuli, which is the transfer point from the Chinese Eastern Railway to the Transsiberian. His being there at that time, just before the outbreak in China, was looked upon as highly suspicious, although it could not be determined whether he was coming from or going to Moscow. And paradoxically, he is the most popular figure in Japan, next to the Emperor.

Every country Mickey visits calls him by some variant of his name—or pseudonym, for his real name is unknown; once it was said to be Hilarity Jones. Under that variant as a flag it is apparently his purpose to rally his followers. The complete record of his aliases has never been compiled, but the following list of countries and the names they give him will show his international character.

Germany . . . . Michael Maus
France . . . . Michel Souris
Japan . . . . Miki Kuchi
Spain . . . . Miguel Ratoncito
Italy . . . . Topolino
Greece . . . . Mikel Mus
Sweden . . . . Musse Pigg
Brazil . . . . Camondongo Mickey
Argentina . . . . El Raton Mickey
Central America. . . . . El Raton Miguelito

Mickey is not only appealing to the grown-up mob in the countries of the world; he has taken a leaf from the dictators and is organizing youth movements. These exist almost everywhere, from east to west, and from Singapore to Juneau, Alaska. Nearly every nationality is represented in the Singapore Mickey Mouse Club, but this cell of agitation has apparently not yet aroused the British Government to take action against it as protection for the Singapore naval base. Low, the British cartoonist, has pointed out that Mickey must appeal to the sophisticated before he can be completely successful. Mr. Low thinks Mickey lacks subtlety, and that his antics merely titillate the lower nervous system; but Low may have underestimated Mickey.

The Singapore club happens to be composed of adults, but it is one of the few exceptions. Most of the organizations take in only children, who carry a Mickey Mouse emblem and take a Mickey Mouse oath, which on its face is an innocuous pledge of goodwill and patriotism. But they have a Mickey song, and a grip, and a password. There are 1,500 of these clubs in the United States alone.

Whether Mickey is secretly building up cells in all these countries is not known, although the OGPU and the secret police of Germany might investigate. None of these nations so far has been able to agree upon an interpretation of either Mickey or his activities. They see in him merely a reflection of their own ideologies or those of their enemies, according to their national psychology. His apparent simplicity, the fact he is on the surface a gay creature who dashes madly into impossible situations, and escapes, giving the tail-waving, nose-thumbing Mickey salute—these things completely evade somber analysis.

There are continual attempts by the intelligentsia to interpret him, but he escapes them as easily as he avoided Mr. Low. Searching inquiry into Mickey has been made by a writer in The London Spectator, with the resulting judgment that he is an ebullient little rat, without an ounce of brains, half mug and half gallant, who by turns is meek and brave, and who represents the fantasy world in which adults, as well as children, may wander in a kind of Nirvana.

That there are no limits to his kingdom is also one of the allurements of Mickey which appeal to all the world. The air armadas of Europe, the plunging submarines, the skittering destroyers and dignified battleships cannot compete with the creatures which Mickey can call forth to battle if he chooses. He can scuttle a pirate with the aid of a sawfish and turn tortoises into tanks.

The capacity of such a Mouse for trouble is enormous, and those who pry into his motives cannot believe that he does everything for fun. He has appeared in international cartoons as a figure of importance. Newspapers in France and Italy and Russia speculate on his future and ineffectually try to link him with Br'er Rabbit and Krazy Kat as one who will have his day and be forgotten. But Mickey shrugs his shoulders and bides his time, while his comic strips are in twenty-seven languages, and he speaks fluently four languages to hundreds of millions of people.

Now for his Eastern mysticism. The simplicity of Mickey is denied by one simple fact which has been overlooked by all the sage commentators and interpreters. Mickey can and does appear in thirty-eight countries at once. He is the most omniscient mouse in the world. Whether he is an Eastern Yogi, or Mahatma, or a Lama from Tibet, in the abbreviated raiment of a mouse, some odd victim of transmigration, has never been revealed since he was discovered seven years ago. But his Eastern origin may be assumed from the fact that he has such an affinity for Asiatic peoples—the Chinese seem to recognize in him much of their own guileful humor. Perhaps only as a Mouse could he have won such world-wide fame, and if so, it rather confutes Mr. Low's theory of his lack of subtlety.

There is one other significant point to be made in any review of Mickey's international career. It is nothing that he is in Who's Who, the Encyclopaedia Britannica, and has been decorated many times. But it is something that he has found a niche among the world's great in Mme. Tussauds Wax Works in London. Somebody has recognized him for what he is; somebody knows his future.

Can it be possible that Mickey is waiting patiently for the collapse of civilization, waiting until the nations shall have pulled down their house of cards and destroyed all their own pretentions? Does he believe that the broken and oppressed people, wallowing in despond, will then turn to the one person whom they can depend upon for happiness, and demand that Mickey shall become Emperor of the World? Perhaps Mickey isn't as dumb as he looks. Maybe that is why he is winning the ordinary folk and the great, building his youth movement through clubs, boring from within in Europe, Asia, Africa, India, and the Americas.

And what a Cabinet he would have! Prime Minister, Walt Disney; Empress and Minister of Education, the ubiquitous Minnie; Minister of International Police, Pluto the Pup; Minister of Propaganda and Enlightenment, that notoriously bad egg, Donald Duck; and last, but not least, Minister of Nutrition, Clarabelle Cow.

The only trouble with the idea of this world conspiracy of Mickey's is that its headquarters are in Hollywood.

• The "searching inquiry" in the *Spectator* referenced here was E. M. Forster's essay "Mickey and Minnie."* Russell's statement that in the opinion of the Soviet leadership Mickey Mouse "represents the meekness and mildness of the masses under capitalism," reflects a report in the *Times* ("Mickey Mouse Portrays Capitalist, Reds Assert") affirming that Mickey "is a capitalist in disguise and all his antics are social satire, according to Soviet critics." The source of Russell's comment that David Low felt that "Mickey must appeal to the sophisticated before he can be completely successful" is not known. Low later published an oft-cited piece in the *New Republic* (1942) entitled "Leonardo da Disney," and since 1930 had used Mickey as an occasional motif in his editorial cartoons in the *London Evening Standard*. In the summer of 1935, Walt and Low met in London at a lunch hosted by H. G. Wells.

Walt Disney, M.S., M.A.

Art Digest, July 1, 1938

In almost a bandwagon rush great American universities are hastening to confer academic degrees upon Walter Elias Disney, pictorial historian to Snow White and father of Mickey and Minnie Mouse. Yale has just honored him with the degree of master of arts, two weeks after he was made a master of science by the University of California. To quote Prof. William Lyon Phelps of Yale, Disney was honored "for his feat of laboring like a mountain and bringing forth a mouse. With this mouse he conquered the world."

The citation said in part: "He has the originality characteristic of genius, creating the demand as well as the supply . . . No other artist in history has ever drawn so many spectators at any one time. He has accomplished something that has defied all the efforts and experiments of the laboratories in zoology and biology; he has given impressive significance to the word anima in animated; he has given animals souls. His work has the elements of great romantic art; the beautiful, the fantastic, the grotesque all combining in irresistible and ineffable charm . . ."

• Phelps actually said, "With this mouse he conquers the world." Among other honorees at the ceremony, on June 22nd, were the German novelist Thomas Mann, and Lord Tweedsmuir, Governor General of Canada, better known as John Buchan, author of *The Thirty-Nine Steps*, the spy thriller turned into a film by Alfred Hitchcock in 1935. On June 4, 1938, Disney received an honorary M.S. degree from the University of Southern California (USC), not the "University of California." Harvard gave Disney an honorary M.A. on June 23, 1938, one day after Yale honored him.

Mickey Mouse Celebrates His Tenth Birthday . . . By Capturing a Giant

Look, September 27, 1938

Mickey Mouse is back, with a feather in his hat. For months, Mickey has been taking it rather easy, not loafing, but chivalrously staying out of the spotlight as much as possible while the world was applauding his good friend, Snow White.

Now, in return, for Mickey's co-operation, his boss, Walt Disney, is giving him a giant to kill for a birthday celebration (above and next page). It's Mickey's tenth anniversary—in fact, it's a double anniversary, since Mickey was born and became a movie star at the same time.

Mickey's first roles, back in 1928, were in "Plane Crazy"—inspired by Lindbergh's great flight the year before—and "Steamboat Willie," the first animated sound cartoon.

Disney, who first went to Hollywood in 1923, created Mickey as a successor to Oswald the Rabbit. Disney first called him Mortimer, but Mrs. Disney suggested Mickey.

One reason Mickey gets his chance to kill a giant is that Disney likes, and always has liked fairy tales. ("Brave Little Tailor," the title of this picture, is one of Grimms' fairy stories.) Disney takes only the incidents he remembers from such stories and builds his pictures from those incidents.

In the old days, Disney himself used to do much of the drawing, but now he draws just enough to keep in practice while 75 animators put Mickey and Mickey's friends through their paces. The studio employs 650 persons, soon to be housed in a new million-dollar building just outside Hollywood, thanks to Mickey and Snow White.

For a short cartoon such as "Brave Little Tailor," Disney's artists

147

draw, color and photograph 15,000 sketches. Disney, himself, is always Mickey's voice (he's just 26 years older than Mickey), but he doesn't like real mice—he jumps out of their way.

• The "rough sketch" that accompanied this brief article (see below) is from a set of layout drawings by Ub Iwerks (not Disney, as stated in the caption) for *Plane Crazy*, the only film in which Mickey Mouse appeared barefoot. This image and a much larger one of Mickey wagging his shears at the giant in *The Brave Little Tailor* were used to illustrate the article. On the page facing the text were twelve screen shots summarizing the action in the cartoon, which *Look* called "Disney's First Fairy Tale Since Snow White." Like *Cinderella* (from 1950), *Snow White* and *The Brave Little Tailor* were based on the folk tales of the brothers Grimm, which the poet W. H. Auden, in a *New York Times* book review (1944), said "rank next to the Bible in importance." Auden then added: "A comparison of 'Grimm's Fairy Tales' with our movies, radio serials, comic strips and slick magazines reveals that what today passes for popular art is not the creation of simple 'lowbrow' men and women," but a "degenerate 'middlebrow' horror, mass-produced for profit by fully conscious, well-educated young men who read the classics in their spare time." One can only wonder how Walt might have reacted to that implicit critique of much of his life's work.

Ten Years Ago, in 1928, Mickey Mouse made his movie debut as a student pilot in a film called "Plane Crazy." Above is a rough sketch Disney made for that film

Illustration for "Mickey Mouse Celebrates His Tenth Birthday . . . By Capturing a Giant." © The Walt Disney Company.

A Tale of Six

Harvard Crimson, February 17, 1939 (editorial)

Five hundred disappointed lecture-goers were turned away yesterday afternoon from a Fogg lecture room in which Professor Robin Feild was extolling the merits of Mickey Mouse and associates. Each of the five hundred bore witness to the wide interest which has been evoked by the summary dismissal of the department of Fine Arts' most popular professor. The spontaneous outburst of student indignation and the formation of a Fine Arts Concentrators' committee to make formal protests are other danger signals indicating that the Feild Case is by no means closed. Much as it would like to, the department will find it difficult if not impossible to end the affair on the present note of "regrettable but necessary."

Aside from the clash of personalities inevitably involved in a case of this sort, Professor Feild's concluding appointment is the result of a fundamental difference of opinion within the department. At present, overwhelming stress is laid on the historical and factual approach to the Fine Arts. Students are filled with names and dates, are taught to recognize famous pictures, to distinguish the works of one master from those of another. While there is a branch of the department devoted to design and actual drawing, it is isolated and disconnected from everything else, and no one seemingly knows why it exists or where it fits in with the rest.

The Fine Arts department thus fails to accomplish what should be its highest goal to teach a student the method by which he can judge art for himself, to show him the universal essentials which lie behind all art. The attainment of such a goal entails far less emphasis on facts and chronology—these become a means to an end rather than an end in themselves. It means greater stress on practical art and design; and more than this, a close integration of practical work and history. It means the coordination of art with other branches of knowledge. It means finally the demonstration of the connection between the Fine Arts and the present-day world. The arts would consequently cease to be beautiful expressions from a past period of history, and would become something of living significance.

The introduction of such ideas would involve revolution in the Fine Arts department. It is this revolution of which Professor Feild is the tribune. But the revolution cannot come, and Feild must go because of Harvard's teacher-tenure and departmental-autonomy systems. By these, the committee of six permanent fine arts professors are entrusted with the final decision as to who shall teach under them. Thus they are able to choose their own successors, perpetuate their own ideas, prevent any change, and eliminate unwanted personalities. So long as they remain in control, the department will be static—as it was at its founding.

For the present, it is not necessary to revamp the whole system of appointments and tenure. It is only necessary for President Conant to act over the heads of the Fine Arts Six and reinstate Professor Feild. Although departmental autonomy may be desirable as a general rule, the president in exceptional circumstances is fully justified in exercising his prerogative of superior authority. Beyond this, it would be well for the Faculty Committee of Nine to undertake an investigation of the complete fine arts set-up, with a view toward evaluating the methods now used and those which might be introduced.

These steps: would prevent the commission of a grave injustice. They would forestall the loss of the most popular and successful teacher in Fine Arts. But beyond this, they would possibly lead to fundamental changes in the department which, in view of its unparalleled resources, would make Harvard one of the world's leading centers of art culture.

• This piece may have been written by Harry S. Hammond, Jr., Harvard class of 1941, identified on the *Crimson* masthead as "Editor for this issue." Starting in 1955, and for several decades thereafter, Hammond was the owner of the Channel Bookshop in New Haven, Connecticut.

5. World War II into the Seventies

1941–1977

During World War II, Mickey's name and image—like scores of other Disney cartoon characters—supplied wry comfort to American and Allied servicemen: as insignia for military units, nicknames and emblems for ships, planes, sundry gear and devices (gas masks, bomb-release mechanisms on aircraft, etc.), and as the password for a major pre-D-Day invasion briefing on the south coast of England.*

After the war, however, barely a decade after his triumphal turn in *Fantasia*, Mickey's on-screen career came to a halt. The last Mouse animated short to be made for thirty years, *The Simple Things*, was released in 1953. Shedding his trademark red shorts and yellow dinner-roll shoes, Mickey soon shifted gears and assumed his now familiar, fully-clothed duties as a greeter at Disneyland and cartoon emcee of the *Mickey Mouse Club* TV show.

It was in the mid '50s, as well, that two new, essentially eyewitness accounts emerged describing how Walt's greatest star was born. In a *McCall's* magazine piece, "I Live with a Genius" (Feb. 1953),* Lillian Disney said that when her husband created Mickey "there was no symbolism or background for the idea. He simply thought the mouse would make a cute character to animate." In November 1956, the *Saturday Evening Post* began an eight-part series, "My Dad, Walt Disney," published one year later in book form as *The Story of Walt Disney* (Henry Holt). The book, like the serialized version, was credited to Walt and Lilly's daughter, Diane Disney Miller, "as told to Pete Martin." Both texts relied primarily on interviews with Walt by Martin, a veteran *Saturday Evening Post* journalist and editor, but in reality it was Martin who authored the entire book himself.

Here, from *The Story of Walt Disney*, are the details of Mickey's conception—starting with Disney's fateful showdown in New York over Oswald with

Charles Mintz—as recalled by Walt and written up in crisp, plain-spoken prose by Martin:

"Either you come with me at my price, the Eastern distributor [Powers] told Father, "or I'll take your organization away from you. I have your key men all signed."

"Go ahead," Father told him. "I'll build a new organization."

He sounded a lot braver than he felt. When he got back to his hotel he told Mother that the bottom had fallen out of the Disney studio, but he didn't let Uncle Roy know that their enterprise had been sabotaged. He was worried sick himself but he didn't want Uncle Roy to have to worry during the days and nights that would intervene until he could get home and tell him all about it in person. He sent Uncle Roy a telegram: EVERYTHING O.K. COMING HOME.

Then he said to Mother, "Let's get the first train out of here. I can't do any good in New York. I have to hire new artists and get a new series going. I can't sell a new series with talk. I've got to have it on film.

So they boarded a westbound train, and all the way across the continent father tried to think up a cartoon built around a new character. Somewhere west of the Mississippi he decided upon a mouse.

Several stories have been told about Father's having had a mouse who lived in his desk during his Newman Laugh-O-Gram days in Kansas City. The thought back of this tale is that the mouse had given Father a special fondness for mice. "Unlike most of the stories that have been printed," Father told me, "that one is true. I do have a special feeling for mice. Mice gathered in my wastebasket when I worked late at night. I lifted them out and kept them in little cages on my desk. One of them was a particular friend. Then before I left Kansas City I carefully carried him out into a field and let him go."

Mice had been used in cartoons before, but until then they'd never been featured. "I think I've got something," Father told Mother. "It's a mouse. I'll call him Mortimer. Mortimer Mouse. I like that, don't you?"

Mother thought it over and shook her head. "I like the mouse idea," she said, "but Mortimer sounds wrong. Too sissy."

"What's wrong with it?" Father asked. "Mortimer Mouse. Mortimer Mouse. It swings, Lilly."

But Mother didn't buy it. She couldn't explain why "Mortimer" grated on her. It just did.

"All right," Father said. "How about Mickey? Mickey Mouse?"

The Story of Walt Disney contains the last and most satisfying iteration, published during Walt's lifetime, of what may be termed the "legend" of the making of Mickey. The only critical element still missing was Ub Iwerks's part in the process. Because of his bitter break with Walt in 1930 (and for PR and proprietary reasons too, no doubt), Ub's name had long been scrubbed from the studio record. It simply was not yet possible to give Walt's old friend and former partner his due. Nevertheless, compared to earlier narratives, by Harry Carr,* for instance, and in the *Windsor* articles published under Walt's name,* the story of how Mickey came to be was by 1956–1957 relatively complete.

Meanwhile, thanks to his cuddly, costumed presence at the Magic Kingdom and cheery role as host of the *Mickey Mouse Club*, Mickey was now assuming a softer, more mellow persona—in contrast with the antic character of his former pre-color days—thereby fueling the rise of "Mickey Mouse" as a put-down in common, everyday speech.

By the 1960s, the comradely relationship Mickey once enjoyed with our men in uniform also had changed. At the height of the Vietnam War, Admiral Elmo Zumwalt, Chief of Naval Operations, felt compelled, as he explained in an op-ed piece in the *New York Times* in 1977,* to confront petty "Mickey Mouse" regulations in order to raise morale in the fleet. This pejorative or mocking usage of the words "Mickey Mouse," as Maurice Crane noted ("Vox Bop," Oct. 1958),* had "been around almost as long as Mickey Mouse himself," with roots in jazz circles dating back to the 1930s. But by the 1960s, the expression was employed by hipsters and the unhip alike to trash anything, from college courses to institutions and activities—social, corporate, civilian, and military—judged to be preposterous, trivial, or patently dumb.

In *Playboy* in 1973, in an article titled "A Real Mickey Mouse Operation," D. Keith Mano even served up a peevish assessment of post-Walt values at the Disney Company itself. Richard Schickel, film critic for *Time* and *Life* magazines, in a letter to the editor of *Playboy*, saluted Mano's critique, adding: "If fascism ever comes to America, it will probably be wearing mouse ears."

As over-the-top as that line is, perhaps the most extreme verbal assault on Mickey in this period came from the novelist James Michener in an essay in the *New York Times Magazine*, in August 1968, titled "The Revolution in Middle-Class Values." In this fervent, often bitter (though not entirely flawed) screed, blasting bourgeois culture in the United States in general, and U.S. involvement in Vietnam specifically, Michener denounced Mickey as one "of the most disastrous cultural influences ever to hit America."

Nineteen sixty-eight was a big year for the naysayers. That spring, Schickel published his own biography of Walt, *The Disney Version: The Life, Times, Art and Commerce of Walt Disney* (Simon & Schuster), a tome that William Paul, in the *Village Voice* in 1973, characterized as "ungenerous" and Leonard Maltin, in 1968, called "evil" and "a cruel book which is a study in propaganda." Ironically, concurrent with the appearance of *The Disney Version*, in a remarkably friendly piece in *American Heritage* ("Bringing Forth the Mouse," April 1968), Schickel expanded upon the core facts laid out in "I Live with a Genius" and *The Story of Walt Disney* to produce the most extensive summation till then of Mickey's creation.

This fifth stage in Mickey's ascent to the status of global icon, extending from the Age of Franklin D. Roosevelt to the post-Watergate presidency of Jimmy Carter, was closed out—in terms of Disney studies—by a third biography, *Walt Disney: An American Original* (Simon & Schuster, 1976), by the late Bob Thomas. Thomas was another veteran reporter and author, whose book, like Pete Martin's, was based in part on interviews with Walt from as far back as 1946, and privileged access to the Walt Disney Archives. It remains, some thirty-five years later, the most readable and, in some ways, informed chronicle of Walt's life and career.

In his biography of Walt, Thomas allotted a full eleven pages to "the birth of Mickey Mouse," and for the first time in a Disney-sanctioned article or book mentioned Patrick A. Powers by name and brought Ub Iwerks into the picture as well. Alas, having passed away five years earlier, Ub could not enjoy this belated recognition. In his obituary in the *New York Times*, he was called "the man who helped create Mickey Mouse." Bob Thomas, rather more generously, declared: "The real genesis of Mickey Mouse appears to have been an inspired collaboration between Walt Disney, who supplied the zestful personality and voice for Mickey, and Ub Iwerks, who gave Mickey form and movement."

New British Army Slang Less Colorful Than Old

North American Newspaper Alliance

New York Times, April 6, 1941

LONDON, April 5-This war is producing a new batch of army slang, though so far it is neither so picturesque nor so extensive as it was in 1914–1918. Many of the words are peculiar to certain units, and very few are yet in general use.

The most universal expression—equivalent to the now obsolete "fed up," is "browned off." One stage further than "browned off" is "well baked." "Rompers" is the army word for battle-dress; a truck, car or lorry is a "bug." "On the peg" means being under charge for misdemeanor; a "regatta" is the cleaning and scrubbing of barrack rooms.

A "winkle-bag" is a cigarette. "Going on the stunt" is going on manoeuvres. "F. A. Q." means "I am going now"—from the command "file away quietly." An "old bull" is bluff to conceal ignorance, and a "gin palace" is a big wireless truck.

An R. A. F. pilot calls his cockpit the "pulpit" or the "office." "Driving the train" is leading two squadrons into battle. The instrument releasing the bombs, an electrical distributor, is called a "Mickey Mouse."

• During the war Royal Navy Minesweepers also were known as "Mickey Mouses," "Mickey Mice," "Mickeys," or "MMs." In the Royal Air Force, a Lancaster Mk III bomber was christened "Mickey the Moocher," and its nose adorned with a crudely drawn sketch of a pot-bellied Mickey pulling a bomb on a trolley.

"Mickey Mouse"
Was Invasion Password

Johannesburg Sunday Times, South Africa, June 11, 1944.
Courtesy *Sunday Times* (South Africa).

EISENHOWER DIRECTS WAR FROM MOTOR CARAVAN

LONDON, Saturday. — General Eisenhower has directed the first 100 hours of the Second Front from a motor caravan bare of maps and documents, says Stanley Burch, Reuter's special correspondent, in a dispatch to-day from an Advanced Command post.

His simple personal home in a secluded British woodland is the focal point of a command post so compact and mobile that it can at any moment move over to the Continent within a few hours.

The Supreme Commander will take his personal camp across the Channel when the time comes. He does not want to add fresh responsibility or inconvenience to his field commanders by living in their bivouacs.

His conferences are held in the war room—a big tent where all battle secrets are mapped on

"MICKEY MOUSE" WAS INVASION PASSWORD

LONDON, Saturday.—Senior naval officers passing into a naval cinema at a southern port a few days before the invasion had to whisper furtively into the ear of the sentry the magic words "Mickey Mouse," writes the "Sunday Times" correspondent.

This was the password selected during the briefing of nearly 200 naval officers, most of whom are commanding ships and craft in the invasion.

It was at this briefing that they learnt for the first time where the landings were to take place, and there was a buzz of surprise as an enormous map was unrolled at the back of the stage showing the north coast of France.

The atmosphere is friendly and informal

a quilt for the bed. A single dun-coloured leather armchair stands on a brown rug. Visitors squat on the bed. There are no maps, charts or photographs. Behind a screen is a shower and wash-basin, which provides hot water.

There are two telephones on a desk and a pile of "Westerns" with which the General reads himself to sleep.

Normally he is in bed by midnight and five or six hours sleep are enough for him.

In the morning General Eisenhower is brought coffee and fruit-juice, reads the London newspapers and the American army paper "Stars and Stripes," and by 7.30 a.m. he is ready for a substantial breakfast in a mess tent which he shares with his aides.

U.S. CHIEFS OF STAFF
LONDON, Saturday — It was

Courtesy the *Times* (South Africa).

LONDON, Saturday.—Senior naval officers passing into a naval cinema at a southern port a few days before the invasion had to whisper furtively into the ear of the sentry the magic words "Mickey Mouse," writes the "Sunday Times" correspondent.

This was the password selected during the briefing of nearly 200 naval officers, most of whom are commanding ships and craft in the invasion.

It was at this briefing that they learnt for the first time where the landings were to take place, and there was a buzz of surprise as an enormous map was unrolled at the back of the stage showing the north coast of France.

• This briefing probably took place in late May—presumably, by June 4th at the latest—and most likely at Portsmouth, Plymouth, or Southampton, on the English Channel. The hour-by-hour printed charts used by ships for crossing the Channel during the invasion, incidentally, were formally designated "Mickey Mouse Diagrams," in part perhaps because of the circular figures on them indicating holding patterns.

That Million-Dollar Mouse

Frank S. Nugent

New York Times Magazine, September 21, 1947

LOS ANGELES. Twenty years ago a man labored and brought forth a mouse and the civilized world still hasn't stopped applauding the miracle. Mickey Mouse is the goshdarndest single act of creation in the history of our civilization. He probably is more widely known than any President, King, artist, actor, poet, composer or tycoon who ever lived. The worlds that Alexander the Great conquered and Julius Caesar ruled were nutshell microcosms compared with that over which Mickey holds sway. His sovereignty is all but universal, yet he is as American as Kansas City; he was born on a westbound Pullman and his harried parent, Walt Disney, can't for the life of him remember exactly when or where. It was "somewhere out of Chicago," and there wasn't a midwife on the train.

It was to the Disney studio in Burbank—the $2,000,000 plant which Mickey built—that I went last week for a first-hand account of the creation and development of Walt's colossal mouse.

Most Hollywood studios look like storage warehouses: Disney's mulberry-and-green layout is more of a cross between a country club and a sanitarium. It has a baseball diamond, a battery of pingpong tables, a couple of horseshoe-pitching lanes and a penthouse sun-deck where the male employees acquire an all-over tan. The workaday buildings are air-conditioned and reasonably dustproof. Walt's office suite has a stainless steel kitchen, a dressing room and shower, a piano, radio-phonograph, couches, coffee tables and a desk which has acquired an inferiority complex through his consistent disuse of it.

"I want to interview Mickey," I said, taking the mouse by the horns.

Walt looked down his nose at me.

"I dunno," he said. "It's a little irregular. We've kinda frowned on direct interviews. The Mouse's private life isn't especially colorful. He's never been the type that would go in for swimming pools and night clubs; more the simple country boy at heart. Lives on a quiet residential street, has occasional dates with his girl friend, Minnie, doesn't drink or smoke, likes the movies and band concerts, things like that."

"I'd still like to ask him some questions," I said firmly.

Walt's fingers drubbed the desk. His employees recognize it as a danger signal, once removed from his rubbing the side of his nose with a straight Index finger. But I wasn't on the payroll so I just waited.

"I've always done The Mouse's talking," Walt said. [He never calls Mickey by his first name; he's always The Mouse just as Donald is always The Duck]. "He's a shy little feller, so I've provided the voice. I use a falsetto, like this. [And he demonstrated.] His voice changed after I had my tonsils out. It became a little deeper. But no one noticed it. I kind of like it better. Sometimes I'm sorry I started the voice. It takes a lot of time and I feel silly doing The Mouse in front of the sound crew.

"But I'm sentimental about him, I guess, and it wouldn't be the same if anyone else did the speaking. We've had several girls for Minnie. The original got married and had a couple of kids and that was that. What sort of questions?"

Was Mickey born in an upper berth or a lower? Did he spring full-grown onto a drawing pad, and how about his family background? How tall is he, what's his attitude toward Donald Duck, how much does he make a year, any chance of his retirement, how does he stand politically?"

"One at a time," said Walt. "He was born in a section. Things weren't that tough. But it wasn't a good train. I remember there was no diner and we stopped for meals. I was going to call him Mortimer Mouse, but my wife suggested 'Mickey' and that sounded better.

"Now he's Mikki Maus In Russia, Miki Kuchi in Japan, Miguel Ratoncito in Spanish-speaking countries, Michel Souris in France and Topolino in Italy.

"Sure he was born full-grown, but he wasn't fully developed. That took a lot of time—twenty years so far. He'll probably keep on developing. Why don't you look at some of his early pictures and talk to the boys? Then you'll see how he's changed through the years."

The Disney family album is a film storage vault. In it are the 118 shorts

Mickey has appeared in since "Steamboat Willie" opened at the Colony Theatre exactly nineteen years ago today. In it, also, are Mickey's two features, "Fantasia" and the current "Fun and Fancy Free." Technically, "Steamboat Willie" was the first Mickey Mouse cartoon; actually two others, "Plane Crazy" and "Galloping Gaucho," had been made before it, but sound had come in meanwhile and the two silent shorts were held back while "Willie" got the benefit of synchronization—though by today's perfectionist standards, it wasn't much of a benefit. The sound seems to come from some place ten years behind the screen. Still Mickey makes you forget that. Even then he had personality.

But he wasn't the Mickey we know now. His legs were pipestems and he had only black dots for eyes. His muzzle and nose were longer and so was his tail. He was thinner and more angular then and his movements were on the jerky side. His acting was influenced by the Keystone Comedy school; he would jump in the air before starting to run and when an idea dawned you could see it climbing the horizon. He indulged in some cruelties and crudities that would shock his fans today—like pulling a cat's tail and using a goose as a bagpipe while playing a one-man band.

The projectionist turned the pages of the family album rapidly. There was Mickey as a convict in "Chain Gang" in 1930; among the prisoners were two hounds—one of them later became Pluto. Mickey shared the stage and spotlight with an irascible duck in "The Orphan's Benefit" in 1934; Donald had made his bow as a heavy in a Silly Symphony called "The Wise Little Hen" a few months before, but it was as the frustrated reciter of "Little Boy Blue" that he really wowed 'em.

Somewhere in the late thirties Mickey lost his tail; a canny production man had figured that thousands of dollars would be saved by not having to animate that eloquent little appendage. But Mickey didn't seem the same without it and the tail was restored.

Mickey acquired color in "The Band Concert" in 1935 and never has reverted to black and white. As the mouse grew older his black-dot eyes were replaced with expressive, rollable eyeballs. He began wearing "longies" to hide the pipestem legs and the stems themselves thickened. He gained a little weight and acquired a flexible body. His knees and elbows lost their angularity.

But the most important development was in his acting ability. He learned to emote without calisthenics and, with that advance, the basic character of the Mickey Mouse comedies underwent a radical change. Instead of the slapdash chases and slapstick climaxes of "The Fire Chief" and "Building a Building," Mickey began giving us the gentler comedy, tinged with pathos, of "Brave Little Tailor." He became a situation comedian, not just a funny man—or mouse; a Harold Lloyd, say, rather than a Chaplin—or a Donald Duck.

No one can tell at Disney's—Walt least of all—just to what extent Mickey is a self-made mouse. Artists like Fred Moore, Marvin Woodward, Les Clark and Kenny Muse have helped him to express himself. They taught him a lot of tricks—how to let his shoulders droop and his feet drag when he is despondent, how to strut on his way to a date with Minnie, how to convey by an eye-brow's lift an emotion that he used to project by leaping a yard in the air. But not even Disney can explain why he sometimes sits with his story men and solemnly asks: "But would The Mouse do a thing like that?" And if the conclave decides that he wouldn't, then out it goes—no matter how funny the gag.

The modern Mickey—they now know—wouldn't pull a cat's tail to make music and couldn't be found on a chain gang without there being some innocent explanation of it. Mickey is ringed about with musts and must-nots. In addition to not smoking and not drinking, he doesn't use any language stronger than a "shucks."

Donald has no such limitations; he can be diabolic even to the point of looting his nephews' piggy bank. Some of the heretics at Disney's will confide that they have more fun working with The Duck than with The Mouse for just this reason and hint that the public's current preference for Donald over Mickey (the Gallup Audience Research Institute puts Donald first, Bugs Bunny second and Mickey third) is a vote for human fallibility.

Walt only smiled wisely when I brought this treasonable report to his office. "Sure," he admitted. "After 120 pictures, it's only natural for them to get a little tired of The Mouse. It's tough to come up with new ideas, to keep him fresh and at the same time in character. The Duck's a lot easier. You can do anything with him. But what they forget is that The Mouse hasn't made a picture since the war. He was in one short released in '42. Five years off the screen and he still rates third! Is there any star in Hollywood with a public that loyal?"

Then it was safe to state—I ventured—that Mickey is not jealous of the upstart duck?

"His attitude," replied Walt pontifically, "is that of the older master who's glad to give the youngsters a hand. After all, this is a big place and there's room for everybody. The Mouse knows we have to keep bringing new people along, new faces. It makes his job that much easier. It was pretty tough when he was carrying the whole studio. But now he's got The Duck and Pluto and The Goof and our feature program. Quite an accomplishment for a mouse."

Walt wouldn't tell me about Mickey's politics, except to say that they do not resemble Chaplin's, and he was a bit vague when I tried to find out exactly how tall The Mouse was. The best I could get was that he's three quarters the size of The Goof, about a head taller than the Duck, and a third bigger than Pluto. He stands about even with the coloratura, Clara Cluck, and is exactly level with Minnie—which may be due to the fact that Minnie originally was Mickey with eyelashes, a skirt and feminine footgear; otherwise the drawing was identical.

"What's he make a year?" I asked.

"What year?" countered Walt, and stopped me cold.

"Well, what's he made in all, over the twenty years?" I asked finally.

"Me," Walt said and I had to let it go at that.

Kay Kamen was more specific. Mr. Kamen is the Kansas City advertising man who has been Disney's licensing agent since 1932. He is the middleman between Walt and the thousand-and-one manufacturers and advertisers who use the Disney characters on their products.

The Disney label, says Mr. Kamen, helps to sell about $100,000,000 worth of goods each year and Mickey is the best salesman of the lot. Books are the chief item, going at the rate of 10,000,000 a year and ranging in price from kindergarten primers at $1 a copy to a deluxe Deems Taylor edition of "Fantasia" at $3.75. A Walt Disney illustrated "Uncle Remus" ran through a first printing of 150,000 in practically no time and another is on the presses. The Walt Disney Comics, a monthly comic-strip magazine, sells to the merry tune of 30,000,000 a year and rates fourth on newsstand sales of all national magazines.

Mickey is a consistent salesman of cereals, soaps, dolls, toys, sweaters, sweatshirts, phonographs and records, radios, hot-water bottles, hairbrushes, caps, robes, slippers, footballs, baseballs, paint sets, porringers and, most notably, the Mickey Mouse watches—600,000 of them sold so far this year.

A Los Angeles ceramics plant stacks its kilns exclusively with Disney figurines; one of the nation's largest doll manufacturers gives Mickey top priority. A New York department store sold $10,000 worth of Disney-decorated sweaters in a day.

No small-time operator, Mickey has made tie-ups with Standard Oil, General Foods, Standard Brands, National Biscuit Company, du Pont and National Dairy Products. He has declined bids from liquor companies, cigarette manufacturers, makers of patent medicines.

The net income to Disney from all these sidelines has been, Mr. Kamen estimates, from $500,000 to $800,000 a year. "No doubt of it," says Mr. Kamen, "Mickey Mouse is the greatest thing in the history of merchandising."

What this means to The Mouse himself, how it affects his standard of living, whether he is any closer now to being able to support a wife called Minnie than he was twenty years ago, what kind of a car he drives, what he thinks of screen vs. stage and his opinion of the English tax on Hollywood films are, unfortunately, questions I have been unable to clear up satisfactorily.

I can only add that as I left Walt's office, I heard behind me the sounds of a drawer rattling in that unused desk and then a voice in a familiar falsetto. "It's the next birthday that worries me," it said. "Tell me, boss: When I'm 21 will I be a man, or a mouse?" I dashed back into the room. Walt looked up in surprise.

"I thought I heard something," I explained.

"Probably a mouse," he said, and went on working.

What Mickey Means to Me

Walt Disney

Who's Who in Hollywood, April–June 1948

Mickey Mouse to me is a symbol of independence. He was a means to an end. He popped out of my mind onto a drawing pad 20 years ago on a train ride from Manhattan to Hollywood at a time when the business fortunes of my brother, Roy, and myself were at lowest ebb.

Born of necessity, the little fellow literally freed us of immediate worry, provided the means for expanding our organization to its present dimensions and for extending the medium of cartoon animation toward new entertainment levels.

His first actual screen appearance was in 1928 at the old Colony Theater in New York in *Steamboat Willie,* with its sound effects and cautious "speech." Since then, he has appeared in more pictures than any flesh-and-blood star. He was the first cartoon character to stress personality and to be consistently kept in character.

I thought of him from the first as a distinct individual, not just a cartoon type or symbol going through comedy routines. I kept him away from stock symbols and situations. We exposed him to closeups. Instead of speeding the cartoons as was then the fashion, we were not afraid to slow down the tempo and let Mickey emote.

Mickey soon searched the stage where we had to be very careful about what we permitted him to do.

Mickey could never be a rat . . .

He had become a hero in the eyes of his audiences, especially the youngsters. Mickey could do no wrong. I could never attribute any meanness or callow traits to him. We kept him lovable although ludicrous in his blundering heroics. And that's the way he's remained, despite any outside influences.

Naturally, I am pleased with his continued popularity, here and abroad, with the esteem he has won as an entertainment name, among youngsters and grownups. With the honors he has brought our studio. With the high compliment bestowed when his name was the password for the invasion of France, and with his selection for insignia by scores of fighting units during the war years. These are tributes beyond all words of appreciation.

In his immediate and continuously successful appeal to all kinds of audiences, Mickey first subsidized our Silly Symphony series. From there he sustained other ventures, plugging along as our bread-and-butter hero. He was the studio prodigy and pet. And we treated him accordingly.

Mickey still speaks in my own falsetto-pitched voice, as he has from the first. In the early days I did the voice of most of the other characters, too. It wasn't financially feasible to hire people for such assignments. In *Steamboat Willie*, in addition to speaking for Mickey, I also supplied a few sound effects for Minnie, his girl friend, and for the parrot.

For Mickey's first picture, I planned to go all out on sound. And those plans came very near spelling a major disaster for us.

To launch our picture impressively, I had hired a full New York orchestra with a famous director to do the recording. The musicians were to cost $10 an hour. I thought 15 men would be enough. But the director insisted on having 30 pieces. Because I was awed by him, I was finally persuaded to take the 30. The upshot was that I had to borrow on my auto and Roy and I had to mortgage our homes as well, to cover the cost of that first synchronization for *Steamboat Willie*. And when it was finished, the thing wasn't in sync. We had to do it all over again!

What I wanted most of all, I didn't get: a bull-fiddle for the bass. The recording room was so small that the orchestra could hardly be jammed into it. The bull-fiddle blasted so loudly it ruined the other sound and kept blowing out the lamps.

A sad thing, I thought at the time, to launch our Mickey without benefit of a bull-fiddle in so precarious a world of new possibilities and increased competitions.

Million-dollar mouse . . .

But he survived and thrived and set the pace in his entertainment field. The cost of his vehicles increased from the bare $1,200 for *Steamboat Willie* to seven figures for *Fun and Fancy Free*.

I often find myself surprised at what has been said about our re-
doubtable little Mickey, who was never really a mouse not yet wholly a
man—although always recognizably human.

Psycho-analysts have probed him. Wise men have pondered him.
Columnists have kidded him. Admirers have saluted him. The League
of Nations gave him a special medal as a symbol of international good
will. Hitler was infuriated by him and thunderingly forbade his people
to wear the then popular Mickey Mouse lapel button in place of the
Swastika.

But all we ever intended for him was that he should make people
everywhere chuckle with him and at him.

And it is certainly gratifying that the public which first welcomed
him two decades ago, as well as their children, have not permitted us,
even if we had wished so to do, to change him in any manner or degree
other than a few minor revisions of his physical appearance.

In a sense, he was never young. In the same sense, he never grows
old in our eyes. All we can do is to give him things to overcome in his
own rather stubborn way in his cartoon universe.

There is much nostalgia for me in these reflections.

The life and ventures of Mickey Mouse have been closely bound up
with my own personal and professional life. It is understandable that I
should have sentimental attachment for the little personage who played
so big a part in the course of Disney Productions and who has been
so happily accepted as an amusing friend wherever films are shown
around the world.

• "Compiled by the editors of Modern Screen," Who's Who in Hollywood
was published in a format akin to that of a mass-market magazine. The
ninety-eight-page annual contained primarily "pictures and biographies of
some 1,000 of the screen's most familiar faces," including the character actor
Jane Darwell, who would play the Bird Woman in Mary Poppins. There were
just eight other articles in the book, one by Ronald Reagan, president of the
Screen Actors Guild, another by John Mills, who later co-starred in the Disney
film Swiss Family Robinson.

Unlike his Windsor articles, "What Mickey Means to Me" sounds very
much like Walt. That is because it is a version of an account in his own words,
"The Story of Mickey Mouse," recorded for broadcast in 1948 on the NBC ra-

dio show, *University of the Air*. As we've seen, Walt was mistaken in his recollection that Mickey's "name was the password for the invasion of France."
He repeated the story in 1953 to Ed Sullivan, host of the Sunday evening CBS
TV show *The Toast of the Town* (reported by Larry Wolters in the *Chicago
Tribune*). Barbara Berch Jamison further propagated this nascent urban legend
in her *New York Times Magazine* story, "Of Mouse and Man," * in which she
said that "Mickey Mouse" had been "the password for the troops landing on
the Normandy beaches on D-Day."

Mickey Mouse and How He Grew

Irving Wallace

Collier's, April 9, 1949

Not so many years ago there was a lady scribbler in Hollywood who made her living ghostwriting a monthly gossip column called Mickey Mouse's Diary. She pretended she was actually Mickey Mouse, relating day-to-day adventures, to the delight of all juveniles under sixty who read the popular comic book in which the column appeared. A condition of her job, however, was that she submit all copy, before it was published, to the Walt Disney publicity department for approval. In one of her monthly whimsies, the lady scribbler, playing Mickey Mouse, wrote:

"This afternoon, I went to a birthday party for Freddie Frog over at M-G-M—"

When the Disney censor-publicist read this line, he was horrified. With trembling hands, he grabbed for his phone, and called the lady scribe.

"You've got to kill that line!" he ordered. "Really, you know very well Mickey Mouse would *never* go to anything at M-G-M—and *you* know those people at M-G-M, they might expect a present!"

The lady scribbler insists she was not being kidded, that the veteran Disney publicist was dead serious, and that she was forced to expurgate immediately the offensive line of gossip.

All of which is by way of final answer to the inevitable question: Is Mickey a man or a mouse? Those who write about him, who write for him, ballyhoo him, dress him, think for him and live by him treat him as a full-fledged member in good standing of the run-down human race.

Though the men who make Mickey always refer to him as the Mouse, it is their policy never to treat him as one. To them he is a very real person. For years, Mickey Mouse pictures have been minus mousetraps, cheese gags or cat villains. Disney animators think he's a lot like Walt Disney. "The same soulful eyes," they say, "the same beaky face, the same trick of falling into pantomime when at a loss for words."

When he was only three years old, there were 1,000,000 youngsters in America who belonged to his fan clubs and believed in him as a person. He still receives a steady flow of mail he is expected to read and answer. He has appeared in Who's Who and the Encyclopaedia Britannica, won a special gold Oscar from the Academy of Motion Picture Arts and Sciences, received a medal from the late League of Nations, been reproduced in Madame Tussaud's Waxworks along with President Truman and Princess Elizabeth, been made an honorary citizen of France and, with his creator, Walt Disney, been made a member of the Artworker's Guild of London, a society to which George Bernard Shaw also belongs.

So far have his associates and his fans gone in pretending Mickey is a man, not a mouse, that they have burdened him with the most insidious and unhappy baggage of the human race—a birthday. They have celebrated his birthday annually, but this year the celebration is the biggest of them all—he is twenty-one years old.

There are dissenters, a few vocal human beings around who feel Mickey should not be messed up with man-made maturity. They feel that Mickey Mouse is not twenty-one at all, and never will be, but is instead a legend, a folklore, a part of the American scene that is ageless.

Mickey Mouse, either by name or by image, is better known in more places on this mud-ball earth than any human being in all history. In their day neither Caesar nor Napoleon were half so widely known. During the greatest wartime invasion in world history, the Allied landing in Europe on D-Day, one instantly recognizable name was picked as the password at SHAEF—Mickey Mouse. More, recently, the American Army asked a group of prominent Koreans to suggest what sign over the doors of its information center would immediately tell their countrymen it was American. After a brief consultation the Koreans' vote went 100 per cent for Mickey Mouse.

A Fantastic Record of Success

But whether the world is celebrating Mickey's coming of age as a man or a mouse or a legend, upon one fact all hands heartily agree. In his 21st year as a movie star, Mickey's record of success is the most fantastic in Hollywood history. During the first three years of his long career, among his most potent rivals were Emil Jannings, Bessie Love, Lon Chaney, George Arliss, Norma Talmadge, Colleen Moore and Nancy Carroll. Today of the five who've survived, not one is active, yet Mickey is more popular than ever.

In 21 years, Mickey has starred in 118 short comedies, and in two full-length features, Fantasia and the more recent Fun and Fancy Free. In the fall he will appear in a full-length feature called Adventures of Ichabod and Mr. Toad. He was off the screen for only one period. That was during war when Walt Disney converted 90 per cent of his mammoth plant into wartime production.

Today, by public demand, the Mouse is again fully active, ranking a step behind Donald Duck and Bugs Bunny in popularity among people under the age of thirty, and second to Donald Duck among persons over thirty.

In all other, and more profitable fields, he still maintains an overwhelming lead. His name and face, on 2,000 articles of merchandise, including bath towels, wrist watches, Belgian candy, fruit juices, British milk of magnesia and weather vanes, has saved two companies from bankruptcy, and helped gross upward of $100,000,000 a year for manufacturers using Disney labels.

He first appeared in newspaper comics in 1929, and today, two decades later, an estimated 30,000,000 readers follow his antics in 300 different outlets.

Now Mickey is being wooed by television.

Disney makes 18 shorts a year. Of these Mickey Mouse is allotted four, Donald Duck nine. This ratio is maintained not because the Duck has become more popular, but because the Duck is infinitely easier to put on the screen.

Recently, when letters flooded the Disney Studios demanding to know why more Mickey Mouse cartoons aren't made, Walt Disney tried to explain. "Mickey's decline was due to his heroic nature. He grew into such a legend that we couldn't gag around with him. He acquired as many taboos as a Western hero—no smoking, no drinking, no violence."

A salty Disney writer elaborated: "Mickey is limited today because public idealization has turned him into a Boy Scout. Every time we put him into a trick, a temper, a joke, thousands of people would belabor us with nasty letters. That's what made Donald Duck so easy. He was our outlet. We could use all the ideas for him we couldn't use on Mickey. Donald became our ham, a mean, irascible little buzzard. Everyone knew he was bad and didn't give a damn. So we can whip out three Donald Duck stories in the time it takes us to work out one for the Mouse."

It is as an actor that Mickey Mouse has most definitely shown the marks of time. While taking wild risks in those early films to save Minnie Mouse from villains like Pegleg Pete, Mickey committed all kinds of atrocities on good manners—pulling a cat's tail, being sentenced to a chain gang, using a goose for a bagpipe, committing every comedy cliché except catching a Keystone pie on his kisser. Through the years he mellowed, until today his taste and temper are strictly a cross between Emily Post and Frank Merriwell. No expletives, violence, practical jokes, double dealings, cruelty, nor arrogance may be found in his present-day make-up.

Physically, too, Mickey has changed with the years. In the beginning, he had black dots for eyes, a long nose and tail, pencil legs, a skinny stringbean body and a jerky walk. Today, Mickey has expressive white eyeballs in which realistic eyes roll, a slight nose bob, handsomely rounded legs encased usually in shorts or trousers.

Mickey, has had, and still has, certain physical deformities, mainly because these deformities save the Disney Studios considerable cash. An animator once discovered that a fortune could be saved on each movie simply by leaving off Mickey's tail. This omission cut down countless hours of sketching, copying, inking. In several, shorts, Mickey's tail was left off, but when the animator realized it reduced Mickey's expressiveness, like wiping a feature off his face, it was hastily restored.

Missing Fingers Aren't Noticed

Mickey is lacking a finger. From 1928 on, he has been drawn with three fingers and a thumb. "No one seemed to notice," says Disney. The experiment of the missing finger on each hand was so successful with Mickey, that all other Disney wild life was thereafter drawn with digits missing.

"Leaving the finger off was a great assist artistically and financially," insists Disney. "Artistically, five digits are too many for a mouse. His hand would look like a bunch of bananas. Financially, not having an extra finger in each of 45,000 drawings that make up a six and one-half minute short has saved the studio millions."

Around the Disney factory today, many of the old-timers still retain ancient portraits of the early, skinny Mickey Mouse. Even Walt Disney seems more devoted to the youthful Mickey than to the newer, stream-lined one. Either because of pure sentiment, or because he himself has not actually drawn the Mouse very much in the last twelve years, Disney is often placed in embarrassing predicaments.

On a recent trip to South America he was begged by the Latins time and again to sketch Mickey as a souvenir. When he complied, the only Mickey Mouse he could draw, or perhaps would draw, was the out-moded, string-bean Mickey of a decade or two ago.

There have been many stories of how Mickey Mouse was born. The actual true story is probably buried deep under a thousand mimeo-graphed publicity handouts, and too much has happened since for Walt Disney to remember the exact details. This much is known definitely: The brain child occurred on a westbound train between Chicago and Los Angeles, in 1927.

Walt Disney, who was to sire the Mouse, was the son of a contrac-tor. He was born in Chicago and raised in Kansas City along with three brothers and a sister. Besides a brief session studying cartooning nights at the Chicago Academy of Fine Arts, Disney never had a lesson in drawing in his life. After World War I he went into illustrating adver-tisements for farm magazines, working in Kansas City. The room in which he worked swarmed with mice. One particularly brave mouse, soon to become as immortal as Shelley's Skylark, used to prance across Disney's easel.

The Public Was Apathetic

Seeking to improve his position, Disney answered an ad placed by a commercial slide company and found himself sketching his first ani-mated cartoons. Later, going into business for himself, he tried a movie on Little Red Riding Hood, another, on Goldilocks, and finally one called Alice in Cartoonland in which a real live girl had adventures with animated make-believe figures. This stirred Kansas City not at all, and when his distributor went on the rocks and was unable to pay him, Disney decided to pull stakes and go West, young man.

He reached Hollywood and Vine with one suit, $40 inside it, and a print of his Alice in Cartoonland. His older brother Roy, already in Hollywood, had $250. An uncle had $500. A garage was rented, two girls hired to draw and ink in the figures, and Disney was in business. He made and sold 60 different episodes of Alice in Cartoonland and introduced a series called Oswald the Rabbit. Meantime, one of the two women on Disney's staff, Lillian Bounds, an Idaho girl in the big city, salary $15, seemed too attractive to confine to business. So Disney married her. Later, on a trip to New York, Disney had a falling out with the distributor of his Oswald the Rabbit films, which ended with the distributor holding the rabbit, and Disney holding the bag.

On the train home to Hollywood, Disney sat brooding, with his wife. He had $15,000, his own talent, a whole animation setup and nothing to animate. Trying to think of a new character, he examined the possibilities of a dog, a cat, a rabbit, and discarded them all because they were being done elsewhere. He remembered the animals he's seen on a farm, and in zoos. He remembered the days when he sketched ads for farm journals and—lo, he had it! The mouse! "Mortimer Mouse!" he cried.

"Mickey Mouse!" his wife corrected.

Unlike Byron, who woke up famous, Mickey Mouse fell on his face in his initial two jousts with fame. His first film, Plane Crazy, diverted few fans from John Gilbert. A second film, Gallopin' Gaucho, crawled out of theaters fast.

It was 1928, and Hollywood had found its voice. Disney had completed his third Mickey Mouse, an item called Steamboat Willie, and put his own voice in Mickey's mouth, making it register as a squeaking falsetto. Disney used his voice because he couldn't afford to hire one. (He remains Mickey's voice today, because the public might be too used to it to tolerate a change.) Besides adding voice to this early film, Disney attempted music and sound effects—Mickey playing a xylophone solo on a cow's teeth and giving a loud concert on dishpans. The audience loved it.

In quick succession, Mickey made a musical comedy, The Opry

House, a Western, The Cactus Kid, and appeared as Robinson Crusoe in The Castaway. The stampede was on. Through the terrible thirties, Mickey Mouse grew until his shadow fell across the globe. He did 12 to 15 pictures a year.

One year 468,000,000 paid admission. Eskimos in Alaska formed a Mickey Mouse fan igloo. Kaffirs, natives of South Africa, who once refused to take coins unless Queen Victoria's image was on them, refused to buy soap unless Mickey Mouse's image was on all brands. Argentina awarded Mickey a giant gourd, Australia sent live kangaroos, and the Nizam of Hyderabad, richest man in the world, selected Mickey as his favorite actor.

The sun never set on Mickey Mouse. In Japan he performed as Miki Kuchi, in France he was Michel Souris, in Spain he was Miguel Ratoncito, in Italy he was Topolino.

He even pierced the Iron Curtain, before Churchill coined the phrase. Appearing in The Band Concert, Peculiar Penguins and Three Little Pigs, he excited enthusiasm from Smolensk to Siberia, with one Soviet critic explaining to the masses, "Disney is really showing us the people of the capitalistic world under the masks of mice, pigs and penguins. A definite social satire."

Having become the darling of the proletariat, Mickey was then adopted by the carriage trade and the lorgnette set. The gentlemen of the Metropolitan Museum in New York called Mickey's creator "the greatest historical figure in the development of American art." David Low, the English cartoonist, added, "Disney is the most significant figure in graphic art since Leonardo da Vinci." In the Leicester Galleries, London, Mickey Mouse was stuck on a wall between a Picasso painting and an Epstein sculpture.

Symbolism in Disney's Art?

It was getting thoroughly out of hand. People were yammering about expressionism and the dynamics of art and the symbolism inherent in Mickey. Disney, while ranked among the world's top living artists working in a new form, is regarded as somewhat less than *avant-garde* by several of his ex-employees and colleagues.

There is the story that when Disney saw the first cut of Fantasia, and heard Beethoven's Sixth on its sound track, he reared back in his projection-room seat and bellowed, "Gee, this'll *make* Beethoven!" If that one is true or not, there *are* several persons who overheard the discussions between the learned and literary Aldous Huxley and Walt Disney. Huxley wondered what made Mickey Mouse and Company tick. "Hell, Doc, I don't know," replied Disney. "We just try to make a good picture. And then the professors come along and tell us what we do."

As a matter of fact, there is little in common between the assembly-line methods of producing a Mickey Mouse short and hoity-toity art. At the 51-acre Disney Studios—which contain thoroughfares like Dopey Drive and Mouse Street—over 500 highly trained employees grind out the cartoons.

The method is simple. Almost no one writes at Disney's. Writers, so-called, actually draw. Stories, as such, are never submitted, but rather drawing strips pinned to boards are submitted.

With the story line set, senior animators sketch out the main story steps. It takes 16 drawings to make Mickey move once on the screen. The senior animators might draw the 1st, the 10th and the 16th of these drawings, and let their assistants fill in. The studio is closed on week ends, and on these days, usually, Disney will wander through the rooms alone, studying the drawings up on boards, often leaving notes of criticism. When Disney approves a story, it is transferred from white paper to celluloid sheets, inked and painted by a staff of girls, and photographed with special cameras.

Since picture costs have doubled, even tripled, in the last decade, all kinds of trick short cuts are used to save money. Mickey has no soles on his shoes, because it saves cash. Elaborate costume pictures are avoided, because they give the animators extra work. Whenever possible, lions are used to harass Mickey instead of tigers, because tigers have stripes. Situations demanding crowds are rare; too many people to draw.

There have been mixed opinions concerning Walt Disney's main contribution to Mickey Mouse, beyond the original act of creation. A former employee said, "Walt is not an artist. He doesn't have the instincts or the imagination of an artist. His little-known virtue is that of a great promoter, who happens to recognize the importance of putting out a product technically better than anyone else's."

But whatever Disney's talent, exactly, the fact is that it is a mighty talent. Most of his underlings, though speaking from the safety of anonymity, acknowledge his daily contribution to Mickey Mouse and the other characters. "When we have a tough problem, we bring it to him and he solves it," says a veteran Disney writer. "When we leave his office, we don't say, 'What a brain to think of that!' We say, 'It's so simple. Why didn't we see it ourselves?' Walt is always clear and direct. He always delivers."

Disney—called Walt to his face by everyone in the studio—directs his $7,000,000 firm from a three-room office suite. Visitors enter through an outer office, between two secretaries and a glass trophy case, into Disney's personal study in brown. Behind the big desk is a dark-haired, slight-framed, rather shy man of forty-eight years, who works from nine to five daily. His office is dotted with framed photographs of his wife, Lillian, and his two daughters, Diane Marie, aged fifteen, and Sharon Mae, aged twelve.

Disney is not a wealthy man. For years some of his employees made more money than he did. He dwells quite modestly—using the Hollywood definition of the word—in a Los Feliz Hills home.

If the movies of Mickey Mouse and company have not made Walt Disney rich, at least the by-products of their fame have given him promise of security for years to come. In 1932, a bouncy gentleman named Kay Kamen, who'd been a department-store sales promotion man in Kansas City where he first met the struggling Disney, realized the full potentialities of hiring Mickey Mouse to sell merchandise. He rushed to Hollywood and sewed up Disney.

Working out of a Manhattan office, Kamen became the middleman between Disney and manufacturers the world over. And Mickey Mouse went into a new career as salesman for a variety of products ranging from sweat shirts and Halloween masks to greeting cards and fruit juices. Mickey promptly greatly increased the sales of two major manufacturers. The Lionel Corporation, makers of toy electric trains, tied up with Mickey and sold 253,000 Mickey Mouse handcars during a Christmas season for a profit of about $150,000.

Another more important assist was given by Mickey to the lngersoll Waterbury Company (now U.S. Time Corp.), makers of watches. Kamen suggested a Mickey Mouse watch to Disney, who insisted, "It'll never sell." Today, the Mickey Mouse watch outsells its nearest children's watch competitor ten to one and the 5,000,000th manufactured Mickey Mouse watch is now under glass in Disney's office.

In a few years Mickey's products had taken the world by storm. There have been Mickey Mouse bracelets of platinum set with diamonds selling for $1,200 on Fifth Avenue. There was a Mickey Mouse wallpaper praised by the present King of England. There were Mickey Mouse sandals that sold 2,000 pairs in one day at a New York store.

Kamen has 2,000 different products tied up with Disney characters. Last year they provided a gross take of $1,000,000—of which Kamen took $300,000 and Disney $700,000.

But those who profit by cash have less to thank Mickey Mouse for than those who profit by the escape he provided. For the peoples of the earth, Mickey is a miracle. In an uncomplicated way, he is always good for a laugh, for a moment away from man-made headaches, the taxes and the troubles of this civilization. He is of a special planet where we never grow old, or achy, or vain, a perfect place without sarcasm and sinus, without politicians and poorness—that is the world of Mickey Mouse on this, his happy birthday.

• The English writer Aldous Huxley briefly worked for the Disney studio in 1945 on a script for an *Alice in Wonderland* film which was never made. However, his query about "what made Mickey Mouse and Company tick" and Walt's answer to the question date from circa 1938. Huxley arrived in Hollywood in 1937, and the first known appearance in print of Walt's reply (there are several versions) was by Frank Nugent in "Disney Is Now Art—But He Wonders" in the *New York Times Magazine* (February 26, 1939). According to Nugent, Walt said: "Hell, Doc, I don't know! We just make a picture and then you professors come along and tell us what we do!"

I Live with a Genius— a Conversation with Mrs. Walt Disney (*excerpt*)

Lillian Disney and Isabella Taves

Originally published in the February 1953 *McCall's® Magazine*.

Right here I want to say another thing about Mickey Mouse. Stories have been printed about how Walt got interested in mice back on the farm in Marceline, Missouri, when he was a kid. Newspaper articles have told how Walt used to have a pet mouse named Mickey, which lived in his wastebasket during the free-lance cartoon days in Kansas City. Walt loves all animals—he won't even let the gardener and me put out traps for the little ones that are garden pests—but when he created Mickey Mouse there was no symbolism or background for the idea. He simply thought the mouse would make a cute character to animate.

I'm getting ahead of my story, however, Roy and Walt were still working with Oswald the Rabbit when the New York distributor notified them that from now on he was cutting the price per picture almost in half. Walt went to New York to argue that they couldn't break even that way. I went along too, for a second honeymoon. It didn't turn out quite that way.

Walt discovered that the distributor owned all the rights to Oswald and intended to go on making Oswald shorts without Walt if he refused to knuckle down to the cut price. Walt got mad and told the distributor what he thought of him. He came back to the hotel and announced that he was out of a job and glad, because he would never again work for anybody else. He never has, either.

I know now how right his decision was, for to function, Walt has to be free. I didn't have the long-range viewpoint that day. I was scared to death. Walt didn't even tell Roy what had happened, but wired him that he was coming home with a great new idea. On the way back, on the train, he wrote a scenario for a cartoon short to be called *Plane Crazy* and starring a mouse named Mortimer.

As for me, I was plain crazy. I sat watching the green of the Middle West change to sagebrush and desert. I remembered the early Hollywood days when Walt and Roy were so broke that they would go to a restaurant and order one dinner, splitting the courses between them. I knew I wouldn't care much for that. I couldn't believe that my husband meant to produce and distribute pictures himself, like the big companies. He and Roy had only a few thousand dollars between them. Pictures needed a lot of financing, even in 1927. And what if Walt failed? He had insulted his distributor and hadn't even looked for a new connection.

By the time Walt finished the scenario I was practically in a state of shock. He read it to me, and suddenly all my personal anguish focused on one violent objection to the script. "Mortimer is a horrible name for a mouse!" I exclaimed.

Walt argued—he can be very persuasive—but I stood firm. Finally, to placate his stubborn wife, Walt came up with a substitute: "Mickey Mouse." At this late date I have no idea whether it is a better name than "Mortimer." Nobody will ever know. I only feel a special affinity to Mickey because I helped name him. And, besides, Mickey taught me a lot about what it was going to be like married to Walt Disney. We've never been so broke since, at least quite so visibly. But I have been plenty worried on occasion. It has often helped to look back on that period.

Everybody helped Walt. Roy was Jack-of-all-trades, and Edna and I stopped being ladies of leisure and filled in celluloids. We worked night and day. We ate stews and pot roasts which luckily were cheap in those days. We were down so low that we had a major budget crisis one night when I tripped on the garage stairs and ruined my last pair of silk stockings. Then when we had finished three Mickeys we had an even worse blow. Nobody was interested in them because talkies had just come in and the theaters wanted shorts with sound.

I shall never forget the conversation between Roy and Walt when we made that discovery.

Roy: "What will we do?"

Walt: "We'll make them over with sound."

Roy: "How?"

Walt: "I don't know, but we'll do it."

Walt can do pretty nearly anything he puts his mind to. That is the way in which he is a great artist, not as a manipulator of crayon, chalk or paint. As a matter of fact, he does very little drawing these days, and never did care much for it. He knew nothing about music, but he began to study it. To this day he cannot carry a tune, but he has a vast knowledge and understanding of all kinds of music. He seldom wastes time being proud of anything he has finished, but of everything he has made he is most pleased with certain sections of *Fantasia*, which showed music as it looks to Walt Disney in cartoon and color. I feel, too, that a large part of the charm of his nature films, particularly the recent *Water Birds*, is due to the musical backgrounds.

The first Mickey Mouse opened in September, 1928, in New York. It had music behind it, but the animals had not yet learned to talk; they made grunting noises. Talking animals were a later brainstorm of Walt's.

Of Mouse and Man, or Mickey Reaches 25: Time Has Slowed His Step, But Walt Disney's Remarkable Rodent Has Come Smiling through Depression, Wars, A-bombs and H-Bombs

Barbara Berch Jamison

HOLLYWOOD. This week Mickey Mouse will be 25 years old, and although the average life expectancy of a mouse is four years, millions of Mickey's friends the world over—among them children, kings, college presidents and African bushmen—will not feel at all absurd to be wishing him a happy birthday. For Mickey has come through a quarter of a century of prosperity, flappers, depression, zoot suits, war, inflation and atom bombs the same skinny-shouldered, freckle-voiced, unmatchable little dandy he was the day he was born in an abandoned Hollywood real estate office and, according to Walt Disney, the man who knows, Mickey will go on forever.

True, Mickey is not the active little mouse he used to be. Today his cartoons turn up perhaps twice a year, in contrast to his heyday in the early Thirties, when he romped through twelve or fifteen shorts each year. Today some children have never seen—or heard of—Mickey, and other cartoon characters have far surpassed him in popularity. "But as long as there's a Disney studio," Disney flatly states, "there'll be Mickey Mouse cartoons. I can't live without him!"

Looking back, have there been any significant changes in Mickey through the years? Well, he's thickened a bit through the middle, Mickey has: he wears shoes now, cuts a sharper figure sartorially, and lives in a more fashionable neighborhood. He once lost his tail—"as an economy move," says Disney—but it so threw him out of balance that it was quickly replaced. He still has only four fingers on each hand, but no wrinkles and no gray hair. But he no longer carries the load himself, usually requiring an all-star cast (Donald Duck, Goofy, and/or Pluto) to see him through his twice-yearly appearances.

Mickey was conceived, back there in 1927, somewhere in Nebraska, on a train between New York and Hollywood as Disney and his wife were returning from an unhappy trip East. Disney had just lost the rights to his cartoon character, Oswald the Rabbit, along with most of his staff, and was muttering miserably to his wife. "What now?" he moaned. "All the other animals have been used—cats, dogs, rabbits—about all that's left is a mouse—" he jerked upright as though one of the little creatures had veritably scooted up his leg. "A mouse! Of course—a mouse—!" Six weeks later Mickey Mouse came to life in a one-reeler called "Plane Crazy," and within the year—with his third appearance in "Steamboat Willie," in which his actions were synchronized with a high-pitched, boyishly-breathless voice which was Disney's own (and still is), he became the star of the first sound cartoon ever released.

At that time Disney did all the work on the Disney cartoons himself—the ideas, the drawing, the animation, everything. "A twenty-hour-a-day job," he recalls. "I tried to keep my wife from knowing how hard I was working—so we'd go out to dinner, then we'd casually stop by the shop and I'd turn the clock to eleven while she took a quick nap on the couch. At 2 or 3 in the morning I'd wake her, tell her it was 11 o'clock, and we'd go home. She never did find out"—he looks around him—"or did she?"

Since then, Mickey, born of one-tenth inspiration and nine-tenths perspiration, has soared onward and upward to win for himself (and

Disney) the most impressive display of admiration, honors and trophies ever to come to a single entertainment figure in all history, human or rodent. He's considered far more than an American property; his appeal is international. He's known by a dozen different names in as many countries: Michel Souris in France, Topolino in Italy, Miki Kichi in Japan, Miguel Ratoncito in Spain, Mikki Maus in Soviet Russia.

During the war he disappeared almost completely from the screen to devote his time to being the leading character in a staggering number of insignia the Disney staff presented to the armed forces, by request, "Mickey Mouse" was the password for the troops landing on the Normandy beaches on D-Day.

Mickey Mouse watches pulled prices higher than expensive Swiss or American makes, some selling for $1,000 each, in the bartering between American and Russian soldiers in Berlin in 1945. Mrs. Roosevelt reports that her husband requested a Mickey Mouse cartoon to be included in nearly every film program shown at the White House.

"And," adds Disney, "there'd be no beautiful studio like this without him." His eyes gaze over the fifty-one acres that make up the lavish Disney studio in Burbank. "I owe it all to Mickey and I'm plenty grateful." But he's less knowing in trying to explain Mickey's phenomenal appeal. "Everybody's tried to figure it out," Disney goes on. "So far as I know, nobody has. I don't know. I guess Mickey's the good Sam most of us really are—a pretty nice little fellow who never does anybody any harm, who gets into a lot of scrapes through no fault of his own but always manages to come up grinning. Why, Mickey's even been faithful to one girl all of his life!" Disney smiles. "This is tough, trying to explain Mickey. It's been done by experts and the best any of us have been able to come up with is the fact that Mickey is so simple and uncomplicated, so easy to understand, that you can't help liking him.

"You know, I've seen babies reach for the stuffed Mickey toy instinctively, out of a pile of other finer and more expensive toys. There's something about his shape—a little ridiculous, a little pathetic, a little gay.

"And Mickey's been my passport to everything I've wanted to do," Disney continues. "When I felt I should branch out a little—I wanted to try pure beauty in cartoons, I wanted to try animating great music, I had a lot of ideas—but all the exhibitors wanted was Mickey. Okay, I gave them Mickey, but they had to take my Silly Symphonies too. Mickey was the club I used over their heads."

Even "Snow White and the Seven Dwarfs," the now-historic first all-cartoon feature, was due to Mickey. "We raised the money on the strength of Mickey's popularity. It took us years to finish—but we managed to do it between, over, and under the Mickey cartoons."

Since "Snow White," of course, it's been easier, Disney admits, but he still thanks his wonder mouse for all the other things he's been able to do—"Dumbo," "Fantasia," "Bambi," "Peter Pan," the live-action pictures, "Treasure Island," "Robin Hood," and the real-life adventures, "Seal Island," "The Alaskan Eskimo," "The Living Desert."

Disney hopes he's been able to show Mickey his appreciation with more than words. "That's why we put him in 'Fantasia'—in the 'Sorcerer's Apprentice' sequence," Disney grins. "There he was, prancing around pure art, great music. We showed the old boy we thought he could hold his own with any of the masters. And he did, didn't he?" Next month, too, Mickey's coming out in "Mickey's Birthday Party," a full-length feature, which will be a compilation of some of his most popular cartoons. "More gratitude," Disney says, with a wink. "We love the little fellow."

Why, then, is Mickey practically dead now? Why are his appearances limited to a scant two cartoons a year? Disney leans back, scratching his head. "Mickey's our problem child. He's so much of an institution that we're limited in what we can do with him. If we have Mickey kicking someone in the pants we get a million letters from mother telling us we're giving their kids the wrong ideas. Mickey must always be sweet, always lovable. What can you do with such a leading man?"

With Donald Duck, it's different. "He can yell at his nephews that he could kill them for scribbling up the living room walls—just as any mother would—then soften a few minutes later and cry like a baby because he thinks they're burned up in the stove. The duck's allowed to have a temper. Mickey isn't. And the tempo of the times demands more violence—but not from Mickey."

Vox Bop (*excerpt*)

Maurice A. Crane

American Speech 33, no. 3. Copyright 1958, the American Dialect Society
(Columbia University Press). Reprinted by permission of the
present publisher, Duke University Press. www.dukepress.edu

A considerable amount of anything is *bogoobs* (e.g., 'It's a mickey band,' but there's bogoobs bread'), quite obviously from *beaucoup*. Incidentally, a *mickey* or *Mickey Mouse* band is not merely a 'pop tune' band, as Gold indicated, but the kind of pop band that sounds as if it is playing background for an animated cartoon. Listen to Lawrence Welk, if you will, and discover how apt the expression is. (The term, which has been around almost as long as Mickey Mouse himself, has also come into common parlance in another sense at Michigan State, where a 'Mickey Mouse course' means a *snap* course, or what Princeton undergraduates in my day called a *gut* course.)

• The sobriquet "Mickey Mouse band" likely derives from "Mickey Mouse music," an expression long used in Hollywood to describe the harmonized union of screen action with song and sound effects innovated by Disney. In 1936, Jerome Kern said that Walt "made use of music as language. In the synchronization of humorous episodes with humorous music, he has unquestionably given us the outstanding contribution of our time." As a term for "uncool" music, "Mickey Mouse" appeared in the first published lexicon of jazz slang, authored by Carl Cons (Nov. 1935). Robert S. Gold, cited here by Crane, had footnoted Crane in "The Vernacular of the Jazz World," *American Speech*, December 1957.

... on the Navy

Elmo R. Zumwalt Jr.

New York Times, December 3, 1977

MILWAUKEE—To many Navy men, the term "Mickey Mouse" some-times means laughter—but not at a cartoon character. Sometimes it isn't a laughing matter.

Who doesn't know that unnecessary or demeaning regulations are "Mickey Mouse"?

If a sailor working frantically to repair urgently needed equipment must change into and out of another uniform in order to have his meal in the mess hall, that's Mickey Mouse.

If sailors are ordered to slap paint over rusted decks to make the ship look temporarily good for visiting brass, that's Mickey Mouse.

If sailors are ordered to do dirty work, not in dungarees but in blue uniforms, which must then be dry-cleaned at personal expense, that is Mickey Mouse.

If a commanding officer violates that article of Navy Regulations that has always permitted beards, and, on personal whim, prohibits them, that is *very* Mickey Mouse. Very.

Navy's Mickey Mouse was very impressive before World War II. By 1941, it had swollen considerably. But the war nearly killed the creature. Millions of citizen-soldiers who didn't know about the Navy version of Mickey Mouse—there are indeed other versions, lest other armed forces take false comfort—filled jobs at all levels. In their innocence, they disregarded the cheese—or was it cheesiness?—that fed the beast: they used common sense. By 1945, Mickey Mouse had deteriorated from dragon to—well, insect-size.

Then, slowly, over the years Mickey Mouse recovered. His basic ra-tions—excessive regulations—proliferated. By 1970, sailors were leav-ing the naval service in ever-increasing numbers at the end of their first four-year cruise; almost as much as the very unpopular Vietnam War,

Mickey Mouse contributed to 1970's all-time historic low in re-enlist-ments—9.5 percent.

Like Navy knights before me, I set out in 1970 with a mighty sword and a worthy following to slay Mickey Mouse. A memorandum was fashioned, in all its beauty, proclaiming throughout Navy's Camelot an intention to do battle with the dragon-sized rodent and declaring it un-wanted. My loyal subjects rose up and followed. It came to pass that a great battle—indeed, another Midway—took place. We smote the foe hearty blows! Mickey Mouse, wounded, retreated. But no doubt he still lives somewhere. Hidden.

Sailor, beware.

• An editorial note accompanying this essay stated: "Elmo R. Zumwalt Jr., while Chief of Naval Operations (from July 1, 1970, to June 30, 1974), sent out certain kinds of naval directives that sailors dubbed 'Z-Grams.' One was titled: 'Mickey Mouse, Elimination Of.' Admiral Zumwalt is now a business-man."

6. The Nostalgia Begins

1978–1989

Mickey's fiftieth anniversary in 1978 provoked much hoopla, and broad-based stirrings of nostalgia for the Mouse of yore. A series of month-long screenings of his cartoons at MoMA ("Modern Museum Celebrates Mickey"*) was a major factor in his resurrection. That resurgence was evident as far afield as France, where a collection of Mouse memorabilia went on display at the Paris department store, Au Printemps, as noted here in my item on Mickey and Charles de Gaulle as iconic effigies of their respective countries.*

In 1948 and 1950, the proto-Pop English artist Eduardo Paolozzi had included vintage clippings of Mickey and Minnie in two witty collages now at the Tate Gallery, London. But the first true Pop artist—probably the first American artist of note since John Steuart Curry—to insert Mickey in a painting was Roy Lichtenstein, in a 1961 canvas depicting Donald Duck and his disk-eared pal fishing together off a dock (National Gallery of Art, Washington, D.C.).

Lichtenstein made that picture mainly for fun, to amuse his small children. But it was nostalgia that infused the various versions of the Mouse produced a generation later by Andy Warhol. Warhol's Mickeys were silkscreen multiples—originally part of a "portfolio" of images from 1981 entitled *Myths* that featured Warhol himself (as "The Shadow"), Greta Garbo, Uncle Sam, Superman, the Wicked Witch of the West, plus four other familiar faces from modern American popular culture.

Maurice Sendak, like Warhol, was born in 1928, and both men were members of what Robert W. Brockway, a professor of theology in Canada, later branded "the Mickey Mouse generation."* In an article in *TV Guide* in 1978,* Sendak said that "growing up with Mickey" was "the best of relationships and one of the few genuine joys of my childhood"—a statement Andy himself might well have endorsed.

Also in 1978, in the *Saturday Review*, John Culhane called Mickey "the best-known imaginary creature in history,"* and Anna Quindlen, in the *New York Times*, described him as "a guy who made the big time but always kept the old friends and never deserted the gal who stood by him in his spaghetti days."* One year later, in 1979, Harvard biologist and professor Stephen Jay Gould* published a now classic analysis of what it was in Mickey's graphic DNA that made him so lovable.

In the 1980s, Mickey Mouse t-shirts became big, and even President Ronald Reagan's press secretary, Lyn Nofziger, was seen in public wearing a necktie with Disney's iconic rodent on it. Mickey's entry into the realm of adult sportswear, as Irene Daria reported in *Women's Wear Daily* in the fall of 1984, was the brainchild of clothier Max Raab, who declared: "We figured any clothing that could handle a polo pony or an alligator could handle Mickey Mouse." Raab's "Mickey & Co." line, marketed by his apparel firm, J. G. Hook, helped plant the seed for the Disney Store global retail chain, which was launched in 1987.

By the end of the 1980s, in his essay on the mythic "masks" of Mickey Mouse, Professor Brockway would proclaim the Disney character to be "an archetypal symbol, not only to Americans but to people everywhere, especially to the generation that was young during the thirties." Mickey had, in other words, become a planetary emblem of America, and the American spirit.

Growing Up with Mickey

Maurice Sendak

TV Guide Magazine, November 11, 1978. Courtesy of *TV Guide Magazine*, LLC © 1978.

This year Mickey Mouse and I will be celebrating our 50th birthdays. We shared, at least for our first decade, much more than a common first initial; it was the best of relationships and one of the few genuine joys of my childhood in Brooklyn during the early '30s.

Those were the Depression years and we had to make do. Making do—for kids, at least—was mostly a matter of comic books and movies. Mickey Mouse, unlike the great gaggle of child movie stars of that period, did not make me feel inferior. Perhaps it was typical for kids of my generation to suffer badly from unthinking parental comparisons with the then-famous silver-screen moppets. There is no forgetting the cheated, missed-luck look in my father's eyes as he turned from the radiant image of Shirley Temple back to the three ungolden children he'd begotten. Ah, the wonderful, rich, American-dream blessing of having a Shirley Temple girl and a Bobby Breen boy! I never forgave those yodeling, tap-dancing, brimming-with-glittering-life miniature monsters.

But Mickey had nothing to do with any of them. He was our common street friend. My brother and sister and I chewed his gum, brushed our teeth with his toothbrush, played with him in a seemingly endless variety of games and read about his adventures in comic strips and storybooks. Best of all, our street pal was also a movie star, in the darkened theater, the sudden flash of his brilliant, wild, joyful face—radiating great golden beams—filled me with an intoxicating, unalloyed pleasure.

In school I learned to despise Walt Disney. I was told that he corrupted the fairy tale and that he was the personification of poor taste. I began to suspect my own instinctual response to Mickey. It took me nearly 20 years to rediscover the pleasure of that first, truthful response and to fuse it with my own work as an artist. It took me just as long to forget the corrupting effect of school. A Renaissance child, growing up in the shadow of the Sistine Chapel, would perhaps have been more fortunate—his instincts sharpened by "the real thing." I had to make do with Mickey Mouse.

Though I wasn't aware of it at the time, I now know that a good deal of my pleasure in Mickey—a rich, sensual pleasure—had to do with his bizarre but gratifying proportions, the great rounded head extended still farther by those black saucer ears, the black trunk fitting snugly into ballooning red shorts, the tiny legs stuffed into delicious doughy yellow shoes. The giant white gloves, yellow buttons, pie-cut eyes and bewitching grin were the delectable finishing touches. I am describing, of course, the Mickey of early color cartoons (his first being "The Band Concert" of 1935). The black-and-white Mickey of the late '20s and early '30s had a wilder, rattier look. The golden age of Mickey for me is that of the middle '30s. An ingenious shape, fashioned primarily to facilitate the needs of the animator, he exuded a wonderful sense of physical satisfaction and pleasure—a piece of art that powerfully affected and stimulated the imagination.

I'm less a lover of Mickey's character and personality—that of the actor/boy next door, man about town—than I am of him as pure graphic image. (His provincialism disturbed me even as a child.) That golden-age Mickey metamorphosed, alas, into less original forms at the end of his first decade. Every addition and modification to Mickey's proportions after that time was, in my opinion, a mistake. He became a suburbanite, abandoning his street friends and turning into a shapeless, mindless bon vivant. Those subtle and sometimes not-so-subtle nuances pushed Mickey out of art into commerce. (Mickey, surely, was *always* commercial, but now he *looked* commercial.) This transformation, which I take so to heart, apparently made not a jot of difference to following generations. Mickey is as popular as ever. But those kids, like Mickey, were missing the best.

My own collection of Mickey Mousiana is rigidly bound by that first decade of his life. There is no end to such a collection, nor, oddly, is there any wish to end it. Happily and incredibly, there was an infinitude of Mouses manufactured in those early days (as there still is), and the search for an early Mouse becomes a delightful obsession. To seek out that face—that completely nuts look of fiery, intense animation—to find it on a post card, box top, piece of tin or porcelain is an enduring pleasure.

The Mickey who exerted an influence on me as an artist is the Mickey of that early time—my early time. Playing a Kafka-game of shared first initial with most of the heroes in my own picture books, I only once broke cover and fused a very particular character with the famous Mouse. That is the Mickey who was the hero of my book "In the Night Kitchen," written in 1970. It seemed natural and honest to reach out openly to that early best friend while eagerly exploring a very private, favorite childhood fantasy. "In the Night Kitchen" is a kind of homage to old times and places—to Laurel and Hardy comedies and the film "King Kong," as well as to the art of Disney, comic books in general and the turn-of-the-century, funny-papers fantasist, the artist Winsor Mc-Cay, in particular. It was also an attempt to synthesize past and present, with Mickey as my trusty medium. And if the Disney studio irritatingly refused to let me paint this revered image on a cooking stove that figured in my plot, I put it down to the general decay of civilization.

Fifty is the notorious middle age of crisis and flux, and certainly, as an artist, I am going through the obligatory creative bumps. But I have a fantasy of Mickey at this great age busting loose—à la Steamboat Willie—and declaring his independence by demanding back the original idiosyncratic self that prosperity and indifference have robbed him of. A trifling conceit, no doubt, but if middle age hopefully precedes a rebirth of spirit and inspiration, then maybe the Mouse has a chance. Good luck, Mickey—and happy birthday.

• It's been said that Sendak's first color drawing as a child was a depiction of Mickey, and that he decided to become an artist after seeing *Fantasia*. In 1945, he wrote in his high-school magazine that "Walt Disney is the greatest exponent of a new art form which will leave its imprint on civilization" (Lanes, "Sendak at 50"). Max, the pajama-clad hero in Sendak's most famous book, *Where the Wild Things Are* (Harper & Row, 1963), was partly modeled after Mickey, who figures overtly in Sendak's *In the Night Kitchen* (Harper & Row, 1970). This article, with very slight variations, was reprinted in Sendak's anthology *Caldecott & Co.: Notes on Books & Pictures* (Farrar, Straus & Giroux, 1988). The only notable change came in the last two sentences, where what appeared in *TV Guide* (and here) as "A trifling conceit . . ." was replaced with: "Hardly likely, I suppose. But middle age has been known to precede a rebirth of spirit and inspiration, so maybe the Mouse has a chance."

A Mouse for All Seasons

John Culhane

Saturday Review, November 11, 1978. Used by permission of the author.

"You're the top!
You're the Colosseum,
You're the top!
You're the Louvre Museum,
You're a melody from a symphony by Strauss,
You're a Bendel bonnet,
A Shakespeare sonnet,
You're Mickey Mouse." *

Mickey Mouse has always been a star. When Mickey first played New York City's Music Hall, Cole Porter would bring his dinner guests there just to see the cartoon. In 1935, Arturo Toscanini asked that *The Band Concert* be stopped and re-run because he so enjoyed the Mousetro's sly caricature.

Arguably the best-known imaginary creature in history, Mickey Mouse will be 50 years old on November 18. From poor kids to presidents and once-and-future kings, millions have given their hearts to this cartoon personality. *The New York Times* reported in 1935 that "the King of England won't go to the movies unless Mickey Mouse is on the bill. Today, Emperor Hirohito wears a Mickey Mouse watch."

That this mouse is still so loved is indicated by the dimensions of his 50th birthday party. Celebrations will include a black-tie dinner attended by the President of the United States at the Library of Congress; a party at the White House for Mickey and some heretofore underprivileged children, hosted by Amy Carter; an NBC television special; and retrospectives at the Chicago Film Festival, the American Film Institute Theater at the John F. Kennedy Center for the Performing Arts in Washington, D.C., and the Museum of Modern Art in Manhattan.

At New York's Broadway Theater—which was called the Colony when Mickey made his debut in *Steamboat Willie*, "the FIRST animated cartoon with SOUND," at 2 PM on Sunday, November 18, 1928—a plaque will be dedicated exactly a half century later.

Mickey began life as an expression of Walt Disney's innate optimism. The cartoonist had just lost his job—making Oswald the Rabbit cartoons for a New York distributor named Mintz—but instead of sinking into depression, Walt came up with Mickey.

"Walt designed a mouse, but it wasn't very good," Otto Messmer, creator and designer of Felix the Cat, once told me. "He was long and skinny. Ub Iwerks redesigned the character."

"It was the standardized thing," Iwerks—the one animator on Disney's staff who had not stayed with Mintz—told me in 1967. "Pear-shaped body, ball on top, couple of thin legs. If you gave it long ears, it was a rabbit. Short ears, it was a cat. Ears hanging down, a dog. With an elongated nose it became a mouse. Mickey was the same basic figure initially."

Initially. But Iwerks made the ears big circles—no matter which way the head turned. In fact, Mickey's face is a trinity of wafers—and the circular symbol, as C. G. Jung has told us, "always points to the single most vital aspect of life—its ultimate wholeness." Simple round forms portray "the archetype of self," he said, "which, as we know from experience, plays the chief role in uniting apparently irreconcilable opposites and is therefore best suited to compensate the split-mindedness of the age."

Personally, I have always thought that the secret of Mickey's appeal lies in the fact that his design is the perfect expression of what he symbolizes—survival. "Our work is a caricature of life," Disney told me in 1951. Mickey is a caricature of the optimistic adventurer that mankind has had to be to survive through the centuries. Somehow, the three interlocked circles that make up his famous face communicate that.

This is pretty heavy to hang on a cartoon rodent, and yet, things kept happening involving Mickey for half a century now that suggest he is communicating something more profound than did Felix the Cat or the Kewpie Doll—or any of the other fads he has outlived.

There is even a fairy-tale ring to the fact that it was Disney's third try that succeeded. The first Mickey Mouse cartoon, *Plane Crazy*, in which

Mickey burlesqued Lindbergh's conquest of the Atlantic, could not find a distributor; nor could the second, *Gallopin' Gaucho*, in which the mouse caricatures Douglas Fairbanks the swashbuckler and rescues Minnie from Peg-Leg Pete. Part of the reason was that they were silent cartoons. Al Jolson's *Jazz Singer* had already created a demand for sound pictures, as the indomitable Disney made his third attempt, *Steamboat Willie*, the first synchronized sound cartoon.

Before Mickey was a year old, the stock market crashed. The optimistic mouse may have succeeded initially because of his winning looks and the novelty of sound, but now he was an idea whose time had come. In the long days of the Depression, fellow optimist FDR found Mickey a tonic. "My husband always loved Mickey Mouse," Eleanor Roosevelt later wrote, "and he always had to have the cartoon in the White House." While Roosevelt battled economic royalists, the epidemic world lawlessness, and fear itself, Mickey took care of a mail bandit (*The Mail Pilot*, 1933), an escaped gorilla (*The Pet Store*, 1933), and a small-time gang of cutthroats (*Shanghaied*, 1934).

It wasn't just morale-building. The mouse is credited with saving at least two other corporations besides the Disney Studio—the Lionel Corporation, manufacturer of toy trains, which was rescued from receivership by the sale of 254,000 handcars carrying Mickey and his girlfriend Minnie, and Ingersoll, which brought out the Mickey Mouse wristwatch just in the nick of time.

Sadly, in the Fifties, the Disney Studio stopped making new Mickey Mouse cartoons. Television had destroyed the old market for theatrical short subjects, and the production costs of new Mickey Mouse cartoons were beyond the budgets of television. Kids could still see the old cartoons on Disney's new television series, "The Mickey Mouse Club," which caused those large, round mouse ears to sprout on youngsters all over the nation. But Mickey, like America, was losing his identity as an optimistic adventurer—though not as a survivor.

The continuing power of his form to communicate was never in question. In the late Fifties, Dr. Tom Dooley, the "jungle doctor" and founder of Medico, was running a hospital ship off the coast of Southeast Asia that provided free medical care for whoever would come out of the jungle to his clinic. "Dooley had a problem getting children," recalled John Hench, an artist who is one of the key figures in the ongoing design of Disneyland and Disney World. "He wanted to know if he could use our characters—Mickey particularly. . . . Dooley didn't understand what was wrong at the time, but he knew from the experience he had that the Red Cross didn't work well—so he put Mickey on the side of his ship. Suddenly, kids who had refused to come out of the bush happily stood in line for a medical examination. Obviously, hardly any of them had ever seen a picture of Mickey. But they recognized something. It wasn't the cartoon character, it was the symbol. . . .

"Walt had an instinct for these very old survival patterns," said Hench. "I think that if anyone really wanted to take the time to examine it, he would see that these survival patterns are the basis of our esthetics, our sense of pleasure. And Walt was always interested in why designs had their power. After all, he was in the business of communicating with form."

I remember two moments in the Sixties and Seventies in which I felt the force of Mickey as symbol of survival. In 1969 I went to the Middle East as a foreign correspondent and visited a border kibbutz in Israel and a Palestinian refugee camp in Jordan. Children on both sides of the barbed-wire frontier immediately pointed to the tiny figure on my wristwatch and said the name that is the same in Hebrew and Arabic: "Mickey Mouse."

And I recall seeing, in 1971, a bootleg cartoon called Mickey Mouse in Vietnam that some artist not with the Disney Studio had taken the risk and the trouble to animate in defiance of copyright law. In this short cartoon, Mickey Mouse is an American soldier. He lands in Vietnam. And is immediately shot dead. End of cartoon.

At the Disney Studio today, a new generation of artists wants to make Mickey Mouse cartoons for the Eighties—but Ron Miller, the company's executive vice president in charge of production and creative affairs, contends there is no more market for theatrical shorts now than there was when the studio stopped making them, and still no way to turn a profit on Disney-style animation for TV.

But if they were able to do more Mickey Mouse shorts, the young animators would be unlikely to pick up where Mickey was left in the early Fifties, a suburban householder living in a quiet middle-class neighborhood with his sadly subdued pup, Pluto.

"The Mickey who was an adventurer—that's the real thing," said

Andy Gaskill, probably the finest all-around artist of the new Disney generation. "He had a case of schizophrenia right after the war and he's never been the same since. You have to take him into the realm of fantasy," said Gaskill. "You can't keep him in the suburban home. Imagine Mickey in space, battling old Peg-Leg Pete—except now, Pete has retrojets in his peg-leg."

I suppose it does no harm for Disney employees to dress up in Mickey Mouse costumes and shake hands and have their pictures taken with children at Disneyland or Disney World. But this is not the historic Mickey Mouse, the maker of an era, an animated cartoon character whose personality is so definite that you were sure he must get itchy being merely a greeter or a master-of-ceremonies or a corporate symbol. Having vanquished Peg-Leg Pete in countless tight spots, from the Wild West in *Two-Gun Mickey* to the Frozen North in *The Klondike Kid*; having toppled giants in *Giantland*, *The Brave Little Tailor*, and *Mickey and the Beanstalk*; having conducted a band in a tornado in *The Band Concert*; having commanded even the oceans and the planets in *The Sorcerer's Apprentice*, he would surely now be eager to blast off into the farthest reaches of outer space. Then woe be unto Darth Vader if he should venture so far out of his class as to kidnap Minnie Mouse!

* Cole Porter, "You're the Top" © 1934, Warner Bros. Inc. Copyright renewed and all rights reserved.

Modern Museum
Celebrates Mickey

Anna Quindlen

Here's to a character who's been a superstar for half a century and only gotten sweeter, who's always worn the same unassuming garb and simple smile. Here's to a guy who made the big time but always kept the old friends and never deserted the gal who stood by him in his spaghetti days. Here's to an actor who's 50 years old but hasn't lost his hair, his teeth, or his recognition factor.

Happy birthday, Mickey Mouse.

Yes, the four-foot-tall mouse who has contributed to the fortunes of the Ingersoll-Waterbury watch company, Annette Funicello and a guy named Disney is turning 50 tomorrow, and though his mellifluous little name has become a synonym for the banal and the bush league, that's hardly what his birthday celebration will be.

The party for the world's most famous mouse in the city where he was horn on Nov. 18, 1928, will go on for more than a month at the Museum of Modern Art. Starting tomorrow, the museum will be showing five-weekends worth of Mickey Mouse cartoons, with six different screenings planned this weekend.

"Steamboat Willie," the film that launched Mickey 50 years ago at the Colony Theater, now the Broadway (at 53d Street), will kick off the noon and 1:15 P.M. shows tomorrow. Those screenings will also include the 1942 "Mickey's Birthday Party," naturally, as well as one of Mickey's later cartoons, "The Simple Things," made in 1953. The 1930's, Mickey's heyday, will he highlighted during the shows at 2:30 and 3:45 P.M., and the 5 P.M. show will not only feature "The Sorcerer's Apprentice" segment of "Fantasia," Mickey's first feature film, but also an introduction by the longtime Disney animator Ward Kimball. The shows are free with admission to the museum, which is $2.50 for adults, $1.25 for students and 75 cents for the elderly and children under 16.

A Career of Five Decades

As befits a mouse whose career has spanned five decades, the celebration will continue Sunday at noon with a repeat of the "Sorcerer's Apprentice" show, which also includes excerpts from two other feature-length films, and at noon every Saturday and Sunday to come though Dec. 17, the museum will present an hour-long show of seven cartoons, most of them from the 30's. Mickey's fans win be able to see him as a musician, a physician, a football player, an ice skater, on the high seas, down on the farm, and up in the wild blue yonder. He will appear in black-and-white in his pre-1935 movies and in color after that. The director of the museum, Richard Oldenburg, explained Mickey's presence among the Maillols and Matisses in these words: "Mickey Mouse represented a kind of simple classic design that has an effect on many of the visual arts. Does that sound pompous?"

Mickey, long the friend of Presidents, also will be honored today at a party given by Amy Carter in the White House, and tomorrow morning at the Broadway he will be feted at a party to be given by New York Bell, whose early sound system provided the rinkety-tink of "Willie," the first sound cartoon. Plaques and proclamations will inevitably follow.

This is only the latest in a series of honors for a mouse who was once classed by the artist Ernest Trova with the swastika and the Coca Cola bottle as the most powerful graphic images of 20th century culture. Franklin D. Roosevelt and Mary Pickford publicly mentioned Mickey in his younger days, as their favorite movie star. Madame Tussaud put him in the waxworks, and the Dictionary of American Slang puts him under M. He won an Oscar, received a medal from the League of Nations, and eventually, as all Americans know, got his own adventure park in California and later in Florida. It may be an indication of his devotion to those who knew him when, that there is no record that he objected when the original name of Mickey Mouse Park was changed to Disneyland.

But behind the smiling facade, behind the dinner-plate ears and the enigmatic four-finger gloves, there is another Mickey Mouse. What is he really like?

His Master's Voice

His creator, Walt Disney, once described him thus: "A tiny bit of a mouse that would have something of the wistfulness of Chaplin." Some say that Mickey was patterned after a pet mouse Disney once befriended in his original Kansas City workroom, a mouse named Mortimer whose name in his cartoon reincarnation was mercifully changed at Mrs. Disney's suggestion. Mickey's falsetto voice was supplied for two decades by Disney himself—to his increasing embarrassment—and his animated mouseplay was originally provided by Ub Iwerks. Some intimate that Mickey, in his good-natured, little-guy guise, was much like Disney himself; Lilly Disney once remarked that Mickey was her favorite of all her husband's characters because "there's so much of Walt in him," and like his creator, Mickey stayed with his Minnie and never even played opposite another Mouselet.

Naturally, a Kansas City mouse who began acting before he could even talk was changed by all this attention. Ward Kimball, who himself was responsible for creating the mice in "Cinderella" ("which were meant to be real mice, which clearly Mickey was not"), recalled the other day that Mickey was originally a collection of quick and easy-to-draw circles with no whiskers, and a vaguely rodentlike face. But as he did more and more films, and spent an increasing amount of time with humans instead of his old friends Goofy and Donald Duck, Mickey developed cheeks and pupils, neither of which are noticeable in most mice. He became, in effect, a mouse parodying a person.

His personality changed, too. Although some fans would say it improved, Mr. Kimball, who will accompany Mickey on this week's train trip, has his doubts. "There was a touch of cruelty and violence in the earlier cartoons," he said. "Mickey and Minnie would play cruel tricks on other animals. But as he became a worldwide figure who was seen by so many children, that side of him had to go; he had to clean up his act. Trouble is that then you don't have much of a character. Now, it's not so important because Mickey doesn't make films anymore so he can just stand as the symbol of the parks."

In fact Mickey became the symbol of something more; he came to represent the all-American individual, a peppy, cheerful, never-say-die guy. It obviously worked. Over the years almost every conceivable product, from stationery to shirts, has been stamped with Mickey's smiling face, and the Ingersoll-Waterbury company, which had been In financial trouble in the early 30's, rose to prosperity again when it made Mickey's spindly limbs the hands on its wristwatches.

Let it not be said, however, that Mickey Mouse did not pay his dues. In "Plane Crazy," made, but not shown, before "Willie," he had neither gloves nor shoes, and he spends most of his time in his strange little red shorts, not the loud sports shirts he has affected in some of the later cartoons. (In fact Minnie was topless in many of the films but now always wears a blouse.)

Although Mickey has in his time made more than 100 movies and was the world's No. 1 ranked cartoon character in the 30's, he was on light duty during World War II while the men he worked with produced things unsuitable for his gifts with names like "Aircraft Carrier Landing Signals" and "Four Methods of Flush Riveting." It must have been some solace to him during this slow period that his name was used as the code for D-Day and that the Germans banned his films. "The wearing of German military helmets by an army of cats which oppose a militia of mice is offensive to national dignity," they said at the time.

The war changed the world, and Mickey changed with it. When television became the media to watch, the mouse was right there with it, grabbing the imagination of a whole new generation of children and selling 24,000 pairs of ears a day with the Mickey Mouse Club, which made his name a tune as familiar as the National Anthem. On any day at Disneyland or Disney World, hundreds of people vie for the privilege of having their picture taken with Mickey, wearing, as always, his gloves and his red shorts. He is expected to be wearing them on Saturday, and Mr. Kimball says that while Mickey will be attending a black-tie dinner in Washington during his trip, he will wear his customary garb there, too.

"Mickey," Mr. Kimball said, "will look as he's always looked. He's too old to start dressing up now."

Le Grand Charlie et le Petit Mickey

Garry Apgar

Paris Metro, November 22, 1978

Prominent proboscis aside, what on earth could Mickey Mouse and Charles de Gaulle possibly have in common? De Gaulle, after all, was on record as a Tintin fan, whilst what the Mouse thought of the General—well—God only knows.

Still, they do have this in common: they both became national symbols. De Gaulle has come to stand for *"une certaine idée de la France,"* while, like it or not, Mickey Mouse (like Uncle Sam or Coca-Cola) is America. Quite coincidentally, 1978 is a landmark year for them both. It's the Mouse's 50th birthday and it's the 20th anniversary of de Gaulle's return to power. And two first-rate *manifestations* help commemorate the occasions.

The "Exposition Charles de Gaulle" has three unbeatable virtues: it's about a remarkable man, it's intelligently planned, and it's free. The emphasis of the show is almost entirely visual. There is a multi-screen slide and sound show at one end of the hall, and photos, cartoons and other art galore, tracing his life starting as a young WW I officer, through his activities during WW II, the Liberation, and the years as head of the Ve République.

De Gaulle was undeniably, as they say, *quelqu'un*, one of the last of the giants. As Mao observed, "People like De Gaulle and myself have no successors." De Gaulle also became a symbol of overpowering Gallic cultural confidence and national pride that the French call *grandeur* and *gloire*. This show may not make you a believer, i.e. a De Gaulle fan, but even a quickie visit is worth while. The show, *chez* Chirac, is on the rue Lobau side of the Hôtel de Ville—but hurry, it only runs through November 15.

If ever there were a symbol of America's naïve, optimistic brand of confidence, it would be Mickey Mouse. Mickey's got his own show going over at the Printemps department store, up on the terrasse of the 9th floor of the Magasin du Havre. The highlight of the goings-on is an exhibition of 300 Disney toys, dating as far back as 1929, from the collection of Honoré Bostel—who's been known to appear, to the astonishment of diners at his restaurant, Chez Honoré, in a Mickey Mouse outfit.

Bostel's collection will be on display until December 4, when it will be sold at auction on the premises. Why? Because for the middle-aged Bostel, the real Mickey Mouse, the spunky little rodent of his youth, died back in the 1950s when *"le trust Disney"* started running out animated cartoons wanting in "soul."

Mickey probably did peak around 1940 with his role as the sorcerer's apprentice in *Fantasia*. Thereafter it was downhill—reaching a sort of

Garry Apgar, illustration for "Le Grand Charlie et le Petit Mickey" in *Paris Metro*, pen and ink, screentone, and Chinese white, on Bristol board, 1978. Walt Disney Family Foundation, San Francisco, Calif.

saccharine nadir with the Mickey Mouse Club of the 1950s. In 1944 "Mickey Mouse" had been the code during the Normandy landings; by the 1960s it had become another military code, standing this time for petty harassment.

Yet, the Mouse remains an image of optimism and pluck, and nowhere more than in France. This is one Disney crazed country! You're liable to run into Walt's progeny decorating custard cups, mustard jars, or postcard racks anywhere in town. And Uncle Scrooge—*Onc' Picsou*—has even graced magazine advertisements for a serious business weekly, *le Nouvel Economiste*. But for the biggest splash of Disneyana this side of Disneyworld, head over to Printemps' *"Boutique Mickey,"* where they've got a selection of Mickey Mouse and Disney toys from all over the world on sale. There are Disney puzzles, jewelry, games, posters, towels, you name it: in short, more Mouseware than Scrooge has got gold.

It's a Christmas season natural for kids because in addition to the Bostel exhibit they're also running several short films every hour (a promo film for Florida and Disneyworld)—and best of all, a 15-minute short dedicated to Mickey's 50th birthday celebration, featuring such sequences as the opening theme song from the Mouse Club and Donald Duck reciting "Mary had a little lamb" from an early color film.

• Jacques Chirac, future president of France, was mayor of Paris in 1978. During his tenure in office the palatial Hôtel de Ville or town hall (*"chez* Chirac"*) often was mockingly referred to by the French as "château Chirac." In French, "Petit Mickey," "petit miquet," or "petit micquet," are all slang terms for what, in English, we call cartoons.

Mickey Mouse
Meets Konrad Lorenz

Stephen Jay Gould

Natural History, May 1979

Age often turns fire to placidity. Lytton Strachey, in his incisive portrait of Florence Nightingale, writes of her declining years:

> Destiny, having waited very patiently, played a cruel trick on Miss Nightingale. The benevolence and public spirit of that long life had only been equalled by its acerbity. Her virtue had dwelt in hardness. . . . And now the sarcastic years brought the proud woman her punishment. She was not to die as she had lived. The sting was to be taken out of her; she was to be made soft; she was to be reduced to compliance and complacency.

I was therefore not surprised—although the analogy may strike some as sacrilegious—to discover that the creature who gave his name as a synonym for insipidity had a gutsier youth. Mickey Mouse turned a respectable fifty last year. To mark the occasion, many theaters replayed his debut performance in *Steamboat Willie* (1928). The original Mickey was a rambunctious, even slightly sadistic fellow. In a remarkable sequence, exploiting the exciting new development of sound, Mickey and Minnie pummel, squeeze, and twist the animals on board to produce a rousing chorus of "Turkey in the Straw." They honk a duck with a tight embrace, crank a goat's tail, tweak a pig's nipples, bang cow's teeth as a stand-in xylophone, and play bagpipe on her udder. Christopher Finch, in his semiofficial pictorial history of Disney's work, comments: "The Mickey Mouse who hit the movie houses in the late twenties was not quite the well-behaved character most of us are familiar with today. He was mischievous, to say the least, and even displayed a streak of cruelty" (*The Art of Walt Disney*). But Mickey soon cleaned up his act, leaving to gossip and speculation only his unresolved relationship with Minnie and the status of Morty and Ferdie. Finch continues: "Mickey . . . had become virtually a national symbol, and as such he was expected to behave properly at all times. If he occasionally stepped out of line, any number of letters would arrive at the Studio from citizens and organizations who felt that the nation's moral well-being was in their hands. . . . Eventually he would be pressured into the role of straight man."

As Mickey's personality softened, his appearance changed. Many Disney fans are aware of this transformation through time, but few (I suspect) have recognized the coordinating theme behind all the alterations—in fact, I am not sure that the Disney artists themselves explicitly realized what they were doing, since the changes appeared in such a halting and piecemeal fashion. In short, the blander and inoffensive Mickey became progressively more juvenile in appearance. (Since Mickey's chronological age never altered—like most cartoon characters he stands impervious to the ravages of time—this change in appearance at a constant age is a true evolutionary transformation. Progressive juvenilization as an evolutionary phenomenon is called neoteny. More on this later.)

The characteristic changes of form during human growth have inspired a substantial biological literature. Since the head-end of an embryo differentiates first and grows more rapidly in utero than the foot-end (an antero-posterior gradient, in technical language), a newborn child possesses a relatively large head attached to a medium sized body with diminutive legs and feet. This gradient is reversed through growth as legs and feet overtake the front end. Heads continue to grow but so much more slowly than the rest of the body that relative head size decreases.

During human growth, a suite of changes pervades the head itself. The brain grows very slowly after age three, and the bulbous cranium of a young child gives way to the more slanted, lower-browed configuration of adulthood. The eyes scarcely grow at all and relative eye size declines precipitously. But the jaw gets bigger and bigger. Children, compared with adults, have larger heads and eyes, smaller jaws, a more prominent, bulging cranium, and smaller, pudgier legs and feet. Adult heads are altogether more apish, I'm sorry to say.

As Mickey became increasingly well behaved over the years, his appearance became more youthful. Measurements of three stages in his development revealed a larger relative head size, larger eyes, and an enlarged cranium—all traits of juvenility. © The Walt Disney Company (this caption accompanied the image in Gould's original article).

Mickey, however, has traveled this ontogenetic pathway in reverse during fifty years among us. He has assumed an ever more childlike appearance as the ratty character of *Steamboat Willie* became the cute and inoffensive host to a magic kingdom. By 1940, the former tweaker of pig's nipples gets a kick in the ass for insubordination (as the *Sorcerer's Apprentice* in *Fantasia*). By 1953, his last cartoon, he has gone fishing and cannot even subdue a squirting clam.

The Disney artists transformed Mickey in clever silence, often using suggestive devices that mimic nature's own changes by different routes. To give him the shorter and pudgier legs of youth, they lowered his pants line and covered his spindly legs with a baggy outfit. (His arms and legs also thickened substantially—and acquired joints for a floppier appearance.) His head grew relatively larger and its features more youthful. The length of Mickey's snout has not altered, but decreasing protrusion is more subtly suggested by a pronounced thickening. Mickey's eye has grown in two modes: first, by a major, discontinuous evolutionary shift as the entire eye of ancestral Mickey became the pupil of his descendants, and second, by gradual increase thereafter.

Mickey's improvement in cranial bulging followed an interesting path since his evolution has always been constrained by the unaltered convention of representing his head as a circle with appended ears and an oblong snout. The circle's form could not be altered to provide a bulging cranium directly. Instead, Mickey's ears moved back, increasing the distance between nose and ears, and giving him a rounded, rather sloping forehead.

To give these observations the cachet of quantitative science, I applied my best pair of dial calipers to three stages of the official phylogeny—the thin-nosed, ears-forward figure of the early 1930s (stage 1), the latter-day Jack of *Mickey and the Beanstalk* (1947, stage 2), and the modern mouse (stage 3). I measured three signs of Mickey's creeping juvenility: increasing eye size (maximum height) as a percentage of head length (base of the nose to the top of rear ear); increasing head length as a percentage of body length; and increasing cranial vault size measured by rearward displacement of the front ear (base of the nose to top of front ear as a percentage of base of the nose to top of rear ear).

All three percentages increased steadily—eye size from 27 to 42 percent of head length; head length from 42.7 to 48.1 percent of body length; and nose to front ear from 71.7 to a whopping 95.6 percent of nose to rear ear. For comparison, I measured Mickey's young "nephew" Morty Mouse. In each case, Mickey has clearly been evolving toward youthful stages of his stock, although he still has a way to go for head length.

You may, indeed, now ask what an at least marginally respectable scientist has been doing with a mouse like that. In part, fiddling around and having fun, of course. (I still prefer *Pinocchio* to *Citizen Kane*.) But I do have a serious point—two in fact—to make. First, why did Disney choose to change his most famous character so gradually and persistently in the same direction? National symbols are not altered capriciously and market researchers (for the doll industry in particular) have spent a good deal of time and practical effort learning what features appeal to people as cute and friendly. Biologists also have spent a great deal of time studying a wide range of animals.

In one of his most famous articles, Konrad Lorenz argues that humans use the characteristic differences in form between babies and adults as important behavioral cues. He believes that features of juvenility trigger "innate releasing mechanisms" for affection and nurturing in adult humans. When we see a living creature with babyish features, we feel an automatic surge of disarming tenderness. The adaptive value of this response can scarcely be questioned, for we must nurture our babies. Lorenz, by the way, lists among his releasers the very features of babyhood that Disney affixed progressively to Mickey: "a relatively large head, predominance of the brain capsule, large and low-lying eyes, bulging cheek region, short and thick extremities, a springy elastic consistency, and clumsy movements."

I propose to leave aside for this article the contentious issue of whether or not our affectionate response to babyish features is truly innate and inherited directly from ancestral primates—as Lorenz argues—or whether it is simply learned from our immediate experience with babies and grafted upon an evolutionary predisposition for attaching ties of affection to certain learned signals. My argument works equally well in either case for I only claim that babyish features tend to elicit strong feelings of affection in adult humans.

Lorenz emphasizes the power that juvenile features hold over us, and the abstract quality of their influence, by pointing out that we judge other animals by the same criteria—although the judgment may be utterly inappropriate in an evolutionary context. We are, in short, fooled by an evolved response to our own babies, and we transfer our reaction to the same set of features in other animals.

Many animals, for reasons having nothing to do with the inspiration of affection in humans, possess some features also shared by human babies but not by human adults—large eyes and a bulging forehead with retreating chin, in particular. We are drawn to them, we cultivate them as pets, we stop and admire them in the wild—while we reject their small-eyed, long-snouted relatives who might make more affectionate companions or objects of admiration. Lorenz points out that the German names of many animals with features mimicking human babies end in the diminutive suffix *chen*, even though the animals are often larger than close relatives without such features—*Kotkehlchen* ("robin"), *Eichhörnchen* ("squirrel"), and *Kaninchen* ("rabbit"), for example.

In a fascinating section, Lorenz then enlarges upon our capacity for biologically inappropriate response to other animals, or even to inanimate objects that mimic human features. "The most amazing objects can acquire remarkable, highly emotional values by 'experiential attachment' of human properties. . . . Steeply rising, somewhat overhanging cliff faces or dark storm-clouds piling up have the same, immediate display value as a human being who is standing at full height and leaning slightly forwards"—that is, threatening.

We cannot help regarding a camel as aloof and unfriendly because it mimics, quite unwittingly and for other reasons, the "gesture of haughty rejection" common to so many human cultures. In this gesture, we raise our heads, placing our nose above our eyes. We then half-close our eyes and blow out through our nose—the "harumph" of the stereotyped upper-class Englishman or his well-trained servant. "All this," Lorenz argues quite cogently, "symbolizes resistance against all sensory modalities emanating from the disdained counterpart." But the poor camel cannot help carrying its nose above its elongated eyes, with mouth drawn down. As Lorenz reminds us, if you wish to know whether a camel will eat out of your hand or spit, look at its ears, not the rest of its face.

In his important book *Expression of the Emotions in Man and Animals*, published in 1872, Charles Darwin traced the evolutionary basis of many common gestures to originally adaptive actions in animals later internalized as symbols in humans. Thus, he argued for evolutionary continuity of emotion, not only of form. We snarl and raise our upper lip in fierce anger—to expose our nonexistent fighting canine tooth. Our gesture of disgust repeats the facial actions associated with the highly adaptive act of vomiting in necessary circumstances. Darwin concluded, much to the distress of many Victorian contemporaries: "With mankind some expressions, such as the bristling of the hair under the influence of extreme terror, or the uncovering of the teeth under that of furious rage, can hardly be understood, except on the belief that man once existed in a much lower and animal-like condition."

In any case, the abstract features of human childhood elicit powerful emotional responses in us, even when they occur in other animals. I submit that Mickey Mouse's evolutionary road down the course of his own growth in reverse reflects the unconscious discovery of this very biological principle by Disney and his artists. In fact, the emotional status of most Disney characters rests on the same set of distinctions. And to this extent, the magic kingdom trades on a biological illusion— our ability to abstract and our propensity to transfer inappropriately to other animals the fitting responses we make to changing form in the growth of our own species.

Donald Duck also adopts more juvenile features through time. His elongated beak recedes and his eyes enlarge; he converges on Huey, Louie, and Dewey as surely as Mickey approaches Morty. But Donald,

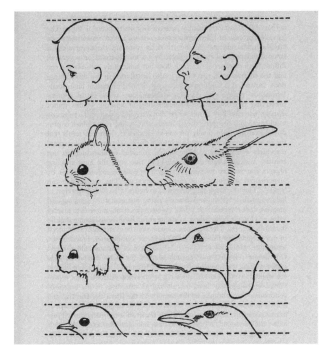

Humans feel affection for animals with juvenile features: large eyes, bulging craniums, retreating chins (left column). Small-snouted animals (right column) do not elicit the same response (illustration and caption from Gould's original article).

having inherited the mantle of Mickey's original misbehavior, remains more adult in form with his projecting beak and more sloping forehead.

Mouse villains or sharpies, contrasted with Mickey, are always more adult in appearance, although they often share Mickey's chronological age. In 1936, for example, Disney made a short entitled *Mickey's Rival.* Mortimer, a dandy in a yellow sports car, intrudes upon Mickey and Minnie's quiet country picnic. The thoroughly disreputable Mortimer has a head only 29 percent of body length, to Mickey's 45, and a snout 80 percent of head length compared with Mickey's 49. (Nonetheless, and was it ever different, Minnie transfers her affection until an obliging bull from a neighboring field dispatches Mickey's rival.) Consider also the exaggerated adult features of other Disney characters—the swaggering bully Peg-leg Pete or the simple, lovable, dolt Goofy.

As a second, serious biological comment on Mickey's odyssey in form, I note that his path to eternal youth repeats, in epitome, our own evolutionary story. For humans are neotenic. We have evolved by retaining to adulthood the originally juvenile features of our ancestors. Our australiopithecene forebears, like Mickey in *Steamboat Willie*, had projecting jaws and low vaulted craniums.

Our embryonic skulls scarcely differ from those of chimpanzees. And we follow the same path of changing form through growth: relative decrease of the cranial vault since brains grow so much more slowly than bodies after birth, and continuous relative increase of the jaw. But while chimps accelerate these changes, producing an adult strikingly different in form from a baby, we proceed much more slowly down the same path and never get nearly so far. Thus, as adults, we retain juvenile features. To be sure, we change enough to produce a notable difference between baby and adult, but our alteration is far smaller than that experienced by chimps and other primates.

A marked slowdown of developmental rates has triggered our neoteny. Primates are slow developers among mammals. We have very long periods of gestation, markedly extended childhoods, and the longest life span of any mammal. The morphological features of eternal youth have served us well. Our enlarged brain is, at least in part, a result of extending rapid prenatal growth rates to later ages. (In all mammals, the brain grows rapidly in utero but often very little after birth. We have extended this fetal phase into postnatal life.)

And the changes in timing themselves have been just as important. We are preeminently learning animals, and our extended childhood permits the transference of culture by education. Many animals display flexibility and play in childhood but follow rigidly programmed patterns as adults. Lorenz writes, in the same article above: "The characteristic which is so vital for the human peculiarity of the true man—that of always remaining: in a state of development—is quite certainly a gift which we owe to the neotenous nature of mankind."

In short, we, like Mickey, never grow up although we, alas, do grow old. Best wishes to you, Mickey, for your next half century. May we stay as young as you, but grow a bit wiser.

We Are Mickey:
Meet the Men behind the Mouse

Charles Solomon

People Weekly, November 7, 1988

Mickey Mouse's familiar personality is actually a mosaic. Each of the animators, artists, writers and voice actors who worked with him has seen him a little differently and added a little of his own vision to the world's most recognized cartoon character.

Wayne Allwine: "The tendency to make him too nice has limited him. But he's an actor, and he's capable of doing whatever he's given to do—provided it's kept in the context of what Mickey would and wouldn't do. I've had people ask to hear him swear, but I'd never do that—he's too special. With the prospect of more short subjects coming up, we're trying to direct him more toward Walt's version of Mickey, who was an actor. I think the character is still as Walt envisioned him: forever young and forever optimistic. Walt always has been very much alive in Mickey Mouse."

Floyd Norman: "By the time I picked him up in 1986, Mickey just seemed to be hanging around the house. He was sort of a laid-back, middle-aged guy who reacted to his nephews or Goofy or whatever happened around him. I try to push him in a more vigorous direction and to think of him as being a little younger—certainly not a retiree."

Roman Arambula: "Mickey is not just one personality—he couldn't be, because he's been done by so many artists. As an artist, I have to be myself, so the Mickey I draw is my Mickey. When Mickey's talking to his nephews, I can relate to him because I talk to my children or my nephews the same way. When he talks to Minnie, I'm talking to my girlfriend. I make him act by giving him life the way I feel it."

Glen Keane: "Mickey takes a leap forward whenever an animator makes him his own and isn't afraid of flexing the design a little to personalize him. The worst thing for animators is to be afraid of Mickey, so they don't put something of themselves into him. If you approach him too reverently, you end up with a lifeless, stiff icon, instead of a real flesh-and-blood character."

Ollie Johnston: "I never felt that Mickey was a part of me, the way other characters I've drawn were—like Pinocchio or Thumper in *Bambi*. I always felt Walt's presence very strongly when I worked with him. Mickey reflected Walt's boyhood personality and did a lot of the things Walt had wanted to do himself—rescuing princesses, beating up bullies, putting on variety shows."

Frank Thomas: "I think Walt saw Mickey as having the spirit of a nine-year-old boy with the capability of a 14 year old—but he also thought of him as ageless. In the beginning, Mickey was a different character in each picture, but all the Mickeys had something of Chaplin in them."

Mark Henn: "There are definitely some limits to the character. He's not clumsy or mean-spirited or hot-tempered. But he can get angry—and should, I think, when the situation calls for it. He's a hero; he represents all the good things in people. But even good people get angry at bad things, so why can't Mickey? Just to say he's a good guy who would never hurt a fly is too extreme. I like to think of him as the kind of person who's good at whatever he does. I'd liken him to the stars of the golden era, who could play any role, from tragedy to comedy. Like Cary Grant or Fred Astaire or Laurence Olivier. Mickey represents class."

• Of Solomon's seven interviewees four were animators (Keane, Johnston, Thomas, and Henn), one a voice actor (Allwine), another a comic-strip writer (Norman), and the last of the group a comic-strip artist (Arambula).

Mickey Mouse's Age

Lawrence Van Gelder

By now, is there anyone from the Hudson to the Dnieper and beyond who doesn't know that today is Mickey Mouse's 60th birthday?

But how do we know?

Meet David R. Smith.

The 48-year-old Mr. Smith bears the title of archivist of the Walt Disney Company, a position he has held since 1970. He established the archives during what he thought was a two-month leave of absence from his job as librarian at the University of California at Los Angeles.

These days, Mr. Smith presides over a six-member department occupying 8,000 square feet of space—about the size of three three-bedroom houses, he said—in the Roy O. Disney Building, named for Walt's brother, on the grounds of the Disney Studio in Burbank, Calif.

The domain includes the business records of the company, from 1923 to the present, the creative records (everything from artwork and scripts for movies to blueprints and models for Disneyland) and a catch-all category that covers films, books, recordings, merchandise, publicity materials and newspaper articles (including, soon, this one).

"One of my favorite things," Mr. Smith said, noting that some historians had asserted that the company founder was incapable of drawing Mickey Mouse, "is an actual drawing of Mickey Mouse by Walt Disney."

Over the years, Mr. Smith added, the archive has made a determined effort to build up a sample collection of the toys, games and other merchandise licensed by the company. "The earliest one we have is a stencil set of Oswald the Lucky Rabbit, a character Walt Disney had prior to

Mickey Mouse," Mr. Smith said. "It dates to early 1928. Mickey came in Nov. 18, 1928. That's one point I'm very proud of."

"I'm the one who established the date of Mickey's birth," he continued. "It needs a little background. When I got to the archives in 1970, I discovered many different dates had been used for Mickey's birthdays. This had started back in the early 30's, when Mickey was celebrating his fifth birthday or his seventh birthday. They would pick a nice Saturday in the fall when they could get a lot of kids in the theaters.

"But all along, they had said Mickey was born essentially when his first film was seen by the public at the Colony Theater in New York, and that was 'Steamboat Willie.' But nobody had ever bothered to look up to see what date that was. So we started doing the research, and I actually found the program from the Colony Theater for that particular night." Other supporting evidence was found as well.

"So," Mr. Smith said, "from then on, we have used that date."

Mr. Smith, who is the son of librarians, said, "Probably, if you think of all the companies in the world, there is no other company that re-uses its history so much as Disney." Donald Duck's 50th birthday was celebrated in 1984, and the 50th anniversary of "Snow White and the Seven Dwarfs" was observed last year.

Coming up in 1990: 50th anniversaries for "Fantasia" and "Pinocchio."

Mr. Smith says so. And he knows what happens if you tell a lie.

The Masks of Mickey Mouse

Robert W. Brockway

Journal of Popular Culture 22, no. 4. Copyright © 1989.
Reproduced with permission of Blackwell Publishing Ltd.

From time to time in his later years, Walt Disney tried to explain the
enduring popularity of Mickey Mouse. The animated cartoon character he created in 1928 always baffled him. Mickey continues to baffle
critics today. Over the years since Mickey Mouse first appeared, just
before the Wall Street Crash, he has undergone a series of metamorphoses, and has actually grown up with the generation born during the
teens and twenties. He was still popular when Disney died in 1966, and
his fiftieth birthday was celebrated by national festivities including a
black tie party at the Library of Congress attended by the President of
the United States.[1] In part, the continued popularity of Mickey Mouse
has been whimsey, in part nostalgia, but some critics find deeper significance in the little chap made of circles and clad in red short pants
with white buttons. He has become an archetypal symbol, not only to
Americans but to people everywhere, especially to the generation that
was young during the thirties. They are the Mickey Mouse Generation.

The meteoric rise of Mickey Mouse and Disney astonished the film
industry. In later years Disney sometimes mused over the vastness of
his corporate empire and murmured, "We must never forget that it was
all built by a mouse." The phenomenal success of his character never
ceased to fascinate him and the critics. Not only was Mickey instantly
popular among ordinary people young and old, but with intellectuals,
artists, and heads of state.

By 1933 the Mickey Mouse craze was global. George V decreed that
there must be a Mickey Mouse cartoon at all film performances attended at the palace by the royal family and their guests. The Emperor
of Japan wore a Mickey Mouse watch. Known by many names in many
languages, Mickey was adored by the whole world. He was listed in

Who's Who and *Encyclopedia Britannica* devoted an article to him. What is most intriguing, the global fondness for Mickey Mouse has endured more than five decades.[2] What is most fascinating is his complexity. Disney once tried to account for Mickey's appeal by his simplicity, saying that he is easy to understand. He is not. He is as complex as Disney was himself and as profound in his symbolic and mythic implications as any mythic or fairy tale character. He is what Harold Schechter calls a "new god."

Being composed of wafers, he also evokes the mysteries of the circular design which some authorities find profoundly significant as an archetypal figure. Such a phenomenon can scarcely be dismissed as frivolous. While technical innovation and commercial promotion account for some of Mickey's popularity as a film star, his remarkable endurance shows that his creator unwittingly touched something deep in the human psyche.

Although the ultimate origin of Mickey Mouse may have been a pet field mouse named Mortimer, whom Disney tamed when he was in Kansas City, and mice appear in an early *Alice's Wonderland* film, Disney claims to have conceived of the Mouse during a train trip back to Los Angeles from New York in March, 1927. He had just lost his Oswald the Rabbit series and nearly all of his animators to the New York distributor Charles Mintz. "But was I downhearted?" he later wrote, "Not a bit! For out of the trouble and confusion stood a mocking, merry little figure. Vague and indefinite at first. But it grew and grew and grew. And finally arrived-a mouse. A romping, rollicking, little mouse. . . . The idea completely engulfed me. The wheels turned to the tune of 'Chug, chug mouse! Chug, chug, mouse! The whistle screeched it. 'A m-moua-ouse,' it wailed. By the time the train had reached the Middle West I had dressed my dream mouse in a pair of red velvet pants with two huge pearl button, had composed the first scenario and was all set."[3]

On his return to California, with all of his staff but one signed up [by] Mintz and producing Oswald films, the Disney brothers and the one loyal animator secretly created the new character. He called the mouse Mortimer until his wife Lillian persuaded him to change the name to Mickey, which she thought was less pompous. (According to another version of the story, the name was suggested by a distributor.)

Mickey Mouse was drawn by Ubbe Ert Iwerks, the son of a Missouri barber from Holland with a first name which sounds odd even to most Dutchmen. Iwerks shortened it to Ub. Walt and Ub, who were the same age, met in 1919. Both were trying to become animators. Of the two, Ub was by far the more talented at the drawing board. In fact, Disney was never able to draw his own creation, Mickey Mouse.

Ub secretly drew the first two films, producing seven hundred frames a day. They were *Plane Crazy*, inspired by the Lindbergh flight, and *The Gallopin' Gaucho*, in which Mickey was a swashbuckler like Douglas Fairbanks. Both animated cartoons were silent films. None of the distributors were interested in Mickey Mouse, and Disney decided to make an animated cartoon with sound. Although Lee DeForest had developed a practical sound system for film in 1923, none of the studios showed interest until Warner Brothers staved off bankruptcy in 1927 by producing *The Jazz Singer* with Al Jolson. After that all the studios produced talkies, but none of the animators except Disney dared to try the new technique. Disney made another trip to New York and contracted use of the Cinephone sound equipment from a freebooter in the film industry named Pat Powers. On his return to Los Angeles, the Disneys hired a new staff of animators and, after much experimentation, developed a workable technique for making animated cartoons with sound. They made *Steamboat Willie* in which Mickey and Minnie Mouse cavort aboard a boat carrying animals, piloted by Pegleg Pete who was to become Mickey's arch-rival. Mickey rescues Minnie from Pegleg Pete's unwelcome advances and, in the course of the river journey, plays a cow's teeth like a xylophone, her udder as bagpipes, and Minnie twists a goat's tail and plays him like a hurdy-gurdy.

Steamboat Willie opened at the Colony Theater in New York on November 18, 1928. And thus Mickey Mouse was born. He appeared in theaters all over America during 1930. Powers, the distributor, contracted for more Mickey Mouse cartoons. Disney studio hired more staff and remade and released *Plane Crazy* and *The Gallopin' Gaucho*. They also agreed to make six more and soon were producing Mickey Mouse reels at the rate of one every four weeks. Early in 1931 a syndicated Mickey Mouse comic strip drawn by Iwerks appeared and Herman (Kay) Kamen, a New York merchandiser, licensed the manufacture of figurines, dolls, and other items including a Mickey/Minnie handcar on a circular rail and Mickey Mouse watches. The first saved the Lionel

Company from bankruptcy and the second the Ingersoll-Waterbury Watch Company. The tiny, obscure Disney studio became a corporate success, and Mickey Mouse was popular throughout the entire world.

Mickey's chief rival was Pat Sullivan's Felix the Cat, created by Pat Sullivan and drawn by Otto Messmer. Felix was sometimes called the Charlie Chaplin of cartoon characters. "Like Chaplin, Felix is a loner in a hostile world, who combines resourcefulness and a touch of viciousness to survive."

According to Mark Langer, "What was most appealing about Felix was his personality. He had his distinctive pensive walk, head down and hands clasped behind . . . " His versatile, prehensile tail could be a baseball bat, fishing hook, or telescope. The stories concocted by Raoul Barré were good. Leonard Maltin considers Felix to have been the equal of Mickey Mouse in every respect save sound. "Felix is as recognizable and rounded a character as any later cartoon character. Mickey's only initial advantage was sound. As the aging Iwerks recently told John Culhane, Mickey "was the standardized thing . . . , Pear shaped body, ball on top, couple of thin legs. You gave it long ears and it was a rabbit. Short ears, it was a cat, Ears hanging down, a dog . . . With an elongated nose it became a mouse. . . ." Iwerks' comment is overly modest. He improved the animating style of the day. The conventional style of drawing originated with animated cartooning itself, an art invented at the turn-of-the-century by French and American pioneers such as J. S. Blackton. During the teens, the art was developed by animators such as Winsor McCay with his "Gertie the Dinosaur." Little progress was made in drawing style during the twenties until Ub Iwerks (who is sometimes called the forgotten man of animation), introduced a more fluid style as well as more refined drawing technique.[4]

The cartoon style of the twenties was slapstick. While it has ancient and medieval antecedents, slapstick as a comic film style originated in France at the turn of the century; it was enormously popular among the urban proletariat. According to Durgnat, ". . . French comedies swarmed with comic stuntmen called *cascadeurs*, who, in Nicole Védrès's words, 'really did perform the plunge from the third storey into a tub of washing; and at the exact moment that the floor of a room fell through, each man knew precisely where to leap—one onto the piano, another onto the aspidistra—silk hats still on their heads, lorgnettes dangling, beards a-quiver."[5]

The comic style which Disney exploited in the Mickey Mouse films of the early thirties was derived from Mack Sennett's slapstick comedy. Sennett studied the French slapstick films and adapted the technique to produce the "Keystone Kops." According to Durgnat, "American comedy continued to derive poetry from coupling simple and violent attitudes with a delirium of physical and mechanical knockabout." With Sennett there was a shift from the American music hall's older style of character comedy to that of the mechanized man. "Thus Sennett's films register not only the shock of speed but the spreading concept of man as an impersonal physical object existing only to work rapidly, rhythmically, repetitively. But Sennett parodies the conception, to concoct a universe where authority, routine, and the monotony of factory days are shattered as cars burst into bedrooms and beds race down the highway. Comedy, by exaggeration, veers toward revolt, an orgy of disorder, a Saturnalia of chaos."

According to Durgnat, slapstick emerges from childlike impulsiveness, dream fantasy, and visual poetry. The "slapstick comedians are childlike, and . . . act out impulses which as adults we suppress."[6] This was the style of comedians who delighted audiences during the twenties. Chaplin, Arbuckle, Keaton, and Lloyd learned their craft from Sennett's "Keystone Kops" and went on to develop their own styles. The early animators such as Sullivan and Fleischer exploited the same slapstick style and so did Disney.

During the thirties, tastes changed. Durgnat notes that "if anything, the comic tone took an upbeat turn. The earlier movies took poverty matter-of-factly. But when it became a national problem too, and the subject of optimistic pronouncements from complacent Republicans as from dynamic New Dealers, a more optimistic frame of reference was introduced. The cinema had, from its very beginnings, been steadily rising in the social scale, and the middle classes are far more decorous and squeamish about the seamy side of life than the lower classes; the Hays Code (1933) marks the middle class dominance. Further, the grimness of life made everyone all the more responsive to sentimental escapism."[7] While slapstick continued to delight, there was public demand for new comic modes, and so Disney started *Silly Symphonies* in 1932. These short cartoons were masterpieces of charm, sentiment, and escape.

By 1934 Disney was complaining that Mickey had become a problem child. "He's such an institution that we're limited in what we can do with him. If we have Mickey kicking someone in the pants, we get a million letters from mothers scolding us for giving kids the wrong idea."[8] The problem was solved by introducing a supporting cast which included Donald Duck who made his debut in *The Wise Little Hen* in 1934. He soon upstaged Mickey as slapstick comic and the latter became a straight man. Mickey was born again. The barnyard bratty kid gave way to the likeable small town fellow in oversize coat with brass buttons and braid who conducts the band in the town park on a Sunday afternoon. He is plagued by a bratty Donald Duck who keeps playing a flute while the band is trying to perform "The William Tell Overture." If *Steamboat Willie* was the *rite de passage* marking Mickey's birth, *The Band Concert* was his initiation into maturity. There was a new Mickey Mouse audience, and Mickey was born again

In later years, Disney said that the Mickey Mouse film was addressed to an audience "made up of parts of people; of that deathless, ageless, absolutely primitive remnant of something in every world-wracked human being which makes us play with children's toys and laugh without self-consciousness at silly things, and sing in the bathtub, and dream ..."[9]

The Mickey Mouse film was primarily addressed to the inner child in the adult rather than to actual children, few of whom had money of their own for theater tickets. While Mickey was ostensibly reborn for commercial reasons, the change had profound psychological implications. Disney often said, "There's a lot of Mickey in me!" There was. There was also a lot of Mickey in the Mickey Mouse audience. He and they were growing up.

As Jacobs noted in 1939, Disney exhibited rare artistic idealism and integrity for a business man, especially during the 1930s. "Money is important indirectly," Disney said, "experimentation comes first. Quality is the thing we have striven most to put in our pictures." He added, "... I don't favor much commercialization. Most producers think it is better to get while the getting is good. We have not operated that way."[10]

Disney was attuned to the soul of Middle America, he shared its values himself, and was exceptionally sensitive to its changing moods. A theater-going public which liked Andy Hardy, the bashful Jimmy Stewart of *You Can't Take It With You*, and, above all, the Chaplin of *Modern Times* wanted a kindhearted and gentle, youthful but grown up Mickey Mouse. The new Mickey of the middle and late thirties was sometimes the heroic dragon-slayer who rescues Minnie from the pirates, the desperadoes and Pegleg Pete. More often he was the bourgeois do-gooder. He moved from the farm to the small town and from there to the suburbs. He became the neighborly Middle American young fellow who lives next door, "Mr. Nice Guy."

New in-house instructions for drawing Mickey were prepared in 1934 by Ted Sears and Fred Moore. They wrote: "Mickey is not a clown . . . he is neither silly nor dumb. His comedy depends entirely upon the situation he is placed in. His age varies with the situation . . . sometimes his character is that of a young boy, and at times, as in the adventure type of picture, he appears quite grown up. . . . Mickey is most amusing when he is in a serious predicament trying to accomplish some purpose under difficulties or against time. . . ." Moore adds[,] "Mickey seems to be the average young boy of no particular age, living in a small town, clean living, fun loving, bashful around girls, polite and clever. . . . In some stories he has a touch of Fred Astaire, in others of Charlie Chaplin, and in some of Douglas Fairbanks, but in all of these there should be some of the young boy."[11]

Fantasia (1940) was Mickey's finest hour. Here Mickey is the apprentice in Paul Dukas's *The Sorcerer and the Apprentice*, a story by Goethe. Mickey, when in the sorcerer's cap, commands the sea, winds, clouds, and stars like a god.

No Mickey Mouse films were made during the war years. The few films made during the late 1940s and early 1950s portray Mickey as the likeable suburbanite in pastoral settings, with the comic roles entirely taken over by Pluto and other supporting characters. His last movie was *The Simple Things* in 1954. The short film had become too expensive to produce and the thirties-type presentation with short subjects and cartoon followed by feature, gave way to the double feature just before Hollywood succumbed to television. Again, Disney and his alter ego Mickey were quick to adapt to the new medium and the Mickey Mouse Club appeared.

During the mid-fifties, as the genial host of Disneyland in tails, Mickey underwent a third *rite de passage* in his life journey. He climbed to the top of the Disney corporate empire as the corporate image. This was his most recent metamorphosis. The middle-aged Mickey mirrors the world of the corporate executive. He became an "organization man." He also became the king of the Magic Kingdom and his appearances took on the mystique of monarchy. He acquired *noblesse oblige* and patrician charm. He became avuncular; he was often seen nuzzling small children with nurturant affection on Main Street, U.S.A., in Disneyland. He became gentle and sentimental.

Disney was often taciturn in his later years. Mickey was not. When Disney died in 1966, *Paris Match* featured a cover in which a sad Mickey has a large tear in his eye.

The recent founding of Magic Kingdoms in Japan and France attest to Mickey's continued popularity abroad. He remains well beloved throughout the world. By no means all of his loyal devotees are either very old or very young. Many are youthful and middle-aged. Many experience something akin to mystical experience in his presence.

Recently he was in trouble. Trade articles with titles like "Wishing Upon a Falling Star at Disney" lamented "What a great studio Disney used to be."[12] The crowds who attended Disneyland during the Los Angeles Summer Olympics in 1984 fell below corporation hopes and expectations. But both Disney Studios and Mickey have since recovered. Mickey continues to be a symbol. To test this point, David Bain showed the cartoon title card with Mickey's beaming face in a sunburst to an infant who reached out for the cheerful image which made him feel happy. He invites anyone to try the same experiment.[13] During the late fifties, Dr. Tom Dooley, who ran a hospital ship off the coast of Southeast Asia, found that he could not entice children to come for medical help until he obtained permission to paint Mickey Mouse on the hull of the ship. The children never had seen Mickey before, but were drawn by the figure. Such experiences as these, and they have been numerous, intrigue commentators familiar with the archetypal theories of C. G. Jung.

Among those who have attempted to interpret the popularity of Mickey Mouse in terms of analytic psychology are the aging Ub Iwerks, who drew him, and John Hench, who was the vice-President of WED, the Disney corporation which manages Disneyland and Disneyworld.

According to Iwerks, ". . . Mickey's face is a trinity of wafers—and the circular symbol, as C. G. Jung has told us, always points to the single most vital aspect of life—its ultimate wholeness." "Simple round forms portray the archetype of self which, as we know, in experience, play the chief role in uniting irreconcilable opposites and is therefore best suited to compensate the single-mindedness of the age."[14]

Hench, who came to Disney studio in 1939 as an artist, suggests that Disney art was able "to exploit very old survival patterns, a case in point being Mickey Mouse who is composed of circles." Mickey "has been accepted all over the world, and there is obviously no problem of people responding to this set of circles. I'm going to oversimplify this, but circles never cause anybody any trouble. We have had bad experiences with sharp points, with angles, but circles are things we have fun with—babies, women's behinds, breasts. So Mickey was made this way, while a contemporary known as Felix the Cat didn't get anywhere. He has points all over him like a cactus. He has practically disappeared while we couldn't get rid of Mickey if we tried . . ."[15] Circles are "very reassuring—people have had millions of years experience with curved objects and they have never been hurt by them. It's the pointed things that give you trouble. Imagine putting a set of dynamic curves together around a design that has the power that this one does, so that he goes all around the world and no one thinks of him as an American import. They give him a name and then it's all a déjà vu experience. They respond to the curves.[16]

According to Harold Schecter, who interprets popular culture in Jungian terms, Mickey is a trickster, the archaic and universally encountered god who, according to Jung, evokes the shadow, the seamy side of the personal unconscious, akin to the Freudian id. According to Jung, the shadow refers to impulses "which appear morally, aesthetically, or intellectually inadmissible, and are repressed on account of their incompatibility." When the shadow appears in dreams it represents that which is bestial. "The dream confronts the individual with the very thing which he resents; it is presented as an integral part of his own personality and as one that may not be disregarded without danger."[17]

According to Edward Whitmont, "The shadow can also stand for the less individualized part of the personality, the *collective* shadow which

corresponds of the most primitive, archaic level of the human mind—
the level which links us with our animal past—often symbolized by a
beast or some sort of anthropomorphized animal.[18]

In myth the shadow is encountered as the trickster. The latter is an
archaic and virtually universal mythic figure such as Coyote among
some American Indians and Loki among the ancient Norse. According
to Jung, the trickster has persisted from archaic times to the present
in the medieval jester and Punch and Judy. Since the antecedents of
slapstick comics such as Sennett's "Keystone Kops" are of this tradition
of farce, it follows that Krazy Kat, Felix the Cat, and Mickey Mouse are
as well. Because of his various metamorphoses in the course of his development, Mickey Mouse is much more complex than the other animated figures, none of which progressed past the slapstick stage.

Disney posed as a philistine and often ridiculed intellectuals and
their theories about his characters and creations. He always insisted
that he was only an entertainer. Yet, though inarticulate in the expression of ideas, he frequently disclosed deep intuitive understanding and
philosophical wisdom. He, too, recognized the archetypal nature of
Mickey Mouse, though he did not put it in theoretical terms. Disney
realized that he had unwittingly touched a very deep chord in the human psyche and that Mickey Mouse was far more than a comic-strip
character.

Mickey may live to see the year 2001, the centennial of Disney's
birth, but he may not survive much beyond. As an archetypal form,
Mickey Mouse seems to be temporally bound to those generations
who grew up during the teens, twenties, and thirties of the present century. Only they seem to respond to him. In essence, the Mickey Mouse
Generation is the Depression Generation. Mickey has some impact on
younger people but far less than upon those born during the inter-war
years. That generation is now senior and it is also diminishing. All gods
eventually die, and Mickey is no exception. But, being immortals, all
gods rise. Mickey, too, may be reborn in some future imaginary character of the popular culture of which he is an avatar. In past ages we knew
him as Dionysus and Pan. Future generations will encounter him again.

Notes

[**ed.**: Brockway's essay as first published in 1989 was marred by a number of errors or lapses, primarily in the endnote apparatus. In 1993, a second version of the essay appeared in a collection of Brockway's writings, *Myth From the Ice Age to Mickey Mouse* (State University of New York Press), with significant changes to the original—deletions, additions, but with the introduction of further editorial errors. The text in this anthology follows the original 1989 essay. Several errors in the endnotes have been addressed here in editorial remarks appended to the affected notes. Three endnotes had no corresponding endnote marks in the body of the text. Those phantom notes were deleted and the remaining notes renumbered.]

1. John Culhane, "A Mouse For All Seasons," *Saturday Review*, November 11, 1978, p. 50.

2. Richard Schickel, *The Disney Version*, New York: Avon Books, 1968, p. 125.

3. Ibid., p. 116.

4. Leonard Maltin, *Of Mice and Magic: A History of American Animated Cartoons*, New York: New American Library, 1980, pp. 2, 4, 23. [**ed.:** These pages relate chiefly to Winsor McKay's *Gertie the Dinosaur*. The comment in Brockway's article about Felix the Cat being "as recognizable and rounded a character as any later cartoon character," is a garbled version of what Maltin said on p. 26 in *Mice and Magic*. The quote at the end of the preceding paragraph in Brockway's text ("Like Chaplin, Felix is a loner in a hostile world . . .") should have been credited to Mark Langer, from a program note by Langer for a Messmer-Felix retrospective at MoMA in 1976. The lead quote in this paragraph ("What was most appealing about Felix . . ."), misattributed in Brockway's original essay, to "Max" Langer, is a jumbled conflation of separate remarks by Leonard Maltin in *Mice and Magic*, 24.]

5. Raymond Durgnat, *The Crazy Mirror: Hollywood Comedy and the American Image*, New York: Dell Publishing Co., 1969, p. 67.

6. Ibid., pp. 69, 71, 72.

7. Ibid., p. 117.

8. Christopher Finch, *Walt Disney From Mickey Mouse to Magic Kingdom*, New York: Harry M. Abrams, 1973, p. 137 [**ed.:** There is no textual material at

all on p. 137 of Finch's book, which Brockway may have confused with a book by Maltin, *The Disney Film*, also published in 1973, in which Walt is quoted saying: "If we have Mickey kicking someone in the pants, we get a million letters from mothers telling us we're giving their kids wrong ideas."]

9. Ibid., p. 139. [**ed.**: Another dead-end; the quote from Walt regarding "something in every world-wracked human being" appears on the last page of an article by Roy Disney in *Reader's Digest* in 1969.]

10. Lewis Jacobs, *The Rise of the American Film*, New York: Teachers College Press, 1968, p. 499.

11. Culhane, "A Mouse For All Seasons," *Saturday Review*, p. 51. [**ed.**: 50, not 51.]

12. Bart Mills, "Disney Looks for a Happy Ending to Its Grim Fairy Tales," *American Film*, July–August 1982, p. 52.

13. David Bain, Bruce Harris, *Mickey Mouse: Fifty Happy Years*, New York: Harmony Books, 1977, p. 1.

14. Culhane, "A Mouse For All Seasons," *Saturday Review*, p. 51 [**ed.**: 50, where Culhane himself, not Iwerks, said that "Mickey's face is a trinity of wafers."].

15. "Two Disney Artists," *The Harvard Journal of Pictorial Fiction*, spring 1975, p. 35.

16. Charles Haas, "Disneyland is Good For You," *New West*, December 4, 1978, p. 18.

17. C. G. Jung, *The Structure and Dynamics of the Psyche*, CW VIII, par. 310.

18. Edward C. Whitmont, *The Symbolic Quest: Basic Concepts of Analytical Psychology*, New York: Harper & Row, 1973, pp. 161f.

7. Into a New Millennium

1991–2012

There has been a boom over the past quarter-century in research and writings about Walt Disney and Mickey Mouse, with a noticeable uptick in contributions from Academe. As a result, over three-fifths of the principal bibliography at the back of this book date from 1991 or later. None of which, incidentally, reflects an almost decade-long proliferation of Internet activity. The best of the Web in terms of material relating to Walt and his flagship character are probably a pair of Internet sites managed, respectively, by Michael Barrier and Didier Ghez: MichaelBarrier.com, subtitled "Exploring the World of Animated Films and Comic Art," and "Disney History" (http://disneybooks.blogspot .com).

It may be no coincidence that John Updike's "The Mystery of Mickey Mouse,"* arguably the most satisfying single work thus far on the Mouse, appeared in 1991, just as this surge in interest was gathering steam. Updike's essay was followed, in 1992, by "Mickey, A Mouse of Influence Around The World," a brisk op-ed piece by Marshall Fishwick,* one of the founding fathers of American pop-culture studies, and, in 1994, by *Disney Discourse: Producing the Magic Kingdom* (Routledge), a collection of interdisciplinary essays in the critical spirit of Richard Schickel's *The Disney Version*. Richard DeCordova's analysis of the marketing of Mickey Mouse in the 1930s* was a highlight of *Disney Discourse*, edited by Eric Smoodin, professor of American Studies at the University of California-Davis, whose writings on Disney have helped sustain a growing corpus of theory-driven scholarship on the subject.

In 1995, "An American Icon Scampers in for a Makeover," by the distinguished historian of animation at New York University, John Canemaker, appeared in the *New York Times*,* and in 1996, the founder of the Walt Disney Archives in Burbank, Dave Smith (profiled in the previous section by Lawrence Van Gelder*), published *Disney A to Z: The Official Encyclopedia*, now in its third revised edition, which remains a handy resource for research and reflection on Mickey and all things Disney.

Finally, it is fitting that the three items that close out this *Reader*, like many during Mickey's early years, are relatively short . . . and pegged to current events, thereby proving that "Disney discourse" is far from being a solely academic matter. Bill Hutchinson's 2007 piece in the *New York Daily News* focused on Diane Disney Miller's reaction to a rip-off Mickey character that was "used on a new Hamas TV show to encourage Palestinian children to take up arms against Israel and America." Sean Alfano's 2010 *Daily News* story describes a provocative image in Poland involving Mickey, while AP writer Sarah El Deeb, in 2012, reported on a media magnate in Egypt prosecuted for tweeting a cartoon of "a bearded Mickey Mouse and veiled Minnie."

Clearly, Mickey is, and promises to remain, a lively and consequential figure in global and American culture.

The Mystery of Mickey Mouse

John Updike

Untitled introduction to Craig Yoe and Janet Morra-Yoe, eds., *The Art of Mickey Mouse* (Hyperion, 1991). From *More Matter: Essays and Criticism*, by John Updike. Used by permission of Alfred A. Knopf, a division of Random House, Inc. Any third party use of this material, outside of this publication, is prohibited. Interested parties must apply directly to Random House, Inc. for permission. For on-line information about other Random House, Inc. books and authors, see the Internet web site at http://www.randomhouse.com.

It's all in the ears. When Mickey Mouse was born, in 1927, the world of early cartoon animation was filled with two-legged zoomorphic humanoids, whose strange half-black faces were distinguished one from another chiefly by the ears. Felix the Cat had pointed triangular ears and Oswald the Rabbit—Walt Disney's first successful cartoon creation, which he abandoned when his New York distributor, Charles Mintz, attempted to swindle him—had long floppy ears, with a few notches in the end to suggest fur. Disney's Oswald films, and the Alice animations that precede them, had mice in them, with linear limbs, wiry tails, and ears that are oblong, not yet round. On the way back to California from New York by train, having left Oswald enmeshed for good in the machinations of Mr. Mintz, Walt and his wife Lillian invented another character based—the genesis legend claims—on the tame field mice that used to wander into Disney's old studio in Kansas City. His first thought was to call the mouse Mortimer; Lillian proposed instead the less pretentious name Mickey. Somewhere between Chicago and Los Angeles, the young couple concocted the plot of Mickey's first cartoon short, *Plane Crazy*, co-starring Minnie and capitalizing on 1927's Lindbergh craze. The next short produced by Disney's fledgling studio—which included, besides himself and his brother Roy, and his old Kansas City associate, Ub Iwerks—was *Gallopin' Gaucho*, and introduced a fat and wicked cat who did not yet wear the prosthesis that would give him his name of Pegleg Pete. The third short, *Steamboat Willie*, incorporated that brand-new novelty, a sound track, and was released first. In 1928 Mickey Mouse entered history as the most persistent and pervasive figment of American popular culture in this century.

His ears are two solid black circles, no matter the angle at which he holds his head. Three-dimensional images of Mickey Mouse—toy dolls, of the papier-mâché heads the grotesque Disneyland Mickeys wear—make us uneasy, since the ears inevitably exist edgewise as well as frontally. These ears properly belong not to three-dimensional space but to an ideal realm of notation, of symbolization, of cartoon resilience and indestructibility. In drawings, when Mickey is in profile, one ear is at the back of his head like a spherical ponytail, or like a secondary bubble in a computer-generated Mandelbrot set. We accept it, as we accepted Li'l Abner's hair always being parted on the side facing the viewer. A surreal optical consistency is part of the cartoon world, halfway between our world and the plane of pure signs, of alphabets and trademarks.

In the sixty-four years since Mickey Mouse's image was promulgated, the ears, though a bit more organically irregular and flexible than the classic 1930s appendages, have not been essentially modified. Many other modifications have, however, overtaken that first crude cartoon, born of an era of starker stylizations. White gloves, like the gloves worn in minstrel shows, appeared after those early Twenties movies, to cover the black hands. The infantile bare chest and shorts with two buttons were phased out in the Forties. The eyes have undergone a number of changes, most drastically in the late Thirties, when, as some historians mistakenly claim, they acquired pupils. Not so: the old eyes, the black oblongs that acquired a nick of reflection in the sides, *were* the pupils; the eye-whites filled the entire space beneath Mickey's cap of black, its widow's peak marking the division between these enormous oculi. This can be seen clearly in the face of the classic Minnie; when she bats her eyelids, their lashed shades lower over the full width of what might be thought to be her brow. But all the old animated animals were built this way from Felix the Cat on; Felix had lower lids, and the Mickey of *Plane Crazy* also. So it was an evolutionary misstep that, beginning in 1938, replaced the old shiny black pupils with entire oval eyes, containing pupils of their own. No such mutation has overtaken Pluto, Goofy, or Donald Duck. The change brought Mickey closer to us humans, but also took away something of his vitality, his alertness, his bug-eyed cartoon readiness for adventure. It made him less abstract, less iconic, more merely cute and dwarfish. The original Mickey, as he scuttles and bounces through those early animated shorts, was angular and wiry, with much of the impudence and desperation of a true rodent. He was gradually rounded to the proportions of a child, a regression sealed by his Fifties manifestation as the genius of the children's television show, *The Mickey Mouse Club*, with its live Mouseketeers. But most of the artists in this album, though too young to have grown up, as I did, with the old form of Mickey, have instinctively reverted to it; it is the bare-chested basic Mickey, with his yellow shoes and oval buttons on his shorts, who is the icon, beside whom his modified later version is a mere mousy trousered pipsqueak.

His first, iconic manifestation had something of Chaplin to it: he was the little guy, just over the border of the respectable. His circular ears, like two minimal cents, bespeak the smallest economic unit, the over-lookable democratic man. His name has passed in the language as a byword for the small, the weak—a "Mickey Mouse operation" means an undercapitalized company or minor surgery. Children of my genera-tion—wearing our Mickey Mouse watches, prying pennies from our Mickey Mouse piggy banks (I won one in a third-grade spelling bee, my first intellectual triumph), following his running combat with Pegleg Pete in the daily funnies, going to the local movie-house movies every Saturday afternoon and cheering when his cheerful visage burst onto the screen to introduce a cartoon—felt Mickey was one of us, a bridge to the adult world of which Donald Duck was, for all of his childish sailor suit, an irascible, tyrannical member. Mickey didn't seek trou-ble, and he didn't complain; he rolled with the punches, and surprised himself as much as us when, as in *The Little Tailor*, he showed warrior resourcefulness and won, once again, a blushing kiss from dear, all but identical Minnie. His minimal, decent nature meant that he would yield, in the Disney animated cartoons, the starring role to combative, sput-tering Donald Duck and even to Goofy, with his "gawshes" and Gary Cooper–like gawkiness. But for an occasional comeback like the Sor-cerer's Apprentice episode of *Fantasia*, and last year's rather souped-up *The Prince and the Pauper*, Mickey was through as a star by 1940. But, as with Marilyn Monroe when her career was over, his life as an icon gathered strength. The America that is not symbolized by the imperial Yankee Uncle Sam is symbolized by Mickey Mouse. He is America as it feels itself—plucky, put-on, inventive, resilient, good-natured, game.

Like America, Mickey has a lot of black blood. This fact was revealed to me in conversation by Saul Steinberg, who, in attempting to depict the racially mixed reality of New York streets for the supersensitive and race-blind *New Yorker* of the Sixties and Seventies, hit upon scribbling numerous Mickeys as a way of representing what was jaunty and scruffily and unignorably there. From just the way Mickey swings along in his classic, trademark pose, one three-fingered gloved hand held on high, he is jiving. Along with round black ears and yellow shoes, Mickey has a soul. Looking back to such early animations as the early Looney Tunes' Bosko and Honey series (1930–36) and the Arab figures in Disney's own *Mickey in Arabia* of 1932, we see that blacks were drawn much like the cartoon animals, with round button noses and great white eyes creating the double arch of the curious peaked scullcaps. Cartoon characters' rubberiness, their jazziness, their cheerful buoyance and idleness, all chimed with popular images of African Americans, earlier embodied in minstrel shows and in Joel Chandler Harris's tales of Uncle Remus, which Disney was to make into an animated feature, *Song of the South*, in 1946.

Up to 1950, animated cartoons, like films in general, contained caricature of blacks that would be unacceptable now; in fact, *Song of the South* raised objections from the NAACP when it was released. In recent reissues of *Fantasia*, two Nubian centaurettes and a pickaninny centaurette who shines the others' hooves have been edited out. Not even the superb crows section of *Dumbo* would be made now. But there is a sense in which all animated cartoon characters are more or less black. Steven Spielberg's hectic tribute to animation, *Who Framed Roger Rabbit*, has them all, from the singing trees of Silly Symphonies to Daffy Duck and Woody Woodpecker, living in a Los Angeles ghetto, Toonville. As blacks were second-class citizens with entertaining qualities, so the animated shorts were second-class movies, with unreal actors, who mocked and illuminated from underneath the real world, the live-actor cinema. Of course, even in a ghetto there are class distinctions. Porky Pig and Bugs Bunny have homes that they tend and defend, whereas Mickey started out, like those other raffish stick figures and dancing blots from the Twenties, as a free spirit, a wanderer. As Richard Schickel has pointed out, "The locales of his adventures throughout the 1930s ranged from the South Seas to the Alps to the deserts of Africa. He was, at various times, a gaucho, teamster, explorer, swimmer, cowboy, fireman, convict, pioneer, taxi driver, castaway, fisherman, cyclist, Arab, football player, inventor, jockey, storekeeper, camper, sailor, Gulliver, boxer" and so forth. He was, in short, a rootless vaudevillian who would play any part that the bosses at Disney Studios assigned him. And though the comic strip, which still persists, has fitted him with all of a white man's household comforts and headaches, it is as an unencumbered drifter whistling along on the road of hard knocks, ready for whatever adventure waits at the next turning, that he lives in our minds.

Cartoon characters have soul as Carl Jung defined it in his *Archetypes and the Collective Unconscious*: "soul is a life-giving demon who plays his elfin game above and below human existence." Without the "leaping and twinkling of the soul," Jung says, "man would rot away in his greatest passion, idleness." The Mickey Mouse of the Thirties shorts was a whirlwind of activity, with a host of unsuspected skills and a reluctant heroism that rose to every occasion. Like Chaplin and Douglas Fairbanks and Fred Astaire, he acted out our fantasies of endless nimbleness, of perfect weightlessness. Yet, withal, there was nothing aggressive or self-promoting about him, as there was about, say, Popeye. Disney, interviewed in the Thirties, said, "Sometimes I've tried to figure out why Mickey appealed to the whole world. Everybody's tried to figure it out. So far as I know, nobody has. He's a pretty nice fellow who never does anybody any harm, who gets into scrapes through no fault of his own, but always managed to come up grinning." This was perhaps Disney's image of himself; for twenty years he did Mickey's voice in the films, and would often say, "there's a lot of the Mouse in me." Mickey was a character created with his own pen, and nurtured on Disney's memories of his mouseridden Kansas City studio and of the Missouri farm where his struggling father tried for a time to make a living. Walt's humble, scrambling beginnings remained embodied in the mouse, whom the Nazis, in a fury against the Mickey-inspired Allied legions (the Allied code word on D-Day was "Mickey Mouse"), called "the most miserable ideal ever revealed . . . mice are dirty."

But was Disney, like Mickey, just "a pretty nice fellow"? He was until crossed in his driving perfectionism, his Napoleonic capacity to marshal men and take risks in the service of an artistic and entrepreneurial vision. He was one of those great Americans, like Edison and Henry Ford, who invented themselves in terms of a new technology. The technology—in Disney's case, film animation—would have been there anyway, but only a few driven men seized the full possibilities, and made empires. In the dozen years between *Steamboat Willie* and *Fantasia*, the Disney studios took the art of animation to heights of ambition and accomplishment it would never have reached otherwise, and Disney's personal zeal was the animating force. He created an empire of the mind, and its emperor was Mickey Mouse.

The Thirties were Mickey's conquering decade. His image circled the globe. In Africa, tribesmen painfully had tiny mosaic Mickey Mouses inset into their front teeth, and a South African tribe refused to buy soap unless the cakes were embossed with Mickey's image, and a revolt of some native bearers was quelled when the safari masters projected some Mickey Mouse cartoons for them. Nor were the high and mighty immune to Mickey's elemental appeal—King George V and Franklin Roosevelt insisted that all film showings they attended include a dose of Mickey Mouse. But other popular phantoms, like Felix the Cat, have faded, where Mickey has settled into the national consciousness. The television program revived him for my children's generation, and the theme parks make him live for my grandchildren's. Yet survival cannot be imposed through weight of publicity; Mickey's persistence springs from something timeless in the image that has allowed it to pass in status from a fad to an icon.

To take a bite out of our imaginations, an icon must be simple. The ears, the wiggily tail, the red shorts, give us a Mickey. Donald Duck and Goofy, Bugs Bunny and Woody Woodpecker are inextricably bound up with the draughtmanship of the artists who make them move and squawk, but Mickey floats free. It was Claes Oldenburg's work that first alerted me to the fact that Mickey Mouse had passed out of the realm of commercially generated image into that of artifact, so that the basic configuration, like that of hamburgers and pay telephones, could be used as an immediately graspable referent in a piece of art. The young Andy Warhol committed Dick Tracy, Nancy, Batman, and Popeye to canvas, but not, until 1981, Mickey. Perhaps Pop Art could most resonantly recycle comic strips with a romantic appeal to adolescents. Mickey's appeal is pre-romantic, a matter of latency's relatively abstract manipulations. Hajime Sorayama's shiny piece of airbrush art and Gary Baseman's scribbled scraps, both in this volume, capture textures of the developmental stage at which Mickey's image penetrated. Sorayama, by adding a few features not present in the cartoon image—supplying knobs to the elbows and knees and some anatomy to the ears—subtly carries forward Disney's creativity without violating it. Baseman's reference to Mouseketeer ears is important; their invention further abstractified Mickey and turned him into a kind of power we could put on while remaining, facially, ourselves. The ancient notion of transforming hat crowns, dunce caps, "thinking caps," football helmets, spaceman gear acquires new potency in the age of the television set, which sports its own "ears," gathering magic from the air. As John Berg's painting shows, ears are everywhere. To recognize Mickey, as Heinz Edelmann's drawing demonstrates, we need very little. Round ears will do it. A new Disney gadget, advertised on television, is a camera-like box that spouts bubbles when a key is turned; the key consists of three circles, two mounted on a larger one, and the image is unmistakably Mickey. Like yin and yang, like the Christian cross and the star of Israel, Mickey can be seen everywhere a sign, a rune, a hieroglyphic trace of a secret power, an electricity we want to plug into. Like totem poles, like African masks, Mickey stands at that intersection of abstraction and representation where magic connects.

Milton Glaser's charming reprise of Mickey wearing glasses, though still engaged in his jivey stride, lightly touches on the question of iconic mortality. Usually, cartoon figures do not age, and yet their audience does age, as generation succeeds generation, so that a weight of allusion and sentimental reference increases. To the movie audiences of the early Thirties, Mickey Mouse was a piping-voiced live wire, the latest thing in entertainment; by the time of the Sorcerer's Apprentice episode of *Fantasia* he was already a somewhat sentimental figure, welcomed back. *The Mickey Mouse Club*, with its slightly melancholy pack-leader Jimmie Dodd, created a Mickey more removed and marginal than in the first. The generation that watched it grew up into the rebels of the Sixties, to whom Mickey became camp, a symbol of U.S.

cultural fast food, with a touch (see the drawing by Rick Griffin) of the old rodent raffishness. Politically, Walt, stung by the studio strike of 1940, moved to the right, but Mickey remains one of the Thirties proletariat, not uncomfortable in the cartoon-rickety, cheerfully verminous crash pads of the counterculture. At the Florida and California theme parks, Mickey manifests himself as a short real person wearing an awkward giant head, costumed as a ringmaster; he is in a danger, in these Nineties, of seeming not merely venerable kitsch but part of the great trash problem, one more piece of visual litter being moved back and forth by the bulldozers of consumerism.

But never fear, his basic goodness will shine through. Beyond recall, perhaps, is the simple love felt by us of the generation that grew up with him. I remember crying when the local newspaper, cutting down its comic pages to help us win World War II, eliminated the Mickey Mouse strip. I was old enough, nine or ten, to write an angry letter to the editor. In fact, the strips had been eliminated by the votes of a readership poll, and my indignation and sorrow stemmed from my incredulous realization that not everybody loved Mickey Mouse as I did. In an account of my boyhood written over thirty years ago, "The Dogwood Tree," I find these sentences concerning another boy, a rival: "When we both collected Big Little Books, he outbid me for my supreme find (in the attic of a third boy), the first Mickey Mouse. I wanted it so badly, its paper tan with age and its drawings done in Disney's primitive style, when Mickey's black chest is naked like a child's and his eyes are two nicked oblongs." And I once tried to write a short story called "A Sensation of Mickey Mouse," trying to superimpose on adult experience, as a shiver-inducing revenant, that indescribable childhood sensation— a rubbery taste, a licorice smell, a feeling of supernatural clarity and close-in excitation that Mickey Mouse gave me, and gives me, much dimmed by the years, still. He is a "genius" in the primary dictionary sense of "an attendant spirit," his vulnerable bare black chest, his touchingly big yellow shoes, the mysterious place at the back of his shorts where his tail came out, the little cleft cushion of a tongue, red as a valentine and glossy as candy, always peeping through the catenary curves of his undiscourageable smile. Not to mention his ears.

• This essay served as the introduction to *The Art of Mickey Mouse*, an album of visual reimaginings of Mickey, which explains Updike's references to graphic artists like Hajime Sorayama, Gary Baseman, and Milton Glaser. The text is an expanded version of an article in *Art & Antiques* (Nov. 1991), and has appeared in two other anthologies: Susan Sontag, ed., *The Best American Essays 1992* (New York, 1992), and Donald McQuade, Robert Atwan, eds., *Popular Writing in America: The Interaction of Style and Audience*, 5th ed. (Oxford, 1993). One lapse made it through all previous editions: "Toonville" should be "Toontown." Updike's original mention in *Art & Antiques* of Franklin Roosevelt, morphed for some reason into "Teddy" Roosevelt in *The Art of Mickey Mouse*, has been restored here.

Mickey, A Mouse of Influence around the World

Marshall Fishwick

Orlando Sentinel, June 14, 1992

Join in the celebration for the 65th birthday of one of the best-loved Americans. But don't ask him to retire at 65. He's too busy conquering France.

I speak of Mickey Mouse, and the Euro Disneyland that has become the new rage of Europe. It opened last month, and is fast becoming the continent's leading tourist attraction.

Is that any way for an aging mouse to act? But then, Mickey never ages. He is our Peter Pan, our perennial dream and our hope of perpetual childhood. His mission is to keep us young.

Like many folk heroes, Mickey's birth on June 14, 1927, was miraculous. He popped full-blown out of the brain of Walt Disney, who was traveling by train to the West coast to make animated cartoons.

Disney's troubled sleep was interrupted by a romping, rollicking, little mouse. The train wheels seemed to say, "Chug chug mouse, chug chug mouse." Disney got up and started sketching. A mouse was born.

There were ample precedents. Stories abound of magic miceskin, mice transformed into humans, town and country mice rivalries. A German mouse put his tail in a sleeping thief's mouth, making him cough up a magic ring. Three Blind Mice ran after the farmer's wife. Now everybody runs after Mickey.

He's not handsome—black dots for eyes, a string-bean body. We love him anyway. An instant success in Hollywood, he inspired Mickey Mouse Clubs that had a million members by 1931. Defying time, space, and gravity, he was irresistible. The famed cartoonist David Low called Disney "the most significant graphic artist since Leonardo da Vinci."

Mickey entered the service in World War II, starring in numerous training films and amusing troops. And what was the code word American intelligence used for the Normandy invasion? Mickey Mouse. It was tribute enough to turn the average rodent's head. But then, Mickey is not your average rodent.

After the war, he continued his civilian success. By 1950, more than 2,000 companies teamed up with Disney Studios. The Lionel Corporation sold a quarter-million toy handcars in a single Christmas season. That year, Ingersoll Watch company made its five millionth Mickey Mouse watch. There were Mickey Mouse toys, games, books, mugs, posters.

The basis of this early popularity was Disney's animation. Mickey was an actor before he became an icon. It takes 16 drawings to make him move once on the screen; 14,400 for a ten-minute cartoon; and 144,000 for a full-length feature. An army of artists gave him a mechanical, if not biological, life. The secret was that while Mickey was mechanical, he was never mechanized. Because his world has laws of its own, he achieves the illusion of independence from his creators. He does not belong to Disney; he is ours. At Disney World, I heard a father tell a son, "There's the guy dressed up like Mickey Mouse."

"You're wrong, Dad," came the reply. "That is Mickey Mouse."

Now Mickey is surrounded by a galaxy of Disney characters, including the ever-faithful Minnie. Disney Studios have created a Noah's Ark to carry us joyfully through the waves of the chaotic modern world.

Though he belongs to the world, Mickey is the electronic embodiment of the American spirit and the know-how that has served us well in war and peace.

Disneyland opened in California in 1955—an isle of pastoral innocence in a sea of urban sprawl and smog. A generation later, a much more elaborate Disney World opened in Florida. These were dream cities, not only for children, but those who wanted to remember childhood. They were our utopias.

Another utopian, whose career was strikingly similar to Disney's, was Henry Ford. He put America on wheels. Like Disney, he believed in small-town America and old-time values. Mickey was Disney's Model T—simple, sturdy, and functional. You could have any color you liked, Ford said, as long as it was black.

Ford and Disney were single minded, and they knew America well.

So did Lindbergh—who flew the Atlantic solo the same year Mickey was born.

These men, like the legends they created, are part of our national treasures. On them, we have built our popular culture. Norwegian scholar Helge Ronning believes this is becoming everyone's second culture, fostering world-wide cultural bilingualism. People from Australia to Zimbabwe tune in to our movies, TV, magazines, dreams. The new mythology is electronic, and they are part of it. Disneyland belongs to them, too.

That was confirmed recently when an amazed Japanese girl, emerging from the Tokyo Disneyland, asked an American visitor, "Is there really a Disneyland in America?"

Happy birthday, Mickey. Keep up the good work.

The Mickey in Macy's Window: Childhood, Consumerism, and Disney Animation

Richard deCordova

In Eric Smoodin, ed., *Disney Discourse: Producing the Magic Kingdom* (Routledge, 1994)

Walt Disney's Mickey Mouse films emerged against the backdrop of a complex set of debates about children's leisure and the role of the cinema in children's lives. During the late 1920s and early 1930s the cinema's address to children was contested ground and a matter of frenzied concern. Reformers denounced the movies' influence on children and mounted well-organized efforts across the country to regulate and control this aspect of children's leisure. One particularly important aspect of these efforts involved the creation and supervision of a canon of films for children. Reformers asked whether a given film addressed the young moviegoer as a "true" and "proper" child.

Disney's films entered and achieved a privileged position in this canon of films for children. In Mickey Mouse, the cultural interests of children, the business interests of the film industry, and the political and cultural interests of reformers seemingly merged. And today, something like a sacred connection exists between Mickey Mouse and idealized childhood. However, as the occasional early references to Mickey's vulgarity attest, that connection was by no means natural or unproblematic. It was the result of a particular historical work, a work that I want to begin to examine in this essay.

My focus here is not so much on the films themselves as it is on the marketing and merchandising strategies that "sold" the cartoons (and the characters) to children and assured reform-minded adults that this was a healthful purchase. It is at this level that we see the most explicit and emphatic attempts to assure Disney animation's uncontested address to children.

My title's reference to Charles Eckert's famous article, "The Carole Lombard in Macy's Window," gives an indication of the direction of my argument. In that article, Eckert describes a significant transformation in the American film industry. From the late 1920s to the middle 1930s there was an intensification and rationalization of the process through which films were linked to consumer goods. Such organizations as Hollywood Fashion Associates and the Modern Merchandising Bureau emerged to coordinate the display of fashions in Hollywood films and fan magazines with the subsequent production and marketing of those fashions to the public. And the studio exploitation departments systematically began to conceive of story ideas and scripts as opportunities for a wide range of lucrative product tie-ins. For Eckert these developments consolidated the cinema's role as a force in the rise of American consumerism.[1]

Several scholarly works, by contrast, have followed from Eckert to produce compelling arguments about the relations between film and consumerism in the first decades of the century. This work however, like Eckert's, has ignored Disney, in large part, no doubt, because it has concerned itself with consumers other than children. The situation beyond film studies, in the fields of social and cultural history, is much the same: a body of knowledge about the rise of consumerism but very little on children's participation in that process.[2] In short, a kind of gap exists in the research, a gap that prevents us from thinking as clearly as we might about Disney animation's address to children and particularly its address through the mechanisms of consumerism.

We should begin by distinguishing between two different registers of consumption that tied the child to the cinema.

First, the child was a consumer of films, someone who paid a certain amount to see a show. Second, the child was a consumer of products displayed through films. The system of merchandising and promotion employed by Disney and the other studios in the early 1930s worked by creating elaborate networks of mutual reference between these two registers of consumption.

Particularly elaborate networks formed around Mickey Mouse. In Cecil Munsey's account, the beginnings of Mickey Mouse merchandising can be traced to three events. In late 1929, Walt Disney sold the rights to use Mickey on school tablets to a New York company. In January 1930, Charlotte Clark began the small-scale production of Mickey Mouse dolls in a house rented by the Disney Company. And finally, and most importantly, in February 1930, Disney signed a contract with the George Borgfeldt Company for the international licensing, production, and distribution of Mickey Mouse merchandise.[3] Although the Disney Company was never satisfied with Borgfeldt's efforts, the merchandising of Mickey Mouse was soon astoundingly successful. By the beginning of 1932 there were twenty-one licensees in the United States alone, most producing a number of different Mickey Mouse products. Children could, with enough money, have the image of the mouse on almost all of their possessions—their underwear, pajamas, neckties, handkerchiefs, and jewelry; their tooth brushes, hot water bottles, and bathroom accessories; their silverware and china; their toys and games; and their school supplies.[4]

The Disney Company was interested in the publicity value of these items as much as the substantial royalties they would generate. As Roy Disney noted in a letter to Borgfeldt, "The sale of a doll to any member of a household is a daily advertisement in that household for our cartoons and keeps them all 'Mickey Mouse Minded.'"[5] When Borgfeldt's Carl Sollmann expressed his concern that business would be hurt by the saturation of the market with Disney toys, Roy Disney replied, "we feel that we should publicize our character from every angle and accept every opportunity."[6] Sollmann looked at the toy business as a producer; Disney looked at it more as an advertiser. The more publicity the better.

In this sense, Disney and Borgfeldt's interests were complementary more than convergent. They were each interested in consolidating half of the circuit between the two forms of consumption noted above. For Disney, the consumption of the toy would lead to the consumption of the movie; for Borgfeldt, the consumption of the movie would lead to the consumption of the toy. At the local level at which consumption actually took place, this network might better be described as a path, a path that connected the worlds of film exhibition and retailing, and therefore led (in its ideal form at least) from the movie theater to the department store and back. The activities in these two spaces were, as we shall see, strategically linked.

In 1931 and 1932, Mickey Mouse became a fixture in department stores across the country. Mickey Mouse items began to be grouped together in toy departments, and given their own separate displays.[7] And Mickey Mouse became the prominent figure in store windows targeted at the young consumer. The toy trade press of these years reproduced numerous store windows built around Mickey and Minnie Mouse, windows at Gimbel Brothers' in Philadelphia, Kresge's in Newark, Nugent's in St. Louis, Bullock's in Los Angeles, Stearn's in Cleveland and Bloomingdale's, Lord and Taylor's, Stern Brothers' and the Grand Central Toy Shop in New York.[8] The following description, from 1932, gives some sense of the spectacular nature of these windows:

> For stopping crowds, O'Connor-Moffatt certainly took the prize for the early trade. The wonderful Mickey Mouse show with Minnie Mouse at the piano, and a world of little Mickey's and other animals about, caught and held constant crowds. Meanwhile a talking machine mechanism, attached by a vibrating mechanism to the windows, gave out a cheerful mousey melody to the bystanders on either side of the corner.[9]

Mickey Mouse became a kind of star of the toy department, around which could be assembled a large supporting cast of other dolls and toys. This is particularly evident in the description of the Christmas festivities for children at Kresge's in 1932. Mickey Mouse passed out presents and acted as "master of ceremonies" for a show in the Mickey Mouse Barn on the fifth floor. And on the sixth floor, Mickey introduced Santa and Mrs. Claus, who were placed on thrones in the rear of the toy department's Mickey Mouse section.

Borgfeldt helped organize a certain amount of this publicity for its products. It built a Mickey Mouse booth at Bloomingdale's, provided large fake cheeses for Mickey Mouse window displays, and had Charlotte Clark make costumes so that Mickey and Minnie could appear "live" at stores. But it seems that much of the impetus for these extravagant promotions came from the stores themselves.

The stores' enthusiasm for Mickey Mouse is not difficult to understand given the popularity of the films and the early signs of the toys' success. One less obvious source of this enthusiasm should be stressed, however. The toy industry's greatest problem during this period was that it was too much of a seasonal business; the majority of purchases took place in the month before Christmas and the rest of the year was comparatively slow. The trade struggled to find ways to overcome this problem. For the toy industry to flourish, the child's consumption patterns had to be modernized, wrested from the stranglehold of the yearly ritual and connected to other rituals and, particularly, to the flux of everyday life. The movies played an important role in most stores' efforts for year-round sales. One Kansas store explained its success in this regard by pointing to its windows that tied in with movies at the local theaters. *Playthings*, a trade paper for the toy industry, explained the extra stock dividends that Lord and Taylor paid by noting the store's unique window displays and including, as an example, a Mickey Mouse window.[10] By tying toys to movies, stores tied the consumption of toys to the everyday rituals of moviegoing, and a different kind of temporality. Mickey Mouse, as a regularly recurring character, was especially suited for this strategy.

Mickey Mouse was also important in the toy industry's efforts to generate other yearly rituals, notably Children's Day in June and Mickey Mouse's birthday in October. *Playthings*, in fact, urged stores to arrange Mickey Mouse birthday parties as a way of livening up a dull season. It specifically encouraged stores to cooperate with local movie theaters and to offer to dress up their lobbies with a display of Mickey Mouse toys. Here the theater became quite explicitly an extension of the department store.[11]

If the department stores' activities served as an elaborate advertisement for Mickey Mouse films, the theater's activities served as an equally elaborate advertisement for the department stores and particularly for Mickey Mouse toys. The films themselves, of course, popular as they were, served as such an advertisement. But to these films we must add another set of practices, the display and giveaway of Mickey Mouse toys at the theaters. By 1931, at least, theaters across the country had begun to receive a stream of Mickey Mouse dolls and toys for display and giveaways. These were occasionally supplied by Disney, Borgfeldt, or Columbia, the studio that distributed Disney films, or bought by the theater itself, but, in what seems to have been the standard formula, they were also supplied by individual department stores.[12] Stores got involved through the most elegant scheme of Mickey Mouse merchandising of the period, the Mickey Mouse Clubs.

The principal elements of the Mickey Mouse Club scheme were outlined in a general campaign booklet published in 1930 by the Disney Company. According to the plan, exhibitors would arrange a series of Saturday matinees for children, organizing the audience for these matinees into a club built around the character of Mickey Mouse. Each matinee, or "meeting" of the club would consist of a Mickey Mouse cartoon, followed by the introduction of the club's officers, the recitation of the Mickey Mouse Club Creed, the singing of "America," a stage show and/or contest, the Mickey Mouse Club Yell, the Mickey Mouse Club Song and then, finally, the films featured for the day.[13]

The club programs were not designed simply to appeal to children, but to incorporate as fully as possible the cultural activities of children within a community. Children enrolled in local music, dance, and dramatic schools, for instance, found themselves drawn or directed to the Mickey Mouse Clubs, because the stage shows were used as showcases for their talent. Marble shooting contests, doll dressing contests, model airplane making contests, ice-cream eating contests, Easter egg hunts, and dog parades functioned similarly, taking interests and activities unrelated to moviegoing and incorporating them into the flow of the matinee. Some clubs even tried to bring outdoor activities, which were seen as the greatest threat to children's attendance on Saturdays, within their orbit by sponsoring baseball teams or summer picnics.

The clubs extended their reach in another way, by forming networks of tie-ins with local businesses that catered to children. Department stores, dairies, candy stores, banks, newspapers, and sporting goods stores—all businesses that served as points of contact between children and the world of commerce—became potential sponsors. Sponsors split the cost of running the clubs, and in return received advertising at club meetings and the right to use the image of Mickey Mouse in their store windows and newspaper ads.

Tie-ins with department stores were the most common. Those tie-ins linked the club's activities with the selling of toys quite effectively. To join the club, children had to go to the department store's toy department for an application. At club meetings, the department store's sponsorship would be noted, and the latest Mickey Mouse toys would be given away in contests to a handful of very lucky children. The rest of the children would then covet the toys and, ideally, figure out a way to return to the store to buy one.

The growth of the Mickey Mouse Clubs was impressive. By the end of 1930, a hundred and fifty theaters across the country had clubs and, according to Disney's estimates, there were a hundred and fifty to two hundred thousand members.[14] By 1932, *Photoplay* magazine claimed that the clubs had one million members.[15] Although these figures may exaggerate actual membership, they are credible. Between 1930 and 1932, local papers, the national trade press, and the semimonthly "Official Bulletin of the Mickey Mouse Club" chronicled the successes of the clubs in every part of the country. Milwaukee alone had ten clubs and twenty thousand members. Chicago had at least twenty-five clubs. Los Angeles had still more.[16] In 1932, new club chapters were being formed at the rate of about thirty per month. A writer in the *Motion Picture Herald* claimed that the membership of the Mickey Mouse Club approximated "that of the Boy Scouts of America and the Girl Scouts combined."[17]

The idea of a children's cinema club was not an original one. The *Film Daily Yearbook* had recommended juvenile booster clubs in its *Exploitation Guides* in the three years prior to 1930, so it is very likely that exhibitors had been experimenting with the idea for some time. In fact, in 1927, the *Exhibitor's Herald* devoted an article to an "Our Gang" Matinee Club that had been organized by a Chicago exhibitor. That club, and perhaps others like it, existed as a precedent for a children's club based on the characters in a short subject film series.[18]

The Mickey Mouse Club was not, in any case, the only children's cinema club operating between 1930 and 1933. The Loew's and Warner Bros. theater circuits had kiddie clubs during these years, and dozens, if not hundreds, of individual theater managers devised their own clubs. The Capitol Theater Booster Club, the Indians are Coming Club, the Do Right Club, the Young-Timers and the Ancient Order of the Tom Cats are among many mentioned in the trades.[19]

All of the clubs worked to consolidate around the moviegoing experience what Daniel Boorstin has called consumption communities.[20]

What set the Mickey Mouse Clubs apart from these other clubs was the extent to which they organized these communities not only around the consumption of movies but also around the consumption of toys. It is significant that the toy press during these years was encouraging toy departments to organize children's clubs to promote year-round sales. Mickey Mouse clubs, designed by Disney and run by theater managers, provided them an ideal, ready-made vehicle to achieve these goals.[21]

The picture I have drawn is far from complete, but it does give some sense of the elaborate ways that the child was interpellated as consumer through the merchandising of Mickey Mouse. At this point it is possible to return to the question of address, and ask what if any relationship existed between this merchandising, the broad debates about the movies and children, and the canonization of Mickey Mouse.

Let me begin by merely noting that the merchandising of Mickey Mouse toys to children seems to have proceeded in the early 1930s without any criticism from reformers. I would like to suggest that this is more perplexing than it may, on its surface, seem. The Mickey Mouse films, after all, elicited at least scattered signs of resistance. And the values of consumerism were contested from a variety of fronts during the period. Daniel Horowitz has traced the history of moral arguments against consumerism, arguments which, in the 1920s and 1930s, centered on the middle class's susceptibility and conformity to standardized culture.[22] And Roland Marchand has described the ambivalence that even advertisers felt when contemplating the logic of waste and extravagance that characterized consumerism.[23] Today, of course, activists reflexively bring these kinds of arguments to the merchandising of cartoon character toys. They did not, however, bring such arguments to the merchandising of Mickey Mouse in the early 1930s; nor do they generally bring those arguments to Mickey today. It is important to ask: Why not?

It would be misleading to say that issues of consumerism did not enter into the debates over the cinema and children during this period. In fact, most reformist discourse in the first decades of the century related fairly directly to the child's new status as a consumer of films. The movies were part of a new marketplace of culture to which children had unprecedented access. Their freedom of choice as consumers blurred traditional distinctions between child and adult culture, and placed the authority that parents and teachers had normally had in the social-ization of children in crisis. The numerous studies done of children's movie attendance and movie preferences reveal a fundamental concern with the effects of consumerism. Some studies, moreover, called criti-cal attention to the ability of movies to prompt desires for the products they picture, especially products such as cigarettes and clothing.[24]

But it is clear that ancillary products relating to Mickey Mouse were not an issue. In fact, it can be argued that these products played an important role in naturalizing Disney animation's address to children, consolidating the sacred bond I mentioned earlier. I would like to offer two broad and brief explanations for this, explanations for the ways in which the reading of toys worked to consolidate Disney animation's ad-dress to children.

The first has to do with the new valuation of play in the first decades of the century. Both the film industry and the toy industry were singled out in the 1920s and 1930s as arenas of reform. There are, in fact, some interesting parallels between reform activity in the two industries. Re-formers in both arenas stressed character education, criticized the glo-rification of gunplay, and produced elaborate age-grading schemes to guide children's consumption. However, there is a particularly striking difference between the voices of reform in the two industries. The vision of the toy reformers is obviously a much more affirmative one. Very few specific toys are criticized, and though the distinction between educa-tional and noneducational toys is frequently made, the former category was quite large and its boundaries not well defined. The rhetoric of toy reform was informed by the idea that play itself, in itself, was valuable for the child.[25]

A 1931 article in *Toys and Novelties* reveals for us the ways that the interests of reform and the dictates of consumerism could so unprob-lematically converge around toys:

> We are continually purchasing new toys for our kiddies because we be-lieve it is one of the finest investments we could possibly make toward their proper growth and development. It is up to you to sell the same idea to every home in America.[26]

A similarly general statement during this period about "continually sending the child to the movies" would have sounded ludicrous. In 1934, Mickey Mouse Doll houses, playhouses, pencil sets, paint sets, dial phones, and chime sets were put forward as evidence that Mickey had turned educator.[27] In fact, not all of these toys are obviously educational. But, according to the rhetoric of the day, toys generally were educational. For this reason, the toys offered more solid ground on which to assure the sacredness of Mickey Mouse's address to children than did the films.

A second explanation centers on the ideology implicit in the iconography of toys, an iconography shared by animation. Mary Ann Doane has examined the intertwining of identification and object choice—being and having—in the female spectator's simultaneous address by the movies and consumerism.[28] Although the comparison holds some dangers, it is clear that a similar sort of intertwining occurs in children's address by Mickey Mouse films and toys. This is illustrated most vividly in the widespread popularity of Mickey Mouse playsuits, which allowed children to dress up as Mickey or Minnie Mouse. Photos of Mickey Mouse Club activities typically show the officers dressed in such costumes. Members, in fact, were instructed to greet one another by saying "Hi Mickey!" or "Hi Minnie!" What does it mean for a child to "be" a mouse? And what does it mean for a child to "have" a mouse? During the early decades of the century, as today, there was an enormous cultural investment in the association of childhood with animality. The most lauded forms of children's culture—toys, zoos, circuses, children's literature—were built on that investment, and the structured set of fantasies it offered.

The animalization of the juvenile world arguably had a very specific and powerful function in relation to the changing historical construction of childhood in the nineteenth and early twentieth centuries. This might be explained broadly through reference to the increasing currency of Romanticism, which linked the child with nature. Jackson Lears has identified two strains in the new construction of childhood that follow from links Romanticism made between childhood and nature. In the first, nature was a way of establishing children's innocence, their distance from the corrupting influence of social life. In the second, nature was a way of establishing children's vitality, their distance from the stultifying elements of social life. The child's relationship with nature and its association with innocence on the one hand and primitivist vitality on the other could be effectively concretized through symbolic procedures that linked the child to animals.[29]

The fantasy positions laid out (for both children and adults) in the association of children with animals circulated around and conflated two paradigmatic distinctions, that between child and adult and that between animal and human. Reformers were interested in conserving the set of traditional distinctions between child and adult, which the cinema presumably blurred. One way of bringing those distinctions back into focus was to superimpose them on the more culturally stable distinction between animals and humans. That is what the association of animals and children worked to do.[30]

We may look to the work of G. Stanley Hall for a more specific sense of the context in which the connection between animals and children gained its significance. Hall's writing at the turn of the century melded Romantic notions of childhood with theories about evolution and psychological development. As a founder of the Child Studies Movement in this country, Hall was an instrumental force in articulating and carrying forward central tendencies in the discourses of reform. His theories held that the various stages of the child's development recapitulated, through a genetically inscribed memory, the history of the race. Therefore, childhood recapitulated the social and instinctual impulses of the so-called Age of Savagery, while adolescence similarly recapitulated the Age of Chivalry. Proper parental and educational guidance avoided the "omnipresent dangers of precocity" by guiding the child through each stage of its development and by encouraging, at each stage, the proper exercise of the tendencies of the race's past. The child that did not fully live out its savage impulses would be scarred in its development and therefore unable to function properly as an adult in the modern world.[31]

This paleopsychic theory gave animals a very special place in the consideration of childhood, for it held that at the earliest stages of the race's development, humans were very close to animals. Therefore, Hall could argue, "children . . . in their incomplete stage of development are nearer the animals in some respects than they are to adults."[32] The tendency to anthropomorphize animals is established as a particular result of the child's ancestral link with animals.

To the young child, there is no gap between his soul and the soul of animals. They think, feel, act much as he does. They love, hate, fear, learn, sleep, make toilets, sympathize and have nearly all of the basal psychic qualities that the child has.[33]

Hall's description of the paleopsychic connection between children and animals becomes the basis for his argument for the centrality of animals in education. As Hall puts it,

Just as man's development would have been very different without animals and the fishing, hunting and pastoral stages, so childhood is maimed if long robbed of its due measure of influences from this comprehensive arsenal of educational material. Instead, I can almost believe that, if pedagogy is ever to become adequate to the needs of the soul the time will come when animals will play a far larger educational role than has as yet been conceived, that they will be curricularized, will require a new and higher humanistic or culture value in the future comparable with their utility in the past.[34]

Hall therefore pleads for "menageries . . . in every public park, pets, familiarity with stables, for school museums of stuffed specimens," and for "instruction in every school concerning insects, birds and animals. . . ."[35] He might as well have called for Mickey Mouse. Although Hall's chapter gives some clues about the ways that animals can serve the needs of scientific, psychological, and moral education, it is clear that he is concerned not with ends so much as means, that is, with the contact that is established and maintained between the child and the world of animals.

What is particularly important to note here is that animals tended to link children to a different time. Johannes Fabian has argued that the West has constituted the other as occupying not simply a different space (conceived geographically, hierarchically, or taxonomically) but a different time. Such distinctions as nature/culture, traditional/modern, and child/adult (and we might add animal/human) are central to Western society as temporalizing strategies.

The world of toys was built around this primitivist impulse. It was a world of animals, racial others, and figures from the near or distant past. The playsuits available during the period—the Indian, Cowboy, Scout, and Mickey Mouse suits—all depend on this impulse. Yet we must admit that the Mickey Mouse films and the Mickey character itself were in many ways aggressively modern. In fact, children during this period were in many ways on the very cutting edge of modernity. Reformers were disturbed about the movies in large part because the cultural construction of childhood had traditionally depended so much on the child's association with the past. Generally, for them, the more modern a film, the less suitable it was for children. Mickey's association with animality and particularly with the iconography of toys worked to counterbalance his modernity and place him more on the side of traditional childhood.

In *The World of Goods*, Mary Douglas and Baron Isherwood have argued that the primary function of goods is to make "visible and stable the categories of culture."[36] Film reformers acknowledged this view in their refusal to demonize consumerism and oppose it to notions of traditional childhood. These reformers were preoccupied with the cinema's address to children because the cinema mixed adults and children and called into question the hallowed distinction between the two. They were particularly concerned with adolescence because that was where the distinction became particularly problematic. If, as I have argued, the merchandising of Mickey Mouse toys was important in making sacred Disney's address to children, it is because that merchandising worked more assuredly than the movies to push the image of the child back into traditional categories of childhood.

Notes

1. Charles Eckert, "The Carole Lombard in Macy's Window," *Quarterly Review of Film Studies*, vol. 3, No. 1 (Winter 1978), pp. 1–22.

2. For an excellent bibliography of much of this work, see Lynn Spigel and Denise Mann, "Women and Consumer Culture: A Selective Bibliography," *Quarterly Review of Film and Video*, vol. 11, No. 1 (1989), pp. 85–105.

3. Cecil Munsey. *Disneyana: Walt Disney Collectibles* (New York: Hawthorne Books, 1974), pp. 31–32, 39.

4. *Official Bulletin of the Mickey Mouse Club*, January 1, 1932, p. 4.

5. Letter from Roy Disney to Carl Sollmann, March 4, 1931. Unless otherwise noted, all letters are from the Borgfeldt Files, the Walt Disney Archives.

6. Letter from Carl Sollmann to Walt Disney, March 27, 1931.

7. Letter from Carl Sollmann to Roy O. Disney, August 27, 1931.

8. *Toys and Novelties* (December 1932), p. 42 (September 1931), p. 66 (October 1931), pp. 41–45; *Playthings* (October 1931), pp. 60, 90 (January 1932), pp. 117, 159 (December 1932), pp. 23, 43.

9. *Playthings* (December 1932), p. 33.

10. *Toys and Novelties* (January 1929), p. 290; *Playthings* (December 1932) p. 49. Of course, much could be said about the ways in which the aesthetics of window dressing borrowed from the aesthetics of the movies.

11. *Playthings* (July 1932), p. 47 (October 1932), p. 83.

12. *Film Daily* (April 12, 1931), unpaginated clipping, Disney Archives; Carl Sollmann to Walt Disney Productions, December 8, 1930; Carl Sollmann to Walt Disney Productions, May 13, 1931; Walt Disney Productions to Carl Sollmann, September 27, 1930.

13. "General Campaign Covering the Launching and Operation of the Mickey Mouse Club, An Organization for Boys and Girls," 1930.

14. Letter from George E. Morris to Carl Sollmann, September 2, 1930.

15. *Photoplay Magazine* (June 1932), p. 46.

16. "Official Bulletin of the Mickey Mouse Club," April 1, 1932, and *Greater Amusements* (April 21, 1931), unpaginated clipping, Disney Archives.

17. *Motion Picture Herald* (October 1, 1932), quoted in Cecil Munsey, *Disneyana*, p. 102.

18. "Theatres Form Matinee Clubs and Business Begins to Soar," *Exhibitor's Herald* (November 12, 1927), p. 41. The precedent of children's clubs based on predominantly noncinematic fictional characters should also be noted here. See the discussion of the Tribes of Tarzan in Eugene Provenzo, *Edgar Rice Burroughs: The Man Who Created Tarzan* (Provo: Brigham Young University Press, 1975). For an overview of commercial children's clubs in the 1930s, see E. Evalyn Grumbine, *Reaching Juvenile Markets* (New York: McGraw-Hill, 1938), pp. 176–195.

19. See the following clippings in the Disney Archives: *Motion Picture Daily* (January 16, 1931); *Variety* (November 5, 1930), p. 745; *Exhibitor's Herald World* (October 18, 1930), p. 63; *Motion Picture Herald* (January 3, 1931), pp. 121, 126.

20. Daniel Boorstin, *The Americans: The Democratic Experience* (New York: Random House, 1973).

21. For a more detailed account of the Mickey Mouse Clubs see my article, "Tracing the Child Audience: The Case of Disney, 1929–1933," in *Prima del codici 2: Alle porte de Hays* (La Biennale de Venezie, 1991), pp. 213–223.

22. Daniel Horowitz, *The Morality of Spending: Attitudes Toward the Consumer Society in America, 1875–1940* (Baltimore: Johns Hopkins University Press, 1985), pp. 134–166.

23. Roland Marchand, *Advertising the American Dream* (Berkeley: University of California Press, 1985), pp. 134–166.

24. See, for instance, Harold O. Berg, "One Week's Attendance of Children at Motion Picture Entertainments," *Playground* (June 1923), p. 165; Clarence Arthur Perry, "Frequency of Attendance of High-School Students at the Movies," *School Review* (October 1923), pp. 573–587; and Henry James Forman, *Our Movie-Made Children* (New York: Macmillan, 1933), pp. 12–27, 183–190.

25. There are obvious connections between the discourse around toys and the rhetoric of the play movement. Notable work on the play movement includes Dominick Cavallo, *Muscles and Morals: Organized Playgrounds and Urban Reform, 1880–1920* (Philadelphia: University of Pennsylvania Press, 1981); David Glassberg, "Restoring a 'Forgotten Childhood': American Play and the Progressive Era's Elizabethan Past," *American Quarterly*, vol. 32, No. 4 (1980), pp. 351–368; Stephen Hardy and Alan Ingham, "Games, Structures, and Agency: Historians on the American Play Movement," *Journal of Social History*, vol. 17, No. 2 (1983), pp. 285–301; and Alessandra Lorini, "The Progressives' Rhetoric on National Recreation: The Play Movement in New York City (1880–1917)," *Storia Nordamericana*, vol. 1, No. 1 (1984), pp. 334–371.

26. *Toys and Novelties* (February 1931), p. 223.

27. *New York American* (December 9, 1934), unpaginated clippings, Disney Archives.

28. Mary Ann Doane, *The Desire to Desire: The Woman's Film of the 1940s* (Bloomington: Indiana University Press, 1987), pp. 22–33.

29. T. J. Jackson Lears, *No Place of Grace: Antimodernism and the Transformation of American Culture, 1880–1920* (New York: Pantheon Books, 1981), pp. 144–149.

30. Little historical or theoretical work has been done on the representation of animals in the cinema. In the early 1980s, Raymond Bellour's Paris seminar focused attention on animality and the articulation of sexual difference in films such as *Bringing Up Baby*, though Bellour has not, to my knowledge, published any of his work in this area. Anne Friedberg organized an innovative

panel, "The Other Species: Animals and Film," for the 1990 Society for Cinema Studies Conference, with papers by Friedberg, Kay Armatage, Marsha Kinder, and Holly Kruse. Finally, Ariel Dorfman's work on comic strips and animation offers a number of suggestive insights on this topic. See Ariel Dorfman, *The Empire's Old Clothes* (New York: Pantheon Press, 1983), and Dorfman and Armand Mattelart, *How to Read Donald Duck: Imperialist Ideology in the Disney Comic*, David Kunzle, trans. (New York: International General, 1975).

31. G. Stanley Hall, *Adolescence*, two volumes (New York: Amo Press, 1969). See also Lears, *No Place of Grace*, pp. 146–149.

32. Hall, *Adolescence*, vol. 2, p. 221.

33. *Ibid.*, p. 220.

34. *Ibid.*, pp. 227–228.

35. *Ibid.*, pp. 220–221.

36. Mary Douglas and Baron Isherwood, *The World of Goods* (New York: Basic Books, 1979), p. 59.

An American Icon Scampers In for a Makeover

John Canemaker

The rumors were true. Mickey has had a mouse-lift. The beloved
67-year-old star took the big step in Paris at a Disney animation studio
where he was filming "Runaway Brain," his first cartoon short in more
than 40 years. Although public relations executives at the Walt Disney
Company in Burbank, Calif., were hush-hush about the seven-minute
film, to be coupled with "A Kid in King Arthur's Court," a Disney feature opening at theaters on Friday, they have now confirmed that audiences will see a refurbished rodent.

Nothing radical, mind you. Having learned from the past, the Disney
artists didn't dare tamper with the famed circular head and ears, an
internationally recognizable icon. No, the change is more a *return* to
the insouciant Mickey of the mid-1930's. Audiences will also see a more
active and more emotive performer than the previous model.

A (Film) Star Is Born

The basic elements of Mickey's look first appeared in "Plane Crazy," a
silent film made in 1928: a white mask on a black circular head with
pie-shaped eyes, two smaller ear-circles and two-button short pants
on a round black body. But Mickey was also a grungy, goggle-eyed,
long-snouted ratlike creature, with tubular arms and legs, no gloves, no
shoes and no class.

This first creation, a hurried collaboration between the struggling cartoon producer Walt Disney and the animator Ub Iwerks, was based on the generic rubber-hose-and-circle design used by animated-cartoon studios of the period, ear shapes distinguished one rounded character from another. The style derived from Felix the Cat (until Mickey, the world's most popular 1920's cartoon film star), who had a white face surrounded by a black double-arched skullcap.

Originally a boxy critter until his animators discovered circles were easier to draw than angular shapes, Felix was all circular except for sharply pointed ears. This design was adapted from an earlier animated character, a black child named Sammy Johnsin. As John Updike wrote in a 1991 picture book, "The Art of Mickey Mouse," "Like America, Mickey has had a lot of black blood."

Changes in the rodent's appearance came that same year, 1928. In a second film, "Gallopin' Gaucho," also silent, he wore oversize clodhoppers, giving him "the look of a kid wearing his father's shoes," said Walt Disney. His next picture, and the first to be released, "Steamboat Willie," had an innovative soundtrack, which for the first time successfully combined synchronized sound effects, voice and music. This greatly helped the public accept the antics of the roughneck runt. In it, Mickey forces "music" from animals by pulling on a goose's neck, twirling a cat by its tail as if it were a lasso, and tweaking a pig's teats.

Soon, white gloves were added to his black hands. "We didn't want him to have mouse hands," Disney told his biographer, Bob Thomas, in 1957, "because he was supposed to be more human. So we gave him gloves. Five fingers seemed like too much on such a little figure, so we took away one. That was just one less finger to animate.

Mickey's easy-to-draw circular shape helped the animators meet their film-footage requirement. "He had to be simple," Mr. Disney said. "We had to push out 700 feet of film every two weeks . . . There was no mouse hair or any other frills that would slow down animation."

Indeed, simplicity ruled when the animator Ward Kimball, now 80, arrived at the Disney studio in Hollywood in 1934. "Animators were using coins to establish where the head circle and pants circle would be," Mr. Kimball said. "For close-ups we used the silver dollar everybody carried around with them, a 50-cent piece for a medium-close shot, a nickel for medium-long and a dime for a real long shot."

Personality Plus

Loose-change animation may have speeded up production, but the rigid circles did nothing for Mickey's expressiveness. The 1930's were a period of experimentation at Disney in which animators tried to bring a new believability to their characters, many of whom were based on aspects of the animators themselves. It was Fred Moore, a young, small, mouselike animator, who changed Mickey's head and body shapes.

"Fred was the first to escape from the rubber-hose, round-circle school," said Mr. Kimball. "He gave Mickey cheeks so they could work with the dialogue. When he opened his mouth, his head became longer; when it closed, the cheeks squashed. The body became more fruit-shaped. He was trying to get looseness."

In a 1935 in-house how-to-draw manual, Moore wrote, "This is a new procedure on Mickey and is not meant to change him so much as to improve him." Moore noted that the body "should be pliable at all times" and "can assume anatomy as it is needed, such as a chest, stomach, fanny." The animator found that "Mickey is cuter when drawn with small shoulders . . . and I like him pigeon-toed." "The ears are better kept far back on the head," he wrote.

In their book "Disney Animation: The Illusion of Life," the animators Frank Thomas and Ollie Johnston (both now 82 and subjects of a forthcoming documentary, "Frank and Ollie") wrote that with the new shape relationships, Moore "began to get a very appealing Mickey with stronger attitudes, better acting and more personality. Mickey could be anything now." And he was, in classic shorts like "Two-Gun Mickey" (1934), "Mickey's Service Station" and "The Band Concert" (1935), "Thru the Mirror" and "Mickey's Rival" (1936) and "Brave Little Tailor" (1938).

Moore's redesign is considered by most cartoon connoisseurs to be the classic image of Mickey Mouse. "Fred Moore *was* Disney drawing!" says Marc Davis, 82, one of the "nine old men" (including Messrs. Kimball, Thomas and Johnston) whom Disney jokingly referred to as his Supreme Court of animation.

The Image Evolves

Mickey's enduring popularity very likely has much to do with the more youthful and cute appearance given him by Moore. Perhaps because, as the Harvard paleontologist Stephen Jay Gould wrote in a 1979 article titled "The Neotenic Evolution of Mickey Mouse," "babyish features tend to elicit strong feeling of affection in adult humans," a theory attributed to the animal behaviorist Konrad Lorenz.

The famous mouse's power as an image may also derive from the circle shape itself, a symbol of continuity, perfection, survival, eternity and sensuality. "Circles never cause anybody any troubles," said the Disney artist John Hench, now 86. "We have had bad experiences with sharp points, with angles, but circles are things we have fun with."

Yet two changes were in store for Mickey in 1938, both controversial: the addition of eyeballs to replace the sliced pie-shape eyes, and a pinkish flesh tone on his face instead of stark white. Mr. Kimball was the first to draw Mickey's new eyes, on a Disney studio staff-party invitation to celebrate the completion of "Snow White and the Seven Dwarfs" (1937), Disney's first full-length feature.

For the invitation," Mr. Kimball recalled, "I did a drawing of Mickey addressing a golf ball; a three-quarter view of the head tipped down, two eyes showed. He is looking at you and also off into the distance beyond you. It would have been impossible to do that drawing before, to make him look at you without rolling . . . the pie eyes over to the scalloped section of his head."

The animators were delighted with the increased possibilities for facial expressions that the new eyes gave them. Mr. Thomas liked the flesh color "because it made Mickey more realistic and it was in keeping with the new pictures we were doing that were making him popular, like the "Brave Little Tailor" and "The Pointer," films requiring strong attitudes and acting." In the first film (1938), Mickey slays a giant and wins the hand of the fair maid Minnie; in "The Pointer" (1939), Mickey and his dog, Pluto, encounter a bear.

Consternation, however, was the response to the changed mouse in the Disney comic-strip department, Mr. Kimball said. "Is that the way you guys are drawing him?" department members said. "Why didn't we know about it?"

To this day the change remains a sore point with toy collectors. Many wish Mickey's design had stayed fixed in the rigid circles of the pre-Moore 1930 advertising and comic-strip version, complete with a tiny slice cut from his pie-shape eyes, simulating light reflection.

The public first saw the new Mickey in 1940, in the sorcerer's-apprentice segment of "Fantasia." Expecting another "Snow White and the Seven Dwarfs," or "Pinocchio," moviegoers instead saw what some considered a silent film, with no dialogue between the characters, only pantomime. But while "Fantasia" was not a box-office success, the new Mickey found acceptance, with some exceptions.

Mel Birnkrant, a major Mickey toy collector, lamenting the attempt to improve what he thought was "already, in 1930, a perfect image," said, "The perfection was lost."

And recently the artist and author Maurice Sendak said of the post-1930 Moore mouse: "I have nothing good to say about the fat Mickey. It was basically Mickey and Walt selling out to Hollywood. It was a deliberate attempt to make him softer, cuter and cuddlier and to take away any of the spice or acidity of the original. He was a malignant little creature in the beginning, which is why he was so charming."

Mickey purists were in for another shock in 1941. In the short film "The Nifty 90's," a turn-of-the-century nostalgia piece in which Mickey attends a vaudeville show complete with animated caricatures of Moore and Mr. Kimball, the two animators removed the mouse's tail, added a light-colored interior section to his ears and dressed him as a dandy—straw boater and all. "More, quote, experimentation," said Mr. Kimball ruefully.

Mickey's shoes and head were so exaggerated in contrast with his tiny body, and the animation so loose and gooey, that he moved like a quivering water-filled balloon. "I thought it was terrible," Mr. Thomas said. "Audiences didn't care for it. Walt said: 'You took the tail off the guy. He's a mouse, you know!'" A modified Mickey, with the familiar round ears and a tail, followed.

After 1947, Mickey made only six theatrical shorts until his last one, "The Simple Things," in 1953. By then, the once irascible Mickey—dressed in slacks, a short-sleeve shirt and loafers—had evolved into the personification of a Eisenhower-era suburbanite and taken a back seat to characters like Pluto.

Mickey Breaks into TV

With the 1950's, of course, came the golden age of television, and Walt Disney was one of the first film producers to embrace the new technology. His historic "Disneyland" series (which changed names throughout its run) had its premiere in 1954 and was televised through 1990. Mickey appeared from time to time on "Disneyland" and, from 1955 through 1958, regularly as the genial host of "The Mickey Mouse Club." There his tiny shape was encased in a thick black outline and animated with smooth subtlety by Mr. Johnston, who had begun his career at Disney as Moore's assistant two decades earlier.

During those years and after, the peripatetic mouse has also been seen in the Disney theme parks and merchandised in doll form, on T-shirts and greeting cards. He has appeared in comic strips and movie featurettes. In the 1970's, the Disney merchandising folk turned him into a Travolta wannabe called Disco Mickey, a mercifully brief transformation. Two 24-minute featurettes—"Mickey's Christmas Carol" (1982), in which Mickey was Bob Cratchit, and "The Prince and the Pauper" (1990), in which he played both starring roles—brought the mouse back to the screen in costume comedies that cast him again as a less-than-exciting guy.

A Return to His Roots

Each age has had its own horrors. For the 90's, the Disney merchandisers have come up with Rapper Mickey, complete with shades (obscuring the embattled eyes), flipped-back baseball cap, hiking boots and low-rider jeans loose enough to reveal part of the famous red short pants. Perhaps this latest creation indicates that Mickey has been running around in his Calvins for more than six decades. Or maybe the image is a tacit acknowledgment of Mickey's ancestral roots. In any case this, too, shall pass.

For nearly four decades at Disney theme parks worldwide, Mickey Mouse's dominant image has been that of an oversize three-dimensional papier-mâché head with a fixed smile that sits atop a small tuxedo-suited human who mutely greets the parks' visitors. The Disney company hopes to replace this static image, as well as the bland Mickey last seen in featurettes, with a dynamic one in "Runaway Brain." Starring in an action-driven role in the intense short-length medium that made his reputation—and looking great, thanks to a reprise of his sparkling mid-30's design—Mickey Mouse is once again ready for his close-up.

Who Is He?

Edward Lewine

Mickey Mouse has earned fame and fortune, but there have always been those who think of him as a silly little rodent, a nebbish, a lightweight. Until recently, it would have seemed odd to associate him with New York. What would America's biggest, sweatiest, edgiest city have in common with a small, clean, placid cartoon mouse from California?

That was then. Nowadays, the mouse's ears are casting big round shadows across the city. In the past few years, the Walt Disney Company, which Mickey Mouse symbolizes, has opened four retail stores, held a film premiere in Central Park and a parade up Fifth Avenue, and staged a Broadway musical. The Disney store at 42d Street and Seventh Avenue—where hustlers and other night denizens once crawled—is basically a shrine to Mickey Mouse, his visage meshed with New York imagery on T-shirts, hats and mugs.

Suddenly, New York and Mickey Mouse go together like bagels and cream cheese, opening the possibility that some day he might be for New York what the she-wolf suckling Romulus and Remus is for Rome: a municipal symbol. For all his blandness, his power is well proved.

"Like yin and yang, like the Christian cross and the star of Israel, Mickey can be seen everywhere—a sign, a rune, a hieroglyphic trace of a secret power, an electricity we want to plug into," John Updike wrote in his introduction to "The Art of Mickey Mouse," a 1991 collection of Mickey Mouse images by various artists. "Like totem poles, like African masks, Mickey stands at the intersection of abstraction and representation where magic connects."

Nevertheless, Mickey Mouse lacks the depth of King Kong, the city's first great animal avatar who rode to fame atop the Empire State Building. (Now there's a real New Yorker: emotionally scarred, sexually frustrated and an immigrant.) But is Mickey Mouse really that simple? New Yorkers who need a frisson of danger and intellectual heft in their urban symbolism have found his arrival a bit disturbing. There are feelings around town that need working through.

It is not easy to make the case for Mickey Mouse. But the truth is that if you are looking for a place to hang your angst, he is not exactly an impossible bet. An examination of his career shows he may not be the uncomplicated soul many take him to be.

"Mickey is everybody's god," wrote E. M. Forster in a 1934 piece, "Mickey and Minnie," "so that even members of the Film Society cease despising their fellow members when he appears."

His career has not been one-dimensional. He started out in 1928 a nasty barnyard animal and then by hook and by crook managed to stay on the bleeding edge of modern show business. He ushered in that Bill Gates-like technical innovation of the 20's, the talking picture. In 1932 he became the youngest actor to win an Oscar.

In 1940, he starred in "Fantasia," the outlandish animation classic that many consider to be the most sophisticated cartoon ever. In the 70's it inspired many a hallucination. Those in the know could be heard to mutter "trippy" during the dancing mushroom sequence, though Mr. Mouse's turn as the Sorcerer's Apprentice is pretty psychedelic, too.

Mickey Mouse has also been fascinating to various intellectuals and artists. Andy Warhol and Claes Oldenburg have used his image and his character has been dissected by essayists like Forster, Mr. Updike, and Stephen Jay Gould.

But then, of course, there is the anti-Mickey camp—people who say he and his creators have perfected the art of modern celebrity, that he is better known for his marketed image than for any specific talent. There is, they say, no there there.

"He is sort of the Zsa Zsa Gabor of animation," said Chuck Jones, a distinguished animator who worked with Mr. Mouse's spunkier matinee rival, Bugs Bunny. "He's famous for being famous."

To start with, though, Mickey Mouse was not the slick corporate spokesmouse he is today. As legend has it, his story began in 1928 on a train from New York to Los Angeles, when a 26-year-old cartoonist named Walt Disney dreamt him up after money men stole away Mr. Disney's protégé, Oswald the Lucky Rabbit.

Mr. Rabbit may have been known as Lucky, but he quickly became a footnote in history—the Wally Pipp of cartoons.

"Mickey had the classic 42d Street beginning," said Michael Mallory, a cartoon historian. "Mickey was waiting in the wings, got his shot and became much more than Oswald the Rabbit."

It was tough at the beginning. At first Mr. Disney tried his new mouse in two silent shorts, "Plane Crazy," a Charles Lindbergh-inspired romp, and "Gallopin' Gaucho," which spoofed Douglas Fairbanks Sr. Neither found distribution. Then the first successful sound picture, "The Jazz Singer," came out, and Mr. Disney had an idea. Sound was still viewed by many as a gimmick, but he wanted his mouse to be up to date. No one knew how the crowd would react, but when a primitive sound cartoon called "Steamboat Willie" starring Mickey Mouse opened at the Colony Theatre in New York, a mixed audience of critics and fans loved its barnyard sounds and musical gags.

"It is an ingenious piece of work with a good deal of fun," declared The New York Times. "It growls, whines, squeaks and makes various other sounds that add to its mirthful quality."

Sound films became the rage and Mickey had been there first. He immediately eclipsed Felix the Cat as the top cartoon idol. Yet this was not the Mickey Mouse we know today. He was scrawny, with a long, sinister face. His hands and feet knew neither glove nor shoe and he spoke in funny noises, not words. And he was a mean guy. In "Steamboat Willie," among other atrocities, the mouse flings a cat overboard, mercilessly squeezes a duck's midriff and tortures a sow by pinching her nipples.

"He started out as a sadistic, ratlike, sexist pig," said John Canemaker, who heads the animation department at the Tisch School of the Arts at New York University. "He was despicable."

The Roaring 20's were a wicked time, and Mickey Mouse's devilish tone had played well. Then the Great Depression hit and tastes changed. People were looking for a new type of star, a humble person like them who would face down life's adversity with nothing but a smile.

Mickey's creators understood this and immediately made over his image. Gone were the ratlike features and naughty attitude. His features

Illustration for "Who Is He?" from the *New York Times*, by Chester Higgins, Jr., and Naum Kazhdan. The image of Mickey is © The Walt Disney Company.

became rounder, he put on decorous white gloves and round shoes. In essence he aged in reverse.

"Mickey's appeal was that sort of insipid friendliness," said Dr. Gould, a Harvard scientist who has written about Mickey Mouse's physiognomy. "Disney knew instinctively that the features of childhood beget those feelings."

These changes set Mr. Mouse up for his greatest era, the 1930's. By 1930 he was already selling merchandise by the millions and he made 87 of his 119 films during this decade. The six-minute films fell into three basic categories. There were musicals, like "Mickey's Grand Opera" (1936), action pictures like "The Brave Little Tailor" (1938) and more down-to-earth stories.

It was in this last type that he defined his essential character. In the Depression-tinged "Moving Day" (1936), for instance, he has his property confiscated because he cannot pay the rent. He keeps smiling, though, and is saved when a gas explosion sends him and all of his belongings to safety.

"Mickey is an extremely optimistic, often put-upon, but ultimately triumphant little guy," Mr. Mallory, the historian, said. "He shows some fear, some anger, but he is not a coward or a hothead."

The mouse was a star, but almost from the beginning his fame brought detractors. His name quickly became a slang term for silliness.

The upcoming volume of the Random House Historical Dictionary of American Slang records more than 10 examples. The entries range from a 1930's jazz musician's reference to bad music like that played in cartoons, to a 1970's military sense meaning the rigid enforcement of petty rules.

"Mickey Mouse might be a great cartoon," explained Jesse Sheidlower, who edited the dictionary. "But it is something fun and light, and so it would have associations of a lack of seriousness."

It was also around this time that it became fashionable to snicker about Mickey Mouse's relationship to Minnie Mouse, the cute and plucky heroine he appeared with in many films. Somehow, maybe because the two always seemed so chaste, people found it irresistible to accuse them of passionate sexuality or to wonder about their seeming physical indifference to each another.

"It is a forced studio marriage like Troy Donahue and Suzanne Pleshette," sniffed Stefan Kanfer, author of "Serious Business: The Art and Commerce of Animation in America."

While Mickey Mouse was taking off, Mr. Disney was also having great success with his "Silly Symphonies," in which cartoonists would come up with images to fit classical music pieces. In 1939, Mr. Disney put Mickey Mouse in a Silly Symphony based on "The Sorcerer's Apprentice." The short film was beautiful, but so costly that Mr. Disney decided to build an entire feature around it and call it "Fantasia."

The result was the most sophisticated cartoon ever made. It was so fine that the original idea was to screen it in concert halls. Critics agree that his portrayal of the apprentice was his finest performance. In comic pantomime straight from the pages of Charlie Chaplin's Little Tramp character, he expresses the gamut of emotion from joy to contrition.

It was a performance that seemed to herald a new era of acting for him, but "Fantasia" would mark the end of his career as a full-time actor.

World War II killed production at the Disney studios for much of the 1940's, and Mickey Mouse became the good soldier, spending his time promoting war bonds. After the fighting stopped, Mickey Mouse returned to the screen in "Fun and Fancy Free" (1947), in which he played Jack in a "Jack and the Beanstalk" segment. He was still a star, but around the studio the feeling was that his best days were behind him.

"Mickey fell by the wayside," said Ed Benedict, a Disney employee in the 30s. "He was a bit too namby-pamby as the years went on."

That has been the dialectic for Mickey Mouse. Too sweet? Not sweet enough? In the 20's he had made an image change to stay current, but after the war he was not allowed to. Many around the studio say that Mr. Disney was the cause.

"There were people who felt that Mickey should change," said Frank Thomas, who worked with Disney from 1934 to 1978, "but Walt wouldn't let them."

And so here came a plot twist that would sound right at home in the office of an Upper West Side psychiatrist. What seems to have happened is that Mr. Disney came to identify so strongly with Mr. Mouse that he couldn't bear to see him grow up. In "Disney's World," Leonard Mosley's 1986 biography, the animator is described as having walked, talked and even eaten like his prized mouse for long periods of time.

Studio insiders say that by the late 1940's Mickey Mouse had become a son, an alter ego and a good luck charm to Mr. Disney. The mouse would not be allowed to change even if it killed his acting career.

The final death blow to Mickey Mouse's acting aspirations came in the 1950's when theater operators stopped showing shorts in favor of squeezing in an extra feature each day. The rap on Mickey Mouse had always been that he could not carry a full-length picture with his nice personality; his medium had always been the short film. But now there was no venue for shorts. It seemed as though the mouse's career was over.

"They gave him a corner office and secretary," Mr. Kanfer joked.

Yet, true to his plucky, never-say-die attitude, he was not defeated by changing times. In the same way that other old-time stars like George Burns and Groucho Marx were transformed from movie actors into television hosts, so was Mickey Mouse. In 1955 he found important roles for himself pressing the flesh at Disneyland, his newly-opened theme park and as the host of the daily television show "The Mickey Mouse Club." Never mind that he wasn't really performing much at either venue; he was keeping himself in the public eye.

More than 40 years have passed since then, and Mickey Mouse's life has not changed all that much. The mouse we had then ("Gee!" "Gosh!") is the mouse we have now. He is a corporate spokesman and that is all. And that turns out to be the cause of some friction.

There are many in the cartoon community and even within Disney who would like to see him back in movies, acting again. They believe he is capable of change.

But so far this idea has been frustrated. Mickey Mouse's personality is just so specific and his role as corporate symbol so important that it is too risky now to take him in new artistic directions.

"There is so much riding on Mickey," said Andreas Deja, who animated Mickey Mouse in his last short, "Runaway Brain" (1994). "He has become a symbol for Disney so much that finding the right role for him can be so hard."

So where does this leave a skeptical New Yorker? Perhaps Mickey Mouse can be seen as a corporate prisoner, representing suppressed individuality in the name of image and profits.

Or, as his career teaches us, he can be seen as everyman, a survivor, with ups and downs, just like everyone else. Or maybe there's a fatalistic way of looking at things. We must put up with him because he is part of that great irreversible continental cultural exchange that gives us a dose of Middle America but that allows us to find our city in the larger culture.

Or perhaps as you stand in the Disney store and watch children squeal with delight over a Mickey Mouse doll and bargain with parents for one more purchase and see the cash register rushed by customers, you might also look at it this way:

By the ultimate New York measure. Mickey Mouse is one important guy.

As Mr. Disney used to say of his empire, "I hope we never lose sight of one fact. That this was all started by a mouse."

The Meaning of Mickey Mouse

Garry Apgar

Visual Resources: An International Journal of Documentation 14, no. 3, January 1999

In purely biographical or psychological terms, Mickey Mouse was in many ways the fictional extension and alter ego of his creator, Walt Disney, who provided his squeaky voice on film for years. However, Mickey soon took on a life wholly his own. Walt's signature character eventually became not only a Disney corporate symbol but would serve as a generic emblem of cartoons as a whole. In France, for instance, the term *petits micquets* is sometimes used to designate any form of cartoons or comic-book art. Of course, there is much more to the phenomenon that is Mickey Mouse. When his first animated short, *Steamboat Willie*, premièred in December 1929, the Mouse, as John Updike put it, "entered history as the most persistent and pervasive figment of American popular culture in this century."[1]

Mickey's huge popular impact was immediate, in part because, as the *Boston American* pointed out in 1933:

> he came to us at the time the country needed him most—at the beginning of the Depression. He has helped us laugh away our troubles, forget our creditors and keep our chins up.[2]

A few months later, the *Los Angeles Times* observed that "Mickey is 'Everyman'":

> He is little David who slays Goliath. He is that most popular, because most universally conceivable hero—the little man who shuts his eyes and pastes the big bully in the jaw.[3]

All well and good. But what of the enduring pull he has exerted, for more than six decades now, on the elitist hearts and minds of intellectuals, writers and artists? Disney himself could never have answered such a question. When Aldous Huxley asked him in 1945 to account for his creations' success, he replied: "Hell, Doc, I don't know. We just try to make a good picture. And then the professors come along and tell us what we do."[4]

The matter of the Mouse was addressed in print for the first time, at least nominally, in 1934 in a *Scribner's Magazine* piece by Claude Bragdon, "Mickey Mouse and What He Means," which unfortunately did not deliver on the sweeping promise of its title.[5] Also in 1934, E. M. Forster published a witty but brief disquisition on Mickey as leading man and lover.[6] Over time, other writers would tackle the issue at greater length and with greater success. In 1949, for example, the novelist Irving Wallace, penned a breezy, fact-filled essay in *Collier's*, "Mickey Mouse and How He Grew."[7] But there was little more of substance until the golden anniversary of Mickey's "birth," in 1978, when Maurice Sendak's autobiographical piece, "Growing Up With Mickey," and John Culhane's insightful article, "A Mouse for All Seasons," were published in *TV Guide* and *Saturday Review*, respectively.[8] In 1979, Stephen Jay Gould's seminal study, "Mickey Mouse Meets Konrad Lorenz," appeared in *Natural History* magazine.[9] 1986 produced a marvelous, richly documented survey of the character's critical fortunes by Bevis Hillier in his introduction to a book on Mickey memorabilia.[10]

In 1992, the exhibition catalogue *Keith Haring, Andy Warhol, and Walt Disney* put the issue of Disney's creative merits on the table of Post-Modern art history.[11] In the same year, another book did the same for Mickey: *The Art of Mickey Mouse* contains dozens of visual salutes by Warhol, Haring, Eduardo Paolozzi, Wayne Thiebaud,[12] Don Eddy, Milton Glaser and others (including a drawing by Michael Jackson that is truly "bad")—plus John Updike's informed and moving essay from which I have already quoted.[13]

* * *

Naturally, in speaking of Mickey Mouse, one must stipulate which "Mickey" one has in mind. As Stephen Jay Gould demonstrated, the character underwent a remarkable "neotenic" evolution over the years. At first, he was a scamp: more aggressive, more rodent-like than later versions, his snout and body more angular, his actions more slapstick, herky-jerky and even violent. The classic "mature" Mickey of *ca.* 1935, when he began to star in color cartoons, retained his original playful qualities, but his physiognomy and proportions were becoming softer, more rounded. By the 1940s, after he appeared in *Fantasia*, his features more closely resemble those of a small child, thereby, as Gould points out, subliminally triggering instinctive human affection.

One also can view Mickey's formal metamorphosis in terms akin to the standard stylistic trajectory of ancient Greek art. In his earliest incarnation, his physical traits echo those of an Archaic kouros: youthful, primitive, nearly nude, radiating good vibes and raw energy. Mickey's quintessential look and canonical proportions reached perfection during the depths of the Depression. The antique analogue for this archetypal Mickey is the high-Classical, Polykleitan phase of Greek sculpture. Around 1940, a bolder style set in. The gowned Mickey as he appears at one point in the "Sorcerer's Apprentice" segment of *Fantasia*, dramatically poised on a rocky promontory, recalls Grecian goddesses in flowing drapery typified by "Hellenistic Baroque" monuments like the Winged Victory of Samothrace. Finally, there is what, in crypto-Wölfflinian terms, may be referred to as the "Decline-and-Fall" stage: the degeneration of the once-frisky Mouse into a fully clothed, post-war suburbanite, as he was drawn by Floyd Gottfredson in comic strips in the 1950s and 1960s. This is the same figure who, like a former pro athlete, down on his luck, now works the crowd as a "greeter" at the Disney theme parks.

The Mouse is as popular today as ever. In 1996 *Entertainment Weekly* proclaimed him one of the "100 greatest movie stars of all time."[14] But the nature of Mickey's popularity and its novelty have changed tremendously. The first Mickey Mouse clubs were a unique sensation. In 1931, they boasted an unprecedented million members nationwide. Abroad, 20 newspapers carried the Mickey Mouse comic strip and he was immortalized at Madame Tussaud's in London.[15] A 1931 cartoon by Karl Arnold in the German review *Simplicissimus* spotlighted Mickey's cosmopolitan fame, as Frederick the Great joins modern-day celebrities like Chaplin in dumb admiration of this "unreal," pint-size upstart.[16] A contrasting compliment was paid to Mickey and company by a Soviet critic who said:

Disney is really showing us the people of the capitalistic world under the masks of mice, pigs and penguins. A definite social satire.[17]

"Having become the darling of the proletariat," Irving Wallace noted, "Mickey was then adopted by the carriage trade and the lorgnette set."[18] A Mickey-Mouse cartoon-art show ran for six weeks at the Kennedy Galleries in New York in 1932.[19] Another show called "The Art of Mickey Mouse" opened at the Evansville, Indiana, Temple of Fine Arts, in January 1933.[20] In December 1933, an exhibition of Mickey-Mouse and Silly-Symphonies art was organized by the College Art Association. It traveled to numerous venues, including the Art Institute in Disney's birthplace, Chicago. The *New York Herald Tribune* reported that "Mickey Mouse is supreme."[21]

Such success was not without its naysayers. A Midwestern editorialist lamented that he

for one, was sorry to see Mickey Mouse elevated to the plane of high art. Once he was amusing. Now he is significant and at the mercy of every high-browed critic in the nation.[22]

Mickeymania reached an even higher peak of intensity in 1934. A cartoon by Alain in the *New Yorker*'s January 20th issue showed a young man exclaiming to a woman friend: "All you hear is Mickey Mouse, Mickey Mouse, Mickey Mouse! It's as though Chaplin had never lived!" In his 1934 essay, E. M. Forster echoed the point: "Mickey is everybody's god, so that even members of the Film Society cease despising their fellow members when he appears."[23] 1934 was a banner year in many ways. In that year, another Britisher, John Betjman, the future Poet Laureate, praised Mickey Mouse cartoon shorts as among the cinema's "best entertainment,"[24] and Walt Disney became an honorary member of the British Art Workers Guild, joining luminaries like George Bernard Shaw.[25] Also in 1934, the urbane American humorist James Thurber excitedly imagined a Disney animated version of *The Odyssey*. A 50-foot Mickey Mouse balloon appeared in Macy's Thanksgiving Day parade.[26] That demigod of art history, Erwin Panofsky, hailed the Mouse as Felix the Cat's "prodigious offspring."[27] And Cole Porter wrote "You're the Top," with its memorable rhyme:

You're an Bendel bonnet,
A Shakespeare sonnet,
You're Mickey Mouse.

Clearly, by the mid-1930s, Mickey Mouse was the epitome of chic. In 1935, as Irving Wallace wrote, he was "stuck on the wall between a Picasso painting and an Epstein sculpture" at London's Leicester Galleries.[28] In Noel Coward's sophisticated stage production *To-night at 8:30* (1936), one of the characters, referring to a cartoon short at the cinema, laments: "We'll miss the Mickey."

As a show of Disney art toured the United States in 1938, the Metropolitan Museum of Art in New York lauded Disney as "the greatest historical figure in the development of American art."[29] The following year, the Los Angeles County Museum mounted a retrospective exhibition of Disney art that would travel to Cincinnati, St. Louis and, among other venues, Chicago's Art Institute again.[30] Mickey was included in *Vanity Fair*'s pantheon of "1938 Radio Stars,"[31] and his talismanic name was uttered in Howard Hawks' 1938 screw-ball comic film classic, *Bringing Up Baby*. When Cary Grant and Katharine Hepburn are mistakenly jailed in rustic Fairfield County, Connecticut, the constable, who thinks they are hardened criminals, asks Grant to name his accomplices. Grant's exasperated reply: "Mickey the Mouse and Donald the Duck."

* * *

Mickey's "classical" visual persona probably reached its apex with the animated short *The Band Concert* of 1935. The distinguished film critic Gilbert Seldes said he doubted "very much whether half a dozen works produced in America at the same time in all the other arts can stand comparison with this one."[32] The abstract painter Mondrian probably would have nominated another Disney film for top honors. He was hopelessly smitten by Walt's first full-length animated feature and winner of the Oscar for Best Picture in 1937, *Snow White and the Seven Dwarfs*, which he saw in Paris in 1938. Several *Snow White* postcards sent by Mondrian to his brother in that year underscore his fondness for the film.[33]

The high-water mark of Disney's ties to the heady realm of high art involved Salvador Dalí, yet another titan of twentieth-century painting, who worked for several months at Disney's studio in 1946 on a six-minute animated sequence for a sequel to the 1939 feature *Fantasia*. Unsurprisingly, the Dalí project, entitled *Destino*, came to naught.[34] *Fantasia* itself had been a flop.[35] In fact, the film's failure at the box office marked the start of a gradual 20-year downturn in the critical fortunes of both Disney and Mickey. Ernst Gombrich, for one, felt that by "prematurely trivializing" the marriage of "music and pure shapes" in *Fantasia*, Disney brought discredit on the experimental union of different art forms.[36] At the time Gombrich expressed this view, in 1958, Mickey's image, and, to some extent, Disney's, were tainted in the minds of the intelligentsia by the cutesy vulgarity of the Mickey Mouse Club TV show. However, a generation later, in 1980, *Time* art critic Robert Hughes brought the debate back full circle. With specific reference to the scene in the film where Mickey shakes hands with Leopold Stokowski, Hughes spoke of Pop Art's likely debt to *Fantasia* for "the *rapprochement* . . . of high and low."[37]

A harbinger of Mickey's ultimate critical resurgence, and one of the first high-art appropriations of his image, is a pair of collages by the English artist Eduardo Paolozzi, executed in 1948, three years before Paolozzi helped found the proto-Pop, Independent Group. In *Real Gold* (Tate Gallery, London), a pre-war Mickey, counterbalanced by a magazine ad for Real Gold Lemon juice, perches on the haunch of a bikini-clad starlet clipped from a pulp-fiction magazine cover. In the second collage, *Meet the People* (also at the Tate), Minnie Mouse powders her face while surrounded by magazine cuttings of film star Lucille Ball (from pre-"I Love Lucy" days) and mundane emblems of domesticity like a glass of orange juice and a tin of White Star Tuna. The pungent, slightly off-putting tastes we associate with lemon juice and tuna fish, empathically reinforce Paolozzi's subversive jab at bourgeois consumerism.[38] By 1948, Mickey Mouse cartoon shorts were dying out. In 1949, just four were produced (Donald Duck, his star then on the ascendant, appeared in nine that year). By snipping and pasting up 1930s imagery of the cartoon characters, Paolozzi gave an intentionally archaic edge to his kitschy critique of industrial-age home life, and, I suspect, betrayed a degree of affection, even nostalgia, for Disney's cheerful rodent couple.

American Pop artists tended to be more openly fond of the Mouse.

Like Paolozzi, Roy Lichtenstein, Warhol and Claus Oldenburg all were born in the 1920s and had grown up with Mickey. One of the first bona fide Pop pictures, Lichtenstein's 1961 oil on canvas *Look Mickey I've Hooked a Big One!* is a joyous pastiche of a Disney comic of the period (National Gallery of Art, Washington, D.C.).[39]

The man Robert Hughes has called "the thinking person's Walt Disney,"[40] had a more complicated relationship with Mickey Mouse. In 1978, Oldenburg established the definitive inventory of the Mouse Museum, a potpourri of hundreds of pop effluvia that he had collected or made over the years. His *Geometric Mouse*, a stylized sculptural abstraction of Mickey's head, which served as a logo for Oldenburg's 1969 exhibition at New York's Museum of Modern Art, actually had its genesis in an architectural design for the Mouse Museum.[41] Oldenburg also appended to the Mouse Museum what he called the Ray Gun Wing.[42] His partner, Coosje van Bruggen, has explained why Oldenburg chose to link Mickey Mouse to toy pistols and other gun-shaped objects:

> The release of violence is transformed into an energizing force, as it is in George Herriman's *Krazy Kat* comic strip when Ignatz the mouse throws his bricks at the Kat. . . When the brick bounces off Krazy Kat's head, a little heart spirals off it as well, symbolizing [Krazy Kat's] gratitude to the mouse for paying attention. Oldenburg prefers Ignatz, who in his ingenious wickedness is described as "a malignant little tangle of barbed wire," to the welladjusted, conformist Mickey Mouse.[43]

This statement is, however, contradicted by Oldenburg who once told an interviewer: "I'm the *Mouse*," adding that "the Mouse is a state of mind."[44] Lichtenstein's short-lived appropriations of Mickey Mouse, around 1960, began at a time when he was drawing famous cartoon characters to amuse his children.[45] Oldenburg's conflicted take on Mickey is anything but "family-oriented." In a 1967 poster for a gallery show of his work, in which Oldenburg apparently employed the Mouse motif for the first time, a demonic Sorceror's Apprentice glowers at a heart floating in space. This almost obsessive reiteration of the image of Mickey, over a span of more than a decade, suggests a love-hate relationship comparable to Krazy Kat's masochistic response to Ignatz's brickbats.[46]

Unlike Oldenburg, Andy Warhol's Mouse art seems to come straight from the heart. Dave Hickey has surmised that Warhol's soup cans reminded him of "quiet afternoons in Pittsburgh and New York," when mom "would heat him up a can of Campbell's." If that is so, Warhol's silkscreen *Mickey* in the 1981 *Myths* series may well be laden with latent childhood memories too. Warhol's disarmingly simple effigy assumes added weight if we bear in mind what John Culhane has said: firstly, that Mickey's face is "a trinity of wafers" and, secondly, that, as Jung decreed, the circle "always points to the single most vital aspect of life—its ultimate wholeness."[47]

Warhol's cool, totemic design has virtually defined, for most contemporary "adults," our almost mystical mental image of Mickey. It also symbolically capped a popular and critical comeback that had begun in the 1960s and continues to this day. As Updike has remarked, Mickey's "life as an icon," like that of Marilyn Monroe, actually got stronger over time.[48] Indeed, the Mouse is now a world-wide symbol of American cultural, commercial and military clout.

* * *

Over recent decades, Mickey has inspired a wide range of other major artists foreign and domestic, from Europeans like Michael Sandle, Otto Künzli[49] and Rob Birza[50] to Americans such as Saul Steinberg,[51] Dennis Oppenheim[52] and Joyce Pensato.[53] Possibly the most ambitious of their works, Sandle's bronze sculpture, *A Twentieth Century Memorial*, now at the Tate, was completed in 1978. This mock-heroic representation of a malevolent, skeletal Mouse, manning a machine gun, was conceived in response to the Vietnam war.[54] It plays off the Ray-Gun critique of Oldenburg—and Oldenburg's trademark preoccupation with the issue of anti-monumentality.

Left-leaning assaults on Disney came to the fore in the 1960s and '70s, as typified by Sandle's *Memorial*, by Richard Schickel's 1966 book *The Disney Version*, which a revisionist *Village Voice* writer later called "ungenerous,"[55] and by David Kunzle's 1975 introduction to the lively Marxist screed by Ariel Dorfmann and Armand Mattelart, *How To Read Donald Duck*. GIs in Vietnam would grouse about "Mickey Mouse operations" and "Mickey Mouse shit" in general.[56] (In Stanley Kubrick's 1987 film *Full-Metal Jacket*, a platoon of Marines moves out across the rice paddies singing the Mickey Mouse Club march.) Such *lèse-majesté* would have been all but unthinkable a generation earlier. In World War II, Disney characters were used as jolly, reverse-apotropaic devices on military aircraft and vehicles, and "Mickey Mouse" was the codeword for the Normandy invasion.

An ebullient effigy of Ronald Reagan as Mickey Mouse by Robert Grossman, dates from the Vietnam war years (1967). The cartoonist drew the then governor of California in white gloves, red shorts, yellow dinner-roll shoes and the jet black mouse ears, bare chest and tubular legs of the classic Mickey. Grossman's *Ronald Rodent* is a compound image of seemingly simplistic American idealism.[57] It soars, in good measure, on the profoundly ironic and engaging baggage Disney's character carries, just as every other great homage or pastiche, including Warhol's, has.

Like Ronald Reagan, the Mouse may appear to represent the lockstep march of middle-class values and an irrepressible, adolescent optimism utterly free of *Angst* or intellectual curiosity. However, again like Reagan, Mickey also embodies the plucky, can-do spirit of his compatriots and the dynamic, youthful engine that drives the American Dream.

Updike put his finger on at least a partial explanation of why Disney's multi-faceted creation continues to seize our attention:

> The America that is not symbolized by the imperial Yankee Uncle Sam is symbolized by Mickey Mouse. He is America as it feels itself—plucky, put-on, inventive, resilient, good-natured, game.[58]

As an icon of American ideals and values, Mickey is a Happy Face with legs, John Wayne without an attitude.

Small wonder then that Madonna would pose in a saucy, hyper-iconic photo by Herb Ritts in *Rolling Stone* (1987), as Mickey's paramour, clutching a bedsheet to her bosom, à la Marilyn Monroe, and gaily sporting a pair of Minnie Mouse ears on her head.[59]

Notes

This essay is dedicated to two of Mickey's many friends, Francis and Mathew.

1. Updike, "Introduction" to Craig Yoe and Janet Morra-Yoe, *The Art of Mickey Mouse* (New York: Hyperion, 1991), n.p.

2. Article by Edwin C. Hill (8 August 1933); cited in Bevis Hillier's "Introduction" to Hillier and Bernard C. Shine, *Walt Disney's Mickey Mouse Memorabilia: The Vintage Years 1928–1938* (New York: Harry N. Abrams, 1986), 11.

3. Article by Arthur Millier (5 November 1933).

4. Quoted in Irving Wallace, "Mickey Mouse and How He Grew," *Collier's* (9 April 1949): 36.

5. *Scribner's Magazine* (July 1934): 40–43.

6. "Mickey and Minnie," republished in Forster, *Abinger Harvest* (New York: Harcourt, Brace & World, 1964).

7. Wallace, "Mickey Mouse," 20–21, 35–36.

8. *TV Guide* (11 November 1978): 16–17; *Saturday Review* (11 November 1978): 50–51.

9. (May 1979): 30, 32, 24, 36.

10. See Hillier, "Introduction" to Hillier and Shine, *Disney's Mickey Mouse Memorabilia*, 10–27.

11. Bruce D. Kurtz, Bruce Hamilton, Geoffrey Blum and Dave Hickey, *Keith Haring, Andy Warhol, and Walt Disney* (Munich: Prestel, 1992). The itinerary of the show included the Tacoma Art Museum, the Corcoran Gallery of Art and the Worcester Art Museum.

12. Like Walt Kelly, the creator of the comic strip *Pogo*, Thiebaud, as a young man, had been an animator at the Disney studio.

13. "Introduction," n.p.

14. See Steve Daly, "Mickey Mouse: The Mighty Mite" (November 1996): 108.

15. Marshall Fishwick, "Aesop in Hollywood: The Man and the Mouse" (10 July 1954): 39.

16. The cartoon appeared on p. 526. On 28 February 1931, the Seattle (Wash.) *Motion Picture Record* reported that Charlie Chaplin had "requested that his latest production, *City Lights*, be accompanied wherever possible with a Mickey Mouse cartoon. This unusual request bears up Charlie's high regard for . . . the cartoon character and surety in that his own presentation will meet with a greater acclaim after an audience has been amused by Mickey's antics." On March 16th of the same year, a cartoon by George Corley appeared in the Portland (Ore.) *News* showing Chaplin as the Little Tramp presenting a flower to Mickey Mouse. See Hillier, "Introduction," 15–16.

17. Wallace, "Mickey Mouse," 36.

18. *Idem.*

19. See Hillier, "Introduction," 21.

20. Evansville (Indiana) *Press* (8 December 1933), cited in Hillier, "Introduction," 21.

21. See Hillier, "Introduction," 16.

22. Columbus (Ohio) *Dispatch* (16 December 1933); cited in Hillier, "Introduction," 21–22.

23. Forster, "Mickey and Minnie," 53.

24. Betjman's comment came in a piece he published in the *London Evening Standard* (23 April 1934); see Hillier, "Introduction," 16.

25. See Churchill, "Now Mickey Mouse Enters Art's Temple," *New York Times Magazine* (3 June 1934): 12; Hillier, *Disney's Mickey Mouse Memorabilia*, 21. For further proof of the global popularity of Mickey Mouse at this time, see Harold Butcher, "An International Mouse," *New York Times* (28 October 1934): X 4 (section 9, "Drama—Screen—Music").

26. See Hillier, "Introduction," 23 and 15, respectively (Thurber's remark appeared in *The Nation*, in the March 1934 issue).

27. Panofsky, "Style and Medium in the Motion Pictures" in *Critique: A Review of Contemporary Art* I: 3 (January-February 1947); republished in revised form in Daniel Talbot, ed., *Film: An Anthology* (New York, Simon & Schuster, 1959), 23.

28. Wallace, "Mickey Mouse," 36; Hillier, "Introduction," 21.

29. See Wallace, "Mickey Mouse," 36; Fishwick, "Man and the Mouse," 39.

30. The show was entitled a "Retrospective Exhibition of the Walt Disney Medium." See Martin Krause and Linda Witkowski, *Walt Disney's Snow White and the Seven Dwarfs: An Art in its Making* (New York: Hyperion, 1994), 50.

31. A color cartoon by Miguel Covarrubias depicting the stars was reprinted in the December 1996 issue of *Vanity Fair*.

32. Seldes, *Cinema Arts* (July 1937): 24.

33. At the time, Mondrian identified personally with Sleepy. See Els Hoek, "Mondrian in Disneyland," *Art in America* (February 1989): 136–140, 142.

34. Disney had been impressed by Dalí's collaboration with Alfred Hitchcock on the film *Spellbound*. On Dalí and Disney, see: Robert Descharnes (Eleanor R. Morse, trans.), *Salvador Dalí: The Work: The Man* (New York: Abrams, 1984), 289, 309–311; James Bigwood, "Cinquante ans de cinéma dalinien," pp. 349–351 in Pontus Hulten, *et al.*, *Salvador Dalí: rétrospective 1920–1980* (Paris: Centre Georges Pompidou, 1979); Pontus Hulten, *et al.*, *La Vie publique de Salvador Dalí* (Paris: Centre Georges Pompidou, 1980), 120; Leonard Shan-

non, "When Disney Met Dali—the Result Was a Film that Was Never Finished," *Modern Maturity* (December 1978/January 1979).

Curiously, none of the chief Disney detractors (eg., Richard Schickel, David Kunzle) makes mention of Disney's connections with artistic or literary lions like Mondrian, Huxley, Dalí. In his *Walt Disney: Hollywood's Dark Prince* (New York: Birch Lane Press, 1993), 186–187, Marc Eliot does speak of Huxley, but only in the context of Disney's anti-communism and hostility to organized labor.

35. Not everyone, of course, panned *Fantasia*. In the 5 January 1942 issue of *The New Republic*, in an article entitled "Leonardo da Disney," the great British political cartoonist David Low, extolled *Snow White*, *Pinocchio* and *Fantasia* as films which considerably extended the range of animation art (p. 17). The piece is illustrated with six small character sketches, five of which relate to *Fantasia*.

36. "The Vogue of Abstract Art," in Gombrich, *Meditations on a Hobby Horse: And Other Essays on the Theory of Art* (London: Phaidon, 1963), 149 (first published in the *Atlantic Monthly*, April 1958, 43–48).

37. Hughes, *The Shock of the New* (New York: Alfred A. Knopf, 1991, rev. ed.), 341.

38. On Paolozzi's two images, and his connections with the Independent Group (I.G.) in England, see: Thomas Lawson, "Bunk: Eduardo Paolozzi and the Legacy of the Independent Group," in the exhibition catalogue *Modern Dreams: The Rise and Fall of Pop* (Cambridge, Mass., and London, 1988), 19–29; Kirk Varnedoe and Adam Gopnik, *High & Low: Modern Art and Popular Culture*, exhibition catalogue (Museum of Modern Art, New York, 1990), 319 (fig. 141), 425 (n. 184).

39. See Varnedoe and Gopnik, *High & Low*, 196 (fig. 71).

40. Hughes, *Shock of the New*, 356.

41. Oldenburg and Coosje van Bruggen, *A Bottle of Notes and Some Voyages*, exhibition catalogue (Leeds, England: Northern Centre for Contemporary Art, Sunderland, and The Henry Moore Centre for the Study of Sculpture, Leeds City Art Galleries, 1988), 93 (illus.).

42. Claus Oldenburg, "Aboard the Broome Street," in Oldenburg and Van Bruggen, *A Bottle of Notes*, 12. For more on the Mouse Museum and the Ray Gun Wing, see: Oldenburg, *The Mouse Museum: The Ray Gun Wing: Two Collections: Two Buildings*, exhibition catalogue (Chicago: Museum of Contem-

porary Art, 1978); Van Bruggan, *Claes Oldenburg: Mouse Museum: Ray Gun Wing*, exhibition catalogue (Cologne: Museum Ludwig, 1979).

43. Van Bruggen, "The Haunted House: Ghosting," in Oldenburg and Van Bruggen, *A Bottle of Notes*, 193.

44. Interview with Martin Friedman, in Friedman and Oldenburg, *Oldenburg: Six Themes* (Minneapolis: Walker Art Center, 1975), 25.

45. Quoted in David Britt (ed.), *Modern Art: Impressionism to Post-Modernism* (Boston, Toronto & London: 1974), 310. After 1962, Lichtenstein quit using easily identifiable characters like Mickey Mouse "in favor of more anonymous strips"; see Jonathan Fineberg, *Art Since 1940: Strategies of Being* (New York: Harry N. Abrams, 1995), 261. See also: Albert Boime, "Roy Lichtenstein and the Comic Strip," *Art Journal* 28: 2 (Winter 1968–1969), 155–159; Ernst A. Busche, *Roy Lichtenstein: Das Frühwerk 1942–1960* (Berlin: Gebr. Mann Verlag, 1988), 223–231.

46. See Varnedoe and Gopnik, *High & Low*, 208.

47. Quoted in Culhane, "Mouse for All Seasons," 50.

48. Updike, "Introduction," n.p.

49. For Künzli's stylized Mickey art-cum-jewelry, see William Zimmer, "Swiss Artist's Symbol of America," *New York Times* (17 May 1992): CN 24.

50. On the painter Birza, see Jonathan Turner, "The Netherlands: Changing Colors," *Art in America* (December 1992): 83.

51. See, for instance, Jean Leymarie and John Updike, *Saul Steinberg: Fifty Works From the Collection of Sivia and Jeffrey Loria* (Verona, Italy: Jeffrey H. Loria & Co., 1995), 86–91.

52. For Oppenheim's outdoor sculpture *Virus* (1991), in which he used figures of Mickey and Donald Duck, see Robin Cembalest, "The Mouse That Roared," *Artnews* (January 1993): 35.

53. For some of Pensato's "ferocious images of the ur-mouse," see Nancy Princenthal, "Joyce Pensato and Scott Burton at Max Protech," *Art in America* (January 1996): 97–98.

54. Sandle may not actually credit Oldenburg for inspiring this work. The "idea of putting animal heads on human bodies may have been instigated for him by the example of Egyptian art," according to Norbert Lynton, "Michael Sandle: An Introduction," in Lynton and Colin Amery, *Michael Sandle: Memorials for the Twentieth Century*, exhibition catalogue (Liverpool: Tate Gallery, Liverpool, 1995), 8, 17 (n. 8).

55. William Paul, "Disney (1): Pantheon Pantheist," *The Village Voice* (2 August 1973): 71.

56. Disney archivist Dave Smith has reported that the dismissive or derogatory use of the term "Mickey Mouse" dates back to World War II. See William Safire's thumbnail history of its usage in his weekly "On Language" column in the *New York Times Magazine* (9 December 1990): 26.

57. For Grossman's *Ronald Rodent*, see: Brad Benedict, *Fame* (New York: Harmony Books, 1980), 69 (illus.); Steven Heller and Gail Anderson, *The Savage Mirror: The Art of Contemporary Caricature* (New York: Watson-Guptill Publications, 1992), 60–62 (illus.).

58. Updike, "Introduction," n.p.

59. See Todd Gitlin, "Stars Just Want to Have Fun," *New York Times Book Review* (3 December 1989): 14 (illus.).

Through the Years We'll All Be Friends: The "Mickey Mouse Club," Consumerism, and the Cultural Consensus

Barbara J. Coleman

*Visual Resources: An International Journal
of Documentation* 14, no. 3. January 1999

> I remember my mother one day telling me to switch to Howdy Doody. . . . I
> threw a fit when she changed the channel because an episode of my beloved
> "Spin and Marty" was being shown on [the] Mickey Mouse [Club]. . . . And my
> mother wanted me to watch the same old clown blasting the boring old Buf-
> falo with the same old fizz. Who was she kidding? What did she think I was, a
> baby? I was in love with these kids on this new show and no amount of familial
> pressure was going to keep me from watching the Mickey Mouse Club.[1]
> —Stephen Davis

In January 1967 *Time* magazine published its "Man of the Year" issue: the distinction went to the entire postwar Baby Boom generation
of which Stephen Davis was a member. Focusing its attention on the
white, affluent suburban teenager, *Time* characterized the boomers as
"cushioned by unprecedented affluence . . . [with] a sense of economic
security unmatched in history."[2] From the very start, the Baby Boom
generation has been equated with affluence and a bright economic future. Born after World War II, they were acknowledged by advertisers
as both a dynamic social force and an economic one. Even before these
adolescents reached adulthood, marketing executives recognized the
potential of the preteen and teenage markets. According to the United

States Bureau of the Census, by 1960 the percentage of people nineteen and under constituted 38.5% of the total population.[3] Some would argue that this population explosion was the result of postwar euphoria and optimism reignited after the Depression and World War II. Historian Paul Light notes that others "believed this boom merely paralleled a decade of remarkable economic performance with cars and children rolling off the assembly line in unprecedented numbers."[4] In any event, advertisers were quick to appreciate the potential buying power of affluent suburban teenagers. Business strategists suggested that if companies could capture the brand loyalty of the preteen/teen market, they would, through the coming decades, ensure a consistent if not growing market for their products as Baby Boomers matured.[5]

Besides being consumers, this generation of roughly 70,000,000 children born between the years 1946 and 1964 had the distinction of being the first to grow up with television. In 1955, 30.7 million or 64.5% of American homes had televisions. By 1960, 85.9% of households had at least one TV.[6] It has been estimated that by the time the average teenager of the 1950s "reached sixteen, he or she had watched from 12,000 to 15,000 hours of television or the equivalent of 24 hours a day for fifteen to twenty solid months."[7] And it is no wonder that they watched it so much. To the kids, TV was free and intimate. Exciting TV personalities addressed them directly and children could sit as close to the tube as their mothers would allow.

Studies of the media proved that not only were these children watching television, but they were becoming visually astute at identifying advertisers' brand names as well. Inundated with television commercials, the kids effortlessly learned to recognize logos of their favorite products as they bounced across the screen. As art historian Erwin Panofsky noted of this fascination, "the primordial basis of the enjoyment of moving pictures [is] not an objective interest in the specific subject matter, much less aesthetic interest in the formal presentation of the subject matter but the sheer delight in the fact that things seemed to move, no matter what things these were."[8] It did not seem to matter to the kids whether the flickering images depicted were a commercial or a regularly scheduled program. TV was just fun and children could sing along enthusiastically in the privacy of their own living rooms as Bucky Beaver urged them to "brusha, brusha, brusha" with Ipana toothpaste.

Recognizing the television medium as a boon to advertising, marketing strategists wrote books and articles addressed to companies wishing to exploit the television viewer. Walt Disney and the ABC network capitalized on the burgeoning preteen market. Their programming appealed to a generation who had begun to associate fun with technology and advertising. Disney and ABC directly addressed the more sophisticated needs of a television generation of suburban kids who had both security and visual acuity.

Walt Disney's "Mickey Mouse Club" had its television premiere on 3 October 1955 on ABC[9] and was designed for children three to fourteen.[10] It provided variety acts and sophisticated song and dance entertainment for a generation of children who, along with their parents, were watching shows like Jackie Gleason. For kids, TV was a way to participate in an adult culture. Just as "The Honeymooners" (1955–56) opened with a spotlit marquee and a rising moon in the shape of Jackie Gleason's face, so the opening frame of the "Mickey Mouse Club" suggested a show that was visually similar to adult programming. The backlit billboard, framed by modern skyscrapers and shot from a low angle, suggested a momentous occasion. The bright lights of the city and familiar face of Mickey Mouse on the circular logo implied "big doings—adventure, fun, music, cartoons, news!"[11] The show's opening shot of skyscrapers and spotlights promised the excitement of city life to a television population living in the safety of the suburbs.

The "Mickey Mouse Club's" variety format—an Ed Sullivan or Steve Allen show for the prepubescent set—spoke to preteen concerns with sexuality, sociability, group belonging, and consumerism during the 1950s. And unlike the slapstick seltzer gag featured on shows such as "Howdy Doody," the Mouseketeer cast was, as Stephen Davis recalls, "fresh, dynamic and plain sexy" and appealed to a group of children about to enter the self-conscious stage of adolescence.[12] Kids were tired of pie throwing and pratfalls. The "Mickey Mouse Club's" slick variety show numbers and cliff-hanging serials were mini-adult programs and appealed to the kids' maturing tastes.[13]

If the "Mickey Mouse Club" reflected the visual tastes of adults in the 1950s, then it also reflected a successful conflation of traditional Disney values with a new postwar ideology. Disney's "Mickey Mouse Club" seemed acutely aware of the potential malleability of a transient, white suburban television culture. In many of his earlier cartoons such as *The Wise Little Hen* (1934) and *The Pied Piper* (1933), Disney had stressed the importance of "order, community, and safety" and now saw the opportunity, through his television program, to convey these same lessons to a new preteen television audience.[14] The postwar generation was a perfect audience for Disney's messages and a perfect target market for his other products. The "Mickey Mouse Club" was a celebration of the upbeat side of postwar America: contemporary optimism and economic abundance infused with Disney's nostalgia for the mythical good-old days.

Kids clamored for official Mouseketeer rings, cookies, ears, guitars, paper dolls, and records. Parents seemed willing to buy these products for their children, too. As fathers and mothers attempted to cope with their changing socio-economic status, shifting familial ties, and daily living patterns, Disney products were familiar and comfortable. For many Americans raised in the twenties and thirties, Disney motifs constituted, as art historian Karal Ann Marling notes, "a common culture, a kind of civil religion of happy endings . . . and nostalgia for the good old days."[15] Earlier cartoons like the *Three Little Pigs* (1935) espoused hard work, community spirit, friendliness, and frugality. Although the country was experiencing a radical shift of demographics and class structure as a result of postwar economic abundance, many parents adhered to the values they had learned while growing up and, like Disney, relied on the lessons of their youth to sustain them in a time of social change.

As a result of its popularity, the "Mickey Mouse Club" influenced an entire cohort—club—of white, middle-class suburban preteens. As historian Benedict Anderson notes about the imagined community, "the members will never know most of their fellow-members, meet them, or even hear of them, yet in the minds of each lives the image of their communion."[16] The "Mickey Mouse Club" provided the audience with an adult-like form of entertainment and created a sense of group belonging among an imagined community of television Baby Boomers. During a time of economic abundance and Cold War vigilance, it taught group lessons about consumerism, appropriate social behavior, and good citizenship.

Besides providing rudimentary news and entertainment to the Baby

Boomer generation, the "Mickey Mouse Club" was also a potent advertising vehicle designed to promote other aspects of the vast Disney enterprise. In Bill Walsh's general format notes for the "Mickey Mouse Club," he states specifically that "as in the parent Disneyland show, proper exploitation of Disney films and merchandise becomes a basic part of our structure."[17] Disney's marketing strategy consisted of using his television shows to promote his theme park, feature films, and other product lines, and the "Mickey Mouse Club" was no exception to this rule. The Club frequently utilized one of its quarter hours to advertise the theme park, which also premiered in 1955. Unlike other shows such as "I Love Lucy," in which Lucy and Desi interrupted their performance to tell the audience why they smoked Philip Morris cigarettes, "The Mickey Mouse Club" incorporated much of its advertising into the body of the show. Although reviewers panned the show's commercialism, advertising never seemed to bother the exuberant audiences. In 1955, it was estimated that ten million children were faithful members of Walt Disney's "Mickey Mouse Club."[18] And there were no initiation rites. Television was the only key to Club membership. By watching television, they could join the association. To be a member in good standing and to display their group affiliation, however, kids had to do some serious consuming: proper membership cards, Mickey Mouse ears, sweaters, and other memorabilia were a must. Thus Walt Disney's "Mickey Mouse Club" successfully took advantage of two unique aspects of the Baby Boom phenomenon. First, its format spoke to a united television culture of postwar children. And secondly, it addressed their consumer potential. Disney's Club provided a forum in which these two distinctive features met.

Disney's "Mickey Mouse Club" utilized brand loyalty and shared generational values as the linchpin of its marketing strategy. In the opening cartoon segment, as animated ducks, mice, bears, and wolves chant the easy-to-sing theme song, children learned to recognize the round logo with Mickey's face in the center as they learned how to spell M-I-C-K-E-Y M-O-U-S-E. Through a catchy, simple tune, television viewers learned that spelling a brand name with cartoon friends could be fun. Confetti flew, cartoon characters squealed with glee, and Dumbo did loopty-loops. Meanwhile, kids at home, to whom the song was directed, understood from the opening segment that camaraderie in the Mouseketeer community, learning to spell, consuming the club's paraphernalia, enjoying television and advertising were all part of the "Mickey Mouse Club" experience. The Club's song instructed the viewer how to join the Club and have friends; these were important factors for the awkward preteen years and key ingredients of the upcoming corporate and suburban world as well. And Mickey's logo stood for a particular kind of generational unity based on common consumer choices. As children watched the agglomeration of advertising and amusements directed to the postwar generation, they were being initiated into the world of the "outer-directed" where abundance, shopping, and belonging had become increasingly a part of the American experience.[19]

The opening sequence begins with a medium long shot of Jiminy Cricket and Dumbo inciting the audience to "come along and sing the song that's made for you and me." The television audience, at first a passive observer, is encouraged to become an active participant and "join the family." Like a television commercial, the theme song first establishes brand identification (M-I-C-K-E-Y), and then, through a coterie of old Disney characters, entreats the viewer to join the crowd and try the product. As the opening segment comes to a close, the animators position the viewer around the trampoline with Mickey Mouse surrounded by his cartoon friends who celebrate his leadership. As the crowd yells, "Yea, Mickey," we are tossed into the air with Mickey Mouse. This good-natured initiation affirms our position in the sacred inner circle.

As one moves away from the crowd and noise, Donald prepares to ring the gong announcing the official beginning of the show. Donald is the only disruptive element: he refuses to join the good-spirited camaraderie and is never seen within the tightly knit circle of Mickey and his friends. But he is the only dissenter. Even the Big Bad Wolf from the *Three Little Pigs* joins the communal spirit. Although the opening segment was the same five days a week, Donald's antics at the gong changed day to day as he tried to subvert the camaraderie of the group. But with regularity, he is foiled at every turn, ridiculed and humiliated for his efforts. Even his nephews and girlfriend have joined the "Mickey Mouse Club"! Donald appears doomed to the life of a frustrated outsider. By aligning themselves with Mickey Mouse, however, Huey,

Dewey, Louie, and Daisy Duck have become part of the great American consensus.

Unlike other children's shows, the "Mickey Mouse Club" was filmed without a live audience, but it cleverly replaced the peanut gallery of earlier kids' TV with an entire generation of electronic viewers. When Mickey looked directly into the camera and asked, "Is everybody ready?," houses across the nation reverberated with "Ready!" and, like magic, the show would begin.

Although the program was a variety show of sorts, it was, like many of Disney's products, strictly and predictably ordered. Like the Disneyland theme park which was structured into separate thematic areas such as Fantasyland or Frontierland, the "Mickey Mouse Club" had a theme for every day of the week: Monday was "Fun With Music Day"; Tuesday, "Guest Star Day"; Wednesday, "Anything Can Happen Day"; Thursday, "Circus Day"; and Friday, "Talent Round-up Day." Each day began with a distinctive opening segment featuring Mickey Mouse dressed in a costume appropriate to the theme. For example, on "Talent Round-up Day," Mickey sported a ten-gallon hat, six guns, boots, and chaps. Even without sound, the television viewer instantly recognized the theme of the day by simply noting the opening segment. If Mickey were twirling his lasso, it had to be Friday. As such, visual clues sent over the air waves shaped perceptions and expectations of life both inside and outside of the box. And in the tradition of radio and television serials, its predictable format increased anticipation and expectation.

Each hour-long show was divided into four predictable segments. The first quarter hour consisted of a production number revolving around the theme of the day and the introduction of the Mouseketeers. Karen, Cubby, Annette, Bobby and company were all dressed in their Mouseketeer hats and identical turtleneck sweaters with names emblazoned across their chests. The Mouseketeers' uniforms and their synchronized dancing and singing routines embodied group spirit and solidarity. And yet, the individual was never lost in the crowd. The Mouseketeers would line up, and in military style, call off their own names directly into the camera. As historian Lynn Spigel notes, "television—at its most ideal—promis[ed] to bring audiences not merely an illusion of reality as in the cinema, but a sense of 'being there.'"[20] To a television audience used to experiencing a visual intimacy with products and celebrities, it seemed "natural" to feel as if the cast were introducing themselves personally to each child on the other side of the black and white screen.

Before the advent of television, child stars like Shirley Temple, Mickey Rooney, and Judy Garland were movie stars, accessible a couple times a year for a few hours at the neighborhood theater. But like an old friend of the family who never needed to knock, the Mouseketeers could pop into your house with the flick of a switch. Thanks to the marvels of television and the routinized, five-day-a-week format of the "Mickey Mouse Club," children felt they knew the cast personally and perceived them to be friends.

The second quarter hour was devoted to a newsreel either featuring live-action previews of upcoming Disney productions or some newsworthy topic. It was during this quarter hour that Jiminy Cricket would talk to his audience about "curiosity," and provide geography and science lessons from the E-N-C-Y-C-L-O-P-E-D-I-A segment. Tommy Cole, discarding his Mouseketeer outfit for a conservative flannel suit à la J. Edgar Hoover, would solemnly guide television viewers on a tour of the Federal Bureau of Investigation, stressing the government's ability to distinguish spies from "typical American citizens." Although the documentaries appeared "objective" and "factual," they were obviously inculcated with the hegemonic values of the white middle class.

The third quarter hour, similar to a preteen soap opera—a "Guiding Light" or "Search for Tomorrow" for younger viewers—consisted of a continuing series such as "Annette," "Spin and Marty," or "Corky and White Shadow." These serialized dramas were produced especially for the Club. Every episode had a dramatic cliffhanger ending, harking back to the days of Saturday matinees or radio soap operas and often were laden with moral values and social lessons. Numerous series dealt with teenage dating rules. Annette Funicello—she appeared in many Club series—taught adolescents about sex appeal and appropriate etiquette around the punchbowl. Many of these series depicted how couples paired off and began to go steady, teenage paths to future domestic bliss in the 1950s. The "Mickey Mouse Club's" elaborate production numbers, newsreels, and serialized dramas reflected the multiple concerns of a postwar generation growing up in the promise of abundance

and a generation preparing for the world of corporate politics, internationalism, domestic bliss, the space race, and suburban crabgrass.[21]

The fourth quarter hour included a "Mousecartoon," accessible only
to those who knew the secret passwords, "Meeska, Mooseka, Mouseketeer." Following the cartoon, Jimmie Dodd, one of the two adult hosts,
provided some "words to live by" of an ethical or quasi-religious nature.
Then the Mouseketeers would sign off but not before reminding all of
their television buddies that "through the years we'll all be friends."

Whether it was the opening sequence, the cartoon finale or the clos-
ing number, Disney never missed the opportunity to promote the many
goods associated with the Club. Most of these products were designed
in direct reference to the initial shot of the Mickey Mouse symbol.
Whether it was Mickey Mouse ears, a Mousegetar, or a Mouseketeer
sweater or yearbook, the product was stamped with the Mickey Mouse
logo which, after 260 shows per year, any sighted, sensate viewer could
readily identify.

And it was not just the cartoon characters who advertised Disney's
merchandise. Annette Funicello was the most popular Mouseketeer
and was featured in many Disney productions. As soon as she starred
on the "Mickey Mouse Club" as an original Mouseketeer, she became
one of the first televised sex symbols for the prepubescent set and like
Mickey Mouse, her face adorned a plethora of consumer products.[22]
Whether she was featured on albums like "Hawaiiannette" or the suburban girl-next-door in the *Shaggy Dog* (1959), Annette Funicello is remembered today as an all-purpose star who appealed to a diverse audience of television-educated kids.

Whether he featured Mickey Mouse or Annette Funicello, Walt
Disney saw the postwar generation as an ideal audience for selling
both his social messages and products to a television-oriented audience. Through the medium of television, he combined entertainment,
instruction, and advertising. As *TV Guide* stated in its review of the
show, "Disney long ago proved that he [knew] how to educate, inform,
or point a moral for youngsters without cramming dry pedantry down
their throats."[23] The "Mickey Mouse Club" was a celebration of white
suburban culture in postwar America. While the Mouseketeers danced
together in their uniforms, their rapt audience sang the Club's theme
song and wore identical Mouseketeer ears. It is through the visual rep-

resentation of the "Mickey Mouse Club" that we see introduced a new emphasis on generational unity, an imagined unity created through technology and based on shared generational values and purchasing power.

Notes

1. Stephen Davis, *Say Kids! What Time Is It? Notes from the Peanut Gallery* (Boston: Little, Brown, and Company, 1987), 182.

2. *Time* (6 January 1967), 18.

3. United States Department of Commerce: Bureau of the Census, *Statistical Abstract of the United States, 1961* 82d ed. (Washington, D.C.: Government Printing Office, 1961), 6–7, 28.

4. Paul C. Light, *Baby Boomers* (New York: W.W. Norton and Co., 1988), 24.

5. Philip R. Cateora, *An Analysis of the Teen-Age Market* (Austin: The University of Texas Press, 1963), 9–10.

6. Cobbett Steinberg, *TV Facts* (New York: Facts on File Publications, 1985), 86.

7. Light, *Baby Boomers*, 123.

8. Richard Schickel, *The Disney Version: The Life, Times, Art, and Commerce of Walt Disney* (New York: Simon and Schuster, 1985), 130.

9. George W. Woolery, *Children's Television: the First Thirty-Five Years, 1946–1981 Part II: Live, Film and Tapes* (Metuchen, N.J.: The Scarecrow Press, Inc., 1985), 333. The MMC ran for one entire hour from 1955 to September 1957. It ran from 5:30 to 6:00 p.m. from September 1957 to September 1958, and then to alternate days (MWF) from September 1958 to September 1959. Disney's first Mickey Mouse Clubs were organized by Harry Woodin and the studio in the 1930s. These clubs conducted meetings during Saturday matinees and were designed to attract children to the movie theaters. Club activities included birthday celebrations, initiation rites, and sing-alongs. By 1932, the Mickey Mouse Club had over one million members but by 1935, most had dissolved due to unwieldy administrative demands.

10. Keith Keller, *The Mickey Mouse Club Scrapbook* (New York: Grosset and Dunlap, 1975), 20.

11. Opening segment of "Walt Disney's Mickey Mouse Club," produced by Bill Walsh, 1955–1959.

12. Davis, *Say Kids*, 188.

13. The Club's variety format appealed to kids bored with the simple slap-stick humor of "Pinky Lee" and "Howdy Doody." And the "Mickey Mouse Club" went head to head with both: "Pinky Lee" aired daily on NBC from 5:00–5:30 p.m. while "Howdy Doody" ran on the same network from 5:30–6:00 pm. Howdy and Pinky succumbed during the first year of the "Mickey Mouse Club." By 1956, "Howdy Doody" had been relegated to a Saturday morning show and "Pinky Lee" was off the air.

14. Karal Ann Marling, "Disneyland, 1955: Just Take the Santa Ana Freeway to the American Dream," *American Art* 5 (Winter/Spring 1991), 196.

15. Marling, "Disneyland, 1955," 201.

16. Benedict R. Anderson, *Imagined Communities: Reflecting on the Origins and Spread of Nationalism* (London: New York: Verso, 1983), 15.

17. Keller, *Mickey Mouse Club Scrapbook*, 22.

18. Woolery, *Children's Television*, 338.

19. David Reisman, *The Lonely Crowd* (New Haven: Yale University Press, 1954), 35–38.

20. Lynn Spigel, "Installing the Television Set: Popular Discourses on Tele-vision and Domestic Space, 1948–1955," *Camera Obscura* 16 (January 1988), 22.

21. For a discussion of corporation life of the times, see William Whyte, *The Organization Man* (New York: Simon and Schuster, 1956), 3–59. For a discus-sion of internationalism and consensus culture, see David W. Noble, *The End of American History: Democracy, Capitalism, and the Metaphor of Two Worlds in Anglo-American Historical Writing* (Minneapolis: University of Minnesota Press, 1985), 90–114. For an overview of domestic expectations, see Elaine Tyler May, *Homeward Bound: American Families in the Cold War Era* (New York: Basic Books, 1988), 162–82.

22. Annette was the last Mouseketeer chosen for the Mickey Mouse Club and the only one discovered by Walt Disney. By the end of the first season, An-nette had become the most popular member of the cast and it was rumored that she received over six thousand fan letters a month.

23. "Review of the Mickey Mouse Club," *TV Guide* (7–13 January 1956), 20.

"New" Mickey: Big Cheese of "MouseWorks" Television: Animators Look to the Past to Liven Up the Personality of Disney's Star Rodent for a Cartoon Series Starting Saturday

Charles Solomon

Los Angeles Times, April 30, 1999

The idea of Mickey Mouse, who starred in some of the most beautifully animated cartoons in the history of the medium, appearing in limited television animation sounds almost blasphemous. But "Disney's Mickey MouseWorks," the new series from Walt Disney Television Animation premiering Saturday at 11 a.m. on ABC, has a bright, fresh look, and while no one would mistake these cartoons for "The Sorcerer's Apprentice" in "Fantasia," they look downright lavish by TV standards.

One of the toughest problems the "MouseWorks" artists faced was figuring out just who Mickey Mouse is in 1999. Mickey may be the most famous animated character in the world, but his personality and appearance have changed repeatedly over the years. He's been an impetuous rascal, a suave charmer, a loyal patriot, a children's entertainer, a genial suburbanite and a corporate symbol. Which one is the real Mickey?

"It's been difficult, getting a grip on Mickey," says co-executive producer Roberts Gannaway. "We're producing more Mickey films than the studio's done in years and years, so there's going to be a certain amount of exploration. Our goal was to draw some of Mickey's person-ality back into him. For inspiration, we looked to the '30s Mickey, the more mischievous Mickey. Once we get comfortable, we may see how feisty we can make him, without him becoming Bugs Bunny or a Tex Avery character. We're not interested in making him into somebody else."

For the old artists, Mickey was always Walt's alter ego. Roy E. Dis-ney, the son of Walt's brother Roy O. Disney and vice chairman of the Walt Disney Co., agrees: "Mickey really is Walt in a lot of ways. Mickey has all those nice impulses Walt had, the kind of gut-level nice guy he was."

Walt Disney made his first sketches of Mickey in 1928, on the train back to Los Angeles from New York, after he lost the rights to Oswald Rabbit, the star of his fledgling studio's cartoon series. He based the character on a mouse he had adopted as a pet and wanted to call him Mortimer, but his wife rejected the name.

"It's been told so many times that you don't know what's true," adds Roy E. Disney. "The name part I'm sure of: I often heard my father and Walt say, 'Thank God we didn't name him Mortimer!'"

Ub Iwerks, Disney's top animator at the time, designed the first ver-sions of the character, but Walt supplied his personality and—until 1947—his voice.

The early Mickey Mouse was a rubbery-limbed scamp. During 1928–29, the Disney artists added his trademark three-fingered white gloves and replaced his blocky black feet with light-colored shoes. As the animators polished their skills, Mickey grew rounder, more solid and more appealing.

But as Mickey grew more popular, especially with children, he even-tually grew tamer—and less interesting. In a 1949 interview in Collier's magazine, Walt summarized the problem: "[Mickey] grew into such a legend that we couldn't gag around with him. He acquired as many ta-boos as a western hero—no smoking, no drinking, no violence."

As a result, Disney produced fewer and fewer Mickey cartoons. Between 1941 and 1965, the studio released 109 Donald Duck shorts, 49 Goofys and only 14 Mickeys. In most of them, Mickey was just the straight man; Pluto got the laughs. In recent years, the artists at Walt Disney Feature Animation have used the classic characters in "Mickey's

Christmas Carol" (1983), "The Prince and the Pauper" (1990) and the 1995 short "Runaway Brain." Although he was well animated, Mickey generally remained a passive character who responded to actions the others initiated.

But the "MouseWorks" artists hope to keep Mickey from simply being a reactive character.

"Keeping him active has been a challenge," concedes Gannaway. "We're doing a series of 90-second cartoons that were designed to showcase each character's personality. In 'Mickey to the Rescue,' we put him in cliffhanger situations from the first second: Minnie is a damsel in distress and Mickey has to rescue her."

"We went back to Walt's theories about Mickey being the little guy, the underdog who comes out a winner, just because he tries really hard and has determination and spirit," adds co-executive producer Tony Craig. "For the look of the character, we drew our inspiration from the Mickey animated by Fred Moore, Ward Kimball and Walt Kelly in 1941 in 'The Nifty Nineties' and 'The Little Whirlwind.' It's basically that version of the design, with slightly larger hands and feet and a more streamlined body."

Donald Duck's Persona Translates Well to Show

Recapturing the personalities of the other classic Disney characters proved less problematic. Gannaway notes, "Donald translates very well—his impatience is timeless. We're doing a Donald cartoon where he has to set up a computer—it's no different than Donald trying to fix the clock in [1937's] 'Clock Cleaners.'"

"A character whose personality wasn't defined in the old cartoons is Daisy," adds Craig. "We've made Daisy a passive-aggressive character who'll push Mickey and Minnie to the limits—not on purpose, she just takes advantage of them being so nice until they finally crack."

"We felt there should be someone who tests how nice Mickey and Minnie are," says Gannaway.

While the Fox animated prime-time hit "The Simpsons" introduced a new style of storytelling in animation that uses large numbers of characters and celebrity guest voices, Gannaway and Craig deliberately kept the population of their show small. They're introducing a few new characters and reviving a few supporting players—Clarabelle Cow, Chip 'n' Dale and Humphrey, the incorrigible bear who matched wits with Donald in some of the fastest and funniest cartoons Disney produced during the '50s.

"This time, Donald is going to have a modern, up-to-date RV, which is much nicer than Humphrey's cave," says Craig. "When Donald goes out fishing, Humphrey goes in to take advantage of all those amenities."

The question of whether Donald should have a computer or an RV reflects a major problem the "MouseWorks" artists faced: how to make decades-old characters seem fresh without losing the qualities that made them popular.

For years, audiences watched Mickey, both as the host of the original "Mickey Mouse Club" and in the vintage cartoons that aired on ABC's "Disneyland" in the '50s, and NBC's "The Wonderful World of Color" in the '60s. Gannaway, Craig and crew are hoping a new generation of viewers will tune in to see his latest antics. If the handful of cartoons available for preview are an indication of the quality of the series, their chances look good.

* "Disney's Mickey MouseWorks," premieres at 11 a.m. Saturday on ABC. The network has rated it TV-Y (suitable for very young children).

M-I-C-K-E-Y:
He's the Leader of the Brand

Richard Verrier

Los Angeles Times, July 23, Copyright © 2003 *Los Angeles Times*.
Reprinted with permission.

Mickey Mouse, once described by Walt Disney as "a little fellow trying to do the best he could," is now being called on to do even better.

Trying to turn around its flagging merchandising operation, Walt Disney Co. is planting Mickey's vintage visage in some hip new places and planning to roll out the mouse in an aggressive marketing campaign centered on his 75th birthday.

On its face, using Mickey Mouse to full effect as a marketing tool would seem a no-brainer for Disney executives. After all, over the last three-quarters of a century, Mickey has sustained himself as one of the most recognizable figures in America, if not the whole world.

Yet when Andy Mooney arrived at Disney a few years ago to rescue its merchandising division, he was stunned to find how much the Burbank entertainment giant was underutilizing its famous mouse. Mooney had been hired away from sneaker maker Nike Inc., where he had a front-row seat to the marketing power of celebrity endorsements. Think Michael Jordan.

But Mickey, he found, was sitting on the sidelines, tangled in a thicket of marketing do's and don'ts dating back decades. Mooney, chairman of Disney's consumer products unit, was determined to free the mouse, bucking a conservative corporate culture reluctant to tamper with the company's signature image, hand-drawn by Walt Disney himself.

"This is our swoosh," Mooney successfully argued, likening Mickey to Nike's trademark logo. As a result, Mickey Mouse is on the loose.

Already, he has been stretched across a snug T-shirt worn by actress Sarah Jessica Parker during a racy scene on HBO's "Sex and the City" series. Minnie surely would blush. Disney also hired a graffiti artist called Mear, whose most recent work was an antiwar mural, to spray-paint a 1930s-style Mickey Mouse comic strip on the side of a Sunset Boulevard building last week. "Very nice," said one onlooker with an orange Mohawk.

Meanwhile, at trendy Fred Segal in Santa Monica, shoppers are paying top dollar for silk pants (costing $250), belt buckles and purses adorned with Mickey's retro image from the 1920s and '30s. It was enough to make Katie Couric, the host of NBC's "Today Show," ask, "Is it true . . . that Mickey is the new black?" while interviewing the style editor of "People" magazine this month.

Today, the company plans to announce other changes aimed at elevating Mickey's profile. A series of Mickey Mouse U.S. postage stamps is in the works. Classic comic books, as well as a daily syndicated comic strip featuring Mickey and his pals, are being rolled out once again. Two new direct-to-video movies, including a new 3-D version of the mouse, will be released next year. And as part of the hoopla, consumers can expect lots of news footage as 75 artists and celebrities are asked to create their own statues of Mickey Mouse.

Whether the campaign will succeed remains unclear. Operating income for Disney's consumer products group plummeted more than 50% from $893 million in 1997 to $386 million in 2000, and it has remained basically flat since then. As part of a restructuring of the group, the company recently announced plans to close more than 100 of its 500-plus Disney Store outlets and put the rest of the retail chain up for sale.

A national advertising campaign to spur Mickey-related sales three years ago, anchored by the slogan "Why do we love the Mouse," had little effect. Sales of Mickey paraphernalia, which account for about 40% of the company's overall merchandise revenue, have remained stagnant in recent years.

But now Disney is hoping a hipper image will make Mickey more appealing to a new generation of teenagers. The idea is that once kids see stars wearing T-shirts featuring the mouse, they will be drawn to all things Mickey, including a line of vintage apparel that Disney plans to roll out to mass retailers.

"Mickey has always been cool," said Dennis Green, vice president for apparel at Disney consumer products, who also came from Nike. "It's just the way he has been represented hasn't always been cool."

The challenge facing Disney is that its core audience keeps getting younger, shrinking the pool of potential consumers, as the competition grows. The last decade has seen an explosion of animated characters from rival film studios and cable television shows such as "SpongeBob SquarePants" and "Rugrats."

Licensed merchandise drove Disney's growth during the 1980s and '90s, when a string of animated hits including "Beauty and the Beast" and "The Lion King" sparked huge demand for toys, clothes and scores of other items.

When "The Lion King" hit theaters in 1994, it was the only major animated release that year.

This year, 17 animated films were up for Oscar consideration—the bulk of them from studios other than Disney.

The company always has had something of a fluid relationship with its cornerstone character, one that author John Updike once labeled "the most persistent and pervasive figment of American popular culture in this century."

"Mickey Mouse has always been in some phase," said Walt Disney chief Michael Eisner. "He's an actor . . . sometimes he gets work, sometimes he's retiring, and sometimes he's coming back."

Long before he became a corporate icon, Mickey was a mischievous deckhand aboard a riverboat in the 1928 film "Steamboat Willie," his debut. He would go on to star in more than 100 cartoon shorts in the 1920s and '30s. But as his fame grew, so did complaints about his sneaky behavior.

Disney animators eventually softened his appearance, making his body more pear-shaped, expressive and appealing to children. Even though he starred in "The Mickey Mouse Club" television show in the 1950s, Mickey's popularity began to be overtaken by Donald Duck and Goofy, according to Disney archivist Dave Smith. Mickey was featured in fewer and fewer films, bringing a 30-year gap between "The Simple Things" in 1953 and "Mickey's Christmas Carol" in 1983.

Through the 1990s, Mickey was largely underemployed as an entertainer. Besides his role as chief greeter at Disney's theme parks and a few modest film appearances, his only other major gig was on the Saturday morning television cartoon "MouseWorks."

Efforts to spark a commercial revival of the mouse over the years have invariably met with resistance from traditionalists who feared that the company might cheapen the character.

"This is a debate that has gone on for the 75 years since Mickey Mouse has been around," Mooney said. "That's a good thing. If you have people who don't care internally about what to do with the character, you don't have a decent business."

The 1995 "Runaway Brain" marked Mickey's return to animation shorts for the first time in years. Many objected to the plot in which a mad scientist transplants Mickey's brain into a monster's body and vice versa.

"It's clear Mickey is not himself. . . . He overcomes that in the end, but the very fact that Mickey was possessed was very disturbing" to some people, Mooney said.

Some of Mooney's new ideas also have been met with raised eyebrows. "Twice Upon a Christmas," one of the two new Mickey movies appearing on video next year, marks the first digital version of Mickey. "The movement of Mickey to 3-D was hotly debated," Mooney said. "There's a group of folks internally who believe that 2-D animation is the correct form . . . in which to portray Mickey."

Another source of contention was the 2002 interactive video game "Kingdom Hearts," which broke the taboo of having Mickey interact with characters outside his traditional group of friends.

Likewise, there were misgivings about hiring a graffiti artist to spray one of Walt's classic cartoons on a wall. Attitudes changed when Mooney convinced skeptics that the mural was paying homage to Walt. "I don't think embalming is a good thing," Mooney said. "I think the brand needs to be rejuvenated to be relevant to the future."

Experts agree. Revitalizing Mickey's career—especially as an entertainer—"is really, really critical," said Kevin Lane Keller, professor of marketing at Dartmouth College. "There's a stretch of kids who really didn't have much connection to the brand."

Mooney recalled "discovering" Mickey and his pals during his first few months on the job, after he spent a day poring over the company's archives. "There was this treasure trove of art," Mooney recalled. "We just felt that if we could expose it to contemporary consumers, something could happen."

First came a product blitz that put Mickey Mouse and the gang on toothbrushes, cereal boxes and juice cartoons. More recently, Mooney launched a new line of consumer electronics products, including a 13-inch television set that has yellow feet and speakers that look like ears.

The retro-Mickey effort began after Disney executives noticed that shops in Hollywood were selling 30-year-old Mickey T-shirts—some for as much as $100. The company then invited designer Jackie Brander, who has the largest floor space at Fred Segal in Santa Monica, to develop a line of Disney vintage apparel.

Then, instead of just encouraging retailers to push the product, Mooney borrowed a technique commonly used by Nike, Armani and others in the fashion industry called "seeding." That's where marketers "nurture" demand for a new product by encouraging celebrities to wear it.

Disney doled out retro T-shirts to stars at events such as last week's ESPY awards hosted by Disney-owned ESPN, as well as to publicists, fashion editors and designers. Before long, trendsetters—from actress Jennifer Aniston to musician Avril Lavigne—were wearing the T-shirts at events and magazine shoots.

Disney says the stars weren't paid, but the company acknowledges orchestrating at least some things behind the scenes. The appearance on "Sex and the City," for instance, came after Disney contacted two of the show's staff members.

Mooney insists that he is being careful not to exploit Mickey. "If you look at the original cartoon shorts, they were targeted at adults," he said. "Mickey had a little edge, a little attitude. So I don't view anything that's being done now as disrespectful to what Walt would have done."

Disney Presents Mickey Mouse, Again: Media Giant Pushes to Make Cartoon Rodent Hip

Frank Ahrens

GLENDALE, Calif.—If you thought Mickey Mouse was already ubiquitous, you ain't seen nothing yet.

The sainted and globally famous four-fingered trademark of the Walt Disney Co. is about to become the centerpiece of a movie, retail, publishing, video and television campaign aimed at amplifying its marketplace presence.

This year is Mickey's 75th birthday, and the Disney brass is determined not to let the cheerful geriatric rodent fade from public consciousness, the victim of company marketers too afraid to exercise the mouse's branding power for fear of cheapening Walt Disney's most important creation.

On Wednesday at a theater in this Los Angles suburb, Disney Chairman Michael D. Eisner led a parade of company executives in a rally of hundreds of employees to reinforce that message.

Mickey "is from and of every country around the world," said Deborah Dugan, president of Disney publishing. "Bugs Bunny wishes he could say that," she added, referring to the Warner Bros. character.

Beginning this fall, Gemstone Publishing will reintroduce Disney comic books featuring Mickey and his pals, hoping to tap into the robust comic-book sector, which spawned and capitalized on the movie success of "Batman," "Spider-Man" and "The Incredible Hulk." Disney has also launched a retro-Mickey retail blitz by selling the famous Mickey T-shirts, which have in the past two years become hip, worn by such celebrities as rocker Lenny Kravitz and style-maker Sarah Jessica Parker in the HBO comedy, "Sex in the City."

Roger Wyett, executive vice president of Disney's global apparel, noted that Parker wore a Mickey T-shirt on a recent episode of "Sex in the City" and by the following Tuesday, the ultra-chic Fred Segal Hollywood clothing boutique had already sold 60 of the T-shirts—at $43 each.

"We timed it—[Parker] was onscreen with the T-shirt for four minutes," Wyett said. In other words, it was dream marketing for Mickey.

Wyett noted that when Kravitz appeared in a magazine photograph two years ago wearing a vintage Mickey T-shirt, "it hit us like a two-by-four over the head." Trips to vintage-clothing stores—where used Mickey T-shirts were selling for $100 to $300—confirmed that Mickey T's were a growing cultural phenomenon and Disney needed to monetize the trend.

Disney's consumer-products division has been flagging since the decline of the character apparel trend in the mid-90s (Warner Bros. has felt the same pinch on its character wear). Disney hopes that a Mickey full-frontal assault can help the division, though there is no guarantee that consumers have more of an appetite for the mighty Mouse, as evidenced by the division's poor results.

In the second quarter this year, revenue for the consumer-products division was $500 million, down 14 percent from the second quarter of 2002. Much of the drag comes from soft sales at North America's 387 Disney stores, down from 522. Disney sold its stores in Japan last year and said in May that it would also sell its North American and European stores to a retailer practiced in running stores.

At the same time, Disney has turned to alternative ways of marketing its products.

Nina Jacobson, president of Disney's Buena Vista Motion Pictures Group, was asked to hand out Mickey T-shirts to movie stars who visited her office with the hope that they would wear them and be photographed. She gave them to Sharon Stone, Jodie Foster and Freddie Prinze Jr., among others.

Disney is engaging in guerrilla marketing elsewhere in its home city. Disney enlisted a graffiti artist to render classic black-and-white Mickey comic strips on the sides of buildings on chic Sunset Boulevard and Melrose Avenue—with permission, of course.

Mickey's muscling-up is largely the work of Andrew Mooney, head of Disney consumer products. When he arrived four years ago, he found Mickey bound by ancient and Byzantine strictures determining how he could appear and in what form. Mickey was something of a sacred figure, and many in the company feared blaspheming him by putting him on too many products.

Mooney, an early employee of Nike, realized that Mickey was Disney's "swoosh"—the equivalent of the logo on Nike shoes. At the same time, Mooney sought to preserve the aging mouse's dignity, employing him judiciously.

For example, in November, dozens of Mickey statues, painted in various motifs, similar to the "Party Animal" donkeys and elephants around Washington D.C., will debut in Disney World. They will later tour the country.

More Mickey-intensive efforts will roll out over the next three years, including "The Three Musketeers," a straight-to-video movie scheduled to be released in August 2004. In fall of next year, Disney comic strips featuring Mickey will appear in newspapers.

But it's likely that nothing will spread Mickey's mouse-face as widely as a three-year U.S. Postal Service commemorative stamp program that is to begin next year. The stamp designs will debut at Walt Disney World in October. Vivendi Universal's Grinch character from Dr. Seuss books has appeared on a stamp, as well as other trademarked images owned by large corporations.

If the Mickey campaign goes well, Wyett suggested other projects for Disney. "What's next?" he asked the group of employees. "Donald Duck? Tinkerbell?"

If he gets it wrong, if he either sticks with Mickey for too long or downgrades him and that proves an error, he will have been guilty of a monstrous corporate mistake.

My own view? The only way Disney can revive Mickey is by shoving the Mouse in front of kids all over the world—it has to carpet-bomb the market.

Sure it has the muscle to do so, but to succeed it will have to take successful offerings such as its own Winnie the Pooh off the TV, out of the cinemas and out of its stores—to be replaced by Mickey.

If the kids don't like it, which in my view they won't, this will be a classic case of corporate ego crowding out sensible business practice.

And all because the message, in time, became the problem.

Can Disney Build
a Better Mickey Mouse?

Jesse Green

"He was the only time I was happy," said Maurice Sendak.

Mr. Sendak, who based the character of Max in his children's book "Where the Wild Things Are" on Mickey Mouse, is an exact contemporary of the cartoon rodent: both were born in 1928. "I was around 6 when I first saw him," he said. "It filled me with joy. I think it was those primary colors so vivid and pure, taken up with the most incredibly beautiful animation, reminding you of Fred Astaire. Oh! And his character was the kind I wished I'd had as a child: brave and sassy and nasty and crooked and thinking of ways to outdo people." The joy leached from Mr. Sendak's voice. "Not like the lifeless fat pig he is now."

Mr. Sendak is hardly alone in mourning the mouse's decline. "Boring," "embalmed," "neglected," "irrelevant," "deracinated" and, perhaps most damning, "over" are some of the adjectives that cropped up in recent interviews with people in the cartoon, movie and marketing businesses. And strangely for such a well-known figure, Mickey doesn't even have a back story: no clearly defined relations, no hometown, no goals, no weaknesses. According to David Smith, director of the Disney archives, the company maintains no "biography" of the character; he is who he is.

But Mickey is not just another property that Disney owns: he's the hallmark, the frontman, the ambassador for its theme parks, the logo on its business cards. A significant portion of the Disney empire is built around this strange creature. And yet, at a time when the company is already facing an almost cartoonishly daunting litany of travails—a hostile takeover bid, the loss of its highly successful partnership with the animation studio Pixar, mass layoffs at its own animation studio, the very public campaign by Roy E. Disney, nephew of Walt, to dethrone the C.E.O., Michael Eisner—his appeal is apparently starting to slip.

Publicly, the company maintains an optimistic stance. "In my world," said Andy Mooney, chairman of the consumer products division, "a character that generates $4.5 billion a year in retail revenue and is at least four times larger than any other character in the world except Winnie the Pooh"—which Disney also controls—"doesn't need refurbishing." According to Mr. Mooney, Mickey has "98 percent unaided awareness for children 3 to 11 worldwide," and has started to appear again as a "real favorite" among girls 8 to 12 and, surprisingly, boys 13 to 17.

The company acknowledges that revenue from Mickey merchandise, measured as a portion of all consumer products, has shrunk significantly since 1997. What Disney doesn't acknowledge is that Mickey's reputation, measured in conversations with industry watchers, is shrinking even more. Still, signals of the Mouse's distress have lately begun to seep out, almost unconsciously, from the soul of Disney's business: its storytelling. In a video game called "Kingdom Hearts"—which has sold more than 4 million units since its release in 2002 and is frequently cited as evidence of Mickey's continuing relevance—the mouse barely appears. Instead, he is relegated to a subplot that seems eerily allegorical. According to the game's Web site, evil marauding aliens known as the Heartless are threatening the Kingdom. (Roy Disney has called the company under Mr. Eisner's leadership rapacious and soulless.) "There's turmoil in Disney Castle," it says. "King Mickey is missing."

The company has indeed made quiet attempts to find him. In 2002, Disney marketing officials set up a Mickey "situation room," stocked floor to ceiling with thousands of examples of mouse merchandise, to show executives from every division, brought in for tours, that the character was inconsistent and in need of refocusing. (Licensees were somewhat randomly producing four different generations of Mickey likenesses.) At around the same time, said a branding executive who did not wish to risk reprisals by allowing his name to be used, Disney "put out feelers" among animators for ideas about remaking the Mouse. Disney officials deny it, saying that the 18-month program of special events and new product releases that commenced on his 75th birthday, last November, was not an attempt to revive a flagging brand but merely a company-wide effort at "showcasing" Mickey more successfully. But it is not immediately clear how the 75 giant Mickey statues they gave celebrities to decorate might do that.

"Companies at times let a character linger because they are not sure what to do with it and fear going the wrong way," said Avi Arad, CEO of Marvel, which has revived its classic Spiderman character. "So they do nothing. Mickey right now doesn't have a dialogue. He's not carrying any banners. Maybe right now he doesn't stand for anything but nostalgia. Nostalgia is fine, but it is not enough."

Whose nostalgia it is makes a crucial difference. Some marketers said that these days, Mickey merchandise is mostly bought by parents—an ominous sign. Martin Brochstein, executive editor of the "Licensing Letter," calls Mickey "irrelevant to a huge generational chunk that grew up on 'Sesame Street' or Nickelodeon but really had no contact with Mickey unless they went to one of the theme parks." According to Cindy Levitt, vice president of Hot Topic, a mall-based fashion retailer, kids themselves are buying clothing featuring SpongeBob and, of all things, the Care Bears. To be popular with today's hipster teens and 20-somethings, she said, a character "has to have originated in their youth. It has to be from the 1980s." Mickey, she added, doesn't "register" with her clients. "He's too old. He's their parents' character."

So how did Mickey come to be seen by so many people as an out-of-touch Rat Pack leftover, cashiered to Anaheim and Orlando, all but playing golf with Gerald Ford? How can something so beloved become so empty? And what can Disney do about it?

"It all began with a mouse," Walt Disney liked to say. Well, not quite. In 1928, Disney lost control of the rights to a previous creation called Oswald the Rabbit. All but bankrupt, he hastily sought to develop a new character that would be a distinct individual instead of a vaudeville stooge. Along with Ub Iwerks—the only animator who stayed with him—he replaced the rabbit's long floppy ears with two black disks and came up with one weird creature. Not just physically, though as mice go, he was pretty irregular, with his giant feet, widow's peak, plunger hands and hose-like limbs.

More surprising was his personality; if it was based, as many people say, on Disney himself (he provided the voice), you've got to wonder about Walt. The original Mickey—who made his public debut in "Steamboat Willie," the first synchronized-sound cartoon—was only partly civilized: uninhibited, bare-chested, rough-and-ready to the point of sadism. His chums were farmyard animals like Clarabelle Cow and Horace Horsecollar, and, like most cartoon characters of the period, he blithely trafficked in fistfights, drownings, dismemberments. For violence, the shipboard shenanigans of "Steamboat Willie" far exceed those in "Steamboat Bill Jr.," the Buster Keaton feature that inspired it. In one sequence, Mickey tortures various animals—banging cow teeth, tweaking pig nipples—in order to produce a rendition of "Turkey in the Straw."

But that richly drawn, disreputable character, born of desperation and betrayal, got watered down almost from the moment he was introduced. Disney's first licensed merchandise—a Mickey Mouse writing tablet—appeared in 1929, by which point the first Mickey Mouse Club had already been established (along with its code of behavior). The cartoon, originally drawn for adults, was repositioned for the millions of children who took Mickey to heart. And although Mickey for a while remained a playful, conniving underdog, like Huck Finn or Charlie Chaplin's Tramp, he gradually got less mischievous. "He couldn't have any of the naughty qualities he had in his earlier cartoons," said Mr. Smith, of the Disney archives, "because so many people looked up to him. The studio would get complaints in the mail."

So, sometime in the mid- to late 1930s, Mickey settled down. Barnyard cohorts and rail-riding adventures gave way to suburban domesticity with his non-wife Minnie ("They just lived together as friends," said Mr. Smith. "For a very long time") and their unexplained nephews. At the same time, Mickey's perverse qualities were grafted onto his new supporting cast—Donald Duck and Goofy, especially—who by the 1940s, according to Mr. Smith, eclipsed the mouse in popularity. Like Walt, whose politics started a rightward drift after a studio strike in

1941, Mickey was no longer a hungry Depression prole; by the time he started shilling war bonds, the transformation from amoral Huck Finn to virtuous, conservative Aunt Polly was complete.

Mickey had transformed visually, too, from the elegant semi-abstraction of 1928, when his face was basically just an array of seven circles, into something cuter and less boldly graphic. Though the ears were barely altered (they floated around his head so that no matter which way he turned you always saw them straight on), everything else gradually became more "real" and "expressive." The cheeks puffed out, the limbs acquired volume and the eyes, formerly just pupils floating in a vague sea of white, got moored into upright ovals. The overall effect of these changes was that Mickey came to seem less ratlike, more human—and far younger. In an only partly silly investigation, the paleontologist Stephen Jay Gould used calipers to measure drawings of Mickey at three different stages and compared the resulting proportions to those of living animals. His conclusion was that Mickey, while aging chronologically, had become "progressively more juvenile in appearance." Indeed, he had become an infant.

A baby visually yet an upstanding citizen morally, he was so internally contradictory that he ceased to suit any particular story. In any case, as the moviegoing public's taste for shorts diminished, Mickey had fewer animated outlets; he appeared in 118 cartoons before 1960 but in only two thereafter. Disney managed to keep him before the public by having him "play" other characters: Jack in "Mickey and the Beanstalk," for instance, or Bob Cratchit in "Mickey's Christmas Carol." But in the process he shed what was left of his own story. What replaced it, said Jim Hardison, creative director of Character—a company that "revitalizes" icons like Popeye and the Rice Krispies spokes-toons Snap, Crackle and Pop—was the story of Disney itself.

"If I was looking for the crossover point where Mickey's story morphed into the Disney story, it was "The Sorcerer's Apprentice," said Mr. Hardison, referring to the Mickey segment of Disney's 1940 classic, "Fantasia," in which the mouse, as an aspiring magician, attempts to harness his master's tricks. "That's where he cemented his place as the source of Disney magic. Magic is such an important characteristic of Disney, but it wasn't an important characteristic of Mickey. Once he becomes magical, he is no longer the everyman underdog. He went from being the little guy against the world to a symbol of what Disney does."

And so a logo was born. A brilliant one, at that: any close approximation of the two black ear-disks is enough to say "Disney" anywhere in the world. "For the sheer power of the graphics," the sculptor Ernest Trova once said, "Mickey Mouse is rivaled only by the Coca-Cola trademark and the swastika." By making itself inseparable from its beloved mascot, Disney made it impossible to see Mickey and not think of the company that backs him—one whose public profile is a lot more controversial than that of your average stuffed animal.

"There is the dark side of the Disney reputation," said Mr. Hardison, referring to things like the 13-year legal battle over the rights to Pooh and the Sonny Bono Copyright Extension Act, for which Disney lobbied so aggressively that it became known as the Mickey Mouse Protection Act. (Had that bill not passed Congress in 1998, Mickey's 75th birthday would have been his last as an exclusive character; now he belongs to Disney at least until 2023.) "Disney says, 'We are basically selling happiness,'" Mr. Hardison continued. "But that requires a sort of ruthless efficiency that tends to undermine the whole fun-loving image they present. Over time, that shadow story has gained some traction with the audience, and as the symbol of what Disney stands for, Mickey can't help but pick up a little bit of that shadow."

Mickey doesn't have many options, though, for new stories. It's the job of the Corporate Brand Management group—often referred to as the Mickey Police—to ensure, as Maria Gladowski, a consumer products spokeswoman, put it, that the efforts of the company stay true to the core values and personalities of each character. The official list of Mickey's current attributes reads like a Boy Scout pledge: "funny, fun-loving, high-energy, optimistic, good-natured, can-do spirit, helpful, trustworthy and adventurous." As a result, mostly retired from the movies, Mickey only appears where he cannot talk: as merchandise and as a giant mute host at the theme parks. For what would he say? Without a story of his own, he is less and less able to inspire or entertain. "He is in danger," John Updike wrote in the introduction to a book of Mickey art that Disney published in 1991, "of seeming not merely venerable kitsch but part of the great trash problem, one more piece of visual litter being moved back and forth by the bulldozers of consumerism."

Even there, Disney is in a difficult position. The company would like to have Mickey make more money—Mr. Mooney of the Consumer Products division thinks the mouse could bring in an additional $1 billion a year in North America. Some think Disney could do even better; Marshal Cohen, chief analyst at NPD Group, a market research company that has worked with Disney on occasion, said: "The Mickey brand is undervalued in the consumer's purchase power. You could probably grow the brand another 40 percent."

In the past few decades, Disney's attempts to get the mouse out of his trap veered between pathetic stabs at hipness ("Mickey Unrapped," a hip-hop CD) and so-called character-slapping—putting Mickey just about anywhere someone might see him. Mr. Hardison said this technique only works with the youngest consumers—teens are already sophisticated enough to sense the oversell—and thus dilutes the brand. Recognizing this, Disney has, in the last few years, whittled down their Mickey merchandise by as much as 30 percent, said Mr. Mooney. At the same time they've tried to get more bang from the merchandise they've retained. T-shirts featuring the "vintage" Mickey Mouse were given away to youngish celebrities, placed in fashion spreads and on the runway at Dolce & Gabbana—a technique aimed at creating longterm demand instead of instant return.

A new Mickey TV show on the Disney Channel, planned for early 2006, may also help. But the holy grail of character marketing is a blockbuster movie. Disney is making two films for their mascot—one in which, for the first time, the mouse is rendered in 3-D animation. But, as if in acknowledgment of the damage that an unsuccessful film can do, the company is releasing them direct to video.

In any case, the heart of the matter isn't the marketing; it's the storytelling. And while a wide range of industry experts agreed that Disney needed to put new Mickey content in front of kids' eyes, their detailed suggestions for fixing his character were so various and contradictory, it's no surprise that Disney has seemed unsure which way to turn. He needs to be more high-tech. He must go back to his roots. He has to have edge. He should be a patriot. He has to be mischievous like contemporary cartoon characters. He should come in different "flavors," as Spiderman does ("classic" and "theatrical"), to appeal to different audiences. He has to be specific. He has to be universal. Mr. Arad, of Marvel, all but said Mickey needed to have his head examined. "Decide who is the guy under the ears."

Art Spiegelman, author of the "Maus" books, thinks he knows the answer. "How would I renovate Mickey for our times?" he said. "Easy. Make him gay. He's half way there anyway. You keep the voice the same as it's been; beyond having him take a passionate interest in Broadway musicals and occasionally wearing pink shirts, you don't have to do much. You just have to change the world around him."

Underlying Mr. Spiegelman's suggestion is the idea that Mickey should be taken back from children: that his evolution from pig-nipple-tweaker to bland role model should be reversed. After all, Homer Simpson is loved by both kids and parents. Disney can't really afford to turn its figurehead into a controversy, though. "I don't feel the need to present Mickey in a new way," Mr. Mooney said. "In fact, I would say that, with all that's going on in the world, people would prefer Mickey to be this standard bearer for everything that's positive and good in life rather than go back to the presentation that Walt originally did for adults."

But people like Mr. Sendak, who learned to love Mickey as a startling work of art and as an unlikely avatar of survival, don't want him to be more shiny, synthetic and likable. For them, the mystery isn't what Disney should do with him; it's why he lasted so long with nothing left to say. They want him retired if he can't be restored to what he (and America) was in 1930: an underdog struggling to secure his safety in a ridiculously dangerous world.

• According to a note at the end of the piece, "additional reporting" was "contributed by Eric Dash."

Secrets of Steamboat Willie

Jim Korkis

Hogan's Alley: The Magazine of the Cartoon Arts, September 2004

Walt Disney was fond of saying that it should never be forgotten that "it was all started by a mouse." Mickey Mouse was indeed the cornerstone of an entertainment empire that flourished during Walt's lifetime, and still flourishes today.

In the wake of the seventy-fifth anniversary of *Steamboat Willie* and Mickey, celebrated in 2003, it also should not be forgotten that Mickey's first animated cartoon single-handedly revived an art form that was stagnating. For that reason alone, the story of how *Steamboat Willie* was made is well worth exploring.

In early February 1928, Walt Disney and his wife, Lillian, journeyed to New York where Walt was going to negotiate a new contract for his popular Oswald the Rabbit series. Walt wanted a modest $250 increase per cartoon. Distributor Charles Mintz offered $450 *less* per film than what he was currently paying. In addition, Walt discovered that Universal not only owned the rights to Oswald (a common practice in the industry), but that Mintz had contracted with all of Walt's animators except Ub Iwerks to produce future Oswalds for Mintz.

While Walt and Lilly were in New York, his latest Oswald cartoon, *Rival Romeos*, premiered at the Colony Theatre on February 26. *Steamboat Willie* would make its premiere at the Colony later that same year. One of the gags in *Rival Romeos* has a goat eating Oswald's sheet music and Oswald opening the goat's mouth, then cranking its tail to make the music come out. That gag would be repeated in *Willie*.

When Walt returned to Hollywood the last week of March 1928, he and Ub, and probably Walt's brother, Roy O. Disney, developed Mickey Mouse. Disney legend maintains that shortly after the westbound train crossed the Mississippi, Walt created a mouse character initially named "Mortimer," which—at the insistence of his wife—was changed to "Mickey." Today, most animation historians agree that while the idea for Mickey may have been conceived during the train trip, his actual design (which resembled Oswald but with a mouse's ears and tail) and the final decision to go with Mickey did not occur until after Walt arrived back in Hollywood.

Walt and Roy had been able to save over $25,000 and decided to use that money to fund a new series of cartoons to save the studio. Ub was given the entire job of animating the first Mickey Mouse cartoon, *Plane Crazy*, which would exploit the country's new-found passion for flight, especially its fascination with Charles Lindbergh, who had just crossed the Atlantic in his historic solo flight.

Ub began work on *Plane Crazy* during the last week of April 1928. By the second week of May, the cels were ready to be inked and painted. Ub could produce between 600 and 700 drawings a day, a tremendous speed which was only matched by a New York animator named Bill Nolan, who once produced over five hundred drawings a day for an animation series.

The animators who signed with Charles Mintz had not yet left the Disney Studio and were still working on the last three Oswald cartoons Walt had contracted to produce. As a result, Iwerks worked secretly, day and night, on *Plane Crazy*, in a separate area, away from the rest of the studio. Apparently, he also had animation drawings of Oswald close by so that he could make a quick switch and cover the Mickey drawings if anyone unexpectedly barged in.

In his garage at his home on Lyric Avenue, Disney installed three benches for a makeshift studio where Walt and Roy's wives (Lilly and Edna), along with Walt's sister-in-law (Hazel Sewell), inked and painted Iwerks's drawings onto cels. Cameraman Mike Marcus shot the cel artwork at night at the Disney Studio on Hyperion Avenue, after the other animators had gone home. Walt personally eliminated all traces of Mike's work so no one would discover it the next morning.

Plane Crazy was previewed at a theater at Sunset and Gardner in Hollywood on May 15, 1928. Walt had coached the theater organist on how to accompany the action and slipped him a little extra money as well to punch up the music. Reportedly, the picture got quite a few laughs from the audience.

Encouraged by this response, even though they still did not have a distributor for the new series, Walt and Ub began work almost immediately on *Gallopin' Gaucho*, a takeoff on the popular Douglas Fairbanks silent film, *The Gaucho* (1927). By that time, the defecting animators were gone and there was no need for secrecy on the second Mickey cartoon.

Disney was not trying to devise a new series just to save his studio or exact revenge against Mintz. He simply loved producing cartoons. Lillian recalled an incident shortly before they were married: "My sister and I were visiting a friend that night, so Walt decided to go to the movies. A cartoon short by a competitor was advertised outside, but suddenly, as he sat in the darkened theater, his own picture came on. Walt was so excited he rushed down to the manager's office. The manager, misunderstanding, began to apologize for not showing the advertised film. Walt hurried over to my sister's house to break his exciting news, but we weren't home yet. Then he tried to find Roy, but he was out too. Finally he went home alone. Every time we pass a theater where one of his films is advertised on the marquee I can't help but think of that night." It was that same joy that motivated Walt to develop Mickey.

On May 29, 1928, Walt threw a party to come up with gags for *Gallopin' Gaucho*, which was ready for preview on August 28. In the interim, however, Walt became increasingly aware of the sensation caused by 1927's *Jazz Singer*, the first movie with synchronized sound, and realized that distributors would have a diminished interest in a new silent cartoon feature. He became intrigued by the idea of applying synchronized sound to animation, and started production on *Steamboat Willie*.

"Walt didn't know if people would believe that the character on the screen was making the noise," animator Wilfred Jackson later recalled. "Nobody had ever seen a drawing make noise, and there was no way to be sure that the people would believe it. It might just look like some kind of a fake thing, and Walt wanted it to seem real, as if the noise was coming right from what the character was doing. So to find out whether the whole thing would be believable . . . when a few scenes [of *Willie*] had been animated . . . they set up this test."

For the test, which took place in the studio building on Hyperion Avenue, the opening scene was put on a loop of film that would constantly repeat. Roy Disney positioned himself outside a window so that the projector noise would not be audible. Iwerks rigged up a microphone and customized an old crystal radio into a makeshift speaker placed behind a bedsheet hung over a doorway, onto which the film would be projected.

Walt had gone to a five-and-dime store and purchased items like noisemakers, cowbells, tin cans, a frying pan, slide whistles, ocarinas, a washboard, and a plumber's friend. Jackson played his harmonica. Iwerks played the washboard and the slide whistles and produced various sound effects. Les Clark did percussion and sound effects, Johnny Cannon vocalized sounds for the barnyard animals, and Disney supplied the voices and additional sound effects.

"When Roy started the projector up, I furnished the music, with my mouth organ . . . and the other fellows hit things and made sound effects," Jackson said. "We had spittoons everywhere then, and they made a wonderful gong if you hit them with a pencil. We practiced with it several times, and we got so we were hitting it off pretty well. We took turns going out there ourselves, and looking at the thing, and when I went out there wasn't any music, but the noises and voices seemed to come from it just fine. It was really pretty exciting, and it did prove to us that the sound coming from the drawing could be a convincing thing."

Seated on the other side of the bedsheet were the wives of the Disney brothers and Iwerks, as well as Jane Ames, Jackson's girlfriend. Each of the men took turns going out in front of the screen to watch as the loop of film ran over and over. Walt subsequently complained that when it was his turn to go out and view the film, the ladies were paying little attention to the experiment and were instead spending their time gossiping and talking about babies and exchanging recipes. "What did they expect?" Lillian Disney said. "We had absolutely no idea what was going on. And it any case, it sounded terrible."

Iwerks remembered it differently. "It was wonderful," he said. "There was no precedent of any kind. I've never been so thrilled in my life. Nothing since has ever equaled it. That evening proved that an idea could be made to work."

Disney re-ran the film repeatedly, trying to perfect the synchronization of music and sound effects with the cartoon action being projected on the screen. Walt, Iwerks and Jackson needed to come up with a rough score that aligned sound with image. Jackson, a former art student who had joined Disney in order to learn animation, developed the first bar sheet (also known as an exposure sheet or dope sheet). Thanks to his music teacher mother, Jackson—who did not have an extensive background in the field—understood rudimentary musical notation and the principle of using a metronome to keep time.

Jackson played harmonica and worked with Disney to adapt two popular songs, "Steamboat Bill" and "Turkey in the Straw" (one of Jackson's favorite harmonica pieces), for the soundtrack. Although the initial bar sheet devised by Jackson did not contain conventional musical notation, it included a measure-by-measure breakdown of the songs, delineating each musical beat. The orchestra that would record the soundtrack received a musical score using this beat-and-measure breakdown as a guide. Despite its crude form, Jackson's bar sheet represented an important innovation that made it possible to time and synchronize the sound precisely to the picture. Even without the proper musical notation, this bar sheet had all the essential characteristics of the "dope sheets" still used today.

Disney journeyed to New York early in September 1928 to get the film recorded, but encountered chaos as movie companies scrambled to buy or lease recording equipment and line up recording time. He approached Fox, and its Movietone system, but, already overwhelmed with work, Fox was uninterested. The representative at RCA seemed not only to keep padding the estimated price, but was condescending to the idea of accurately synchronizing sound to a cartoon.

When Walt asked for a demonstration of RCA's system, he was shown a copy of *Dinner Time*, an Aesop's Fable cartoon by Paul Terry, for which RCA had done the sound synchronization. *Dinner Time* had just premiered in theaters on September 1, 1928, a full ten weeks before *Steamboat Willie* would debut at the Colony.

"My gosh . . . terrible . . . a lot of racket and nothing else," Walt wrote in a letter to his brother, Roy, "I was terribly disappointed. I had expected to see something halfway decent. But honestly . . . it was nothing but one of the rottenest fables I ever saw and I should know because I have seen almost all of them. It merely had an orchestra playing and adding some noise . . . The talking part does not mean a thing. It doesn't even match . . . We sure have nothing to worry about from these quarters."

RCA and Movietone had secured patents on their sound-on-film systems, but Patrick A. Powers bribed company engineers to provide him with technical information on their designs. With slight modifications he created his own "outlaw" recording process called Cinephone.

Pat Powers was a notorious character in the film business. At one time, he partnered with Carl Laemmle at Universal Pictures. When Laemmle discovered that Powers was cheating him, Laemmle confronted him. Powers protested his innocence, took the doctored financial record books and threw them out his upper-floor office window, where they were retrieved and spirited away by a waiting accomplice.

One reason Walt's cartoon intrigued Powers was that he needed a high-profile project to help publicize and legitimatize his Cinephone system. His warm Irish charisma and acquaintance with important people in the business persuaded Walt that this was the man who would give his cartoon special attention.

Powers arranged for the services of conductor Carl Edouarde, who, until recently, had led the pit orchestra at the Mark Strand Theatre on Broadway. (After the *Gallopin' Gaucho* was fitted with sound, it premiered at the Strand on December 30, 1928.) Despite Disney's detailed instructions, Edouarde was disinterested in the flashes Walt put in the film print to mimic the beat of the metronome, and thus allow the sounds and music to be synchronized.

An orchestra, as Walt later reported, composed of thirty players plus three trap drummers and effects men, was assembled for the recording session. The players received seven dollars an hour, the effects men ten, and Edouarde twenty an hour. As the morning wore on, the expenses quickly mounted, especially since Edouarde insisted on several rehearsals.

Projecting the film on the studio wall distracted the musicians. Often, the film finished with sheets of music yet to be played. Furthermore, the bass player's low notes kept blowing out a bulb in the recording mechanism whenever he sawed his bass, so they kept moving him farther away until he ended up outside the room. One of the first musicians to show up was tired and unshaven from an all-night recording session. Upon opening his music case, he removed a bottle of whisky and took a swig.

In those days, no stopping, editing or layering took place. Everything had to be recorded at the same time in one continuous take, one of which was ruined by a loud cough near a microphone that blew out another bulb. The culprit? Walt himself.

The session was a disaster. In order to finance a second one, Roy had to sell Walt's favorite car, a Moon Roadster. "I think this is Old Man Opportunity rapping at our door," wrote Walt to Roy. "Let's not let the jingle of a few pennies drown out his knock."

For the next session, the orchestra was reduced in size, two of the effects men were let go, and Walt assumed some of their functions. Iwerks had made one other print of the cartoon without the flashes but with a bouncing ball indicating where beats should strike. This film was projected directly onto Edouarde's sheet music. Following this new cue, the effects and music matched the action perfectly.

Carl Stalling, a theater organist from Kansas City and a former acquaintance of Disney, arrived in New York October 26, 1928, and moved into Walt's hotel room. At Walt's request, he had prepared compositions for the sound recordings on *Plane Crazy* and *Gallopin' Gaucho*. Stalling later helped create the *Silly Symphony* series for Disney, and went on to an outstanding career as the musical director for Warner Bros.' cartoons.

Weeks passed with no sales. Powers arranged special showings of *Steamboat Willie* all over town, but, while the bookers enjoyed it, no one bought it. Finally, at one showing, Harry Reichenbach pulled Walt aside. Reichenbach had been one of the most successful press agents in New York and was now handling films for Universal Pictures through its Manhattan outlet, the Colony Theatre.

Reichenbach was a flamboyant personality. As a young man, he gained notoriety when he displayed a print of *September Morn*—a painting that was scandalously nude by 1913 standards—in the window of the Manhattan gallery where he worked, and hired young boys to crowd around and gawk. He then protested to Anthony Comstock, who, as head of the New York Society for the Suppression of Vice, launched a protest against the moral outrage of the lady's nudity. The ensuing publicity caused prints of the painting to sell like hot cakes. It was soon reproduced on postcards and calendars as well, becoming the prototype for modern-day pinup calendars.

Harry Reichenbach was quite the publicist. In 1920, Samuel Goldwyn hired him to save *The Return Of Tarzan*, a film Goldwyn feared would die at the box office. Harry took special delight in promoting this potential bomb because it gave him an opportunity to employ tricks he'd learned working in the circus.

A week before the movie was released, the Hotel Belleclaire in New York City received a guest named Zann. The man arrived with an enormous box he claimed contained a piano, which the hotel obligingly hoisted into his room through a window. The next day, Zann asked room service to send up fifteen pounds of raw meat, which, out of curiosity, was delivered personally by the hotel manager, who, to his surprise, found an adult lion in the room. The police and a boatload of reporters quickly descended, ensuring headlines, and notices in the press soon promised that Mr. "T. Zann" would personally attend the opening of the movie.

Reichenbach advised Disney that he needed a track record to entice a distributor to take *Steamboat Willie*. "Those guys don't know what's good until the public tells them," he reportedly said.

Walt also was concerned that a short New York engagement might discourage a potential distributor since a New York premiere would already have occurred. But Harry Reichenbach convinced him to forget about a distributorship until moviegoers and critics got a chance to see the new short.

Mickey's phenomenal success was partly due to Reichenbach's shrewd sense of publicity. *Willie* was booked in the Colony Theatre for a two-week run beginning November 18, 1928. The Colony announced that it agreed to pay $500 a week for the film, a then unheard-of price for a cartoon. The money provided much needed immediate income enabling the Disney brothers to pay salaries.

Steamboat Willie opened on November 18, 1928, playing on a bill preceding the movie *Gang War*,[1] a standard crime drama starring Jack Pickford, the younger brother of silent-screen star Mary Pickford who would soon become one of Mickey's biggest fans.

Stalling and Disney sat in the back row of the theater and heard a tremendous audience reaction.

Willie was a huge hit. Many critics ignored the main feature and the stage show. *Variety* said it was "a high order of cartoon ingenuity" and "a peach of a synchronization job all the way." The *New York Times* called the film "an ingenious piece of work with a good deal of fun. It growls, whines, squeaks and makes various other sounds that add to its mirthful quality." *Weekly Film Review* reported that the cartoon "kept the audience laughing and chuckling from the moment the lead titles came on the screen, and it left them applauding." And *Exhibitor's Herald* declared, "It is impossible to describe this riot of mirth, but it knocked me out of my seat."

After its two-week run, *Steamboat Willie* moved to the two-year old Roxy Theatre. (Following the cartoon's debut there, the Colony was renamed the Broadway Theatre, and *Fantasia* premiered there twelve years later.) Walt was quickly flooded with offers including one from Charles Mintz and Universal, who were highly complimentary and made a generous offer—but only if Walt surrendered the copyright and control of Mickey to Universal.

Walt seemed to have little choice; every major distributor wanted total control of his work. But that was something, after his experience with Oswald, he would not let happen again. Pat Powers, who needed Disney about as much as Disney needed him (in order to publicize his new sound system), was the only one willing to accept Walt's terms of independence. The deal Walt and Roy Disney struck with Powers gave Powers 10% of the gross of Mickey's films. In addition, it obligated the Disneys to pay him $26,000 a year for exclusive ten-year rights to the Cinephone process. Powers, in return, would handle all expenses involved in booking the product via the "states rights" system.

Powers planned, essentially, to use salesmen to place Mickey Mouse cartoons in theaters on a territorial or state-by-state basis. Most of the best theaters were controlled as part of a national distribution network by large production companies like Paramount or Universal, and were locked into exclusive block-booking agreements. How widely a cartoon could be distributed was, of course, vital to its financial success. The states rights system, despite its limitations, would at least allow Walt's films to be seen. But Walt's arrangement with Pat Powers also allowed Powers and his salesmen the flexibility to perform some financial monkey business in determining fees and expenses before the Disneys ever saw any revenue.

Adding sound tracks to the first two Mouse cartoons meant that by the end of December 1928, three Mickeys were being shown around the country, and Iwerks had already started work—at Walt's insistence—on a fourth, *The Barn Dance*. The world fell in love with the little fellow, and the true world of Disney had officially begun.

It is often stated, erroneously, that *Steamboat Willie* was *the* first sound cartoon (it was advertised that way in the program at the Colony The-atre). Actually, Max Fleischer, one of Walt's successful New York com-petitors, had done a handful of sound cartoons in 1924–25 with the help of Lee De Forest, one of the great, if controversial, pioneers of radio. But these mostly-musical sing-a-longs were unsuccessful and quickly forgotten, just as Paul Terry's *Dinner Time* would be.

Willie was, however, the first cartoon to successfully integrate mu-sic, voice, and special effects into an entertaining and believable prod-uct, with a likeable main character and a clear story line. When Dave Smith founded the Disney Archives in 1970, one of his first tasks was to catalogue what was in Walt Disney's office, which had remained un-touched since Walt's death on December 15, 1966. Smith was surprised to find in Walt's desk the original six-page story outline for *Steamboat Willie*.

"Things were stolen from the company before the Archives was es-tablished," Dave Smith said in a 1997 interview. "Included were some scenes from *Steamboat Willie* and the story sketches for several se-quences of *Snow White*. We have the [story script] for *Steamboat Wil-lie* and most of the other films. I found the *Steamboat Willie* script in Walt's office; which surprised me since everyone told me he wasn't in-terested in the company's past, only the next project."

In 1988, to celebrate the sixtieth birthday of its most famous car-toon character, the Walt Disney Company donated to the Smithsonian (National Museum of American History) six original drawings from *Steamboat Willie* selected personally by Walt's nephew, Roy E. Disney.

Despite his eager fascination with the future and in particular the concept of EPCOT, Walt never did forget that it was all started by a mouse.

Note

1. *Gang War*, directed by Bert Glennon, was primarily silent with some talking sequences. Glennon shot about nine mediocre pictures in Hollywood between 1928–32. He was primarily known as a cinematographer, and worked for John Ford and Cecil B. DeMille. He later did the cinematography for the black-and-white portions of the behind-the-scenes segments in Disney's *Reluctant Dragon* (1941) and also, in color, for Disney's *Davy Crockett and the River Pirates* (1956). The music for *Gang War* was by Alfred Sherman, the father of Disney songwriters Richard and Robert Sherman.

More Secrets of Steamboat Willie

Jim Korkis

Adapted from material published as separate sidebars to "Secrets of Steamboat
Willie," *Hogan's Alley*, September 2004.

Why Is It Called "Steamboat Willie"?

Most articles refer to *Steamboat Willie* as a parody of Buster Keaton's
last independent silent comedy, *Steamboat Bill Jr.*, released earlier
that same year. However, other than the fact that both films feature
a steamboat, and that Keaton's character is nicknamed Willie, the
cartoon makes no direct references to *Steamboat Bill Jr.*, unlike *Gallopin' Gaucho*, which parodies some of the action from the Douglas
Fairbanks silent action picture, *The Gaucho*. No doubt Disney believed
that audiences would associate the title with the Keaton classic, but
direct parody was not intended. In the cartoon, the opening music was
a popular song titled "Steamboat Bill," which also inspired the title and
the hope of audience familiarity. In addition, audiences were aware of
two things: the popular Broadway musical *Showboat*, that premiered
in 1927, and the tragic Mississippi River flood of 1927, which led to vast
improvements in flood control. As a result, Mississippi steamboats
loomed large in the popular imagination.

It is also important to remember that no one had heard of this
"Mickey Mouse" character, so titling the cartoon *Steamboat Mickey*
would have had zero box-office recognition. More importantly, Walt
would insist that when an audience went to see a Mickey Mouse cartoon they were not seeing the adventures of Mickey Mouse. Mickey
was an actor performing a role just as Clark Gable or Cary Grant would.
This conceit was one of the things that positioned Mickey Mouse in the
marketplace differently than other cartoon stars of the time. Mickey
was not Steamboat Willie; he was playing the role of Steamboat Willie.
In his next film, he might be portraying a different character, even if the
character had many of Mickey's own characteristics.

Did Ub Iwerks Animate the Entire Film Himself?

Iwerks animated *Steamboat Willie* virtually by himself in what was known as "straight ahead" animation, a technique in which he did the first drawing, then the second drawing, the third, and so on. It would be a while before production concepts such as key drawings, assistants and inbetweeners became the norm. By this time, Walt had stopped doing any drawing at all—his primary contribution was story and character development. However, unlike the first two Mickey cartoons, Ub had some help on *Willie*.

Wilfred Jackson was so eager to become an animator that he turned up at the Disney Studio one day and offered to pay Walt tuition until he had gained experience. Walt gave him a job washing the ink and paint off cels so that they could be reused. Jackson started work only a week before the Oswald the Rabbit animators left. They were laughing and talking when he arrived, but the following Saturday took all their personal belongings home and didn't return on Monday . . . or any day after that. Jackson quickly moved up into the role of an apprentice animator. His first assignment was the cycle of Minnie Mouse running along the riverbank in *Steamboat Willie*. With Jackson's background in music, he was a natural to become a director of the *Silly Symphonies* and won Oscars for *Tortoise and the Hare*, *The County Cousin* and *The Old Mill*. He also worked as a sequence director on *Snow White* and *Fantasia*, and in the 1950s produced and directed episodes of the Disneyland television series.

Les Clark was the first of Disney's "Nine Old Men." He began his tenure at the Disney Studio in 1927, where, despite his lack of formal animation training, he got some experience on the Alice Comedies and Oswald the Rabbit series. Clark animated the scene in *Steamboat Willie* where Mickey shoves a pitchfork of hay down the cow's throat. When Iwerks left the studio in 1930, Clark became the resident "Mickey and Minnie expert," expanding and defining their personalities. Clark animated major portions of *The Band Concert* and the "Sorcerer's Apprentice" segment of *Fantasia*. He worked on every Disney animated feature from *Snow White* to *Sleeping Beauty*, and directed many episodes of Disney training films and TV series.

What Is the Story behind the Music?

The tune Mickey Mouse is whistling as *Steamboat Willie* opens was a popular parlor song entitled "Steamboat Bill," written by the Leighton Brothers, who also composed "Frankie and Johnny," and Ren Shields, who wrote "In the Good Ol' Summertime." The Leighton Brothers used the song in their minstrel act, encouraging the audience to sing along with each reprise of the chorus:

> "Steamboat Bill, steaming down the Mississippi.
> Steamboat Bill, a mighty man was he.
> Steamboat Bill, steaming down the Mississippi.
> Out to break the record of the Robert E. Lee."

"Steamboat Bill" tells the story of the skipper of the *Whippoorwill.* Bill's boat was attempting to surpass the speed record of the *Robert E. Lee*, set in 1870 for covering the stretch of the Mississippi between New Orleans and St. Louis. In the song, the *Whippoorwill* is pushed beyond its limits, causing its boiler to explode, sending Bill and a gambler high into the air, where Bill bets a thousand dollars that he'll go higher than the gambler.

One of Wilfred Jackson's favorite numbers on the harmonica, "Turkey in the Straw," an old standard long in the public domain, is the other prominent tune in *Steamboat Willie*. The lyrics of the tune that come out of the goat's mouth after eating the sheet music are:

> "Went out to milk, and I didn't know how,
> I milked the goat instead of the cow.
> A monkey sittin' on a pile of straw,
> A-winkin' at his mother-in-law."

What Is a Parrot Doing on a Steamboat?

Before various bans on importation were enacted in the 1930s, parrots often represented prestige and exotic taste. Even President Teddy Roosevelt kept one at the White House. As a major shipping port, New Orleans saw its share of imported parrots and other animals. Occasionally, crates broke open and the birds found new homes, which may be how they became associated with pirates who frequented the port.

A parrot probably was chosen for the same reason it was selected for Disneyland's first audio-animatronics attraction, the Enchanted Tiki Room. Rather than dealing with the problem of matching lip movements, a bird's beak merely opens and closes, making it easier to animate dialogue. In addition, a parrot doesn't merely echo speech, but mimics selectively, which can seem like a taunt, making it an ideal comic foil.

Interestingly, a parrot does not appear in the original script for *Steamboat Willie*. But Walt did provide the bird's voice, including its final words: "Man Overboard!" The parrot mocks Mickey twice during the film, first, near the beginning, after Mickey falls into a bucket of soapy water, with "Hope you don't feel hurt, big boy!" and, second, at the end, when Pete punishes Mickey by making him peel potatoes. In the last comic bit in the cartoon, Mickey hurls a spud at the bird in retaliation for these taunts.

Did Something Disappear?

In the rush to complete *Steamboat Willie*, items continually disappear. Audiences have been so captivated by the cartoon they rarely, if ever, notice.

Mickey starts out wearing a pilot's hat. The pilot actually steers the boat, and on smaller vessels the captain and the pilot may be the same person, or have overlapping job functions. When Mickey's boss—Pete, the captain—appears in exactly the same hat, he grabs his cheeky underling and twirls him around. As Mickey twirls back to face the captain, his cap has disappeared.

The rope for blowing the whistle and the cord for ringing the bell are clearly evident behind Mickey at the start of the film. Once Pete starts chewing a big plug of tobacco, both ropes are gone.

The cow on the dock wears a tag labeled "F.O.B.," which means "Free On Board," referring to the fact that it was being shipped under a rate that included cost of delivery and loading onto a steamboat. When the cow stretches its neck to moo, the tag briefly disappears.

Twice, while the goat eats Minnie's sheet music, its goatee disappears, although this can only be seen by examining the sequence frame by frame. And when Mickey swings a cat by the tail and it hits the lid of a trash can, the lid stays in position, disappears, reappears and eventually vanishes for good.

However, the most famous piece of disappearing animation was missing from the cartoon for decades. Mickey pulls on the tails of baby pigs suckling on their mother. Then, in a sequence that was removed in the 1950s, Mickey picks up the mother, kicks off the piglets still hanging on, and, pushing on her teats, plays the mother pig like an accordion. When the cartoon was shown to a television audience, this bit of barnyard humor was deemed inappropriate and removed, though it's been restored on the recent DVD version.

Where Is Podunk Landing?

"Podunk Landing" is where Mickey's side-wheeler stops to pick up livestock, and where Minnie, arriving late, misses the boat—before being lifted on board by Mickey with the aid of a winch. Originally an Indian name, meaning "lowland" (communities called Podunk tend toward swampiness), the dictionary defines "Podunk" as a small, unimportant, isolated town. However, some people claim the word comes from the sound of a mill wheel going "po-dunk." Others believe that Podunk is a fictional place, though there are several Podunks in the Northeast and Midwest. Podunk is also the town that the country mouse comes from in the Disney cartoon, *The Country Cousin* (1936), directed by Wilfred Jackson.

Haven't I Seen Some of Those Gags Before?

In the days before television and videotape, an audience might see a cartoon only once, so it was not uncommon to recycle the funniest bits from previous cartoons. Apparently, Walt had a great memory for gags. When actor Dean Jones compained to Walt that a gag in one of the live action movies they were making was too corny, Walt said, "It got a laugh in 1923 and it will get a laugh today." At the preview of the film, as the audience howled at the joke, Jones admitted that Disney was right.

When Pete pulls Mickey's stomach and it stretches, Walt's comment on the original story script is, "same as Oswald and the Bear in *Tall Timber*," an Oswald the Rabbit cartoon, released July 9, 1928. As mentioned in "Secrets of Steamboat Willie," Mickey cranking a goat's tail to make music repeats a gag from the Oswald cartoon *Rival Romeos*, released March 5, 1928. And at the end of *Steamboat Willie*, Mickey seen peeling potatoes, making bigger potatoes into smaller ones, is a repeat of a gag of a mouse doing the same thing in *Alice The Whaler*, released July 25, 1927.

Is Pete Doing a Product Placement?

Pete is chewing Star Plug Tobacco; Walt specifically refers to it as such in his script. Star Plug tobacco was an actual existing product at the time and highly popular. Every tobacco chewer prided himself on his aim, whether lobbing it over a piece of furniture without accident or making it ping-pong when it hit the cuspidor. Obviously, Star Plug was popular at the Disney Studio because many years later Goofy uses it as fish bait in 1935 in *On Ice*.

Incidentally, Pete is the longest continually appearing Disney character. He made his first appearance in the Alice Comedy, *Alice Solves The Puzzle*, in 1925, and eventually appeared in four Alice and seven Oswald films prior to his career menacing Mickey Mouse.

Before 1930, he was sometimes called Putrid Pete and Bootleg Pete, and audiences sometimes thought he was a species of bear. However, Walt's original story script refers to him as a "cat Captain" and of course, a cat is a natural enemy for a mouse, even though Walt never considered Mickey and Minnie to be mice. (Walt's script for *Steamboat Willie* always identifies Minnie as "the girl.")

Pete is not really a villain in *Steamboat Willie*. He may be a bully, but as the steamboat captain, he wants his only crewmember, Mickey, to do the job he is supposed to be doing rather than goofing off.

Why Is Mickey Punished by Peeling Potatoes?

Walt's experience in France toward the end of World War I introduced him to the military punishment of peeling potatoes. It was a mindless job that needed to be done to feed the troops, but it also built discipline. (Look how well it's worked for Beetle Bailey!) In fact, in Walt's original script he was going to have Mickey whistle the popular World War I song, "Pack Up Your Troubles."

Potatoes were standard fare on boats since they kept longer and helped prevent scurvy. The *Titanic* carried forty tons of potatoes.

However, even when potatoes became the second-largest food crop in America, they were still used primarily as animal fodder, and that might be their purpose on this steamboat.

How Much Did Steamboat Willie Cost?

In small handwriting, Roy O. Disney entered into his ledger the amounts (which included production and prints) for the first three Mickey Mouse cartoons:

Plane Crazy: $3,528.50
Gallopin' Gaucho: $4,249.73
Steamboat Willie: $4,986.69

Mouse Trap

Garnering a great deal of media attention last year was the Supreme Court's decision to uphold the 1998 ruling by Congress to extend the length of copyright protection to match the term of protection in Europe. This extension, keeping material out of the public domain for an additional twenty years, was challenged as unconstitutional by Eric Eldred, who runs an online archive of published works. The Supreme Court determined that, because Congress had granted enlargements of copyright protection three times since the original copyright statute was enacted in 1790, this latest extension was within its authority.

Much of the debate in this controversy had to do with the prospect that without extended protection, *Steamboat Willie* would enter the public domain in the year 2003. Ignored in all this talk was the fact that Mickey Mouse is also a trademarked character, and trademarks can be kept alive indefinitely as long as they are in use. (Disney filed his application to trademark Mickey Mouse with the U.S. Patent Office on May 21, 1928, and the trademark was granted the following September 18.) So while someone might hope to sell copies of *Steamboat Willie* or merchandise inspired by images from the film, Disney's legal team could legitimately argue that such actions, while legal, were creating "confusion in the marketplace." Disney would no doubt maintain that the items were actually infringing on its existing trademark and thereby prevent the sale of such material.

Using its legal resources, the Disney Company could make any attempt to capitalize on *Steamboat Willie* an uncomfortably expensive and time-consuming series of court challenges that would, to say the least, make any merchandising efforts unprofitable. That was the company's strategy many years ago when Malibu Graphics, a small comic-book company, attempted to reprint early installments of the Mickey Mouse comic strip that had fallen into the public domain.

For the foreseable future, when it concerns the Mouse, let the seller beware.

• As first published in *Hogan's Alley*, this piece was divided into ten parts (with the eleventh part dropped), and scattered as sidebars throughout the preceding essay, "Secrets of Steamboat Willie." The text as reprinted here reflects the way the author originally intended it to be presented. He took this opportunity to slightly revise both articles specifically for this *Reader*.

Mickey Mouse

M. Thomas Inge

In Dennis R. Hall and Susan Grove Hall, eds., *American Icons: An Encyclopedia of the People, Places, and Things That Have Shaped Our Culture* (Greenwood Press, 2006). Reprinted by permission of the author.

There is no more widely known an iconic figure out of American culture in the world at large than Mickey Mouse. So successful have been the marketing strategies of the Walt Disney Company, so widely distributed have been the films and comics, and so strongly appealing is the image of the mouse to children and adults alike that there are few small corners of the earth where Mickey is not instantly recognizable, if by nothing more than a set of round ears. Crude reproductions of Mickey and his girl friend Minnie Mouse appear on the walls of bus stops and telephone booths in remote African villages, and children everywhere decorate the walls of their nurseries and schools with their images. In China the folk figure of the Monkey King has been known to appear with Mickey's face, and a 2003 exhibition of postmodern Russian art in Moscow featured a bronze statue by Alexander Kosolapov of Lenin with the head of Mickey Mouse. In Italy he is known as Topolino, in Sweden Musse Pigg, in Spain Miguelito, in China Mi Lao Shu, and in Vietnam Mic-Kay. His admirers have included Sergei Eisenstein, E. M. Forster, William Faulkner, Charlie Chaplin, Franklin D. Roosevelt, John Updike, Maurice Sendak, Andy Warhol, Roy Lichtenstein, and George Lucas.

For socialists and left leaning intellectuals, Mickey represents American capitalism and cultural imperialism at its most unscrupulous. For conservatives and those on the right, he represents the sweet success of free enterprise and capitalism at its most admirable. For ordinary people, however, Mickey is a symbol of what's good about America and its culture. Gentle but self-confident, sentimental but not maudlin, and naïve without being foolish, Mickey epitomizes a kind of character whose appeal cuts across class and national boundaries.

Stories about the creation of Mickey Mouse are legend and contradictory. Walt Disney had been producing a series of successful animated films for Universal Studios about a character called Oswald the Lucky Rabbit. When Disney traveled to New York from Hollywood to renew the contract in 1928, he discovered that the distributor, Charles Mintz, had hired away most of his staff and intended to produce the films at a lower cost with or without Disney. Although created by Disney, the figure of Oswald had been copyrighted by Universal. Disney refused to cooperate with Mintz. At this moment he probably promised himself never to work on a property over which he did not exercise control and to be sure that his own intellectual property was protected to the full extent of the law.

In search of a character for a new series, one story has it that Disney remembered a pet mouse that visited the young aspiring cartoonist's drawing board in Kansas City. Another was that he dreamed up the character and sketched him out on the train on his way back from the dispute over Oswald. He wanted to call him Mortimer, but his wife suggested that a better name was Mickey. The likely truth is that like all of his creations, it was a matter of consultation and collaboration, mainly with his friend and talented artist Ub Iwerks, who had remained faithful and refused to leave Disney for Mintz.

It may partly have been a simple process of elimination. While no one in particular had decided that anthropomorphism was to be the order of the day in animation, it has worked out that way, from Gertie the dinosaur to Ren and Stimpy. The cat had already been used most famously by Otto Messmer in Felix the Cat, as well as by Disney himself in a Felix look-alike named Julius in the early Alice comedies produced before the Oswald films. Dogs were being used by Max and Dave Fleischer in the *Out of the Inkwell* series, specifically in Bimbo and his canine girlfriend Betty (before she metamorphosed into a girl as Betty Boop). Oswald had cornered the market on rabbits for a long time, until Bugs Bunny came along. What they were left with were rats and mice, largely indistinguishable in how they were drawn in animated films. They had already been used by Disney and others as frequent background characters, except for that mouse Ignatz who threw bricks at the love-struck Krazy Kat but who never made a successful transition to the screen from his comic strip existence. If one examines the rodents who cavort in the Alice comedies, one can see Mickey in an early form not unlike the way he would appear in *Plane Crazy*, the first of the Mickey shorts to be drawn. (See especially *Alice Rattled by Rats* of 1925 where dozens of proto-Mickeys play music, dance, and cause chaos in the household. They even have rounded ears, and as in the case of *Alice the Whaler* in 1927, wear small pants.)

The idea may have been Disney's, but likely the physical form of Mickey is attributable to Ub Iwerks. In the operation of the studio, Disney already turned over to Iwerks the painstaking art while he focused on plots, gags, and technical and business matters. Disney would remain strongly attached to and closely identified with Mickey all of his life, doing the voice of the mouse for the films and defending him against all criticism. In fact, many would view Mickey as Disney's alter ego, and on one occasion he made the oddly revealing statement, "I love Mickey Mouse more than any woman I've ever known" (Grant 23).

If the power of Mickey Mouse as an image is as important to his popularity as his character, then Iwerks remains equally responsible for his success. An incredibly rapid artist, Iwerks had finished work almost single-handedly on *Plane Crazy* and *The Gallopin' Gaucho* when Disney was inspired to use in the third film sound and music, which he saw as the wave of the future. Thus *Steamboat Willie* was the first animated film to be drawn in full synchronization with previously selected pieces of music. Then music had to be added to the first two, although the third was the first to be released to the public on November 18, 1928.

It was not until *Steamboat Willie* that Mickey began to assume in full his traditional appearance. In the first film he wore no shoes and had a head more in the shape of a real rodent, except he had the round ears and wore pants. In the opening scene on the steamboat, Mickey is wearing the large round shoes that would become his trademark, adopted from what was known as the "big foot" school of cartooning in the comic strip world, and he has the large circular head that would remain with him. Like Felix, Bimbo, Oswald, most of the animated film characters who preceded him, Mickey had a black body and head, large white eyeballs, and a white area around the mouth—all characteristic of African Americans as portrayed stereotypically in cartoons, illustrations, and advertising of the time and based on the image of minstrel show performers in black face. When white gloves were added, Mickey moved even closer to his sources. None of these characters retained, however, any of the language or cultural nuances of black life, although Mickey has sometimes been thought to retain some of the free-swinging style of the hipster and trickster. Mickey may be "black" in more than one sense of the word.

In terms of conduct, the Mickey Mouse in these early films is unlike the one the world would come to know and love. In *Steamboat Willie* he chews tobacco, commits violence against any number of farmyard animals to make his impromptu music, and apparently drowns a parrot at the end. *The Gallopin' Gaucho* features a Mickey who drinks, smokes, and treats roughly Minnie, who wears pasties over her breasts as a dance hall girl. He commits more violence against animals in *Plane Crazy* and is guilty of sexual harassment against Minnie, who escapes his unwanted advances by bailing out of his airplane. She uses her bloomers as a parachute and arrives on the ground with no pants at the end. All of these capers are laced with crude humor about cow's udders, dropped pants, and chamber pots.

The truth is that this early Mickey had no distinct personality of his own but borrowed it from notable figures of the time. In *Plane Crazy*, he imitates the national hero Charles Lindbergh, who had made the first non-stop transatlantic flight in 1927 and who appears in the film in caricature as Mickey tousles his hair to look like him. As a Latin lover in *The Gallopin' Gaucho*, Mickey is emulating Douglas Fairbanks, Rudolph Valentino, and other romantic leading men of the screen, and *Steamboat Willie*, of course, banks off Buster Keaton's comedy *Steamboat Bill Jr.* released the year before. As parents noticed that children also greatly enjoyed the antics of the mouse, by 1931 they were complaining to Disney about the bad example he was setting.

Under Disney's influence, therefore, Mickey began to develop a carefully delineated personality that would leave behind the early rambunctious Mickey, although he would continue this way for a number of years under the imaginative hand of Floyd Gottfredson in his adventurous comic strip and comic book stories. As Disney would describe the revised mouse, "Mickey's a nice fellow who never does anybody any harm, who gets into scrapes through no fault of his own but always manages to come up grinning" (Thomas 108). Years later he would add,

All we ever intended for him or expected of him was that he could continue to make people everywhere chuckle with him and at him. We didn't burden him with any social symbolism, we made him no mouthpiece for frustrations or harsh satire. Mickey was simply a little personality assigned to the purposes of laughter. (Disney 68)

What is to account for the staying power and the continuing popularity of Mickey Mouse as an icon? There are no easy or quick answers to that question. Writing in one of his columns for *Natural History* magazine in 1979, the popular science writer Stephen Jay Gould applied the psychological theories of Konrad Lorenz to Mickey and came up with this explanation:

In one of his most famous articles, Konrad Lorenz argues that humans use the characteristic differences in form between babies and adults as important behavioral cues. He believes that features of juvenility trigger "innate releasing mechanisms" for affection and nurturing in adult humans. When we see a living creature with babyish features, we feel an automatic surge of disarming tenderness. The adaptive value of this response can scarcely be questioned, for we must nurture our babies. Lorenz, by the way, lists among his releasers the very features of babyhood that Disney affixed progressively to Mickey: "a relatively large head, predominance of the brain capsule, large and low-lying eyes, bulging cheek region, short and thick extremities, a springy elastic consistency, and clumsy movements." (100–101)

Mickey, then, may appeal to innate instincts in all human beings, if Lorenz is right, although Gould would go on to suggest that these strong feelings of affection may be learned from our immediate experience and environment rather than being inherited from ancestral primates.

Another cultural explanation, for Americans anyway, is the heroic folk tradition of the little man, the lost soul, or what Charlie Chaplin called the Little Fellow. Americans have always had a degree of sympa-

thy for the underdog, the person handicapped by injustice or discrimi-
nation, but the little man proves inadequate because he is overwhelmed
by the anxieties and insecurities of the technological society created
in the wake of the Industrial Revolution. This tradition would include
such figures as James Thurber's Walter Mitty, George Herriman's Krazy
Kat, Chic Young's Dagwood Bumstead, the screen personae of Buster
Keaton and Woody Allen, and of course Mickey Mouse.

In fact, Disney borrowed it directly from the artist who may have
been its originator in American culture, Charlie Chaplin. Developed
over the years and through numerous films, Chaplin's Tramp is a
timid but brave soul overcome by the difficulties of life, yet resilient
and cheerful in the face of the struggle for survival, and often wresting
victory out of the jaws of defeat. He is a romantic who brings style to
his meager existence through passion, imagination, and indestructible
hope. Disney admitted the inspiration and influence in 1948 when he
said, "I think we are rather indebted to Charlie Chaplin for the idea [of
Mickey Mouse]. We wanted something appealing, and we thought of
a tiny bit of a mouse that would have something of the wistfulness of
Chaplin—a little fellow trying to do the best he could" (Disney 68).

There is also something powerfully attractive about the very design
of Mickey, the way he is drawn, even though he has slowly but surely
changed over the years in small ways. The scrappy little barefoot mouse
of *Plane Crazy* in 1928, became in the 1930s better dressed with gloves
and yellow bulbous shoes, although he has always worn short pants. By
the 1940s his solid oblong pupils had given way to more clearly defined
eyes, and his snout was elongated somewhat. He later began to wear
a greater variety of clothes in accordance with the roles he played in
the films, as in *Mickey's Chistmas Carol* (1983) or *The Prince and the
Pauper* (1990), although by the time of his last appearance in a short
cartoon in 1995, *Runaway Brain*, he has returned to his familiar clothing as he fights a rampaging monster to save Minnie one more time.

He looks easy to draw, and he has undoubtedly inspired many a child
to want to become a cartoonist. It isn't that easy, however, as any Disney how-to-draw or instructional book makes clear. It is a matter of
concentric circles handled in just the right way, and no matter the angle
at which he holds his head, the ears must remain two black circles. As
John Updike has noted,

These ears properly belong not to three-dimensional space but to an ideal realm of notation, of symbolization, of cartoon resilience and indestructibility. . . . A surreal optical consistency is part of the cartoon world, halfway between our world and the plane of pure signs, of alphabets and trademarks . . . To take a bite out of our imaginations, an icon must be simple. The ears, the wiggily tail, the red shorts, give us a Mickey. . . . Like totem poles, like African masks, Mickey stands at that intersection of abstraction and representation where magic connects. (8, 12–13)

Because of Mickey, Updike first tried his hand at cartooning before turning with greater success to fiction.

Childrens' book author and illustrator Maurice Sendak likewise was inspired by Mickey as a child to enter a creative field where the magic of imagery is the main mode of communications. As he would explain it,

Though I wasn't aware of it at the time, I now know that a good deal of my pleasure in Mickey had to do with his bizarre proportions, the great rounded head extended still farther by those black saucer ears, the black trunk fitting snugly into ballooning red shorts, the tiny legs stuffed into delicious doughy yellow shoes. The giant white gloves, yellow buttons, pie-cut eyes and bewitching grin were the delectable finishing touches. . . . A gratifying shape, fashioned primarily to facilitate the needs of the animator, he exuded a sense of physical satisfaction and pleasure—a piece of art that powerfully affected and stimulated the imagination. (108)

To this day, Sendak surrounds himself with reproductions of Mickey to feed his imagination.

As a result of his continuing appeal, Mickey has found himself at the center of cultural and political controversy. In 1970 a group of young underground cartoonists, led by Dan O'Neill, gathered in San Francisco, called themselves the Air Pirates after a group of villains who opposed Mickey in the comic strips of the 1930s, and set about liberating Mickey from the strictures of corporate ownership. They felt that Mickey had passed into popular folklore and could be claimed by members of their generation as public property. Thus they began to publish a series of comic books beginning with two issues of *Air Pirates Funnies* in the summer of 1971, as well as three issues of *Dan O'Neill's Comics and Stories* (a parodic but close approximation in appearance to *Walt Disney's Comics and Stories*), in which the Disney characters engaged in unusual conduct, with sex being one of the less startling activities. Needless to say, the Disney corporation sued for copyright violation and trademark infringement in a case that went on for ten years, finally to be settled with the cartoonists promising never to draw Disney characters again.

Then in April of 1989 Eternity Comics began to publish a series of reprints of the 1930 comic strips of Mickey under the title *The Uncensored Mouse*. According to copyright law in effect at the time, the strips had fallen into the public domain in 1986. Only two issues appeared before Disney stepped in to claim trademark infringement, although the front covers of the publications were totally black and featured no image of Mickey. Publication ceased as Disney and other corporations lobbied Congress for a change in copyright law. In 1998, Congress passed the Sonny Bono Copyright Extension Act, which extended copyright to the life of the author plus seventy years. The legislation has been called by the press the "Mickey Mouse law."

Although largely absent from the screen since the 1940s, but ever present as a costumed figure at Disneyland and Walt Disney World since the theme parks opened, and a continuing logo and spokesperson for all Disney enterprises, Mickey holds a central position in the popular imagination. Walt Disney himself once ruminated, "Sometimes I've tried to figure out why Mickey appealed to the whole world. Everybody's tried to figure it out. So far as I know, nobody has" (Updike 12). John Updike may have put his finger on a central matter, however, when he wrote, "The America that is not symbolized by the Imperial Uncle Sam is symbolized by Mickey Mouse. He is America as it feels to itself—plucky, put-on, inventive, resilient, good-natured, game" (10).

Works Cited and Recommended

Bain, David, and Bruce Harris, eds. *Mickey Mouse: Fifty Happy Years.* New York: Harmony Books, 1977.

Disney, Walt. *Famous Quotes.* Lake Buena Vista, FL: Walt Disney Co., 1994.

Gould, Stephen Jay. *The Panda's Thumb.* New York: W. W. Norton, 1980.

Grant, John. *Encyclopedia of Walt Disney's Animated Characters.* 2nd ed. New York: Hyperion, 1993.

Heide, Robert, John Gilman, Monique Peterson, and Patrick White. *Mickey Mouse: The Evolution, the Legend, the Phenomenon.* New York: Disney Editions, 2001.

Holliss, Richard, and Brian Sibley. *Walt Disney's Mickey Mouse: His Life and Times.* New York: Harper & Row, 1986.

Jackson, Kathy Merlock. *Walt Disney: A Bio-Bibliography.* Westport, CT: Greenwood Press, 1993.

Lambert, Pierre. *Mickey Mouse.* New York: Hyperion, 1998.

Levin, Bob. *The Pirates and the Mouse: Disney's War Against the Counterculture.* Seattle, WA: Fantagraphics Books, 2003.

Schroeder, Russell. *Walt Disney's Mickey Mouse: My Life in Pictures.* New York: Disney Press, 1997.

Sendak, Maurice. *Caldecott & Co.: Notes on Books & Pictures.* New York: Farrar, Straus, and Giroux, 1988.

Thomas, Bob. *Walt Disney: An American Original.* New York: Hyperion, 1994.

Updike, John. "Introduction." *The Art of Mickey Mouse.* Eds. Craig Yoe and Janet Morra-Yoe. New York: Hyperion, 1991. 7–13.

Watts, Steven. *The Magic Kingdom: Walt Disney and the American Way of Life.* New York: Houghton Mifflin, 1997.

Mock of Mickey Is Pure Evil: Disney's Daughter Rips Hamas over Monster Mouse

Bill Hutchinson

New York Daily News, May 9, 2007.
© Daily News, L.P. (New York). Used with permission.

The only surviving child of Walt Disney is calling Hamas "pure evil" for making a mockery of Mickey Mouse by turning the lovable icon into a propaganda tool for hate.

Diane Disney Miller said she's disgusted that a ripoff of her father's star cartoon character is being used on a new Hamas TV show to encourage Palestinian children to take up arms against Israel and America.

"Of course I feel personal about Mickey Mouse, but it could be Barney as well," Miller, 73, told the Daily News yesterday in a phone interview.

She was more horrified the terror group was using the knockoff Mickey to preach Islamic radicalism to kids throughout the Gaza Strip.

"It's not just Mickey, it's indoctrinating children like this, teaching them to be evil," said Miller, a Northern California winery owner. "The world loves children and this is just going against the grain of humanity."

The News revealed yesterday that Hamas' Al-Aqsa TV station began running the new children's series in April. Called "Tomorrow's Pioneers," it features the life-size clone of Mickey Mouse named "Farfur."

Farfur speaks in a squeaky voice and wears a tuxedo with tails and a red bow tie. He tells youngsters to drink their milk and pray, but also sings about kids arming themselves with AK-47s and striving for world domination "under Islamic leadership."

While the Disney Co. her father founded had no comment, Miller praised the News for informing the public about the perverse program.

"What we're dealing with here is pure evil and you can't ignore that," Miller said. "I'm awful glad you're doing something about it, writing about this and keeping it in the public eye as much as it can be."

Hamas officials denied they were using the show to incite children against Jews.

"Our problem is not with the Jews," said Yehia Moussa, a Hamas leader in the movement's Gaza Strip base. "Our problem is with the occupation and the occupiers."

But the show was getting bad reviews yesterday from Hamas' political rival, the Fatah movement headed by Palestinian President Mahmoud Abbas.

"I don't think it's professional or even humane to use children in such harsh political programs," said Basem Abu Sumaya, head of Fatah's Palestinian Broadcasting Corp. "Children's nationalist spirit must be developed differently."

Mickey Mouse Appears on Poster Atop a Nude Woman's Body beneath a Swastika

Sean Alfano

New York Daily News, July 14, 2010 (online).
© Daily News, L.P. (New York). Used with permission.

Of all the places Mickey Mouse's face has appeared, attached to a nude woman's body beneath a giant swastika on a poster in Poland has to be a new one.

An Italian artist's shocking outdoor exhibit in the city of Poznan aptly titled "NaziSexyMouse," has caused an uproar throughout the country, which was ravaged by the Nazis during World War II.

"This art provocation is a form of violence against the sensitivity of many people," said Norbert Napieraj, a Poznan city council member who wants the poster, which has been on display since June, banned.

The artist, Max Papeschi, explains on his website that the image is a commentary on the lifestyles of Americans, which he calls a "horror."

He says the Mickey Mouse image, along with one showing Ronald McDonald toting a machine gun in Iraq, lose "their reassuring effect and change into a collective nightmare."

The director of the art gallery where the poster is displayed defended the work, saying it does not promote a Nazi agenda.

"The Mickey Mouse head and swastika are on the same level—they don't mean anything, and they are both part of the globalized world," Maria Czarnecka told the Associated Press.

But people who still have horrific memories of the Nazis killing 6 million Poles, half of whom were Jewish, find the artwork revolting.

"It is a shock for people who are still scarred by the hell of the Holocaust," said Alicja Kobus, a spokeswoman for Poznan's Jewish community.

Papeschi's work appeared without controversy in Berlin this week.

He also has a piece portraying Mickey Mouse decked out in a fully decorated Nazi uniform.

Egyptian Christian Faces Trial for Insulting Islam

Sarah El Deeb

Seattle Post-Intelligencer, January 9, 2012. Used with permission of The Associated Press. Copyright © 2013. All rights reserved.

CAIRO (AP)—A prominent Christian Egyptian media mogul faces trial on a charge of insulting Islam, lawyers said Monday, based on his relaying a cartoon on his Twitter account.

The case dates back to June, when Naguib Sawiris posted a cartoon showing a bearded Mickey Mouse and veiled Minnie. He made a public apology after Islamists complained, but his action set off a boycott of his telecom company and other outlets. He said it was supposed to be a joke and apologized, but lawyer Mamdouh Ismail filed a formal complaint against him.

After investigation, the prosecution set the trial for Jan. 14. Sawiris was not available for comment.

The case is linked to developments in Egypt after the ousting of President Hosni Mubarak last February. Sawiris and Ismail belong to competing political parties, and sectarian violence between Christians and Islamists has been on the upswing. In Egypt's parliamentary elections, Islamist parties have won a large majority, leaving liberals far behind.

Sawiris co-founded a liberal party, and Ismail heads a party representing ultraconservative Salafi Muslims.

The case has added to fears among many that ultraconservative Islamists may use their new found powers to try to stifle freedom of expression.

Ismail countered that, saying he took legal action against Sawiris because he wants the law to be respected by all, even a famous businessman and politician, in the post-Mubarak era.

"The revolution came about because we all are seeking the rule of law without any exceptions," he said. The charge is punishable by up to one year in prison.

Rights lawyer Gamal Eid said the contempt of religion law, in place even before Mubarak came to power, has been used against scholars and activists whose comments about Islam angered conservatives.

He warned that the wording of the law is vague, and it can become a tool in the hands of prosecutors to punish opponents and appease authorities.

"Contempt of religion is a very vague term, and the prosecution has taken the radical interpretation," he said, "raising questions of whether this is a legal or a political matter."

Last week, a Coptic Christian student was arrested and referred to trial for posting a drawing of the Prophet Muhammad on Facebook. That triggered two days of violence in southern Egypt.

Muslims generally oppose any depiction of the prophet, even favorable ones, for fear it could lead to idolatry. This drawing showed four women asking for the prophet's hand in marriage.

• The charges against Sawiris were dismissed, according to a report from the Spanish news service EFE, March 1, 2012.

Le Cinéma (*excerpt*)

Pierre Scize

Jazz: l'actualité intellectuelle, December 15, 1929

Aujourd'hui, 15 décembre 1929, *Jazz* peut, sans craindre de donner à rire à ceux qui le feuilleteront en 1960, proclamer ceci : « Il y a, en ce moment sur les boulevards, des films sonores d'un art parfait. »

Songez qu'il y a tout juste un an qu'on nous présentait les premiers et médiocres essais de sonorisation. Et concluez pour l'avenir.

—Mais ces films, quels sont-ils ? *Broadway-Melody, Les Trois Masques*, ces bandes imparfaites ou impossibles, qui tour à tour étonnent et prêtent à rire?

—Non. C'est la prodigieuse série des « Mickey ».

Des dessins animés. Synchronisés avec une pellicule sonore, ils offrent cent purs enchantements. Tout d'abord, ils seraient déjà remarquables s'ils étaient muets. Leur technique, la fantaisie poétique, la liberté, l'imagination inouïes qui président à leur confection toucheraient l'âme d'un sourd. Jamais on ne fit mieux en cette matière, jamais on ne donna plus libre cours à plus de gaminerie enjouée, à plus de délicate drôlerie. Les ressources de l'auteur sont absolument prodigieuses. Rien n'arrête sa verve, rien ne la limite. A chaque instant, l'esprit sollicité par la plus fantasque et la plus gentille extravagance croit avoir touché les bornes du genre—et l'instant d'après, un nouvel et cocasse rebondissement l'entraîne plus loin vers une invention plus extraordinaire, vers plus de drôlerie encore vers une meilleure et plus surprenante qualité du rire.

Mais ce qui augmente encore le mérite de ces petits chefs-d'œuvre, c'est leur synchronisation sonore. Là, nous touchons au miracle. Les techniciens ébaubis se regardent et demandent: « Comment font-ils ? » Quand on connaît la minutie de ce travail, et ce que le repérage sonore suppose de soins et de peine, on frémit, on dit, comme cet ingénieur du micro avec qui j'en parlais, tout à l'heure: « C'est de la mathématique pure ! »

Mais le public lui-même, à qui ces questions demeurent heureusement étrangères, le public subit confusément cette merveille. Elle double son plaisir d'une stupéfaction joyeuse. Et comme les adeptes d'une nouvelle religion, on s'interroge avec des clins d'yeux complices: « Vous avez vu *Virtuose*? Ah ! Et le *Jazz* ? oh! Et ce sont des cris de joie à mesure que la mémoire restitue au souvenir tel trait, tel arpège, tel *gag* savoureux.

Le cheval de *Mickey-Virtuose*, son orchestre où l'on voit le violoniste scier son violon et reprendre le fil de sa mélodie sur les quatre poils de sa barbe, la gamme chromatique de trompettes bouchées executée par des chats à qui l'on tire la queue, les bulles de savon employées à produire des pizzicatti et, pour couronner enfin le tout, la grande scène du piano !

Ah ! ce piano! Nous le voyons, schématique, irréel, figuré, linéairement sur l'écran, et de cette arbitraire silhouette, de cette indication sommaire, issue tout à coup, avec le son magnifique d'un grand Steinway de concert, le prélude de Rachmaninoff, joué par un splendide virtuose.

La superposition d'un bruit réel et d'une apparence, produit un effet bouleversant. On rit, et l'on est inquiet. Une magie nous intimide et nous égaye. Nous retrouvons notre admiration craintive d'enfant pour notre premier jouet mécanique.

Or, soudain, ce piano se débarrasse de la sujetion de son pianiste. Les touches exécutent seules des trilles interminables. Il faut les étirer comme guimauve, les tresser, les attacher ensemble pour qu'elles demeurent immobiles. Est-ce assez? Non! Le tabouret se dérobe sous le séant de son occupant, le piano, désormais révolté, lui décoche un magistral coup de pied et l'envoie explorer le firmament des cauchemars ; après quoi, cet instrument fantasque, riant de tout son clavier, se met à danser en se jouant sur lui-même, à l'aide de ses premiers pieds, un charleston bien rythmé.

Où sommes-nous, sinon dans le libre univers des rêves, au pays sans loi, où vivent les objets inanimés? Et, finalement, qu'est-ce que Mickey et ses amis? Des bêtes, des hommes? On ne sait pas. Des formes. Cela dépasse la création, emprunte à tous les règnes, s'agglomère diverses espèces, tels ce bœuf, ce chien et ce dindon qu'un choc soudain fait se rentrer les uns dans les autres et qui, fondus en une seule creature à douze pattes, à tois tetes, emplumée, poilue, aboyante, fuient par les plaines et les monts . . .

Toutes ces folies soutenues par des bruiteurs et un orchestre admirablement appropriés, déroulent en même temps à notre oreille une espèce de symphonie parodique pleine de sons inattendus et qu'on ne peut se lasser d'entendre tant ils demeurent à leur place, dans *leur ton*, tant ils participent d'un humour vrai, profondément expressif. Certaines trouvailles, par leur rythme et leur à-propos dans le timbre, ravissent les musiciens. Il y a dans les divers *Mickey* que nous avons pu voir des pages désormais célèbres et qui méritent de l'être. Je vous parlais du *Jazz*, tout à l'heure. Mais parlez donc aux initiés de la scène du cheval et de la guêpe . . . Il n'y a qu'un mot, pour parler de ces réussites. Ce mot est: « Chef-d'œuvre ».

Un langage international: le dessin animé (*excerpt*)

Maurice Bessy

Pour Vous, March 27, 1930

Il semble que l'on ait déjà tout dit sur ces merveilleux « talkartoons » qui ont sans doute converti plus de personnes au film sonore que n'importe quel *Trois Masques* ou *Broadway Melody*.

Qui donc ignore maintenant la grande vedette des dessins animés sonores, la malicieuse souris Mickey, fille du dessinateur Ub Iwerks. Mickey impératrice de l'encrier et reine du micro !

Il est donc équitable de donner aussi quelques renseignements sur son père, un des plus anciens « cartoonistes » américains et qu'on oublie un peu trop souvent dans les justes louanges que l'on fait de ses œuvres.

Le succès de Ub Iwerks n'a pas été des plus rapides, puisque ce merveilleux artiste travaille depuis quatorze ans dans les « cartoons » : il demeure au contraire le résultat d'un effort long et concentré.

Il fut tout d'abord durant deux ans assistant d'un dessinateur spécialisé dans le genre et, par la suite, « commercial artist » dans une firme de publicité. C'est pour la Commercial Film Company de Kansas City, dont il dirigeait la section artistique, qu'il exécuta ses premiers sujets animés.

Il fut par là même en rapport avec le dessinateur Disney qui devint bientôt son associé ; tous deux se mirent à produire avec régularité de courtes bandes animées.

Les deux amis maintinrent leur association qui dura jusqu'en février 1930.

Ub Iwerks, auteur de *Mickey*, de *La danse macabre*, préféra en effet se séparer de Walt Disney, père de *Oswald*, « Lucky Rabbit », amusant mais non comparable à Mickey, pour devenir producteur independent et lancer sa nouvelle création : *Flip la Grenouille*, que New-York commence depuis quelques temps seulement à apprécier.

Iwerks estime que la grenouille est l'animal qui, dans la nature, se rapproche le plus de l'être humain, parce qu'elle est le symbole de la paresse et de la vivacité humaines.

Le travail d'Iwerks présente un intérêt rare et étonnant.

Précisons du reste que cette nouvelle série de dessins comportera des versions en couleurs et qu'Iwerks s'est préparé à réaliser un film par mois.

Puisque le public français ne les connaît point, présentons, outre la silhouette bien connue de Mickey et celle, qui le sera bientôt autant, de *Flip la Grenouille*, quelques autres personnages de Ub Iwerks, sa fourmi et son héron, son caméléon et son corbeau, son lapin, sa tortue, son chat et son araignée.

Zu Micki Maus

Walter Benjamin

Private notebook fragment from 1931, unpublished in the author's lifetime; Akademie der Künst, Berlin, Germany, Walter Benjamin Archiv, WBA Ms 778. This text first appeared in print in Benjamin (Rolf Tiedemann, Hermann Hauser Schweppe, eds.), *Gesammelte Schriften* (Frankfurt am Main, 1972-1989), vol. VI (1985), 144–145. In that edition, as noted by Tiedemann (VI, 718), slight editorial alterations were made to the original in terms of capitalization, indentation, punctuation. "Micki Maus," for instance, was changed to "Micky-Maus." The present edition fully adheres to the original manuscript.

Aus einem Gesprach mit Glück und Weill.—Eigentumsverhältnisse im Micki Maus Film: hier erscheint zum ersten Mal, daß einem der eigne Arm, ja der eigne Körper gestohlen werden kann.

Der Weg eines Akts im Amt hat mehr Ähnlichkeit mit einem von jenen, die Micki Maus zurücklegt[,] als mit dem des Marathonläufers.

In diesen Filmen bereitet sich die Menschheit darauf vor, die Zivilisation zu überleben.

Die Micki Maus stellt dar, daß die Kreatur noch bestehen bleibt, auch wenn sie alles Menschenähnliche von sich abgelegt hat. Sie durchbricht die auf den Menschen hin konzipierte Hierarchie der Kreaturen.

Diese Filme desavouieren, radikaler als je der Fall war, alle Erfahrung. Es lohnt sich in einer solchen Welt nicht, Erfahrungen zu machen.

Ähnlichkeit mit dem Märchen. Niemals seitdem sind die wichtigsten und vitalsten Ereignisse unsymbolischer, atmosphärenloser gelebt worden. Der unermeßliche Gegensatz zu Maeterlinck und zu Mary Wigman. Alle Micki Maus Filme haben zum Motiv den Auszug, das Furchten zu lernen.

Also nicht „Mechanisierung", nicht das „Formale", nicht ein „Mißverständnis" hier für den ungeheuren Erfolg dieser Filme die Basis, sondern daß das Publikum sein eignes Leben in ihnen wiedererkennt.

Sie sehen Micky Mäuse tanzen . . .

Film-Kurier, July 28, 1931

Das pommersche Gauorgan der N.S.A.P. „Die Diktatur" veroffentlicht folgenden Aufruf:

„Der Micky Maus Skandal!!!"

„Blonde, freisinnige, deutsche Stadtjugend am Gängelbande des Finanzjuden. Jugend, wo ist dein Stolz? Jugend, wo ist dein Selbstbewußtsein? Die Micky Maus ist das schäbigste, elendste Ideal, das je erfunden wurde. Die Micky-Maus ist eine Verblödungskur des Young-Kapitals. Das gesunde Gefühl sagt eigentlich jedem anständigen Mädchen und jedem ehrlichen Jungen von selbst, daß das schmutzige und mit Dreck behaftete Ungeziefer, der große Bakterienüberträger im Tierreich, nicht zum idealen Tiertypus gemacht werden kann. Haben wir nicht etwas besseres zu tun, als mit schmutzigem Viehzeug unser Kleid zu schmücken, weil amerikanische Geschäftsjuden verdienen wollen? Hinweg mit der jüdischen Volksverdummung! Hinaus mit dem Ungeziefer! Herunter mit der Micky Maus, steckt Hakenkreuze auf!"

*

Her mit Micky Maus! Nehmen wir sie als das frohliche Symbol aller Vernünftigen, die sich gegen Ungeist, Verleugnung und Mord wenden.

Steckt sie an die kleine Micky-Maus als ein Wahrzeichen gegen Hakenkreuz und Verhetzung.

• The text cited herein from *Die Diktatur* ("Der Micky Maus Skandal!!!") and the concluding two-sentence commentary on it by the Berlin *Tageszeitung* (daily newspaper) *Film-Kurier*, were reprinted by Carsten Laqua in his book *Micky unter die Nazis Fiel: Walt Disney und Deutschland* (Rowohlt Verlag, 1992), 35, 243 (note).

Mickey Mouse

Diego Rivera

Unpublished holograph manuscript in Spanish, brown ink on Barbizon-Plaza stationery, probably composed between November 1931 and January 1932; box 114, folder 3, Bertram Wolfe Collection, Hoover Institution Archives, Stanford, Calif. D.R. © 2013 Banco de México, "Fiduciario" en el Fideicomiso relative a los Museos Diego Rivera y Frida Kahlo. Av. 5 de Mayo No. 2, Col. Centro, Del. Cuauhtémoc 06059, México, D.F.

La otra noche, despues de una conferencia y prolongando el tema de ella, la posición del arte y los artistas en la colectiva actual y llegamos rodando alrrededor de ese tema hasta las cosas que no son tomadas en serio como arte solo ni siquiera por los que las hacen.

Recordaba yo mil objetos hechos en mexico. destinados *a ser destruidos*, esculturas en azucar hechas para ser comidas, esculturas en carton y papel precisamente creadas par ser hechas pedazos o quemadas.

Y esas cosas son las que tienen mayor valor plástico en el arte de Mexico.

Si un dia un artista famoso hubiera "no, buscado, sino encontrado" la manera de lograr crear la belleza de uno solo de esos objetos, el "mundo del arte" se hubiera pasmado y los museos de todo el universo hubieran ofrecido cuanto pudieran por adquirir el objeto maravilloso.

Pero todos esos juguetes para niños y adultos viven y pasan sin inquietar al reino de los estetas.

Puede ser que un dia un esteta "descubra" o "encuentre" la belleza de esas cosas y todas las gentes de buen gusto se pasmen con ellas.

Probablemente entonces cesaran de ser producidas esas cosas, o se volveran tan aburridas como el arte de los artistas.

No se alarmen ustedes. No estoy creyendo encontrar la teoria de la creación inconsciente, otros la buscaron y la encontraron hace ya mucho tiempo.

No hago mas que referirme a hechos como el hablábamos esa noche !

Que si se miran las caracteristicas de los dibujos animados que se proyectan en el cine nos vemos forza dos a encontrar las caracteristicas] del estilo mas puro y mas definido como gráfica, de la mayor eficacia como resultado social, dibujos alegres y sencillos que hacen des cansar a las masas de hombres y mujeres fatigados y hacen reír a los niños hasta cansarse y dormirse y no chillando, ya permitir el reposo de los mayores.

Revisamos el estilo la estandardización del dibujo de los detalles y la infinita variedad de los con juntos, como en los egipcios de los pisos pintados y los griegos de los vasos de tierra cocida, con mas, la cualidad de moverse y su manifestación en el cine que según el Señor Eisenstein es el arte de hoy en día.

Felizmente para los medicos oculistas, digo yo y para los enfermos de insomnio si tienen la suerte de encontrar un reproductor de sonidos no muy ruidoso y una butaca cómoda.

Admitimos que esos dibujos animados expresaban los ritmos mas lógicos pero mas inesperados por las necesidades de su técnica que eran expresiones directísimas encontrando la mayor eficacia con la mayor ceremonia.

En fin concluimos que tal vez, si los filmes puedese conservarse, las gentes que al fin poseeran un teatro se negarán a oir que los cinedramas, mas admirados hoy, las masas que ya habran realizado la verdadera revolucion no se interesarán gran cosa por las películas "revolucionarias" de hoy que todo esto y los cuadros y estatuas y poesias y prosa que hayan sobrevivido a la limpieza general del mundo no sean miradas sino compasiva curiosidad pero que probablemente los dibujos inanimados diviertan entonces como ahora a los hombres y hagan morirse de risa a los chiquillos y los artistas de entonces encuentren que Miki Maus fue uno de los verdaderos heroes del arte americano hacia la primera mitad del siglo veinte, del calendario anterior a la revolucion mundial.

• This is the original text in Rivera's native language, penned—with dozens of strikethroughs and amendations—on sixteen sheets of hotel stationery. It was translated into English by Diego's friend, Bert Wolfe (1896–1977), for the quarterly, *Contact.* The title given here, "Mickey Mouse," is inscribed at the top of the first page of the manuscript, no doubt by Wolfe, whose five-page, hand-written English translation of Rivera's text is in Box 117, Folder 15 of the Bertram Wolfe Collection, also at the Hoover Institution Archives. Rivera abbreviated "Ustedes" as "uds" in the Hoover manuscript.

Mickey Mouse au Gaumont-Palace

Jean Laury

© Jean Laury/*Le Figaro*, June 28, 1935 avec l'aimable autorisation du Figaro.

Plus de cinq mille enfants ont acclamé hier matin, au Gaumont-Palace, « Mickey Mouse [»] et son père Walt Disney. De ce gala, organisé par le « Figaro » et qui fut un succès complet, nous rendons compte, en détails, dans notre rubrique cinématographique.

Les prouesses de la souris fameuse et des rusés porcelets, les aventures d'un couple de pingouins et celles de la fée Printemps ont fait battre les petites mains, les jeunes cœurs d'un public tout neuf et point ménager de son enthousiasme : Walt Disney, très ému, pouvait mesurer la portée de son œuvre et la popularité des personnages qu'il créa.

Après que se fussent déroulées à l'écran les « Silly Symphonies », les artistes du Petit-Monde exécutèrent le ballet de Mickey. Sur la scène, les bras chargés de fleurs nouées aux couleurs américaines, Walt Disney écouta le charmant poème composé à son intention par Mme Pierre Humble. Enfin, Mlle Hélène Vacaresco, en remettant la médaille d'or de la C. I. D. A. L. C. à M. Walt Disney, le présenta avec la plus aimable éloquence aux enfants de Paris. « Vous eussiez été ravis, leur dit-elle, de connaître La Fontaine ou Perrault . . . » Et Mlle Hélène Vacaresco, en les termes choisis et vibrants qui lui sont propres, traça un parallèle entre le fabuliste, le conteur et l'auteur des dessins animés à la fois joyeux et poétiques dont la gloire est « une gloire heureuse » . . .

Cependant, au milieu des étoiles du ballet enfantin, Walt Disney s'était accroupi, comme pour se mettre, une fois de plus, à la portée des petits qui lui ont dû, hier soir encore, tant de rêves charmants . . .

BIBLIOGRAPHY

Principal Books on Walt Disney and Mickey Mouse

Apgar, Garry. *Mickey Mouse: Emblem of the American Spirit.* San Francisco: Walt Disney Family Foundation Press, forthcoming.

Bain, David, and Bruce Harris. *Mickey Mouse: Fifty Happy Years.* New York: Harmony Books, 1977.

Barrier, Michael. *Animated Man: A Life of Walt Disney.* Los Angeles and London: University of California Press, 2008.

Feild, Robert D. *The Art of Walt Disney.* New York: MacMillan, 1942.

Finch, Christopher. *The Art of Walt Disney: From Mickey Mouse to the Magic Kingdoms.* New York: Abrams, 1973; 2nd rev. ed., 2004.

Gabler, Neal. *Walt Disney: The Triumph of the American Imagination.* New York: Vintage, 2007.

Ghez, Didier. *Walt's People: Talking Disney with the Artists who Knew Him.* 14 vols. (ongoing). Philadelphia and Orlando: Xlibris and Theme Park Press, 2005–2013.

Girveau, Bruno, et al. *Once Upon a Time Walt Disney: The Sources of Inspiration for the Disney Studios.* Exhibition catalogue: Musée des Beaux-Arts, Montreal, 2007. Munich, Berlin, London, and New York: Prestel, 2007.

Gottfredson, Floyd. *Walt Disney's Mickey Mouse.* In "The Floyd Gottfredson Library," edited by David Gerstein and Gary Groth. Seattle: Fantagraphics Books, 2011–2012. [**ed.:** six volumes published to date in a series devoted to Gottfredson's daily Mickey Mouse newspaper comic strips; expected to total 13 vol.]

——. *Walt Disney's Mickey Mouse: Color Sundays.* In "The Floyd Gottfredson Library," edited by David Gerstein and Gary Groth. Seattle: Fantagraphics Books, 2013. [**ed.:** two volumes, published separately, devoted to Gottfredson's Sunday Mickey Mouse comic strips.]

Hamilton, Bruce, ed. *Mickey Mouse In Color.* New York: Pantheon, 1988.

Heide, Robert, John Gilman, Monique Peterson, and Patrick White. *Mickey Mouse: The Evolution, the Legend, the Phenomenon!* New York: Disney Editions, 2001.

Hiller, Bevis, and Bernard C. Shine. *Mickey Mouse Memorabilia: The Vintage Years, 1928–1938.* New York: Abrams, 1986.

Holliss, Richard, and Brian Sibley. *Walt Disney's Mickey Mouse: His Life and Times.* New York: Harper & Row, 1986.

Jackson, Kathy Merlock. *Walt Disney: A Bio-Bibliography.* Westport, Conn.: Greenwood Press, 1993.

Korkis, Jim. *The Book of Mouse: A Celebration of Walt Disney's Mickey Mouse.* Orlando: Theme Park Press, 2013.

——, with foreword by Diane Disney Miller. *The Revised Vault of Walt: Includes Five New Unofficial, Unauthorized, Uncensored Disney Stories Never Told.* Orlando: Theme Park Press, 2012.

——, with foreword by Diane Disney Miller. *The Vault of Walt: Unofficial, Unauthorized, Uncensored Disney Stories Never Told.* Lexington, Ky.: Ayefour Publishing, 2010.

Lambert, Pierre. *Mickey Mouse.* New York: Disney Editions, 1998.

Merritt, Russell, and J. B. Kaufman. *Walt in Wonderland: The Silent Films of Walt Disney.* Baltimore: Johns Hopkins University Press, 1994.

Miller, Diane Disney, and Pete Martin. *The Story of Walt Disney.* New York: Henry Holt, 1957; repr. New York: Disney Editions, 2005.

Munsey, Cecil. *Disneyana: Walt Disney Collectibles.* New York: Hawthorn Books, 1974.

Schickel, Richard. *The Disney Version: The Life, Times, Art and Commerce of Walt Disney.* New York: Simon & Schuster, 1968 and 1985, 2nd ed.; Chicago: Ivan R. Dee, 1995, 3rd ed.

Schroeder, Russell. *Walt Disney's Mickey Mouse: My Life in Pictures.* New York: Disney Press, 1997.

Smith, Dave. *Disney A to Z: The Official Encyclopedia.* New York: Disney Editions, 1996; 3rd rev. ed., 2006.

Smoodin, Eric, ed. *Disney Discourse: Producing the Magic Kingdom.* London: Routledge, 1994.

Susanin, Timothy. *Walt Before Mickey: Disney's Early Years, 1919–1928.* Jackson: University Press of Mississippi, 2011.

Thomas, Bob. *Walt Disney: An American Original.* New York: Simon & Schuster, 1976; New York: Disney Editions, 1994.

Tieman, Robert. *The Mickey Mouse Treasures.* New York: Disney Editions, 2007.

Watts, Steven. *The Magic Kingdom: Walt Disney and the American Way of Life.* Boston and New York: Houghton Mifflin, 1997.

Yoe, Craig, and Janet Morra-Yoe. *The Art of Mickey Mouse.* New York: Hyperion, 1991.

List of articles and books referenced or reprinted in their entirety in this anthology

"Add Vamp and Mouse." *Springfield* (Mass.) *Evening Union,* Dec. 5, 1935, 22.

Ahrens, Frank. "Disney Presents Mickey Mouse, Again: Media Giant Pushes to Make Cartoon Rodent Hip." *Washington Post,* July 26, 2003, E1.

Alfano, Sean. "Mickey Mouse Appears On Poster Atop a Nude Woman's Body Beneath A Swastika." *New York Daily News,* July 14, 2010 ("With News Wire Services"), online only.

Apgar, Garry. "Le Grand Charlie et le Petit Mickey." *Paris Metro,* Nov. 22, 1978, 6–7.

——. "The Meaning of Mickey Mouse." *Visual Resources: An International Journal of Documentation* 14, no. 3 (Jan. 1999): 263–273.

"Art & Hollywood: Sergei Eisenstein Gives it Up." *Manchester Guardian,* Nov. 5, 1930, 9 ("From our own Correspondent").

Associated Press. "Cartoons Invade Chicago Institute of Art for Exhibit." *Washington Post,* Dec. 14, 1934, 11.

——. "French Honor Disney's Work." *New York Times,* Jan. 9, 1936, 25.

Auden, W. H. "In Praise of the Brothers Grimm." *New York Times Book Review,* Nov. 12, 1944, 1, 28.

Benjamin, Walter. "On Mickey Mouse." In *Walter Benjamin: Selected Writing, Volume 2, 1927–1934,* edited by Michael W. Jennings, Howard Eiland, and Gary Smith, 545. Cambridge, Mass.: The Belknap Press of Harvard University Press, 1999.

——. "Zu Micky-Maus." In *Gesammelte Schriften,* edited by Rolf Tiedemann and Herman Hauser Schweppe, vol. VI, 144–145. Frankfurt am Main: Suhrkamp Verlag, 1985.

Bessy, Maurice. "An International Language: the Animated Cartoon." *Pour Vous,* Mar. 27, 1930, 11.

——. *Walt Disney.* Paris: Seghers, 1970.

"British Art Guild Honors Mickey Mouse Creator." *New York Times,* Apr. 20, 1934, 1.

Brockway, Robert W. "The Masks of Mickey Mouse." *Journal of Popular Culture* 22, no. 4 (spring 1989): 25–34; and, in a revised, extended version in Brockway, *Myth From the Ice Age to Mickey Mouse*, 119–145, 180–181. Albany: State University of New York Press, 1993.

Canemaker, John. "An American Icon Scampers In For a Makeover." *New York Times*, Aug. 6, 1995, H9, H20.

Carr, Harry. "The Lancer." *Los Angeles Times*, Dec. 29, 1930, section II, 1 (subhead, "Turned Down").

———. "The Lancer." *Los Angeles Times*, Jan. 2, 1934, section II, 1 (subhead, "Wisecracking").

———. "The Lancer." *Los Angeles Times*, Jan. 28, 1935, section II, 1 (lead item).

———. "The Only Unpaid Movie Star." *American Magazine*, Mar. 1931, 55–57, 122, 125.

Churchill, Douglas W. "Now Mickey Mouse Enters Art's Temple." *New York Times Magazine*, June 3, 1934, 12–13, 21.

Coleman, Barbara. "Through the Years We'll All Be Friends: The 'Mickey Mouse Club,' Consumerism, and the Cultural Consensus." *Visual Resources: An International Journal of Documentation* 14, no. 3 (Jan. 1999): 297–306.

Cons, Carl. "The Slanguage of Swing Terms the 'Cats' Use." *Down Beat*, Nov. 1935, 1.

Crane, Maurice A. "Vox Bop." *American Speech* 33, no. 3 (Oct. 1958): 225–226.

Crowther, Bosley. "Fantasia." *New York Times*, Nov. 14, 1940, 28.

Culhane, John. "A Mouse for All Seasons." *Saturday Review*, Nov. 11, 1978, 50–51.

"Danes Ban 'Mickey Mouse': Censor Calls the Film Creation of Disney Too Macabre." *New York Times*, Feb. 24, 1931, 11 ("Wireless to the New York Times").

Daria, Irene. "Mickey Mouse Comes of Age on SA." *Women's Wear Daily*, Sept. 25, 1984, 10.

deCordova, Richard. "The Mickey in Macy's Window: Childhood, Consumerism, and Disney Animation." In *Disney Discourse*, edited by Smoodin, 203–213, 249–251. New York and London: Routledge, 1994.

Disney, Lillian, and Isabella Taves. "I Live with a Genius—a Conversation with Mrs. Walt Disney." *McCall's*, Feb. 1953, 38–40, 103–104, 106–107.

Disney, Roy O. "Unforgettable Walt Disney." *Reader's Digest*, Feb. 1969, 212–218.

Disney, Walt. "The Life Story of Mickey Mouse." *Windsor Magazine*, Jan. 1934, 259–263.

——. "'Mickey Mouse': How He Was Born." *Windsor Magazine*, Oct. 1931, 641–645.

——. "The Story of Mickey Mouse." Recorded on Oct. 13, 1947 (11:15 min.), and, according to Steven Watts (*Magic Kingdom*, 265), broadcast in 1948 on the weekly NBC radio program, *The University of the Air*; on track 2 of a CD included in Tieman, *Disney Treasures*, and published in Jackson, *Walt Disney: A Bio-Bibliography*, 118–121.

——. "What Mickey Means To Me." *Who's Who in Hollywood* 1, no. 3 (Apr.–June 1948): 50–51.

El Deeb, Sarah. "Egyptian Christian faces Trial for Insulting Islam." *Seattle Post-Intelligencer*, Jan. 9, 2012 (online only here, but published in print in a number of other newspapers).

Eliot, Alexander (unsigned). "U.S. Scene." *Time*, Dec. 24, 1934, 24–27.

"Europe's Highbrows Hail 'Mickey Mouse.'" *Literary Digest*, Aug. 8, 1931, 19.

"The Evolution of Mickey Mouse." *Motion Picture Daily*, June 20, 1931, 7.

"First Four Cinephone Cartoons Under Way." *Film Daily*, Nov. 13, 1928, 1, 4.

Fishwick, Marshall. "Mickey, A Mouse of Influence Around The World." *Orlando Sentinel*, June 14, 1992, D3.

Forster, E. M. "Mickey and Minnie." *Spectator*, Jan. 19, 1934, 81–82.

"Fox, Disney Add to Museum Film Group." *Motion Picture Daily*, Nov. 30, 1935, 2.

Gabler, Neal. *Life the Movie: How Entertainment Conquered Reality*. New York: Vintage, 2000.

"Gain in Television Is Demonstrated: Philo T. Farnsworth Shows Clear Images Picked Up by His System." *New York Times*, July 31, 1935, 15.

"The Genius of Walt Disney: 'World of Fun and Happiness.'" *London Times*, Dec. 4, 1935, 11.

Gold, Robert S. "The Vernacular of the Jazz World." *American Speech* 32, no. 4 (Dec. 1957): 271–282.

Gould, Stephen Jay. "Mickey Mouse Meets Konrad Lorenz." *Natural History*, May 1979, 30, 32, 34, 36; repr. as "A Biological Homage to Mickey Mouse," in Gould, *The Panda's Thumb* (New York: W. W. Norton, 1980), 95–107.

Grafly, Dorothy (unsigned). "An Artist of Our Time: Walter E. Disney, 1901–." *Philadelphia Public Ledger*, Oct. 23, 1932, 12.

——. "Animated Cartoon Gives the World An American Art: Slips Into Being

Without Benefit of the Orthodox." *Philadelphia Public Ledger,* Oct. 23, 1932, 12.

——. (unsigned). "Disney Has Debut in Art Circles: His Cartoons Given First Recognition by Art Body." *Philadelphia Public Ledger,* Oct. 23, 1932, 12.

Green, Jesse. "Can Disney Build a Better Mickey Mouse?" *New York Times,* Apr. 18, 2004, section 2 ("Arts & Leisure"), AR1, AR18–19.

Greene, Graham. "Joan of Arc, Turn of the Tide, Top Hat, She." In *The Graham Greene Film Reader: Reviews, Essays, Interviews & Film Stories,* edited by David Parkinson, 40. New York: Applause Books, 1995; first published in *Spectator,* Oct. 25, 1935.

Hall, Mordaunt. "The Screen." *New York Times,* Nov. 19, 1928, 16.

Hamilton, Sara. "The True Story of Mickey Mouse." *Movie Mirror,* Dec. 1931, 100–101, 122.

Hill, Edwin C. "Mickey Mouse Goes to Hollywood—How Young Artist Tamed His Models." *Boston Evening American,* Aug. 8, 1933, 26 ("Human Side of the News").

Hughes, Robert. "Disney: Mousebrow to Highbrow." *Time,* Oct. 15, 1973, 88–91.

Hutchinson, Bill. "Mock of Mickey Is Pure Evil: Disney's Daughter Rips Hamas Over Monster Mouse." *New York Daily News,* May 9, 2007, 3.

Inge, M. Thomas. "Mickey Mouse." In *American Icons: An Encyclopedia of the People, Places and Things That Have Shaped Our Culture,* edited by Dennis R. Hall and Susan Grove Hall, vol. 2, 473–480. Westport, Conn.: Greenwood Press, 2006.

Jamison, Barbara Berch. "Amazing Scripts by Animals: It's the Owl, Wise or Not, and a Host of Other Fauna Which Call the Shots in Disney Nature Film." *New York Times Magazine,* July 18, 1954, 16–17, 46–47.

——. "Of Mouse and Man, or Mickey Reaches 25: Time Has Slowed his Step, But Walt Disney's Remarkable Rodent Has Come Smiling through Depression, Wars, A-bombs and H-Bombs." *New York Times Magazine,* Sept. 13, 1953, 26–27.

Jamison, Jack. "He Gave Us Mickey Mouse." *Liberty,* Jan. 14, 1933, 52–54.

Johnston, Alva. "Mickey Mouse." *Woman's Home Companion,* July 1934, 12–13, 92–94.

Korkis, Jim. "Secrets Of Steamboat Willie." *Hogan's Alley: The Magazine of the Cartoon Arts,* Sept. 2004, 57–63.

La Farge, Christopher. "Walt Disney and the Art Form." *Theatre Arts,* Sept. 1941, 673–680.

Lambert, Eleanor. *Notes on The Art of Mickey Mouse and His Creator Walt Disney.* College Art Association, spring 1933.

Land [Robert J. Landry]. "'STEAMBOAT WILLIE' / Animated Cartoon / Powers Cinephone: 7 Mins. / Colony, New York." *Variety,* Nov. 21, 1928, 13.

Lanes, Selma G. "Sendak at 50." *New York Times,* Apr. 29, 1979, BR23, BR48 (Sunday Book Review).

Laqua, Carsten. *Micky unter die Nazis Fiel: Walt Disney und Deutschland.* Reinbeck bei Hamburg: Rowohlt Verlag, 1992.

Laury, Jean [Nicole Boré-Verrier]. "Mickey Mouse at the Gaumont-Palace ("Mickey Mouse au Gaumont-Palace")." *Le Figaro,* June 28, 1935, 1.

"League of Nations Medal For Mr. Disney." *Times* (London), June 18, 1935, 18.

Lejeune, C. A. [Caroline Alice]. "Mickey Mouse." *Observer* (London), Dec. 8, 1929, 20 (in her recurring unsigned column, "The Pictures").

Leslie, Esther. *Hollywood Flatlands: Animation, Critical Theory and the Avant-Garde.* London and New York: Verso, 2002.

Lewine, Edward. "Who Is He?" *New York Times,* Aug. 10, 1997, Section 13 ("The City"), 1.

Low, David. "Leonardo da Disney." *New Republic,* Jan. 5, 1942, 16–18.

Luce, Henry. "The American Century" (editorial). *Life,* Feb. 17, 1941, 61–65.

Maltin, Leonard. untitled introduction. *Film Fan Monthly,* Sept. 1968, 2.

——. "More on The Disney Version." *Film Fan Monthly,* Sept. 1968, 5–6.

Mann, Arthur. "Mickey Mouse's Financial Career." *Harper's,* May 1934, 714–721.

Mano, D. Keith. "A Real Mickey Mouse Operation." *Playboy,* Dec. 1973, 199, 322, 324, 326, 328–330, 332, 334, 336, 338.

Michener, James A. "The Revolution in Middle-Class Values." *New York Times Magazine,* Aug. 18, 1968, 20–21, 85, 87–88, 90, 92–93, 99.

"'Mickey Mouse' at Roxy." *Film Daily,* May 4, 1931, 2.

"Mickey Mouse Celebrates His Tenth Birthday . . . By Capturing a Giant." *Look,* Sept. 27, 1938, 58–59.

"Mickey Mouse Exhibit Will Be Shown Here." *Evansville Press,* Dec. 8, 1933, 9.

"'Mickey Mouse' in Trouble: German Censorship." *Times* (London), July 14, 1930, 12.

"Mickey Mouse Invades Gallery." *Art Digest,* May 1, 1933, 12.

"'Mickey Mouse' is 8 Years Old." *Literary Digest,* Oct. 3, 1936, 18-19.

"Mickey Mouse Makes the Britannica." *New York Times,* July 29, 1934, X2 ("Drama-Screen-Music-Fashions-Art").

"Mickey Mouse Portrays Capitalist, Reds Assert." *New York Times*, Dec. 11, 1935, 29 ("Special Cable to the New York Times").

"Mickey Mouse Saves Jersey Toy Concern; Carries It Back to Solvency on His Railway." *New York Times*, Jan. 22, 1935, 21 ("Special to the New York Times").

"The Mickey Mouse Scandal!!!" from *Die Diktatur*, probably mid to late July 1931; reprinted in the daily publication *Film-Kurier* (Berlin), July 28, 1931.

"'Mickey Mouse' Was Invasion Password." *Johannesburg Sunday Times*, June 11, 1944, 1.

Miller, Diane Disney, and Pete Martin. "My Dad, Walt Disney." *Saturday Evening Post*, Nov. 17, 1956, 25+; Nov. 24, 1956, 26+; Dec. 1, 1956, 28+; Dec. 8, 1956, 38+; Dec. 15, 1956, 36+; Dec. 22, 1956, 24+; Dec. 29, 1956, 24+; Jan. 5, 1957, 24+.

Monahan, Kaspar. "Mickey Mouse, His Vanity Wounded, Declares War On This Column and Writes Reproving Letter." *Pittsburgh Post*, July 18, 1932, 11 ("The Show Stops" column).

North American Newspaper Alliance. "New British Army Slang Less Colorful Than Old." *New York Times*, Apr. 6, 1941, 30.

Nugent, Frank S. "Disney Is Now Art—But He Wonders." *New York Times Magazine*, Feb. 26, 1939, 4–5.

———. "That Million-Dollar Mouse: Twenty Years Ago Mickey Was Born to Win Fame and Fortune and We Still Applaud This Act of Creation." *New York Times Magazine*, Sept. 21, 1947, 22, 60–62.

Paul, William. "Disney (1): Pantheon Pantheist." *Village Voice*, Aug. 2, 1973, 71, 74.

Peet, Creighton. "The Cartoon Comedy." *New Republic*, August 14, 1929, 341–342.

———. "Miraculous Mickey." *Outlook and Independent*, July 23, 1930, 472.

"Profound Mouse." *Time*, May 15, 1933, 37–38.

Quindlen, Anna. "Modern Museum Celebrates Mickey." *New York Times*, Nov. 17, 1978, C1 (Weekend section).

Ramsaye, Terry. "Mickey Mouse: He Stays on the Job." *Motion Picture Herald*, Oct. 1, 1932, 41.

"Regulated Rodent." *Time*, Feb. 16, 1931, 21.

Rivera, Diego. "Mickey Mouse and American Art." *Contact: An American Quarterly Review* 1, no. 1 (Feb. 1932): 37–39.

Robbins, L. H. "Mickey Mouse Emerges as Economist." *New York Times Magazine*, Mar. 10, 1935, 8, 22.

Russell, Herbert. "L'Affaire Mickey Mouse: An Inquiry Into a Plot of World-Wide Scope: Mickey and Company As Arch Conspirators." *New York Times Magazine*, Dec. 26, 1937, 4, 17.

"Santa Is Coming Early for Parade." *New York Times*, Nov. 28, 1934, 18.

Schickel, Richard. "Bringing Forth the Mouse." *American Heritage*, Apr. 1968, 24–29, 90–96.

———. Letter to the editor. *Playboy*, Mar. 1974, 12.

Scize, Pierre [Michel-Joseph Piot]. "Le Cinéma." *Jazz: l'actualité intellectuelle*, Nov. 15, 1929, 547–548; partially reprinted (the section concerning Mickey Mouse) as "Éloge de Mickey" in Maurice Bessy's biography of Walt Disney, 73–75.

Seldes, Gilbert. "Mickey-Mouse Maker." *New Yorker*, Dec. 19, 1931, 23–27.

———. "No Art, Mr. Disney?" *Esquire*, Sept. 1937, 91, 171–172.

Sendak, Maurice. "Growing Up With Mickey." *TV Guide*, Nov. 11, 1978, 16–18; repr. in slightly revised form as "Walt Disney / 1," in Sendak, *Caldecott & Co.: Notes on Books & Pictures* (Farrar, Straus, and Giroux, 1988), 107–110.

"Short Subjects." *Film Daily*, Aug. 7, 1927, 20.

Solomon, Charles. "'New' Mickey: Big Cheese of 'MouseWorks' Television: Animators Look to the Past to Liven Up the Personality of Disney's Star Rodent for a Cartoon Series Starting Saturday." *Los Angeles Times*, Apr. 30, 1999, Part F ("Calendar" section), 2.

———. "We Are Mickey." In "America Celebrates Mickey's 60th Birthday." Special advertising section in *People Weekly*, Nov. 7, 1988, n.p. (pp. 2–3 of a 32-page insert).

"'Steamboat Billie' / Walt Disney Cartoon / Real Entertainment." *Film Daily*, Nov. 25, 1928, 9 (subhead in the recurring unsigned column, "Short Subjects").

"A Tale of Six." *Harvard Crimson*, Feb. 17, 1939, 2 (editorial).

"That Rodent Now Rates a Top Ranking." *Washington Post*, May 17, 1931, 3.

Theisen, Earl. "The History of the Animated Cartoon." *Journal of the Society of Motion Picture Engineers*, Sept. 1933, 239–249.

———. "The History of Cartoons." *International Photographer*, Mar. 1933, 2–4.

Thomas, Bob. *Building a Company: Roy O. Disney and the Creation of an Entertainment Empire*. New York: Hyperion, 1998.

Thomas, Dan. "How They Make Animated Cartoons." *Ohio State Journal*, Mar. 8, 1931, in the Sunday magazine section *EveryWeek*, 4 (*EveryWeek* was a Sunday insert syndicated to many newspapers nationwide).

Thurber, James. In *The Thurber Letters: The Wit, Wisdom, and Surprising Life of James Thurber*, edited by Harrison Kinney. New York: Simon & Schuster, 2002.

United Press, "Mickey Mouse, Big Bad Wolf Reach Walls of Museum," *Cleveland Press*, Dec. 14, 1933, 14.

Updike, John. "The Mystery of Mickey Mouse." *Art & Antiques*, Nov. 1991, 60–65, 98; an expanded version of this article served as the introduction to Yoe, Morra-Yoe, *Art of Mickey Mouse* (1992), reprinted, with four black-and-white illustrations, in Updike, *More Matter: Essays and Criticism* (New York: Random House, 1999), 202–210. The *Art & Antiques* article was reprinted, text only: in Sontag, Atwan, eds., *The Best of American Essays* (New York: Houghton Mifflin, 1992), 306–313, and McQuade, Atwan, eds., *Popular Writing in America: The Interaction of Style and Audience*, 5th ed. (Oxford: Oxford University Press, 1993), 347–351.

Van Gelder, Lawrence. "Mickey Mouse's Age." *New York Times*, Nov. 18, 1988, C8.

Verrier, Richard. "M-I-C-K-E-Y: He's the Leader of the Brand." *Los Angeles Times*, July 23, 2003, A1.

Wallace, Irving. "Mickey Mouse and How He Grew." *Collier's*, Apr. 9, 1949, 20–21, 35–36.

"Walt Disney, M.S., M.A." *Art Digest*, July 1, 1938, 17.

Wolters, Larry. "Fabulous Story." Feb. 9, 1953, *Chicago Daily Tribune*, section 3, B9 (subhead in Wolters's column "Television News and Views").

Wood, Cholly. "Mickey Mouse Is 7 Years Old Today." *Bridgeport Sunday Herald*, Sept. 25, 1935, feature section, 3.

Zumwalt, Elmo R., Jr. ". . . on the Navy." *New York Times*, Dec. 3, 1977, 23.

Frank Ahrens
Charleston, West Virginia, Nov. 24, 1963–

Frank Ahrens worked for eighteen years at the *Washington Post*, primarily as a business reporter covering the media and entertainment industry. In September 2010 he quit the *Post* to accompany his wife, who was assigned by the U.S. government to South Korea, where he accepted a position as Director of Worldwide Corporate Affairs for the Hyundai Motor Co.

Sean Alfano
New York, New York, Aug. 11, 1978–

A graduate of the Columbia School of Journalism, in 2003–2005 Sean Alfano worked as a sports reporter for the *Watertown* (N.Y.) *Daily Times*, and, later, assignment editor at CBSNews.com. In May 2010, he began reporting for the *New York Daily News*, where he is now a senior editor in charge of the homepage.

Garry Apgar
Baton Rouge, Louisiana, Oct. 6, 1945–

Garry Apgar, a former Marine and Vietnam veteran, was from 1972 to 1976 a staff artist and political cartoonist on the *Roanoke Times* in Virginia. He holds a *maîtrise ès lettres* from the Sorbonne and, from Yale University, a Ph.D. in art history, which he has taught at the University of Delaware, Brown, Princeton, and the Université de Lyon. His monograph, *L'art singulier de Jean Huber: Voir Voltaire* (Paris, Adam Biro), was published in 1995. He also wrote the principal essay, "Signs of the Times: Print News Imagery in the Visual Arts," for *The Newspaper in Art* (New Media Ventures, 1996). His book, *Mickey Mouse: Emblem of the American Spirit*, is scheduled to be published in 2015 by the Walt Disney Family Foundation Press.

Walter Benjamin
Berlin, Germany, July 15, 1892–Sept. 26, 1940, Portbou (Catalonia), Spain

Benjamin, a Marxist intellectual, literary and cultural theorist, essayist and critic, associated with the so-called Frankfurt School, is best known for *The Work of Art in the Age of Mechanical Reproduction* (first published in French in 1936). As a Jew, Benjamin tried to flee Nazi-occupied France in 1940, but committed suicide in Spain rather than face deportation back to France.

Maurice Bessy

Nice, France, Dec. 4, 1910–Nov. 15, 1993, Paris, France

Bessy's biography, *Walt Disney*, was published in Paris in 1970. In the early 1930s he was hired by the French movie magazine, *Cinémonde*, where he was editor-in-chief from 1934–1939. A photo of Disney from 1951, signed and dedicated to Bessy, was published in *Il était une fois Walt Disney: Aux sources de l'art des studios Disney*, the exhibition catalogue for the Disney retrospective at the Grand Palais in Paris, 2006–2007. In 1972 Bessy was named managing director of the Cannes Film Festival; he was a member of the jury in 1979. His memoirs, *Les Passagers du souvenir*, were published in 1977 (Albin Michel).

Robert W. Brockway

Washington, D.C., Sept. 10, 1923–Dec. 10, 2001, Brandon (Manitoba), Canada

Robert W. Brockway received an M.A. from Columbia University, an M.Div. from Union Theological Seminary, and a Ph.D. in religion from Columbia. He was active as a Unitarian minister in America and Canada until 1959. A professor of religion at Brandon University, Manitoba, Canada, 1965–1987, he was the author of *Young Carl Jung* (1996) and *A Wonderful Work of God* (2003). The piece in this volume was republished, with significant changes (deletions, additions, intrusion of new editorial errors) in Brockway's book, *Myth From the Ice Age to Mickey Mouse* (1993).

John Canemaker

Waverly, New York, May 28, 1943–

A leading historian and scholar on animation, and an independent animator as well, John Canemaker has been director of the animation program at New York University since 1988. His film, *The Moon and the Son: An Imagined Conversation*, won an Academy Award for Best Animated Short in 2005. Among a host of articles and books he has written are: *Treasures of Disney Animation Art* (1982), *Winsor McCay: His Life and Art* (1987; rev. ed., 2005), *Felix, The Twisted Tale of the World's Most Famous Cat* (Pantheon, 1991), *Before the Animation Begins: The Art and Lives of Disney Inspirational Sketch Artists* (1996),

Paper Dreams: The Art and Artists of Disney Storyboarding (1999), and *Walt Disney's Nine Old Men and the Art of Animation* (2001). The John Canemaker Animation Collection, at NYU's Elmer Holmes Bobst Library (Fales Library & Special Collections), is a multi-faceted archival resource established by Canemaker in 1988.

Harry Carr
Tipton, Iowa, Mar 27, 1877–Jan. 10, 1936, Los Angeles (Tujunga), California

Carr began his career in 1897 with the *Los Angeles Examiner*, but soon switched to the *Los Angeles Times*, where he made his name reporting on the San Francisco earthquake in 1906. He worked at the *Times* till the day he died, as a foreign correspondent, feature writer, editor and columnist, covering everything from sports and entertainment to the Mexican Revolution, World War I and national politics. In 1934 the Pulitzer Prize Commission cited his work as a correspondent. Carr published several books, including *Los Angeles: City of Dreams* (Appleton-Century, 1935), and had a hand in writing, adapting or editing scripts for a number of Hollywood films. His funeral was attended by Harold Lloyd, Cecil B. DeMille, D. W. Griffith, 20th Century-Fox chairman, Joseph M. Schenck, Jack Dempsey, among others.

Barbara J. Coleman
Erie, Pennsylvania, Nov. 11, 1947–

Barbara J. Coleman is an associate professor of art history specializing in 20th century American art at Regis University, Denver, Colorado, where she is the Director of the Art History Program. She earned her Ph.D. at the University of Minnesota, where she studied under Karal Ann Marling.

Maurice A. Crane
Atlantic City, New Jersey, June 6, 1926–June 2, 2014, East Lansing, Michigan

An accomplished jazz musician, Crane earned a Ph.D. in American literature from the University of Illinois. From 1953 until he retired in 2000, Crane taught humanities courses at Michigan State University, where, from 1974–2000, he also served as librarian of the G. Robert Vincent Voice Library.

John Culhane
Rockford, Illinois, Feb. 7, 1934–

John Culhane began his career as a reporter with the *St. Louis Globe-Dem-*

ocrat before joining his hometown paper, the *Rockford Register-Republic* (as he was advised to do when he was a teenager by Walt Disney). Later he was a feature writer and foreign correspondent with the *Chicago Daily News* and *Reader's Digest,* and an associate editor at *Newsweek.* At the School of Visual Arts in New York City in 1972, Culhane created the first course for college credit on the history of animation, which he also taught at New York University, Manhattan's Fashion Institute of Technology, and the Roy Disney Studio for Animation Studies at Mercy College in Westchester County. Among his many articles and books are "The Old Disney Magic," *New York Times Magazine* (1976), and *Walt Disney's Fantasia* (1978). His autobiographical "I Speak for Democracy, Mickey and Minnie Mouse," and interviews with Disney animators "Izzy" Klein and John Hubley appeared in vols. 9 (2010) and 11 (2011), respectively, of *Walt's People,* edited by Didier Ghez. John also has written about the emotions of his cousin, James (Shamus) Culhane, as he animated the "Heigh-Ho" sequence in *Snow White and the Seven Dwarfs.*

Richard deCordova

Denton, Texas, June 14, 1956–Nov. 21, 1996, Chicago, Illinois

A member of the Department of Communication, now the College of Communication, at DePaul University in Chicago, where he taught for twelve years, deCordova was a founding member of the university's interdisciplinary American Studies Program. He received his B.A. in 1977 from Southern Methodist University, and Ph.D. in Theater Arts from UCLA, 1986. His book, *Picture Personalities: The Emergence of the Star System in America,* based on his dissertation, was published in 1990 by the University of Illinois Press.

Lillian Bounds Disney

Spalding, Idaho, Feb. 15, 1899–Dec. 16, 1997, Los Angeles (Holmby Hills), California

Lillian Disney was hired as an inker and painter at the Disney studio in 1924, starting work on Jan. 14th, at $15 a week. Lilly and Walt were married in July 1925, and had two daughters, Diane Disney Miller and Sharon Disney Brown Lund.

Walt Disney

Chicago, Illinois, Dec. 5, 1901–Dec. 15, 1966, Burbank, California

Walt began his career in 1919 in Kansas City with a commercial art firm. In

1923 he moved to Hollywood, where he created the Alice Comedies and Oswald the Lucky Rabbit for Winkler Productions, before striking out on his own with Mickey. In 1939, Disney received a special Academy Award consisting of one standard-size and seven smaller Oscars to honor his first feature-length cartoon, *Snow White and the Seven Dwarfs*. He was nominated for fifty-nine Oscars, and won twenty-two, more than anyone else in history. *The Jungle Book* was the last animation he oversaw before his death. In September 1964, President Lyndon B. Johnson presented Disney with the Presidential Medal of Freedom, the nation's highest civilian award. Over the years dozens of articles like the two in this book—all of them, almost certainly, ghostwritten—were published under Walt's name.

Sarah El Deeb

Sarah El Deeb has worked for twelve years at the Associated Press, primarily reporting on the Middle East, covering Egypt, Iraq, the Palestinian territories, Bahrain as well as Sudan's Darfur conflict. She has recently been focusing on Egypt's political transition after the 2011 uprising that forced Hosni Mubarak to step down. El Deeb is a graduate of the London School of Economics, holding a Master's degree in development studies.

Marshall Fishwick

Roanoke, Virginia, July 5, 1923–May 22, 2006, Blacksburg, Virginia

A graduate of the University of Virginia, with a Ph.D. in American Studies from Yale (1949), Marshall Fishwick has been called "a founding father of popular culture studies." His began his academic career in the history department at Washington and Lee University as Professor of American Studies (1949–1962). One of his students at W&L, Tom Wolfe, later called him "the greatest teacher I ever had." In 1970, with Ray B. Browne and Russel B. Nye, Fishwick established the Popular Culture Association. He joined the faculty at Virginia Tech in 1976, where, upon his retirement in 2003, he was director of both the American Studies and Popular Culture programs. Among many other articles and books he wrote are *Seven Pillars of Popular Culture* (Greenwood Press, 1985) and *Popular Culture in a New Age* (Haworth Press, 2002), which includes the essay, "The Man and the Mouse." An earlier piece by Fishwick on Disney, "Aesop in Hollywood: The Man and the Mouse," appeared in the July 10, 1954, issue of *Saturday Review*.

E. M. Forster
London, England, Jan. 1, 1879–June 7, 1970, Coventry (Warwickshire), England
    In 1900 and 1901, Forster took degrees in classics and history at King's College, Cambridge. A prolific novelist, short fiction writer, critic (for the *Spectator*) and essayist, he is recalled today as the author of the novels *A Room With a View* (1908), *Howards End* (1910), and *A Passage to India* (1924), all of which were turned into major motion pictures.

Stephen Jay Gould
Bayside, Queens, New York, Sept. 10, 1941–May 20, 2002, New York, New York
    Gould earned his Ph.D. at Columbia. He taught paleontology, evolutionary biology, and the history of science at Harvard, from 1967 until he died in 2002. From 1996 till his death, Gould also was a visiting research professor at New York University. Thanks to his many contributions to *Natural History* over the years, and the republication of these essays in book form, Gould was for decades an influential popularizer of science. Among the collections of his writings are *Ever Since Darwin: Reflections in Natural History* (1977) and *Hen's Teeth and Horse's Toes: Further Reflections In Natural History* (1983). The essay in this book from *Natural History* was reprinted in *The Panda's Thumb: More Reflections in Natural History* (1983) as "A Biological Homage to Mickey Mouse."

Dorothy Grafly
Paris, France, July 29, 1896–Nov. 13, 1980, Philadelphia, Pennsylvania
    The daughter of Charles Grafly, a sculptor and instructor at the Pennsylvania Academy of the Fine Arts, Grafly earned a B.A. from Wellesley (1918), and did graduate work at Harvard. In 1946 she married Charles H. Drummond. A teacher, curator, writer, editor, and critic, she worked for four newspapers in Philadelphia: the *North American*, *Public Ledger*, *Record*, and *Evening Bulletin*. From 1942 to 1948 she was contributing editor with *Art Digest*. In addition to the profile of Walt in this volume, she published two other pieces in the same issue of the *Public Ledger* about the Disney show at the Art Alliance of Philadelphia, and was one of four contemporaneous female writers who believed that Disney's animation should be regarded as highly as any of the fine arts. The others were C. A. Lejeune, a British critic at the *Observer*, Eleanor Lambert, who authored "Notes on the Art of Mickey Mouse,"* and Iris Barry,

a second British critic, who formed the Film Library at New York's Museum of Modern Art. In July 1933, Grafly wrote an article about animation, "America's Youngest Art," for the *American Magazine of Art*.

Jesse Green
Philadelphia, Pennsylvania, June 8, 1958–

A graduate of Yale (1980), Green has been, since 2008, a feature writer for *New York* magazine. Previously he wrote about theater and other cultural topics for the Arts & Leisure section of the *New York Times* while covering broader subjects for the *Times Magazine*. In addition to his journalism, Green is the author of *The Velveteen Father: An Unexpected Journey to Parenthood* (Villard, 1999), a memoir that was named one of the best nonfiction books of the year by the *Los Angeles Times Book Review*, and a novel, *O Beautiful* (Ballantine Books; 2000), which *Entertainment Weekly* called "one of the best first novels of the year."

Edwin C. Hill
Aurora, Indiana, Apr. 23, 1884–Feb. 12, 1957, St. Petersburg, Florida

A graduate of the University of Indiana, Edwin C. Hill was a star reporter with the *New York Sun*, and, later, a syndicated columnist. The article in this volume was one such column. In 1933–1934, Hill scripted several news documentaries, and, beginning in 1933, broadcast radio commentary on several national networks as well.

Bill Hutchinson
New York, New York, March 1962–

Bill Hutchinson has been a reporter and senior writer at the *New York Daily News* since 1997. He previously worked for the *Boston Herald*, the *Fresno Bee*, and the *Daily Ledger-Post Dispatch* in Antioch, Calif. He is a graduate of San Francisco State University and is the author of *Sushi and Black-eyed Peas: an All-American Memoir*, published by TheWriteDeal.org in March 2012.

M. Thomas Inge
Newport News, Virginia, March 18, 1936–

An undergraduate at Randolph-Macon College, with a Ph.D. in English from Vanderbilt, from 1969–1980 Inge taught at Virginia Commonwealth University. In 1984 he joined the faculty at Randolph-Macon where he is Blackwell

Professor of Humanities. Among the many books he has written or edited are: *Handbook of American Popular Culture* (Greenwood Press, 1978–1981, 3 vols.; 2nd rev. ed., 1989); *Comics as Culture* (University Press of Mississippi, 1990); *My Life with Charlie Brown* (University Press of Mississipp, 2010), a compilation of writings by Charles M. Schulz; *Will Eisner: Conversations* (University Press of Mississippi, 2011), and, with co-editor Marcel Arbeit, *The (Un)Popular South* (Palacky University Press, 2011), which includes Inge's essay, "Walt Disney's Racial Dilemma in Song of the South." Starting in 1975, he began donating materials that formed the basis of the M. Thomas Inge Collection of Comic Arts Reference Journals at the James Branch Cabell Library at VCU.

Barbara Berch Jamison

Winnipeg, Canada, June 6, 1919–Dec. 31, 2006, Fuengirola, Spain

Though born in Canada, Jamison—née Barbara Berch—grew up in Hollywood where she became a publicist and journalist, specializing in the motion picture industry. She freelanced for *Collier's*, *Lady's Home Journal*, and the *New York Times*, to which she contributed dozens of stories in the '40s and '50s on stars like Barbara Stanwyck, Johnny Weissmuller, and Marilyn Monroe. In the 1970s, she was a documentary filmmaker, first in Guadalajara, Mexico (1972–1975), then in Bournemouth, England. In 1981, she moved to the Costa del Sol, Spain, where she worked as a playwright, radio broadcaster, and freelance writer. An unpublished autobiography in the form of letters to famous people begins with one to Walt, in which she described her "brief interview" with him for the article reprinted in this volume. In 1954, a piece by Jamison on the Disney True-Life nature films appeared the *Times Sunday Magazine*.

Jack Jamison

Jamison was a freelance writer circa 1932–1935. In addition to *Liberty* magazine, Jamison wrote for *Photoplay* ("Cary *versus* Gary," Jan. 1933) and contributed a number of articles to *Modern Screen*, including "Hard Times in Hollywood" (also Jan. 1933).

Alva Johnston

Sacramento, California, Aug. 1, 1888–Nov. 23, 1950, Bronxville, New York

Johnston was a newspaperman, magazine writer, and biographer. He began his career in 1906, directly out of high school, at the *Sacramento Bee*. From 1912–1928, he was a beat reporter at the *New York Times*, where he was awarded the Pulitzer Prize for Reporting in 1923. He moved to the *New York Herald Tribune* in 1928, and, starting in 1932, worked as a freelancer, writing primarily for the *Saturday Evening Post* and the *New Yorker*. In one of three books he published, *The Great Goldwyn* (Random House, 1937), a biography of Samuel Goldwyn, Johnston attributed a number of classic "Goldwynisms" to the legendary movie mogul. Among them: "A verbal contract isn't worth the paper it's printed on," and, during a contentious confab, "Gentlemen, include me out." Upon his death, the *Times* called Johnston "One of the keenest reporters of an era which produced some almost legendary figures in the newspaper writing field." Harold Ross, editor of the *New Yorker*, and novelist John O'Hara attended his funeral. An abbreviated version of the article in this anthology appeared in the August issue of *Reader's Digest*.

Jim Korkis

Tulsa, Oklahoma, August 15, 1950–

Jim Korkis is a Disney scholar, teacher, professional actor, and magician. He has a Masters Degree in English from Occidental College where he graduated with honors. He worked for the Disney Company in a variety of roles including performer, animation instructor, writer, business facilitator, coordinator of College and International programs, Guest Relations host, and coordinator of the Epcot Learning Center. He has written hundreds of articles on Disney history and animation, and in 2004 received the Disney Company *Partners in Excellence* award. His books include *The Vault of Walt* (Ayefour Publishing, 2010) and *Who's Afraid of the Song of the South?* (Theme Park Press, 2012). With John Cawley he co-authored *The Encyclopedia of Cartoon Superstars* (Pioneer Books, 1990), *How to Create Animation* (Pioneer Books, 1990), and *Cartoon Confidential* (Malibu Graphics, 1991).

Eleanor Lambert

Crawfordsville, Indiana, Aug. 10, 1903–Oct. 7, 2003, New York, New York

Lambert, subsequently known as "the doyenne of American fashion," briefly enrolled at the art school at the Art Institute of Chicago before moving to New York in 1925, where she worked for a book publicist, and eventually represented artists like John Steuart Curry, Jacob Epstein, and Isamu Noguchi. In 1930 she took charge of publicity for the new Whitney Museum of American Art, was an early supporter of the Metropolitan Museum of Art's Costume

Institute (created 1937), and in the early 1940s, established the International Best-Dressed List. In 1962 she helped found the Art Dealers Association of America and the Council of Fashion Designers of America. In 1965 she was appointed by President Johnson to the National Council on the Arts of the National Endowment for the Arts. In 1936 Lambert married Seymour Berkson, general manager with International News Service, and, from 1954 until his death in 1959, publisher of the *New York Journal-American*.

Land (Robert J. Landry)

East Haddam, Connecticut, June 14, 1903–May 23, 1991, New York, New York

Landry worked for over fifty years as a critic, columnist, office supervisor, and managing editor at *Variety*. He served as its first radio editor and also was director of program writing at CBS-TV (1942–1948), where he won a Peabody Award in 1946 for a broadcast of *Richard III*. He wrote two books, *Who, What, Why Is Radio?* (George W. Stewart, 1942) and *This Fascinating Radio Business* (Bobbs-Merrill, 1946). Writers for *Variety* often used short forms of their names to sign their work. A squib on the Colony Theatre program in *Variety*, a week after Mickey's debut (Nov. 28, 1928), by "Abel," was written by Abel Green, who helped create the paper's unique jargon (e.g., "Stix Nix Hick Pix").

Jean Laury (Nicole Boré-Verrier)

"Jean Laury" was the pseudonym for Nicole Boré-Verrier, film critic for the French daily *Le Figaro* in the 1930s. In May 1938, she published a review of the French classic by Marcel Carné, *Le Quai des Brumes*, starring Jean Gabin, Michèle Morgan, and Michel Simon. Like Maurice Bessy, earlier in her career Boré-Verrier had written for *Pour Vous*. In 1950, for the French men's fashion magazine, *Adam*, she authored a special issue on marriage ("Mariages—Usages du Temps Présent—Des Fiançailles au Voyage de Noces").

C. A. (Caroline Alice) Lejeune

Didsbury, near Manchester, England, Mar. 27, 1897–Apr. 1, 1973, London

Lejeune began her career as a music critic for the *Manchester Guardian*, but soon switched to writing a weekly film column. In 1928 she became the movie critic for the *Observer*, where she remained until her retirement in 1960. After she died, the *Times* of London called her "the doyen of English film critics." Passages from Lejeune's piece on Mickey Mouse in this anthology were refashioned, along with portions of a subsequent *Observer* column (Mar. 9,

1930), into a chapter in her book, *Cinema* (Alexander Machlehose & Co., 1931), entitled "Disney's Cartoons." A posthumous collection of writings, *The C. A. Lejeune Reader* (Carcanet, 1991), was edited by her son, Anthony Lejeune, who noted, in his preface to the volume: "I have in my bedroom a picture of Mickey Mouse, saying, with a jaunty wave of his four-fingered hand, 'Greetings to Miss C. A. Lejeune!'"

Edward Lewine
New York, New York, Mar. 3, 1967–

Lewine is a writer, journalist, and wine importer. A frequent contributor to the *New York Times*, he has been the *Times Magazine*'s "Domains" columnist since 2004, and is the author of two books, including *Death and the Sun: A Matador's Season in the Heart of Spain* (Houghton Mifflin, 2005). His work has appeared in more than a dozen magazines, including *Details* and *New York*. Lewine, a former head of the Old Master Drawings Department of Christie's auction house, is the son of two art historians: his father, Milton, was a professor at Columbia University; his mother, Carol, at Queens College. For the past year, while continuing his writing career, Lewine has begun importing wine from Spain. He lives in Brooklyn with his wife and two children.

Arthur Mann
Stamford, Connecticut, Sept. 11, 1901–Jan. 3, 1963, New York, New York

Multi-talented artist, actor, musician, and prolific writer, Mann attended the Art Students League in New York. In 1921 he joined the *New York Morning World* as a staff artist, but switched to sports reporting, first for the *World*, then the *Herald-Tribune* (1923–1931), *New York Daily Mirror*, and *Evening World*. In the '30s and '40s he freelanced for the *Saturday Evening Post, Collier's, Liberty, Scribner's, Sporting News*, as well as *Harper's*. After the war, he worked for the Brooklyn Dodgers as an assistant to Branch Rickey. Mann authored several baseball books, including biographies of Rickey and Jackie Robinson, and co-wrote the 1950 biopic *The Jackie Robinson Story*, in which future Mouseketeer MC Jimmie Dodd had a bit part.

Frank S. Nugent New York, New York, May 27, 1908–Dec. 29, 1965, Los Angeles, California

Less than a year after the article in this anthology was published in the *New York Times*, Nugent was lured to Hollywood by Darryl F. Zanuck. He had been a reporter and film critic at the *Times* since 1929. From 1940–1966, he was a highly successful script doctor and screenwriter, who was involved with twenty-one film scripts, mostly for John Ford, including *Mister Roberts* (1955) and *The Searchers* (1956). In 1953 he was nominated for an Academy Award for his work on Ford's *The Quiet Man*. A graduate of the Columbia University School of Journalism, Nugent began his career at the *Times* as a reporter, before shifting, in 1934, into film criticism. He heaped immense praise on *Snow White and the Seven Dwarfs*, in a piece that appeared in the *Times* on January 14, 1938, and wrote a glowing review of *The Wizard of Oz* (1939), as well. In 1957–1958, Nugent served as the President of the Writers Guild of America, West.

Creighton B. Peet
New York, New York, April 1899–May 15, 1977, New York, New York

A leading motion picture critic in the late 1920s and 1930s, whose career lasted into the 1970s, Peet wrote on a host of subjects for numerous magazines and newspapers, including *Life*, *Science Digest*, and the *New York Times*. A graduate of the University of Pennsylvania and Columbia School of Journalism, he was published thirty-one times in the *New Yorker*, typically in the "Talk of the Town" section. He reviewed films for the *New York Post* and wrote children's books as well, like *Mike the Cat* (1934). In 1944 the Museum of Modern Art reported that its "film section has been further strengthened by the purchase of the private clipping file of Creighton Peet, consisting of 12,000 envelopes containing movie and stage reviews of newspapers and trade magazines from 1925–1942." Peet's laudatory article, "Miraculous Mickey," reprinted in this volume, appeared in July 1930. Eleven months earlier, without naming Disney or Mickey, in an article, "The Cartoon Comedy," in the *New Republic*, Peet declared: "When it comes to 'pure cinema,' 'visual flow,' 'graphic representation,' 'the freedom of the cinematic medium,' and all the other things learned cinema enthusiasts talk about, nothing Jannings or Lubitsch or Murnau or Greta Garbo or Rin Tin Tin can do has more than a roll of celluloid's chance in Hell beside Felix Cat and other animated cartoons." "Unhampered by any such classical limitations as dramatic unities, or even such customary necessities as the laws of gravity, common sense, and possibility," Peet also said, "the animated drawing is the only artistic medium ever discovered which is really 'free.'"

Anna Quindlen
Philadelphia, Pennsylvania, July 8, 1952–
   Anna Quindlen, former Pulitzer Prize–winning columnist for the *New York Times*, is the author of six novels and many non-fiction books.

Terry Ramsaye
Tonganoxie, Kansas, Nov. 2, 1885–Aug. 19, 1954, Norwalk, Connecticut
   "Generally regarded as the dean of film historians," as the *New York Times* noted, after his death, Ramsaye was editor of the *Motion Picture Herald* from 1931–1949. A student in engineering at the University of Kansas, he began his career in journalism in 1905 with the *Kansas City Star*, and worked for the *Omaho Bee* and *Chicago Tribune*. In 1915 he was hired by the Mutual Film Corporation, where he, it is said, produced a few Chaplin comedies. Before joining the *Motion Picture Herald*, Ramsaye was editor-in-chief of Pathé News, and also was associated with the legendary "Roxy" Rothafel and the Rialto and Rivoli theaters on Broadway. Ramsaye's two-volume history of film before the advent of sound, *A Million and One Nights*, was published by Simon & Schuster in 1926.

Diego Rivera
Guanajuato, Mexico, Dec. 8, 1886–Nov. 24, 1957, Mexico City, Mexico
   Rivera was, with José Clemente Orozco, a leader of the Mexican Mural Movement. From 1911 to 1920, he lived in Paris, where he knew the painter Modigliani. In the early 1930s he had major commissions for mural designs in San Francisco, Detroit, and New York City, including a project in the lobby of Rockefeller Center, that included a portrait of Lenin and a caricatural head of John D. Rockefeller, Jr. (the mural was destroyed). Rivera's wife, Frida Kahlo, was a famous painter in her own right. Seven years after his essay on Mickey Mouse appeared in *Contact*, Rivera's friend, Jean Charlot, published an article, "But Is It Art? A Disney Disquisition," in the *American Scholar* (summer 1939).

L. H. Robbins
Lincoln, Nebraska, Apr. 2, 1877–June 24, 1947, Wolfeboro, New Hampshire
   L. H. Robbins, who attended the University of Nebraska and, briefly, Princeton, wrote a humor column for the *Newark Evening News* from 1901 to 1917. In 1923 he joined the *New York Times*, working for twenty-four years in the Sunday department, where he contributed to the book review section and the

"Topics of the Times" department. He also published humorous short stories in *Life* and *Everybody's* magazine. Among his books were a collection of light verse, *Jersey Jingles* (Newark, N.J., 1907), and *Mountains of Men* (Dodd, Mead & Co., 1931).

Herbert Russell

Russell, not to be confused with the British war correspondent Sir Herbert Russell, published roughly half a dozen pieces in the *New York Times* in the 1930s and 1940s.

Pierre Scize (Michel-Joseph Piot) Pont-de-Chéruy, near Lyon, France, Feb. 10, 1933–Dec. 10, 1956, Melbourne, Australia

Pierre Scize attended the Conservatoire de Lyon, 1912–1914, and lost an arm in World War I. Between the wars he contributed to *L'Œuvre*, *Bonsoir*, the weekly newspaper *Candide* (as film and theater critic), the monthly *Gazette Dunlop*, and was a *grand reporter* with *Paris-Soir*. After World War II he worked for *Le Figaro* in a similar capacity. He authored a number of books including a biography of Georges Clemenceau (1944). The short-lived French monthly *Jazz* (Dec. 15, 1928–Mar. 15, 1930) was founded by Titaÿna, a journalist with *Paris-Soir*, and the multi-talented screenwriter-director-author-cartoonist, Carlo Rim.

Gilbert Seldes Alliance, New Jersey, Jan. 3, 1893–Sept. 29, 1970, New York, New York

A Harvard grad, early in his career Seldes was a war correspondent and music critic. Having made his mark with *The 7 Lively Arts* (Harper, 1924), "a celebration of popular entertainment," as the *New York Times* later called it, he moved on to magazine work and a syndicated newspaper column. In 1937 he became director of CBS television, and was both professor and founding dean of the Annenberg School for Communication, University of Pennsylvania, 1959–1963. Seldes wrote two other profiles on Disney, in addition to the one included in this anthology: "Disney and Others," the *New Republic*, June 8, 1932, and "No Art, Mr. Disney?," *Esquire*, Sept. 1937. In his *New York Journal* column, June 18, 1932 ("Mouse and News First Triumphs of Talkies"), Seldes restated in simpler terms the view expressed in the *New Yorker* piece reprinted here: "When I say the Silly Symphonies are better I display no prejudice against Mickey Mouse, who is perky and engaging, but a little too much on the teddy-bear fad side for my taste." The frontispiece to Seldes book *The Movies Come From America* (Scribner's, 1937) features a sketch of Mickey and Donald making a movie.

Maurice Sendak
Brooklyn, New York, June 10, 1928–May 8, 2012, Danbury, Connecticut

A prolific children's book writer and illustrator, Sendak is most famous for *Where the Wild Things Are* (Harper & Row, 1963). In 1968, he donated a 10,000-piece collection of art, books other materials to the Rosenbach Museum & Library, Philadelphia. Sendak received the National Book Award in 1982 and the National Medal of Arts in 1996, and was an avid collector of vintage Mickey memorabilia.

Charles Solomon
Animation historian and critic Charles Solomon contributed two essays to the exhibition catalogue *Il était une fois: Walt Disney* (Grand Palais Museum, Paris, Sept. 2006). Among his books are *The Disney That Never Was* (Hyperion, 1995) and *Enchanted Drawings: The History of Animation* (Knopf, 1989; reprinted, Wings, 1994). He has also done animation programming for the Academy of Motion Pictures Arts and Sciences, the Los Angeles County Museum of Art and the Annecy, Ottawa, and Sundance international film festivals, and lectured on animation history and aesthetics at UCLA, USC, CalArts, NYU, and the School of Visual Arts.

Isabella Taves
Lincoln, Nebraska, Sept. 20, 1905–June 25, 2005, New York, New York

A Phi Beta Kappa graduate of Northwestern University, Taves published fiction and non-fiction in *Collier's, Cosmopolitan, McCall's, Today's Woman,* and *Look.* Among her books are *Successful Women and How They Attained Success* (New York: E.P. Dutton, 1943) and *Women Alone: A Practical Handbook for Widows and Divorcees* (Funk and Wagnalls, 1968). She was a dog fancier as well, who bred and showed Dalmatians. Her husband, Daniel D. Mich, was an executive editor at *Look.*

John Updike
Reading, Pennsylvania, Mar. 18, 1932–Jan. 27, 2009, Danvers, Massachusetts

Updike was a novelist, poet, short story writer, and art and literary critic.

He is best known for his quartet of novels, including *Rabbit Is Rich* (Alfred A. Knopf, 1981) and *Rabbit At Rest* (Knopf, 1991), both of which won the Pulitzer Prize for Fiction. His writings appeared regularly in the *New Yorker* and the *New York Review of Books*. As a boy, Updike wanted to be a cartoonist and work for the Disney Studio.

Lawrence Van Gelder
New York, New York, Feb. 1932–

In 2010, Van Gelder retired as senior editor of the Arts and Leisure section of the *New York Times*. Before joining the *Times*, in 1967, he worked for five other New York dailies, including the *Daily Mirror*, *Journal-American*, and *World-Journal-Tribune*. He has taught writing as an adjunct professor in the Creative Writing Program of School of the Arts at Columbia.

Richard Verrier
Sedona, Arizona, Dec. 28, 1965–

Richard Verrier was identified in 2008 on a *Los Angeles Times* blog as a staff "reporter who covers labor and production issues in Hollywood and the exhibition industry."

Irving Wallace
Chicago, Illinois, Mar. 19, 1916–June 29, 1990, Los Angeles, California

Wallace authored several dozen best-selling fiction and non-fiction books, notably *The Chapman Report* (1960), *The Man* (1964), *The Prize* (1962), and *The Word* (1972), all published by Simon & Schuster, and all turned into motion pictures. In the 1940s and 1950s he wrote or co-wrote a number of scripts for Hollywood and television.

Cholly Wood
"Cholly Wood" was the pen name, identity unknown, of a local Bridgeport, Connecticut, journalist or writer active in the 1930s.

Elmo R. Zumwalt
San Francisco, California, Nov. 29, 1920–Jan. 2, 2000, Durham, North Carolina

A graduate of Annapolis, and combat veteran of World War II, in 1970 Admiral Zumwalt was nominated to be Chief of Naval Operations by President

Richard M. Nixon. He was the youngest man to hold that position. His book covering his career through the Vietnam era, *On Watch: a Memoir,* was published in 1976 by Quadrangle Books. For a full biography, see *Zumwalt: The Life and Times of Admiral Elmo Russell "Bud" Zumwalt, Jr.,* by Larry Berman (Harper, 2012).

ACKNOWLEDGMENTS

For, in numerous ways, helping make this anthology possible, I am indebted to many individuals, chief among them: Margaret Adamic and Maxine Hof at Disney Enterprises, Inc., Gunnar Andreassen, Tony Anselmo, Cristina Apgar Pastor, Keith K. Apgar, Michael Barrier, Bill Berkson, Hervé Cabezas, Rebecca Cline and the staff at the Walt Disney Archives, Burbank, Calif., Susan deCordova, David Gerstein, Didier Ghez, my editors at the University Press of Mississippi, Craig W. Gill and Walter Biggins, Tima Good, Shaun O'L. Higgins, Madelyn Holmes, Michael W. Jennings, Ann LaBerge, Michael Labrie, Director of Collections and Exhibitions at the Walt Disney Family Museum, John Langston (for his splendid cover design), Carol A. Leadenham, Jon Lewis, William Maynez, Régis Michel, Linda Olson, Michael O'Malley, Andrea Pereira, David Pierce (Media History Digital Library), Dave Smith, Eric Smoodin, Rog Sphar, Timothy Susanin, Jacqueline Taylor, Peter Tonguette (for his superb copy-editing), Ron Unz (chairman, unz.org), Steven Wander, and Dr. Erdmut Wizisla and Ursula Marx at the Walter Benjamin Archive, Berlin.

Esther Leslie kindly allowed me to use her translation of "Der Micky Maus Skandal!!!" The original Spanish text of the Diego Rivera essay in Appendix E and the English version in the main body of the book were transcribed and translated primarily by María José Pastor, with input from Didier Ghez and David Jacobs (Hoover Institution). Didier and especially Edward Langille assisted me in translating the three French texts. Barbara J. Coleman proofread my transcription of her article from 1999, to which she made a few minor editorial adjustments. Jim Korkis revised material he published in 2004 as "Secrets of Steamboat Willie" into the two pieces included in this volume, in a manner truer to what he originally envisioned.

I am particularly grateful to the late Diane Disney Miller, Ron Miller, and the Walt Disney Family Foundation, San Francisco, Calif., for their generosity in helping fund publication of this project, and to my brother, Stephen M. Apgar, who tracked down rights holders, and transcribed and proofread many of the entries in the book.